Learning to Teach English and the Language Arts

Also available from Bloomsbury

Secondary English Teacher Education in the United States: A Historical and Current Analysis, Donna L. Pasternak, Samantha Caughlan, Heidi L. Hallman, Laura Renzi, Leslie S. Rush
Navigating Teacher Education in Complex and Uncertain Times: Connecting Communities of Practice in a Borderless World, Carmen I. Mercado
The Bloomsbury Handbook of Reading: Perspectives and Practices, Edited by Bethan Marshall, Jackie Manuel, Donna L. Pasternak and Jennifer Roswell
Teachers as Learners, Sharon Feiman-Nemser
Knowledge, Policy and Practice in Teacher Education: A Cross-National Study, Maria Teresa Tatto and Ian Menter
Policy, Belief and Practice in the Secondary English Classroom, Bethan Marshall, Simon Gibbons, Louise Hayward and Ernest Spencer

Learning to Teach English and the Language Arts

A Vygotskian Perspective on Beginning Teachers' Pedagogical Concept Development

Peter Smagorinsky

BLOOMSBURY ACADEMIC
LONDON • NEW YORK • OXFORD • NEW DELHI • SYDNEY

BLOOMSBURY ACADEMIC
An imprint of Bloomsbury Publishing Plc
50 Bedford Square, London, WC1B 3DP, UK
1385 Broadway, New York, NY 10018, USA
29 Earlsfort Terrace, Dublin 2, Ireland

www.bloomsbury.com

BLOOMSBURY and the Diana logo are trademarks of Bloomsbury Publishing Plc

First published 2020
This paperback edition published in 2021

Copyright © Peter Smagorinsky, 2020

Peter Smagorinsky has asserted their right under the Copyright, Designs and Patents Act, 1988, to be identified as Authors of this work.

For legal purposes the Acknowledgments on pp. viii-x constitute an extension of this copyright page.

Cover image © peepo/iStock

All rights reserved. No part of this publication may be reproduced or transmitted in any form or by any means, electronic or mechanical, including photocopying, recording, or any information storage or retrieval system, without prior permission in writing from the publishers.

No responsibility for loss caused to any individual or organization acting on or refraining from action as a result of the material in this publication can be accepted by Bloomsbury or the author.

British Library Cataloguing-in-Publication Data
A catalogue record for this book is available from the British Library.

ISBN: HB: 978-1-3501-4289-3
PB: 978-1-3502-1058-5
ePDF: 978-1-3501-4290-9
ePub: 978-1-3501-4291-6

Library of Congress Cataloging-in-Publication Data
A catalog record for this book is available from the Library of Congress.

Typeset by Deanta Global Publishing Services, Chennai, India

To find out more about our authors and books visit www.bloomsbury.com and sign up for our newsletters.

Dedicated to my first and greatest teacher, my mother
Margaret Smagorinsky (1915–2011)

Contents

Acknowledgments		viii
Author's Preface		xi
1	Vygotsky and Concept Development	1
2	Methodological Implications of Taking a Vygotskian Approach to Teacher Development	19
3	The Apprenticeship of Observation, Updated, and Its Effects on Beginning Teachers' Evolving Pedagogical Conceptions	35
4	Concept Development in Teacher Education Coursework and Practica	49
5	Cultures of Color and the Deep Structure of Schools	79
6	Fuzzy Concepts in Teacher Education and Their Consequences in the Classroom	99
7	Policy, Practice, and Disruptions in Concept Development	121
8	School Settings and Course Assignments in Shaping Conceptions of Curriculum and Instruction	141
9	Competing Centers of Gravity within Settings of Learning to Teach	157
10	Learning to Teach Grammar at the Intersection of Formalism and Flexibility	173
11	Community Contexts and Their Societal Settings, and How They Shape Practice	197
12	Conclusion	217
References		225
Index		242

Acknowledgments

In this book, I take a series of previously published case studies and synthesize them into a broader argument about how novice English teachers and teachers of Elementary Language Arts learn to teach their discipline. These cases studies have produced both empirical research articles and theoretical/conceptual publications that, in this volume, I put in dialogue in newly presented and more comprehensively synthesized versions.

The research came about serendipitously. With Melissa Whiting, a doctoral student at Oklahoma, I did a study of how English teaching methods courses are conducted, relying on syllabi from over eighty universities to make inferences about their structure and emphasis (Smagorinsky & Whiting, 1995). At about this time, researchers at the University at Albany-SUNY (headed by Arthur Applebee and Judith Langer) and the University of Wisconsin at Madison (headed by Marty Nystrand) were putting together a proposal for a federally funded research center to study teaching and learning in the academic domain of English, which has traditionally encompassed the teaching of literature, writing, and language, although which now incorporates more modes of composition than verbal expression. Ultimately, this group became the National Research Center on English Learning and Achievement (CELA).

To round out the portrait of the English-teaching profession, the center organizers recruited a team of Pam Grossman and Sheila Valencia (both then at the University of Washington, Seattle, with Pam since moving to Stanford and now Pennsylvania as dean) and me at Oklahoma (moving to Georgia after two years of the five-year funding period). As part of the CELA Teacher Education and Professional Development research strand,[1] we studied how novices learn to teach the Elementary Language Arts curriculum and the Secondary English curriculum. Pam was (and remains) perhaps the preeminent teacher education researcher of our generation and, with Sheila and her orientation to primary grades literacy, was an obvious choice for this task. My book with Melissa Whiting also caught the research center's attention.

After Pam, Sheila, and I talked through the possibilities of what to study and how to study it across sites, we agreed to become satellite researchers for the CELA proposal. The problem that we identified as providing the best match for our interests and backgrounds was the challenge of how beginning teachers in university teacher education programs take what they have learned and apply that knowledge to their work in schools. Like many teacher educators, we had been frustrated by the ways in which our teacher education students appeared to be on board with a generally progressive set of teaching practices while in our classes, but often gravitated toward the *status quo* once in schools. Why does this seemingly regressive shift take place so often, and what factors contribute to it? Our inquiring minds wanted to know.

---

[1] See http://www.albany.edu/cela/research/strand4.html

The grant was assembled and submitted in 1996, and CELA was awarded the funding for five years (1996–2001) by the US Department of Education's Office of Educational Research and Improvement (Award # R305A60005; the views expressed herein are those of the author and do not necessarily represent the views of the now-defunct OERI). The research was designed in meetings in Seattle that included Pam, Sheila, their graduate students, and me at the outset of the project. Ultimately, our sites took different directions, even though we worked from the same design for collecting and analyzing data. Pam and Sheila preferred to analyze at the level of the cohort, and I preferred the level of the individual case. A second point of difference between my work and that of my colleagues is that Pam and Sheila remained at one institution for the duration of the grant, and so had the opportunity to conduct longitudinal studies of four years with one cohort of participants from one university's elementary and secondary schools (with the grant written to provide one year for writing at the end of the funding period). Meanwhile, I left Oklahoma for Georgia in the summer of 1998, requiring me to uproot my study after two years of following my own initial cohort of elementary and secondary teachers, and begin again at Georgia with a new cohort of Secondary English teachers, whom I followed for two years, with one final year to begin the analysis and writing. Planning one year for analysis and writing turned out, for me, to be insufficient; the last study was published in 2016. It's now time to put it all together so that the articles all make sense together as an aggregation of cases and themes.

Several factors contributed to this lengthy process of production on my end. First, case studies take a long time for me to complete. I undertook each case study with a doctoral student in a research apprenticeship in which we worked three to four hours a week for two to four semesters one-on-one. During this time I also worked other lines of inquiry, and hit a career stage when my professional duties occupied a great deal of time, including a seven-year stretch during which Michael W. Smith and I co-edited *Research in the Teaching of English*, and a lengthier term during which I did a lot of national organizational committee chairing. This divergent set of activities slowed my progress on any one and helps to account for the lengthy period of analysis and writing that finds synthesis in this book.

I could not begin this book without giving my thanks to my CELA colleagues, including faculty members and graduate students who serve as co-authors to the articles originally published from this research. Nor would it have been possible without the guidance of editors and reviewers for the journals in which this work has been published: *American Journal of Education*; *English Education*; *Journal of Research in Character Education*; *Journal of Teacher Education*; *Learning, Culture, and Social Interaction*; *Pedagogies: An International Journal*; *Research in the Teaching of English*; *Teacher Education Quarterly*; *Teachers College Record*; and *The Elementary School Journal*. Thanks are due as well to Viv Ellis for his conversations, feedback, and generous invitations to Oxford, where he organized the small conference that produced an edited volume that assembles papers on activity theoretical perspectives on teachers' learning (Ellis, Edwards, & Smagorinsky 2010). Thanks also to George Newell, with whom I have discussed many of the ideas presented in this book in relation to both his and my research and teaching. Finally, thanks to Merida Lang and Stacia L. Long for their careful reading of and suggestions for improving the first draft of this manuscript.

In many ways this book is a product of a collective effort. In addition to the CELA researchers, I worked with a host of graduate students, occasional colleagues, and participating teachers on the various studies synthesized in this volume. Thanks to my collaborators on these studies, including Sharon Augustine, Meghan Barnes, Steve Bickmore, Susan Bynum, Leslie Cook, Elizabeth Daigle, Pamela Fry, Natalie Gibson, Alecia Jackson, Cori Jakubiak, Tara Star Johnson, Pam Kluver, Bonnie Konopak, Andrea Lakly, Cynthia Moore, Cindy O'Donnell-Allen, Darren Rhym, Amy Sanford, Stephanie Shelton, Leigh Thompson, Amy Alexandra Wilson, and Laura Wright, without whom these pages would be empty. Although they worked on different studies with me, I also am indebted to Joanna Anglin, Chris Clayton, Deavours Hall, Lindy Johnson, Nick Thompson, Maria Winfield, Xiaodi Zhou, and Michelle Zoss for their contributions to my thinking about teaching and teacher education during their doctoral studies with me. And thanks to Alison Baker at Bloomsbury for ushering this book through the review and publication process.

Author's Preface

This book represents the culmination of work I've undertaken since the mid-1990s studying the ways in which beginning English teachers learn to teach. I began my own career as an educator after graduating from Kenyon College in 1974 as an English major. Kenyon is a small liberal arts college that at the time did not provide a way to earn a teaching credential, which was fine because as a college kid I had no idea of what I wanted to do following graduation. We went to Kenyon for something known as "The Kenyon Experience" rather than to master a trade, and I was all the richer for this nebulous possibility than for preparing for a career I probably would never have pursued.

Universities are now, in the eyes of many, in the business of career preparation only, according to people such as the State of Georgia's Higher Education Chancellor Hank Huckaby, who opined in 2013 that many jobs are going unfilled "because students are studying the wrong things. If you can't get a job, and you majored in drama, there's probably a reason"; or Florida Governor Rick Scott, a former entrepreneur who has issued "a challenge to our state colleges to find innovative ways to offer a bachelor's degree at a cost of just $10,000 in fields that will provide graduates with the best opportunity for employment." In the early 1970s, viewing college education as vocational training was considered crass and unseemly. Today, the view of universities as trade schools meets the broader goal of operating educational institutions as just one of many options in the marketplace—not of ideas, but of job training.

Perhaps Huckaby and Scott might look at my career trajectory as a failure of liberal arts education to train me for workforce readiness, because after graduating from Kenyon, I still wasn't quite sure what to do with myself. After working a few jobs in California and New Jersey that paid the bills yet left my soul empty, I began substitute teaching in the schools in and surrounding Trenton, New Jersey, mostly the junior highs of Trenton itself, but also in suburban and what were then rural districts in the area. Subbing in urban middle schools provides a wild and woolly way of entering the profession. Trenton at the time had a colossal dropout rate, and the middle schools enrolled all the kids before they were able to leave at age 16, which meant that the majority of the young people I spent all day with did not see school as the means to a better life. I was rarely left with a lesson plan, and so had to learn how to manage group after group of adolescents with nothing to do and plenty of time to do it in, and had to manage them with virtually no leverage to maintain order.

For some reason, these experiences convinced me that I wanted to teach. I got more steady work as a hall monitor (known in my job description as "administrative aide") in a Trenton-area high school the next year and began getting certified at a nearby regional state university. I left that institution in the middle of my second semester of enrollment after getting accepted into the M.A.T. program at the University of Chicago.

I earned my degree in 1977, teaching in a pull-out program for city kids during my studies and then launching a teaching career that lasted until 1990 at three Illinois high schools. During that time, I worked on my doctorate at Chicago, taking one year's leave of absence where I again worked as a substitute teacher, this time in about twenty-five schools in the city of Chicago, and completing my degree while teaching full time. After graduating in 1989, I taught one final year of high school English and then left to begin my career as a teacher educator at the University of Oklahoma.

I provide this background in part to ground my interest in the problem that this book explores, that of how people learn to teach. As a substitute teacher, I found that at least in central New Jersey in the 1970s and in Chicago in the 1980s, teachers seemed to lack the ability to leave behind a coherent lesson plan, or anything else for that matter, when absent. The routine dearth of any teaching plans beyond the occasional crossword puzzle or word match game suggested to me that there wasn't much going on instructionally. When teachers were absent and subs took over, the kids who showed up were left to sleep, chat, or raise holy hell for the substitute to try to manage. I began to wonder, even at this nascent stage of my career, what went on in teacher education. How do people learn how to teach? Why did the teachers I was subbing for think that leaving little more than the attendance sheet was helping anyone's education? I was at that time close enough in age to the students to empathize with the dreariness of their education, and wonder what they might be capable of doing if taught with commitment and pedagogical knowledge, even if I wasn't really sure what that might be.

My M.A.T. studies at Chicago also contributed to how I thought about learning to teach. First and foremost, my program was designed to provide a coherent approach to English pedagogy. I had one professor, George Hillocks, for all my courses, and we used a book for which he had served as primary author (Hillocks, McCabe, & McCampbell, 1971). We went through the coursework in a cohort, and George held frequent social events through which members of different cohorts met to extend their pedagogical family, form work groups, build friendships, and provide us with what I came to call a *conceptual home base* for our teaching (Smagorinsky, 2002), one that has survived George's death through a listserv and the personal relationships cultivated across the cohorts of his program.

Very early in my first years of teaching, I was surprised at how few people I met in the profession had the same feeling of conceptual unity and affiliation with their teacher education programs that I had shared with my grad school colleagues at Chicago. Many had gone through the sort of program that I had begun in New Jersey: one characterized by true-false and multiple-choice final exams, little writing or thinking, and random sequencing such that two people could start and end their degree programs on the same days and never cross paths or take the same professors for their courses. As might be expected, they had little interest in referring back to their tedious educational training and felt no affection for or connection with their teacher education programs.

I also noted that most of my fellow novices had no idea of how to plan instruction coherently over time, relying instead on swapped lessons, teacher manuals, tips from veterans, and other piecemeal ways of getting through the day. They often spoke of staying up past midnight trying to plan for the next day—a process they needed to repeat almost daily given the absence of long-term planning—and were typically exhausted and run down from the grind of planning each day anew. I felt fortunate that my preparation under George Hillocks had taught me to plan in terms of units of instruction covering four to eight weeks so that I was refining my plans rather than creating them out of whole cloth every night. I can't say that I was inherently more talented than my novice peers, but I was undoubtedly far better prepared to begin teaching and build from my teacher education foundation than others I met on the job.

Early on, then, I began to wonder, why did people come out of the Chicago program with such a distinctive set of experiences and with such clear and applicable preparation to teach? Undoubtedly the fact that it was a graduate program with selective admissions serving small cohorts under one person's guidance helped provide it with conceptual coherence. I later began teaching at larger state universities with multiple faculty members and both undergraduate and graduate certification programs, and saw how unique the Chicago program was under George's management. Elsewhere, the faculties were larger and more diverse, which both added perspectives and introduced conflicts that made running a conceptually unified program difficult. These conflicts affected program structure, course emphases, the role of field experiences, and many other facets of teacher education, at times in divisive ways. I also found that articulation across courses in large institutions might be more difficult than in smaller private institutions under one person's direction. And large universities, I learned, may rely on teaching assistants to serve large groups of students while keeping tuition low, a boon to their preparation for careers in teacher education but a potential problem in establishing continuity across courses and years for teacher candidates (TCs) and program administrators.

Even with these recognitions, I wondered: How does a university program become a conceptual home base for its students such that they regard it as the pedagogical place to which they return when considering how to teach? How does a university program teach so that its graduates have a distinctive approach that enables others to infer where they attended school based on both the quality and practice of its graduates? How does a program "brand" develop based on these unique traits of the people who teach and attend it? As a teacher, I had the opportunity to supervise student teachers from both the Chicago program and those from other universities, and these experiences only amplified my interest in these questions, given the differentiated preparation and supervision provided by different universities for their TCs.

As a teacher educator beginning in 1990, I began to see how such things could happen. As one of two faculty members teaching English Education methods and related courses, and in an environment characterized by academic freedom, I shared little in common with my first colleague in higher education. Our students did not proceed through the program in any sequence, but in a catch-as-catch-can fashion. One might take the methods class first, and another might take it last in the certification sequence. One might take a foundations course from one teaching assistant, another from another, and yet another from yet another; and each might provide contradictory views to each of the others. I began to view the program as one characterized by *structural fragmentation* (Zeichner & Gore, 1990), that is, the absence of a sustained, consistent focus on a pedagogical approach or teaching philosophy. I ultimately became program chair and redesigned the program, so it was better sequenced and more conceptually coherent, at least on paper. These revisions were based on what I was learning from research that I'd undertaken through funding awarded from the CELA, and that provides most of the material in the chapters that follow. I left for Georgia in 1998, however, and never had an opportunity to see the changes through to fruition.

At Oklahoma, and also at Georgia, I experienced the challenges of structuring teacher education so that more graduates consider their programs to be their conceptual home base. The state of Oklahoma at the time required all first-year teachers to be supervised by an entry-year committee consisting of a university professor, a departmental colleague, and a school administrator, with certification only available after one year of teaching and the committee's endorsement. Because our annual travel money came from compensation for this committee service, most faculty members got to observe their graduates teach after leaving the university nest and being free of its evaluative demands. In my university curriculum and instruction department that housed the teacher education faculty, many of us shared the same observation: an alarming number of our own graduates seemed to gravitate quickly to the norms of their schools, rather than serving as the change agents that our university documents claimed they would become. Why, we wondered, was this reversion happening so consistently, and often so quickly? What were we doing wrong, and more concerning, what if we were doing it well and, in spite of our efforts, the *status quo* we believed we were challenging was quickly absorbing our graduates shortly after they left our courses and influence?

This conundrum served as the focal question for the research we undertook through CELA. Over time, as I have engaged with data, and have thought through the challenges of improving secondary school English instruction through university course preparation, my answers to this question have changed and have become more nuanced in light of the complexity of the problem. At first, for instance, I thought that if I could replicate the Chicago program in state universities by making the programs more coherent, I'd resolve the primary issues that presented obstacles to creating a conceptual home base whose principles could be sustained, even when schools had competing priorities. Even with my university programs, however, finding agreement among faculty about how to run a program was difficult and frustrating and, I realized before long, well above my pay grade.

Studying the dynamics of teacher education faculties and their internal disputes, however, is not the purpose of this volume. Rather, it's to synthesize a couple of decades of research into one coherent volume documenting how people learn how to teach, and particularly, how to teach Secondary English or Elementary Language Arts. Often, teacher education research seeks single-cause explanations for why university emphases get abandoned once teachers are working in schools, leading teacher educators to wonder what exactly they are achieving with their teaching and supervision. To some, the problems begin with people's acculturation to school culture throughout their education, leading to selectivity factors in determining who finds teaching to be an attractive profession and who therefore returns to schools for their life's work (Lortie, 1975). In this sense, preservice teachers never integrate university values into their teaching conceptions to begin with and so are amenable to easy absorption into schooling as usual, which Zeichner and Tabachnik (1981) say will *wash out* effects of teacher education programs. To others, schools represent monocultures that are impervious to change, such that even the few teachers who endorse university progressivism that trickle onto staffs make little cumulative impression (Borko & Eisenhart, 1992). This process is abetted by the problem that university programs often emphasize the theoretical more than the practical and thus lose out when students lack the ideal qualities often ascribed to them by university faculty (Baldassarre, 1997; Gallagher, 1996; Kallos, 1999; Voutira, 1996).

Each of these explanations is seductive, because, like my belief in conceptual home bases achieved through coherent program design, it assigns a single, powerful cause to explain a complex phenomenon. My engagement with the cases upon which I base this book has led me to abandon single-source causal arguments that explain teacher development as having one basic pathway. I now recognize that no single explanation accounts for how teachers learn to teach, including the role that university teacher education programs play in that concept development. One advantage of case studies is that they enable careful analyses of the particular, and the particularities of cases help to provide nuance to overgeneralized beliefs.

As I will detail in this book, teachers learn to teach through multiple sources, only one of which is the teacher education program. Learning to teach, like developing any social conception, rarely proceeds along a single pathway. Rather, each case illustrates how a large number of influences are orchestrated idiosyncratically by individuals as a function of how they integrate those experiences into their fundamental belief systems. This book is an effort to explore the dynamics of those processes and to consider the implications of this phenomenon for academics charged with preparing teachers for life in schools.

1

Vygotsky and Concept Development

I'm sure it's just a coincidence, but my father's parents, born in 1880 and 1885 respectively, were Jewish, and came to the United States from the city of Gomel in the Eastern European country of Byelorussia (now Belarus). In 1896, Lev Vygotsky, also from a Byelorussian Jewish family, was born in Gomel. My grandparents ended up fleeing the pogroms and landing in New York City's Jewish ghetto on the Lower East Side of Manhattan, where my grandfather became a painter of signs for small businesses and where my father was born. Vygotsky stuck around and became the Mozart of Psychology. Much later, after getting my doctorate in 1989, I began reading Vygotsky—my graduate education was more in information processing, a very different paradigm—and developed a strong affinity with his ideas. His perspective has had a powerful effect on my thinking about most things, including what I've written for this book. As the old jazz musicians used to say when they heard a serious young talent: "Cat can play."

The work I synthesize for this book was initially planned using what my CELA colleagues and I called an activity theory framework (Grossman, Smagorinsky, & Valencia, 1999). Pam Grossman and I had an interesting conversation during the course of the data collection, when Pam noted that for all the attention we were giving to contexts and collective activity—an activity theorist imperative—my own approach of focusing on individual cases rather than cohorts presented me with a paradox of sorts. That observation turned out to be very generative for me, contributing to my broader decision to drop claims to conducting research according to an activity theory framework and re-claiming Vygotsky as my theoretical source.

Bakhurst (2007) observes that "despite his emphasis on the sociocultural foundations of psychological development, Vygotsky's thought remains centred on the individual subject conceived as a discrete, autonomous self" (p. 63). Vygotsky considered the role of contexts in human development to be of paramount importance, and indeed foregrounded social interaction based on cultural-historical patterns and mediational means as the origin of any individual's cognitive processes. His consideration of social, cultural, and historical mediation in learning to think, however, emerges from the perspective of the individual who appropriates cultural schemata, worldviews, conceptual understandings, and other fundamental aspects of human cognition. His approach is thus amenable to studies that take a cultural-historical perspective, yet do so in service of understanding individual human development in the context of broader collective activity.

Research on teaching has begun to focus on contexts as part of a social turn in educational research (see, for example, the contributors to Smagorinsky, 2006). Historically, teaching has often been depicted as a solitary, lonely, and isolating profession (e.g., Bullough, 1989; Lortie, 1975; Mirel & Golden, 2012). This view has been adopted in recent teacher assessment policies, with teachers individually responsible for raising students' test scores no matter what has happened in their lives in the past or what issues they might face in the present, facing punitive consequences if they do not (Berliner, 2014). This emphasis on insulated individuals teaching behind closed classroom doors is part of the lore of the teaching profession. Yet this image is deceptive given the dialogic (Bakhtin, 1981) nature of all social interaction; that is, the manner in which thinking and speech are in dialogue with and in intertextual relation with prior human exchanges. This sense of dialogism is fundamentally historical and oriented to speech genres, rather than referring to face-to-face or other immediate forms of talking, in spite of the term's frequent recruitment to characterize immediate classroom discourse and participatory discussions.

Teachers, no matter how innovative or maverick in their conduct, do not construct each day out of whole cloth. Rather, they draw on conversations—conducted with corporeal people or the texts through which they more broadly communicate—that take place over time, extending back to prior eras. Understanding teachers as historically and socially situated, yet agentive individuals helps to break the binary images of (1) the individual going through biological stages of growth with contextual factors serving primarily to abet that development, and (2) the socially *determined* individual fated to be the sum of environmental influences and little more.

The case study investigative method provides a promising, if not exclusive, way of getting at how individuals function in social groups, both in terms of what is available for them to appropriate and how they orchestrate a panoply of mediational possibilities into a personalized approach to engaging with the world. Some have interpreted the cultural-historical approach and its various subgroups as fatalistic in that one's circumstances have much to do with how one conducts life. However, the availability of individual free will and manifold means of mediation provide multiple directions in life, even as social conventions and traditional patterns of cultural dominance curtail such possibilities for people born into less agentive circumstances. Such broad possibilities were not available to all in Vygotsky's less connected, more parochial, more geographically isolated, and more authoritarian world of Stalin's rule than is available to most twenty-first-century US teachers.

In this chapter, I lay out how Vygotsky's formulation of socially situated human cognition has helped lead me to *mediated concept development* as the primary focus for how people learn to teach. The development of teaching conceptions relies on social-cultural-historical mediation through engagement with others in order to enable one to arrive at a set of beliefs about the purposes of education, the means of instruction, the role of the classroom in the broader practice of schooling, the ultimate ends of human development, the explicit and implicit means by which people's thinking is externally mediated, and other considerations through which one develops an approach to teaching a particular discipline.

Vygotsky's major work, *Thinking and Speech* (1987), elaborates his view of concepts and concept development. In this chapter, I both rely and build on Vygotsky's outline of concept development in order to construct my own perspective on how people learn to teach, with a focus on my discipline of origin, English/Language Arts, the subject area that provides the emphasis for this research. This academic domain historically has centered on literary interpretation, writing (often about literature), and language use (Applebee, 1974; Pasternak, Caughlan, Hallman, Renzi, & Rush, 2017; Smagorinsky & Whiting, 1995). It has more recently been expanded to include other modes of composition and reading beyond the printed word and the traditional literary text. It is now as much concerned with linguistic variation as with "standard English," at least in teacher education if not always in schools (National Council of Teachers of English, 2005); and semiotic notions of textuality have extended the field's coverage to virtually any sort of composition.

Vygotsky's (1987) outline of concepts helps to resolve a fundamental problem with learning to teach: the presumed conflict between theory and practice. The disjuncture between theory and practice is involved in the *two-worlds pitfall* (Feiman-Nemser & Buchmann, 1985): the differential expectations that beginning teachers face when simultaneously trying to meet the demands of both idealistic and theoretical university faculty and practical school leaders and faculty. I will challenge this dichotomized conception throughout this volume as limited and insufficient, given the abundance of worlds imposing gravitational pulls on teachers. At the surface level, the gap between these two worlds helps explain the limited effects of educational coursework on how education students teach once they begin working in schools, which was the concern that motivated the original conception of the CELA research drawn on for this book. Teachers often complain that teacher education programs are *too theoretical*; that they emphasize ideals and abstractions at the expense of the pedagogical tools needed for effective *practice* (Baldassarre, 1997; Gallagher, 1996; Kallos, 1999; Voutira, 1996). In this view, theory and practice are positioned as having different concerns, with university-based faculty espousing elaborated theoretical models that may or may not correspond to how their prospective teachers' students actually behave, with teacher candidates (TCs) attempting to instruct students under the guidance of mentors who may not adhere to those principles and with students who may not cooperate with theorists' idealistic representation of them.

The metaphors provided to account for the relation between theory and practice suggest that they are often positioned as separate and competing. Theory is pitted *versus* practice (e.g., The Colorado Writing Tutors Conference, 2000) or can be *put into* practice (Kearsley, 1994–2001) or *into practitioners* (Jackson, 1992), or can *translate into* practice (Rita, Richey, Klein, & Tracey (2011). The chasm between theory and practice might be *bridged* (Weaver, 1998), *linked* (Grisham & Brink, 2000), joined in *marriage* (Ballenger, 1999), or *integrated* (Beyer, 1996). This positioning involves a distinct hierarchy, with influence proceeding from theory *to* practice (ERIC Clearinghouse on Reading English and Communication, 1995). All of these phrasings suggest that theory is the more ethereal and authoritative of these distinct domains, that practice is the more protean and pragmatic dimension, and that some sort of merger ought to be available. Further, from the standpoint of the theorist, theory can and should improve practice, but practice has little effect on theory. This thinking has a long history in university thought (e.g., Brownell, 1948), yet it is rejected as patronizing by those practitioners who study their own teaching (e.g., MacLean & Mohr, 1999).

The dichotomous, hierarchical conception of theoreticians and their theories positioned above practitioners and their practice remains axiomatic among many whose scholarly writing provides the grounds for the debate (Stephens et al., 1999). This common bifurcation of theory and practice misses the point of how people learn. I argue in contrast that Vygotsky's (1987) exegesis on the *concept* links abstract understandings and practical activity. Their interdependence is necessary for a person to engage in utilitarian worldly action. I conclude that *the problem with teacher education is not too much theory, but too little concept* (cf. Cook, Smagorinsky, Fry, Konopak, & Moore, 2002; Smagorinsky, Cook, & Johnson, 2003).

Introduction to Concepts

Vosniadou's (2008) volume on conceptual change demonstrates how researchers have focused on different processes by which concepts develop for individuals. Taber (2011), in reviewing Vosniadou's volume, argues that researchers who attend to the social context of development and distributed notions of context do so because it is "easier to access than an intra-mental plane," that which presumably occurs between the ears, which is out of sight and thus inherently more problematic (p. 5). Vosniadou's contributors, for the most part, distance themselves from "radical" views that "eschew notions of personal knowledge" (p. 5), and instead focus on the social, cultural, and historical contexts of development. In contrast, the contributors to Vosniadou's volume regard the individual learner as the primary unit of analysis, with personal learning serving as the focus of research, consistent with the historical tendency to view teachers as isolated individuals.

If Vosniadou's (2008) collection may be considered to be a state-of-the-art volume of psychological studies of concept development, then the social-cultural-historical approach taken by Vygotsky (1987) would be a minor, perhaps fringe, and possibly "radical" perspective, as argued by Levy (1995) of Michael Cole and Yrjo Engeström, two prominent Vygotskian researchers and activity theorists. I would argue instead that Vygotsky's framework enables attention to both the social setting of learning to teach *and* the individual's orchestration of what is contextually available into a personal conception of teaching. The "radical" perspective eschewed by Vosniadou's authors may be somewhat of a straw person when this position is construed primarily as positing the presence of a static monoculture and a deterministic sense of destiny imposed by context. As I will demonstrate throughout this book, however, learning to teach involves immersion in many settings—far more than the two arenas of the two-worlds pitfall—that make navigating a conceptual pathway quite challenging and often contradictory. None is particularly fatalistic in its influence, given that it is inevitably contradicted by another available influence. The presence of multiple means of mediation in concept development calls, I believe, for attention not only to context but also to many contexts and their histories and means of mediation in order to understand which aspects of culture are appropriated, and why, for teachers to integrate into a worldview that encompasses how to teach an academic discipline.

Vygotsky and the Conceptual Pathway

Vygotsky (1987) was concerned with the ways in which people construct concepts over time, particularly through their attribution of meaning to words that they learn through cultural engagement. That is, people's concept development may be ascertained through the ways in which they attribute meaning to a word at different stages of development as mediated by experiences and formal learning. In contrast to the dichotomous approach of focusing on either the social or the personal, Vygotsky viewed concepts as representative of individual mental reconstructions whose associations of meaning find their origins in joint social and cultural practice with others. His early twentieth-century world was far less connected than today's technology-mediated social environment, perhaps making monocultures more possible. His views thus require adaptation to twenty-first-century conditions that provide far more complex social worlds for individuals and collectives to navigate.

Vygotsky focuses on the manner in which children gravitate to the norms of relatively stable adult communities of practice in which a more-or-less broad social agreement confers a general meaning upon a concept. The meaning available among one group of people might be disputed in other communities of practice, or the concept itself might not be available at all if the social activities associated with it are not locally practiced or imaginable. This view is compatible with the "weak" (i.e., less deterministic) version of the Sapir-Whorf hypothesis of linguistic relativity in which thinking and speech are intertwined. This relation is responsible for the manner in which the language of the indigenous Sami people of northern Scandinavia includes around 180 snow- and ice-related words and around 1,000 different words for reindeer, and the vocabularies of the Yanomami of northern Brazil have words for neither.

I next review the fundamental principles of Vygotsky's (1987) outline. I first situate his attention to concepts in his larger effort to outline a comprehensive psychology of socially, culturally, and historically mediated human development. I then review his distinction between scientific and spontaneous concepts. Finally, I detail his developmental sequence of complexes to pseudoconcepts to concepts. Each of these conceptions has consequences for understanding mediated human development, including that experienced by beginning and veteran teachers.

Concept Development and Human Development

Concept development begins with an infant's first exposure to human contact and the expectations that others have for a child in the greater draft of human societal activity. Cole (1996) describes the covert mediational means for advancing a society's practices as instances of *prolepsis*. Through this phenomenon, people are subtly encouraged to take on particular dispositions, attitudes, and beliefs by means of the cultural tools and values made available in the environment, and the goals toward which they are employed. The persistence of proleptic influences helps to account for the fact that women have historically been guided toward careers as teachers (along with other careers—nursing, social work, domestic cleaning and caretaking, and many others) to a far greater extent than men (Acker, 1994).

In schools, students' trajectories are suggested by all manner of activity structures and suggested optimal outcomes, often embedded in the traditions, curriculum, rules, and unwritten routines. Let's focus on one strand of the English/Language Arts curriculum, the literature strand. A teacher might embrace an approach to reading literature based upon the principles of one type of literary criticism or another. A New Critical approach trains readers to study a text for technique and to construct proofs that lead to authoritative interpretations of texts. In contrast, a Marxist critic might examine the text for the ways in which the text depicts economic inequities and power differentials, both deliberate and unconscious on the part of the author. The approach to instruction, often grounded in much broader epistemologies, shapes what sort of reading is preferred, how that reading is undertaken and processed in classrooms, how students' reading competency is assessed, and other consequences of adopting and imposing a perspective on students' reading (Appleman, 2015).

When one method of reading literature becomes dominant in textbooks, reading literature in school serves the values of that approach, with consequences for practice and assessment. New Criticism has historically shaped secondary school English/Language Arts instruction (Applebee, 1993) and has been revived in the Common Core State Curriculum (Shanahan, 2013). Its values suggest the appropriateness of imposing specific interpretations of the author's textual inscriptions. More personal meaning-making responses, in this approach, become less available to students and subject to dismissal as emotional and idiosyncratic. Yet other ways of reading, such as reader response theories (Beach, 1993), would elevate the reader's personal instantiation of meaning over the received knowledge provided by professional literary critics. Reading, in other words, is not a singular phenomenon. Rather, it is culturally shaped by frames of mind suggested by both traditions and specific applications of those traditions in classrooms.

The broader cultural stream sets the terms for any concept that is available within it, providing the mediational channel that in turn conditions how smaller concepts are appropriated within its value system. This broader cultural stream, in an academic discipline, typically involves genres and discourse practices that suggest appropriate means of expression, and that suggest the purpose of the discipline. These purposes might include learning the technical means through which texts are constructed and designed to be read, engaging in self-exploration, becoming a better citizen of communities near and far, and pursuing other goals that in turn suggest appropriate practices. In this sense, any social concept has an ideological dimension that is embedded in a more encompassing, governing worldview that, rather than determining how one thinks, suggests the appropriateness of ways of thinking for the broadest acceptance within a community of practice and discourse.

Differences in worldviews as they apply to education were reported by Benjamin Franklin in his ironically titled *Remarks Concerning the Savages of North-America*. In this widely reprinted excerpt from that essay, Franklin reports that in 1744, in conjunction with the negotiation of the (soon broken) Treaty of Lancaster in Pennsylvania between the Government of Virginia and the Six Nations of the Confederation of the Iroquois, the Virginia Commissions offered to finance the education of a small group of young Iroquois men at Williamsburg College so they could learn "civilized" ways. After considering this generous offer, an Iroquois representative responded as follows:

> We know that you highly esteem the kind of learning taught in those colleges, and that the maintenance of our young men while with you would be very expensive to you. We are convinced, therefore, that you mean to do us good by your proposal, and we thank you heartily. But you who are wise must know that different nations have different conceptions of things, and you will therefore not take it amiss if our ideas of this kind of education happen not to be the same with yours. We have had some experience of it. Several of our young people were formerly brought up at the colleges of the northern provinces, they were instructed in all your science, but when they came back to us they were bad runners, ignorant of every means of living in the woods, unable to bear either cold or hunger, knew neither how to build a cabin, take a deer, or kill an enemy, or speak our language. They were, therefore, neither fit for hunters, warriors, or counselors; they were totally good for nothing. We are not, however, the less obliged by your kind offer, though we decline accepting it, and to show our grateful sense of it, if the gentlemen of Virginia send us a dozen of their sons we will take great care of their education, instruct them in all we know, and make men of them.

This story reveals the ideological underpinnings of an educational conception, one that shapes both a large vision of the purpose of society and the educational processes that serve its interests.

Scientific and Spontaneous Concepts

Vygotsky (1987) distinguished between what have been translated as *scientific* and *spontaneous* concepts. The scientific concept, argues Wertsch (1991, p. 39), is more properly translated as "academic" because people learn such concepts through formal, systematic instruction. This learning usually takes place in schools and colleges, but it also occurs in other formal settings for learning in which the emphasis is on explicit and systematic instruction in rules, conventions, and other governing knowledge. The process of developing such concepts involves appropriating a set of rules that enable a learner to extract a concept's principles from its original context and apply them to new situations where they provide a framework for understanding circumstances and acting on them in fitting fashion.

In the sense that scientific concepts are often emphasized in academic settings, they tend to be associated with the appropriation of increasingly advanced literacy skills. The formalization of a concept in writing enables a high degree of sustained and consistent elaboration, the fixing of ideas in textual form, and the potential for widespread distribution beyond the bounds of its initial exposure. A scientific concept is thus not tied to the setting in which it is originally learned. Instead, its abstract nature gives it generalizable features that make it adaptable, rather than wholly transferable, to new problems in new contexts that share general properties with those settings in which the concept has been employed elsewhere.

Spontaneous concepts are learned in situated, everyday practice, and therefore are applicable primarily in contexts where the circumstances and practices closely resemble those of the original context of learning. Spontaneous concepts are experiential in origin, with governing rules not subjected to the formal textually embodied outlines that are available in school learning. Rather, learning spontaneous concepts is an informal process through which understandings are appropriated through direct practice. Learning to play basketball on one playground court in one neighborhood, for instance, might lead to a specific conception of how to play the game. This conception might be out of place on a different court where other styles of play guide the action. The skills learned on one court, where one is considered a good player, might involve a heavy emphasis on teamwork. This style might make one a poor player on a playground where players rely on individual talent and where a team-oriented approach might obstruct the individualistic style of play. I have known several high school basketball coaches who have said that the most talented players in the school are walking around the hallways rather than playing for the school team, because they cannot adapt what they have learned on their neighborhood court to formal, systematic team competition.

Vygotsky (1987) emphasizes the need for the integration of spontaneous and scientific concepts in order to develop durable, rule-governed, empirically tested concepts. He argues that formal instruction in principles alone will not result in the development of a strong, adaptable concept; principles are of little value without application. Similarly, applied knowledge is of limited value without the availability of broader governing rules. This *interplay between the two conceptual fields* enables people to think about problems beyond their range of experience through the creative use of their imagination and what they can project based on the principles they have developed. Good teacher education does not pit theory against practice. Rather, *it works toward concept development* by extracting the generalizable from the local and by finding applications from the abstract to construct a working theory of how to teach effectively.

The Broad Sequence of Concept Development

In Vygotsky's (1987) outline (see Table 1.1), all of the individual elements encompassed by a concept are unified by a single theme, enabling the concept to serve as a template for organizing thinking in consistent ways. Along the path toward concepts, people develop *complexes* and *pseudoconcepts*, both of which approximate the unity of elements found in concepts in some fashion, but include inconsistencies. I next outline this developmental sequence as described by Vygotsky.

It would be difficult to process the world without approaching it categorically. Concept development involves a process of constructing increasingly consistent, action-oriented categories for sorting the world and its features so that it can be experienced with confidence and a degree of regulation. The process of discrimination

Table 1.1 Development from Complex to Pseudoconcept to Concept

Type of Generalization in Developmental Order	Definition	Child's Example	Teacher's Example
Complex	The individual elements are associated with one another but not all are associated according to the same theme or significant traits.	Learning to label a pet a cat and then labeling any other four-legged creature a cat.	Learning to label a group activity cooperative learning and then labeling any group activity cooperative learning even if students neither cooperate nor learn.
Pseudoconcept	The individual elements appear to be unified but have internal inconsistencies.	Learning to label a pet a cat and then labeling any feline creature (e.g., fox) a cat.	Learning to label a group activity cooperative learning and then labeling any group activity cooperative learning even if it lacks some critical element such as teamwork, a shared goal, individual and group accountability, and so on.
Concept	The individual elements included in the set are unified by a single theme.	Learning to label a pet a cat and discriminating between cats and other cat-like creatures.	Learning to label an activity cooperative learning when small, heterogeneous groups of students work as a team toward a shared goal in such a way as to be both individually and collectively accountable for the work, and work in such a way as to show cooperation and concern for one another and thus raise students' confidence and self-perceptions.

Source: Vygotsky (1987).

and differentiation characterizes the ways in which people move from crude generalizations to those of greater nuance. The increasing precision of these classifications moves a learner through what Vygotsky argues are two stages, the complex and the pseudoconcept. Although the line between these stages is not always distinct, their utility comes from the idea that they represent increasing capacities for discernment and organization of the world and its working parts.

A *complex* is an early stage of concept development, one in which "*any* connection is sufficient to lead to the inclusion of an element in a given complex. . . . The complex is based on heterogeneous empirical connections that frequently have nothing in common with one another" (Vygotsky, 1987, p. 137; emphasis in original). Early in life, for instance, a child might refer to all plants as "flowers," then gradually learn to make broad distinctions between flowers and trees, flowers and grass, and so on within the general class of vegetation. Later distinctions might discriminate between types of flowers: roses and peonies, irises and daylilies, and so on. Through this process of modification and classification, people develop concepts through which they process and act on their worlds.

These classifications can have consequences, such as when two plants look quite similar yet require very different growing conditions. Irises and daylilies have upright spiky foliage, and are similar at a glance; a closer look finds that daylily foliage has a vertical crease in the center, and irises are flat. More importantly, a gardener needs to understand how each fits in with its ecosystem. Deer love to eat daylilies but leave irises alone, so a plant's survival depends on knowledge of where to locate it. Even that basic knowledge is insufficient for a practical concept to guide planting to enhance a plant's survival. There are between 200 and 300 iris species (depending on the source consulted, an indication of conceptual disagreement) and roughly 80,000 daylily cultivars, each with its own requirements, demanding highly refined conceptual knowledge in order to make good planting decisions. My goal with this review is not to get into the finer points of gardening. Nor is it to provide a firm distinction regarding where the complex ends and the pseudoconcept begins in making classifications of increasing accuracy. Rather, my objective is simply to note that in Vygotsky's parlance, they represent the general stages of differentiation that lead toward the development of the more unified concept that allows for knowledgeable and satisfying worldly navigation, including wise and economical plant placement.

Although Vygotsky's (1987) primary concern as a researcher was the young child and adolescent (Vygotsky, 1998), usually in a clinical setting, his work may be extrapolated to account for learning by people at any stage of human development. Adults, particularly when entering new fields or activities, go through a similar process of differentiation and organization. According to Werner's (1957) *orthogenetic principle*, people entering complex new environments initially find them inchoate and undifferentiated. To begin processing their elements, they break the environment into categorical parts that often are unrelated. Over time, to make more sophisticated sense of these disparate parts, they ultimately orchestrate them into a working whole so that relationships and perhaps hierarchies provide a working order to their interpretation of their surroundings. Each categorical process may involve the developmental sequence outlined by Vygotsky, as would the ultimate task of the broader synthesis of the various parts into a coherent whole.

Learning to teach involves the gradual development of pedagogical concepts, with misconceptions formed and discarded along the way, and with a more comprehensive synthesis of concepts occurring later in the process. One might initially conceive of collaborative learning as any group setting in school in which students are grouped to complete a task, whether they collaborate or learn or not. Only when the formal, academic concept of collaborative learning is subjected to empirical testing and reflection can a learner begin to sort out what collaborative learning entails, perhaps in relation to engagement with texts and other people for corroboration and refinement.

The orthogenetic principle further involves synthesizing concepts such as collaborative learning with other understandings about teaching. The problem I emphasize in this book is that this ultimate synthesis is difficult to achieve because teaching involves many tasks that often don't fit well together. Teachers may be charged simultaneously with conducting orderly classes, and allowing students the freedom to chart out and pursue their individual trajectories and the learning processes that facilitate them. Different environmental influences on teachers impose different values, such that being consistent within competing centers of gravity is challenging and perhaps not possible.

The Cultural Nature of Concepts

In that they provide the frameworks for thinking that people appropriate through their social experiences, concepts are fundamentally cultural. One's conceptions are thus not simply individual constructions, sequestered from social and ideological influences. Rather, concepts are culturally mediated constructions that affect one's sense of place in the world and how one navigates life's journey. Even the most seemingly concrete of scientific facts is open to conceptual interpretation. The naturally formed aggregate of mineral matter in my yard, for instance, exists to me and most people I know as inert rock. Yet subjective idealists (e.g., Berkeley, 1901) might deny the existence of physical matter at all, and indigenous people from this continent might take the animistic view that the rock has a living spirit (Jacobs, 1998). If something as seemingly definitive as a rock can be seen as everything from nonexistent to inanimate to spiritually infused, then *social concepts* like "literary understanding" and "instructional scaffolding" stand little chance of finding universal agreement (Smagorinsky, 2013). Academic disciplines typically involve people of varying ideology and orientation, thus complicating any effort to arrive at a coherent understanding of a subject and its content and processes.

Concepts and Societal Telos

Any cultural tool or sign embodies not only the ideology of the individual who uses it but also the historical social practices through which it has come into being and has been incorporated into cultural activity over time. The culture itself evolves in relation to the ways in which that perspective is adapted to new conditions and problems by its members. Although complex societies such as the United States include people of diverse perspectives, on the whole, a culture has a sense of optimal destination toward which activity and thinking are channeled. Wertsch (2000) has termed this phenomenon *telos*, drawing on the Greek term that refers to the end or outcome of a goal-oriented process.

Achieving a whole teleological sense of purpose for a nation can be difficult, if not impossible, even in totalitarian states that seek to produce absolute dedication to a specified ideology (Rancière, 2010). At the same time, without a generally common sense of purpose and outcome, a society would have trouble functioning with any degree of continuity or cohesion. These agreements tend to be written into laws that govern social intercourse and codify behavioral expectations, even when their personal beliefs are out of synch with the legal code. The end of legalized racial segregation in the United States, for instance, did not change everyone's attitude toward people of other races; racism has often persisted through other means (Lipsitz, 2006) in practices that remain institutionalized, are undertaken more covertly and insidiously, and that structure activity and opportunity through less visible means.

Learning how to think, as a fundamentally social process, leads to the appropriation of meanings that have achieved some degree of cultural stability, even if cultures might view one another's values hierarchically. This problem is evident in the current immigration debate, with people from Mesoamerica treated as products of inferior cultures by many in the US, including teachers, as Moll (2000) has found in his studies of the educational experiences of students of Mexican descent in Arizona.

When teachers impress particular concepts on students—for instance, democracy or theocracy in a history class—they are not just teaching an idea. They are asserting an ideology, one that may be contested by others. A US history textbook, for instance, will typically emphasize the nation's achievements without simultaneously attending to the means by which those achievements have come at other people's expense (Loewen, 1996), and will soften the language through which the European conquest of the indigenous people is represented in order to establish the superiority of Judeo-Christian values (Four Arrows, 2013). The moral question of whether a culture is moving in the "right" direction or is making "progress" is highly subjective, yet ideological differences are typically represented in schools as matters of social and cultural progress rather than as more brutal advantages in weaponry, technology, horse domestication, and disease immunity whose origins are more geographic accidents than cultural achievements (Diamond, 1997).

Concepts and Future Action

Concepts enhance people's ability to anticipate how future action will unfold, provided that (1) the new set of circumstances shares enough traits with the contexts of learning, and (2) formal principles are available to guide adaptation and application in newly developing situations (Smagorinsky, 2011). A generalization that is structured with formal principles and grounded in experience enables one to infer what will happen next when one has sufficient information about the present and how it has come into being. Vygotsky (1987) developed his theory of concept development in a world where geographically and socially isolated cultures were quite common, which made the availability of only spontaneous concepts more likely (see Luria, 1976, for an account of remote peasants whose lands were incorporated into the Soviet Union). In contrast, the twenty-first-century world potentially makes social and cultural isolation less possible, at least in nations with a technological emphasis, especially in a discipline like teaching in which university training, professional development, internet connectivity, and other factors easily enable exposure to multiple perspectives.

The idea that concepts can help one anticipate the future is *not* commensurate with saying that concepts enable one to *predict* the future. Rather, they permit a recognition of how things work, allowing one to anticipate, through a combination of generalizable rules and experiential knowledge, how social and natural processes more or less unfold. This anticipation might run aground when a concept is being tested in a wholly new sort of environment. The "best practices" or "high-leverage practices" available in one setting do not necessarily produce the same results when applied in schools with different financing, class size, affordances, student composition, and other factors (Philip et al., 2018; Smagorinsky, 2009, 2018b).

A concept is not simply a generalization that enables taxonomic thinking. More potently, concepts are motivated by an ideology or theory about how its principles function in relation to natural or social processes (Barrett, Abdi, Murphy, & Gallagher, 1993). Concepts thus serve as the basis for the planning of rule-governed, culturally channeled action in relation to challenges presented by the environment (Tulviste, 1991), assuming that a person can interpret the environment in insightful ways. These settings include the actions of people, which are not easy to forecast reliably. Settings like classrooms, for instance, may involve a room of thirty or so students whose socialization and maturity are works in progress and whose responses to a teacher may vary; and likely involve a teacher who is also experiencing concept development, perhaps in opposition to a classroom aide assigned to assist special learners who interpret the situation differently.

A durable, road-tested concept provides a template for anticipating, however tenuously, how to plan instruction and manage student conduct so that educational goals are possible to reach. The studies that I report in this book suggest that beginning (or experienced) teachers with little conceptual understanding of teaching and learning relations tend to engage in trial-and-error instruction, indicating a fragile understanding of how their plans will work in practice. In contrast, beginning teachers who can articulate the purposes behind their decisions based on a synthesis of formal and practical knowledge have better anticipated how their instructional planning will work in the teeming environment of the classroom.

The Affective Dimension of Concept Development

Vygotsky (1987) integrates consciousness with other bodily processes and with the social, cultural, and historical practices through which people learn how to think paradigmatically. He does not understand cognition as something that takes place within the confines of the skull. Rather, he conceives of it as interrelated with the whole of the human body. Further, thinking is mediated by cultural tools, whose potential for practice is a function of the setting and the cultural and historical antecedents that have shaped the present moment. With conceptual understandings serving to formulate future possibilities based on present knowledge, concepts can help individuals develop feelings of order, security, and a state of deep-seated contentedness and satisfaction with their place in the world.

The greater the experiential verification of a concept's formal principles, the more adaptable it is to new settings and situations. This repurposing, in turn, produces fewer disruptive surprises and greater stability in navigating the environment, leading to a feeling of security and confidence. Having reality trump anticipation is not necessarily disruptive or negative, because surprises may bring about welcome change. But in the general conduct of life, a degree of predictability brings continuity and assurance to social processes. Most of the surprises experienced by the beginning teachers in my studies were related to classroom events that were neither anticipated nor welcome and that left them feeling less confident about their ability to teach effectively.

Affect thus is implicated in concept development in reciprocal ways. One's affective experiences both follow from one's degree of conceptual understanding and provide the foundation on which concept development takes place. Not all learners have positive frameworks to enable persistence in new situations. Meta-experience—how one experiences one's experiences (see Smagorinsky & Daigle, 2012)—can thus frame new situations for better or worse, as illustrated by beginning teachers whose good or bad experiences with a pedagogy, group of students, type of school, and other aspect of teaching in turn frame forthcoming experiences as likely to follow a similar pattern.

Creativity in Concept Formation

When people think of creativity, they tend to summon to mind the lone artistic genius inspired by a muse to which others lack access. Yet Smolucha (1992) argues that the culturally mediated nature of creativity reveals how "any individual creative 'genius' is actually building on the collective labor of other people throughout history" (p. 53). Creativity follows from the use of the imagination, which enables one to project possibilities based on both experience and conceptual understandings. This creative potential allows people to avoid the fatalism that some see in what they consider to be the determinism of theories of social-cultural-historical mediation on the individual's thinking (Scribner, 1997). Creative thinking liberates one from material exigencies, serving as one of the *higher mental functions* that Vygotsky (1987) found to characterize thinking in accordance with cultural concepts, which he asserts are available through socialization rather than biological maturity.

Lower functions include those that follow from unmediated biological processes that are largely hereditary rather than culturally learned; these include such maturational phenomena as the increasing capacity for abstract thinking that comes with age for the typical person (Goldberg, 2006). Higher mental functions develop through social interaction and thus give particular cultural shape to concepts, either scientific, spontaneous, or the more robust interplay of the two. Rather than serving as a dichotomous forced choice, biological and cultural development are complementary. The ancient "nature versus nurture" debate is thus misplaced, moot, and obsolete, according to evolutionary psychologists who assume the presence and interdependence of both (Schaller, Norenzayan, Heine, Yamagishi, & Kameda, 2010).

Creativity relies on the ability to use imagination to assemble prior understandings into new possibilities. Because a culture or type of task poses particular challenges to its members and practitioners, creativity takes on the mediated qualities that people appropriate through the use of cultural tools. Broadly speaking, a student from a culture that relies on respect for elders and other authorities will produce creativity that fits within the parameters of this hierarchical relationship. Any creative pedagogical adaptation will come primarily within the contours of authoritarian teaching and learning that suit the socialization of students from such cultures. Teachers who make inappropriate assumptions about their student's socialization may end up assessing them as deviant or below standard, not on the basis of achievement, but on their departure from expected norms (Ballenger, 1999).

Creativity increases with age because one's experiences with the world increase with age. Because imaginative acts of creativity are reliant on prior images, children's ability to conjure images is relatively limited—a counterintuitive claim to those who see children's unfettered expression as a sign of creativity and adults' conformity to convention as a lack of imagination. In contrast, the experience that accrues with age provides increasing material upon which to project creative possibilities, suggesting that adults are capable of richer creative action than are children (Gajdamaschko, 1999). This creativity is not necessarily evident to outsiders, as it is when children more publicly express themselves, because a mature person's creative work is conducted through the generation of abstract mental images. Without a sense of how things work and how this understanding assists with the anticipation of future events through the projection of images, one is left with trial and error, which relies on tenuous possibilities that may or may not work.

The ability to anticipate future outcomes enables imaginative projections that are consistent with conceptual structures to plan and carry out teaching plans with confidence. A teacher's reflective disposition may enable a reconsideration of the effectiveness of the teaching and in turn a reformulation of the motivating conception that led to the planning of instruction. This capacity to reflect, reconsider, and revise gives individuals agency in sifting through their experiences in relation to their formal knowledge to navigate their social worlds.

Concept Development's Twisting Path and Uncertain Destination

Vygotsky (1987) postulates that concept development follows a "twisting" rather than a linear or direct path (p. 156). In his outline, a relatively stable conception is ultimately available. Even with the pathway often meandering down blind alleys and getting sidetracked, one is headed toward a relatively stable concept. Vygotsky's primary illustrations of concepts involve biological phenomena, such as a child's ultimate ability to differentiate a whale from a fish. My own work studying beginning teachers complicates this notion, because adults working toward a conception such as "effective teaching" are not all headed in the same direction (Smagorinsky, 2013). As a social concept, effective teaching may be defined one way in one setting (e.g., according to a university education instructor, as a progressive, student-centered, constructivist set of practices) and another elsewhere (e.g., according to a school principal who works within a neoliberal environment, as an approach that produces orderly classrooms in which students are trained to score as high as possible on standardized tests).

These mediated shifts of direction are often in such conflict with one another that even the notion of a twisting path that has a clear destination is dubious (Smagorinsky, Rhym, & Moore, 2013). In studying beginning teachers, I have found a host of other mediators that introduce additional potential exemplars and influences, many of which have been described in other research on learning to teach:

- *First-order mediational experiences*, such as one's apprenticeship of observation (Lortie, 1975) that produces influences from one's experiences as a student, in terms of both exemplars and antitheses; peer pressure from various mentors and colleagues to conduct classes in particular and at times conflicting ways; administrative pressure to teach and conduct oneself according to specific definitions of effectiveness and professionalism; mandates that impose a curriculum, a teaching script, an assessment, and other structures and processes that standardize their instruction so that all students are exposed to identical material in identical ways; in-service education that may promote a variety of practices and beliefs, at times fundamentally at odds with one another; and the school schedule, such as block scheduling, that constrains and enables particular practices.
- *Second-order mediational experiences*, such as images of teachers from film, television, and online media that may depict effective teaching as authoritarian, inspiring, gentle, demanding, and countless other traits fictionalized to emphasize particular values; and readings—from professional literature to education blogs—with conflicting recommendations for what to emphasize in teaching and how to promote anticipated outcomes.
- *Dispositions*, such as conceptions of students' "character" and how best to align it with social expectations, accompanied by beliefs such as the view that good character produces obedience and thus good character is a prerequisite to developing those behaviors appropriate for good study habits, in contrast with conceptions of character that make informed and conscientious dissent an admirable trait when authority serves its constituents poorly (see Smagorinsky & Taxel, 2005); and one's reliance on faith-based or secular orientations to the world, including those that motivate teaching, that might position teaching as a calling, a duty, an income, a service, a babysitting job, or other perspective that would have consequences for instructional decisions and relationships with students.

These conflictual settings and practices make it difficult to identify a clear teleological destination, or to map a passageway toward it. This amorphous sense of direction is endemic to complex social problems and produces the conundrum that coming to a clear conception of a biological phenomenon, such as what a fish is, and coming to a clear conception of a social phenomenon, such as understanding and putting into practice what "effective teaching" is, are tasks of different degrees of stability. Teachers are continually under pressure to teach effectively; yet what constitutes effective teaching depends on whom one asks and how it is measured, even within the same academic department in the same school. Arriving at a consistent, durable conception of effective teaching in the midst of multiple, conflicting means of mediation thus might involve something more than a twisting path alternating between limited competing sources of influence.

Tulviste (1991) has argued that, from a cultural-historical perspective emerging from Vygotsky, people develop frameworks for thinking by means of their engagement with the problems that occur in their environments. His *heterogeneity principle* assumes that because people live amid competing ideologies and perspectives and appropriate them concurrently, they may simultaneously hold seemingly contradictory beliefs. This idea suggests that when teachers state contradictory beliefs, what they indicate is their *immersion within contradictory environments* more than the intellectual inability to arrive at a unified concept independent of worldly engagement. Tulviste formulated this perspective before the widespread availability of the internet, which has expanded people's exposure to multiple conceptions of the world and multiple versions of each conception, thus making heterogeneity a fact of twenty-first-century life except in the most isolated of communities.

The pervasive presence of competing pedagogical notions suggests that if anything, as one matures as a teacher, more possibilities enter into one's teaching repertoire, not all of which are conceptually unified. This abundant experiential material enables the generation of a host of possible images, each suggesting a unique conceptual pathway upon which to base creative action for the immediate contingencies that arise during the course of teaching. Teaching experiences also contribute to the affective framework, the collection of meta-experiences through which these creative acts are filtered, which may predispose the teacher in particular directions in relation to specific populations of students. This expanded repertoire undoubtedly enables a wide range of solution paths, yet in doing so, it complicates the degree to which they will all be conceptually unified in the ideal manner envisioned by Vygotsky (1987).

The Social Complexion of Practical Concepts

The outline I have provided suggests that, for those engaging in complex social activities such as learning to teach, *practical concepts* may be the best one can hope for. Because they are subject to continual mediation by competing conceptions in the environment, they may never reach the level of unity suggested by Vygotsky and his tendency to illustrate his points with biological examples. Practical concepts call to mind Bettelheim's (1987) *good enough parent*, which follows from his conclusion that the demands of parenthood in an increasingly fragmented and unpredictable world are sufficiently forbidding that being a great parent exceeds human capability. Parents are expected to become proficient at a task with which they have little, if any, experience, and to do so in a setting that is under continual change. The best a parent can expect to become is good enough to manage child-rearing in reasonably effective ways.

Teachers, too, are working within continually morphing environments. Solid principles are difficult to practice without wavering when the contexts themselves are always contradictory and in flux. Practical concepts might, in this sense, serve as *good enough concepts* that are functional, if flawed in that they reflect the broader social dissensus in which concept development takes place and the difficulty of finding a clear pathway amid the ideological discord. For those learning to teach, this uncertain conceptual destination contributes to the difficulties they have in settling on a pedagogical approach. In the next chapter, I give more attention to the ways in which our research design attended to the brick and mortar of concepts: the tools through which teaching is undertaken and the manner in which teachers learn to use them.

2

Methodological Implications of Taking a Vygotskian Approach to Teacher Development

Vygotsky's (1987) theory of human development assumes that a person's frameworks for thinking are developed through problem-solving action carried out in specific settings whose present social structures have been developed through historical, culturally grounded, and collective activity. In terms of learning to teach, these settings and structures may follow from different conceptions invoked by different stakeholders. The beginning teacher is thus faced with the dilemma of being presented with a range of traditions on which to draw, each assuming a different optimal outcome and therefore reliant on different processes and pedagogical tools. This conundrum is grounded in the issues surrounding concept development elaborated in Chapter 1.

A Vygotskian (1987) framework enables an analysis of the process of learning to teach over time, particularly in terms of identifying the pedagogical tools involved in teaching and how the teacher has learned of them, how to use them, and how using them in particular contexts is and is not effective in reaching articulated goals. In order to understand how and why specific pedagogical tools are employed in teaching, it is useful to understand aspects of the settings of learning to teach to understand why particular tools are regarded as efficacious to meet designed ends.

I have found two constructs to be very useful in understanding why people teach as they do, and why they dedicate their teaching toward particular ends. I introduce them in the first chapter, and will briefly review them here. *Telos* refers to the optimal destinations toward which social activity, including teaching, is directed (Wertsch, 2000). This sense of ideal outcome tends to be linked with broader societal goals. A Montessori education, for instance, positions the child as the director of learning, suggesting a belief in individual agency and distrust of adult motives in child development, and ultimately suggesting a goal of producing adults who are self-regulated and self-directed. A military school education, in contrast, emphasizes discipline and chain of command, which are necessary for coordinating fighting units in the violent defeat of enemies. The teleological direction of any teaching and learning environment thus shapes the more routine practices that comprise daily education.

Establishing a teleological direction may take place through the provision of formal rules enforced through a society's disciplinary mechanisms, or may be promoted more subtly. This less visible means of mediating development toward particular ends is known as *prolepsis* (Cole, 1996), and is more difficult to verify empirically than explicit means of mediation such as laws and manifestos. Such aspects of culture as gender norms and expectations, however, serve as covert means by which people's actions, both great and small, are shaped. Young children are socialized to gender norms and trajectories with such mundane mediators as bedroom décor chosen by their parents, such as when boys' rooms are decorated with transportation motifs and other worldly pursuits and girls' rooms are adorned with dolls, lace, and other domesticalia (Rheingold & Cook, 1975). This destination is suggested through images, encouragement, discouragement, and other means that are less tangible and more built into the fabric of daily social commerce.

Teacher educators are tasked with producing graduates who are prepared to teach competently, perhaps exceptionally, and perhaps with leadership abilities, research skills, and other ancillary assets. This challenge is subject to many vicissitudes that provide TCs with multiple destinations and means of instruction. Student teachers often find themselves pushed and pulled in different directions, with university faculty, supervisors, mentor teachers (MTs), and school systems encouraging different approaches to teaching (Barnes & Smagorinsky, 2016). When beginning teachers become subject solely to evaluation from teaching sites, they often gravitate to site-based values, which is where the high-stakes evaluations that lead to retention or termination are established and enforced.

Key Constructs

Next, I review key constructs that are implicated in this confounding process, assuming that as Wertsch (1985) claims, three themes are central in Vygotsky's theoretical framework: a reliance on a genetic (developmental) method, an assumption of the social origins of consciousness, and a claim that mental processes are mediated by tools and signs. The constructs I next elaborate are *settings*, *tools*, and *appropriation*.

Settings

If the origins of consciousness are necessarily social (Cole, 1996; Vygotsky, 1987; Wertsch, 1991), then understanding the settings of human development is critical to analyzing how people learn to think. I follow Lave's (1988) distinction between *arena* and *setting* to introduce the manner in which the setting of one's work as a teacher is an individual construction. An arena has properties that are tangible and indisputable, such as a school building. How that place is constructed by the individuals who populate it—as a prison, as a source of free food, or as a citadel of learning—serves as the setting that people view it as in social terms (Smagorinsky, 2010). Although two teachers may work within the same arena (e.g., a school or department within a school), they may have distinctly different understandings of the school setting based on their own goals, histories, and activities within the arena.

Settings—assuming that a school building includes both individual and collective constructions that ascribe meaning to the institution—encourage particular social practices that presumably participants will come to see as worthwhile, both in the present and as a means toward teleological ends. These social practices may be explicit (the ringing of bells signifying a time of passage and transition) and implicit or proleptic (males steered toward math and science, and females steered toward home economics). When a collective construction of an arena is at work—what Wertsch (1985) refers to as the *motive* of the setting—the resulting setting provides constraints and affordances that channel, limit, and support learners' efforts to adopt the prevailing social practices.

In this sense, a constraint can be a positive set of limitations that provide the structure for productive activity (Valsiner, 1998), while also being limiting when, for instance, those structures assume that students of color belong in low-track classes (Modica, 2015) and that girls are not fit for STEM fields (Dasgupta & Stout, 2014). These existing practices and artifacts channel new action. Without widespread agreement on the motive and mediational means, a setting could not function cohesively, any more than traffic on roadways could proceed in an orderly way without agreement on how to navigate them. Action within settings is thus goal-oriented, with practices and tool-and-sign configurations mediating development toward the setting's motivating endpoints, for good or ill, depending on who gets directed where and in what fashion.

The idea of an institutional motive, however, does not mean that it has universal consensus, given that multiple and competing goals often coexist within a setting, with some being predominant. Indeed, Wertsch (1995) has challenged developmental theorists for underestimating the importance of asking, *Development toward what?* In other words, in order to understand human development, the teleological values that suggest the appropriateness of particular outcomes and destinations need to be understood to identify which developmental ends are being fostered socially. In terms of settings and motives, then, a motive might represent the outcome for which there is the greatest consensus, which in turn suggests this outcome as the goal toward which schooling should work. This phenomenon may be problematic, such as when there was consensus across the Deep South, at least among many White people, that society, including schools, should be racially segregated and thus inequitable in spite of the "separate but equal" slogan originating with the US Supreme Court in the *Plessy v. Ferguson* segregation case of 1896. The motive for a setting provides channels that encourage and discourage particular ways of thinking and acting without necessarily enforcing action toward those ends. For beginning teachers, resisting these predominant ways of navigating school and the teaching profession is a risk of varying peril, depending on the institution's capacity for and willingness to consider alternative perspectives and its tolerance for the views of those considered to be idealistic novices.

Teacher education is comprised of a number of settings: university coursework, field experiences, field supervision, the program administration, and other factors. The more settings that are available, the greater the prospects are for incompatible goals to coexist. The social pressures applied by members of each interest group often lead to competition for primacy in the minds of the TCs that university programs are designed to influence. With each participant involved in overlapping settings based on divergent personal experiences during their educations, the likelihood that all will identify and work toward the same goals is small.

Learning to teach poses a number of challenges for novices, including but not limited to: developing a conception of the subject matter and how to teach it (Grossman & Stodolsky, 1994), developing a conception of teaching and learning and their role as a teacher (Grossman, 1990), learning to manage student behavior (Bullough, 1989), and learning to work with colleagues (Smylie, 1994). These problems all contribute to the development of an *identity* as a teacher (Alsup, 2006), a construct that refers to one's orientation to the work in relation to personal characteristics, ideologies, commitment to teaching, epistemological underpinnings of a teaching approach, and other factors that make up the persona one enacts in the classroom.

A teaching identity is fundamentally grounded in the conceptions one develops about the role of a career in one's broader life, the purposes of schooling, the means by which educational purposes are achieved, views of human nature and the developmental sequence in which students realize their growth, the fundamental makeup of a discipline, and related factors. In other words, concept development and identity development are closely implicated with one another. When one is required to teach in ways that violate a sense of teaching identity and conceptual understandings, teaching may become a very unsatisfying way to undertake a career (Smagorinsky, Gibson, Moore, Bickmore, & Cook, 2004).

Tools

The notion of a psychological tool follows from the history of cultures in which people develop means by which to act on their environments. A hammer was developed in order to provide a means of pounding nails, a configuration that indicates a level of technological reliance in relation to social essentials such as the need for sturdy structures, which in turn suggest a large degree of social stability necessitating permanent structures. Hammers may be adapted to other purposes having nothing to do with nails, such as killing spiders or opening paint cans with the clawed end, and so are not limited in their possibilities.

Teachers employ such material tools in the form of computers, markers and erasable boards for documenting information and ideas, desks and tables configured for designed instructional purposes, and other means of instruction and management. In a shop class and for building theatrical sets, they may also use hammers and other tools. The material tool itself is not sufficient, however; many expensive computer initiatives, for instance, produce a lot of equipment, but little instruction. As Kim (2012) has argued, *technological tools* only make sense when people develop accompanying *psychological tools* for using them. That critical fact is important in understanding how beginning teachers construct the settings of their teaching: material tools may or may not serve their teaching goals, depending on how they conceptualize them psychologically.

Pedagogical tools may be either material or psychological, and they serve as the central means by which instruction is carried out. They are employed in settings that, ideally, sanction them as suitable. Teachers in secondary schools may employ pedagogical tools, such as drama and art, that their colleagues believe to be inappropriately used with older students more suited to abstract intellectualism than playful, joyous interpretation. They might do so deliberately, as Cindy O'Donnell-Allen did in classes I helped to study (e.g., Smagorinsky & O'Donnell-Allen, 1998a, 1998b) as a way to draw on her background as a speech and drama teacher, and to incorporate aspects of play she had observed in her mother's kindergarten classes and in the play-oriented preschool in which her children were enrolled. Or they might simply be violating local norms without understanding the local culture, such as when teachers use "slave games" to teach inequity in ways that deeply offend descendants of slaves (see Collins, 2019, and many such news stories). The relation between settings and tool use, regardless of how it is contextualized, remains a salient aspect of a Vygotskian study of beginning teachers.

In our research design, we identified two primary types of tools. *Conceptual tools* are abstract principles, frameworks, and ideas about teaching, learning, and English/Language Arts acquisition that teachers use to guide decisions about teaching and learning. A conceptual tool would correspond to the theoretical component of the theory/practice binary, including broadly applicable theories such as constructivism, and principles such as instructional scaffolding that can be interpreted and applied in a variety of situations. *Pedagogical* tools are classroom practices, strategies, and resources that have more local and immediate utility. These might include specific texts, an instructional means such as a small-group discussion, or an interpretive procedure such as a jigsaw activity.

The identification of the pedagogical tools employed by our focal teachers served as a crucial analytic means of studying their development of a teaching approach. Just as to Vygotsky (1987) *word meaning* served as the unit of analysis for understanding concept development and thus human development, pedagogical tools served to illuminate what teachers believed about socially situated effective instruction and how to enact it in the classroom. Simply using a tool, however, does not indicate that a teacher has grasped its designed function—that is, that a teacher has developed appropriate psychological tools to employ them—at least according to the consensus of the field. Rather, teachers appropriate tools to different degrees, a phenomenon that obtains in all conceptual learning (Leont'ev, 1981; Newman, Griffin, & Cole, 1989; Wertsch; 1991). Appropriation refers to the process through which a person adopts and modifies the conceptual and pedagogical tools available for use in particular social environments, and through this process takes on ways of thinking endemic to specific cultural practices (Newell, Tallman, & Letcher, 2009).

The extent of appropriation depends on the congruence of a learner's values, prior experiences, and goals with those of more experienced or powerful members of a culture such as school-based teachers or university faculty (Smagorinsky, 1995; Wertsch, 1991). Through the process of appropriation, learners reconstruct the knowledge available to them, thus transforming both their conception of the knowledge and in turn that knowledge as it is construed and used by others. In our formulation of this research (Grossman et al., 1999), we identified five degrees of appropriation of a tool, ranging from a complete lack of appropriation due to misunderstanding or rejection, all the way through mastery. I have since concluded that "mastery" is a condition that is rarely within reach for beginning teachers or, for that matter, experienced teachers, even as it is assumed possible and expected according to the idealistic thinking of accreditation agencies (Darling-Hammond, Wei, Andree, Richardson, & Orphanos, 2009).

Along the way, one may appropriate labels (e.g., knowing that "cooperative learning" is a pedagogical practice), surface features (e.g., knowing that cooperative learning involves small numbers of people working together on a common task), and conceptual underpinnings (e.g., understanding that cooperative learning requires distributed knowledge that is synthesized through discussion in relation to a task). This conceptual pathway assumes that a definitive understanding is available, primarily through the writing of university-based authorities. The studies my colleagues and I have conducted since outlining this sequence, however, have led me to question the degree to which "pure" university concepts may be available to teachers immersed in settings characterized by competing centers of gravity (e.g., Smagorinsky, 2013; Smagorinsky et al., 2013) that complicate matters such that only a practical version of such concepts may be available to teachers.

Methodological Implications

I next review how the research design relies on the Vygotskian theoretical framework I have outlined. In the studies reported in the following chapters, teachers' evolving conceptions were identified through a combination of interviews, observations, the construction of group concept maps, and teaching artifacts such as handouts and instructional plans. This approach allowed for the identification of a conceptual pathway inferred through the research participants' use of pedagogical tools, their reported goals for using those tools, and their sources of attribution for where they learned of the tools and how to use them. These factors were coded as tool, problem, and attribution. In addition, we coded for the area of the curriculum or other area of teacher conduct such as classroom control. Recalling Bakhurst's (2007) conclusion about Vygotsky's orientation to the socially situated individual as the focus of research, this approach enables individual pathways to be mapped in relation to the territorial context and destinations available in individual cases. By compiling these cases in this volume, I attempt to aggregate these individual paths and draw limited generalizations about the complexities of learning to teach.

Data Collection

The research design included a variety of data points. In my piece of the CELA research, the cohort was recruited by asking enrollees in two programs at one institution—the Elementary Education and Secondary English programs—if they were interested in participating in longitudinal research. From the first university in which this appeal was made, there were originally seven volunteers from Elementary Education and six from Secondary English Education, with four elementary and three secondary persisting to provide sufficient data for studies. After I relocated to Georgia following two years of data collection in Oklahoma, I was able to recruit seven additional Secondary English teachers, six of whom persisted with the research such that case studies were available.

The participants provided a "gateway" interview before both their student teaching and, when they took jobs, their first year of full-time teaching (some participants only provided student teaching data before withdrawing from the study). The purpose of these interviews was to elicit background information about their experiences and conceptions of teaching. The interview prior to student teaching (adapted from interview protocols developed originally by Grossman, 1990) was designed to cover four areas of prior experience and beliefs: their apprenticeship of observation, their personal philosophy and conceptions, their preservice teacher education coursework, and their field experiences prior to student teaching. This approach enabled a certain economy of data collection, and also allowed us to jump-start the research at a later point than a strictly longitudinal approach would take. That is, the Year 1 gateway interview allowed for *backmapping*, i.e., the reconstruction of past experiences through recollection and reflection. By using this method, we did not invest time in participants who might have identified teaching as a career early in their college educations but eventually changed majors. Rather, we recruited them after they had declared an education major and had completed their program of study, except student teaching, thus increasing the chances that our participants would persist with both teaching careers and the research.

Box 2.1 Year 1 Gateway Interview Protocol

I. APPRENTICESHIP OF OBSERVATION

1. Tell me about your own experiences as a student in English and Language Arts classes (literature, reading, writing, language study, drama). (Prompt: in elementary school (grades K-6); in secondary school (grades 7-12); in college English classes; in other college classes that required writing.)
2. What teachers stand out for you? Why? (Prompt: K-12, college, outside the classroom [coaches, church, scouting, etc.].)
3. Who were the best and worst teachers you've had? Why do you feel this way about them?

II. PERSONAL PHILOSOPHY/CONCEPTIONS

1. Tell me about your decision to become a teacher.
2. When did you decide to become a teacher?
3. What influenced your decision?
4. What kind of teacher would you like to become?
5. What influenced your ideas about this vision of yourself?
6. In your opinion, what does good teaching in English/Language Arts look like? (Prompt: At elementary level, at secondary level.)
7. What are the major purposes for teaching Language Arts? (Prompt: At elementary level, at secondary level.)
8. What is the most important thing you want students to learn in your classes?
9. What do you think is "basic" in education?

III. PRESERVICE COURSEWORK

1. When you applied to teacher education, what did you expect to learn?
2. Of the things you've been learning in your teacher education program, what has surprised you the most?
3. What are some of the most important things you've learned in your teacher education program so far? (Prompt: methods class, media and technology, school in American culture, developmental psychology.)
4. How does what you have learned in your teaching methods class fit with what you are learning in your other education classes? In your English department classes?
5. What do you think is your teaching methods professor's image of good teaching in English/Language Arts?
6. What are the ideas you've encountered in teacher education that you think will be most valuable as you look ahead and start teaching?

IV. FIELD EXPERIENCES

1. Tell me about your experiences in the field so far in the program.
2. What has stood out for you?
3. What have you learned from the field? What have you learned about the teaching of English/Language Arts?
4. Think of the teacher you've spent the most time with so far. What do you think is his or her[1] image of good teaching in English/Language Arts?
5. How does this fit with what you're learning at the University?
6. In what ways have you had an opportunity to use the methods you've learned in your university courses in your field experiences?
7. What else would you like to say about what you've been learning in teacher education, either in classes or in the field?

On two occasions—immediately before student teaching and immediately after—the whole cohort of research participants, organized by program (one elementary cohort, one Secondary English cohort in Oklahoma; and one Secondary English cohort in Georgia), participated in a collective concept map activity. The purpose of this activity was to characterize the manner in which the preservice teachers constructed and represented what their program was designed to teach them. In conjunction with an interview with the professors teaching the program and the documents they provided to detail the program structure, assignments, syllabus, and other indicators of the approach to teacher education, the concept maps provided additional backmapped data about what the university had taught about teaching Elementary Language Arts or Secondary English and how the students had appropriated that approach.

---

[1] The gender binary employed in this phrasing came before the current effort to recognize a broad array of sexualities and gender identifications, and would need adjustment to meet today's standards for respectful terms.

Box 2.2 Concept Map Activity Purposes and Procedures

PURPOSES:

- Gather information on what the group perceives to be the most important/valuable ideas they gained from their teacher education program (both fieldwork and coursework) about teaching in general and Language Arts specifically.
- Determine how each individual conceptualizes connections among the important ideas (integrated understanding, concept map).
- Determine how the group conceptualizes connections among the important ideas ("We want you to put this together as a group map").
- Determine how the group functions in discussion and deliberation of ideas.
- Compare the group vision (of importance, of connections) with each individual's vision.
- Determine how the individual and group visions (of importance, of connections) change over time (Task repeated at the end of the program).

PROCEDURE:

1. Ask group to discuss what ideas they gained in their teacher education program that were most valuable to them. Prompt for thinking/reasons behind choices.
2. Follow up with ideas about Language Arts (if not mentioned in response to general prompt)—total discussion about 30 minutes.
3. As they discuss, we write these ideas on cards. We add ideas from individual interviews that have not been mentioned.
4. Display cards.
5. Ask each individual to do a free sketch, concept map, of how these ideas are related to one another (approx. 10 minutes). Explain concept map generally.
6. Group develops concept map—during discussion, prompt for thinking/reasons behind connections (approx. 30 minutes).

During the formal semester of student teaching, each participant was observed and interviewed by a researcher in what we called *observation cycles*. Each of the three observation cycles consisted of a pre-observation interview, an observation of at least two classes that produced field notes, and a post-observation interview. The pre-observation interview was designed to obtain information about the teacher's experiences leading to, and plans for, the upcoming observation, with particular attention to understanding the source to which the teacher attributed instructional planning decisions. The post-observation interview's purpose was to verify what the researcher had observed and extend the line of questioning initiated in the pre-observation interview. If the line of questioning may be distilled into one question, it would be this: How are you teaching, and why are you teaching this way?

In conjunction with the second and third observation cycles, interviews were also conducted with the MT and university supervisor about the guidance they were providing. When possible, feedback sessions between mentors and supervisors were also recorded to enable an understanding of how the school-based and university-based supervisors were attempting to shape the participant's practice. Box 2.3 provides a schedule for data collection and the interview protocols for the pre- and post-observation interviews and the accompanying interview with the MT, which is representative of each of the three observation cycles.

Box 2.3 Observation Cycle #2 Interview Protocols

Observation Cycle #2

The second observation cycle will consist of three visits to each site, with each visit encompassing roughly two lessons/class periods. The activity setting for Observation Cycle #2 will observe the intern (student teacher) in relation to the mentoring teacher (site cooperating teacher). The observation cycle will consist of the following:

1. Pre-observation interview with intern.
2. Observations of student teacher in at least partial conjunction with the observations of the mentoring teacher.
3. A recording of the post-observation meeting between the intern and mentoring teacher.
4. Post-observation interview with the intern.
5. Post-observation interview with the mentoring teacher.

Interview protocols for the three scheduled interviews (#s1, 4, 5 above) follow.

Observation Cycle #2: Pre-Observation Interview

1. What instruction led up to the lessons you'll be teaching?
2. What were the main influences behind the instruction that's taken place so far?
3. Describe the lesson(s) that you will teach during the next three days.
4. Describe your reasoning in planning the lessons you'll teach.
5. Were there any other influences on the way you planned these lessons?
6. How do you anticipate that the lesson will go? Why?

Observation Cycle #2: Post-Observation Interview with Intern

1. How do you think the lesson(s) [unit] went?
2. Were there any points where you departed from your teaching plan? If so, please explain which parts, what you did, and why you did it.

3. Which concepts did you emphasize in the lesson(s) [unit]?
4. Which parts do you think were hard for the kids?
5. How will this lesson [unit] help you assess students' learning?
6. How do you think the lesson(s) [unit] worked for the whole range of students in the class?
7. At this grade level, what are the concepts that you think are most important for the students to learn?
8. If this were your classroom, would you teach the lesson(s) [unit] in the same way you did when I observed you?

    If so, how would you teach it? Why?
    If not, what would you do instead? Why?

9. What instruction will follow the lesson(s) [unit]? What will be your role in planning it? What will influence your thinking in planning what to do next?
10. Is there anything else you can tell me about the classes I've observed?

Observation Cycle #2: Post-Observation Interview with Mentor Teacher

1. What are the major purposes for teaching English/Language Arts at this level of schooling?
2. What is the most important thing you want students to learn in your classes?
3. How would you characterize your approach to teaching English/Language Arts?
4. What are the main influences on your approach to teaching English/Language Arts?
5. How would you describe your approach to being a mentoring teacher?
6. What is it you hope to each [your student teacher] through your role as mentor?
7. What do you see as the factors that will most strongly affect your ability to reach your goals as a mentoring teacher?

The first year of research concluded with most participants finding work within driving and observing distance of the university. Some participants took jobs out of state; others did not teach and withdrew from the research. Those who were available for a second year of study at the site of their first teaching jobs provided a second gateway interview, this one covering the new school and community setting, the teaching assignment, their degree of choice in interpreting the curriculum, and other considerations that framed their forthcoming experiences.

Box 2.4 Year 2 Gateway Interview Protocol

1. Please describe to me what your job is, including your title, the grades you teach, the subjects you teach, etc.
2. How big is your school—number of students, number of faculty? What kind of community is it in (urban, suburban, rural; professional, farming, industrial, etc.)? What are the demographics of the student body?
3. Tell me how you got this job. What attracted you to this particular school/district?
4. Now that you've been teaching for a few weeks, tell me what it's like so to be an (English/Elementary) teacher at this school? In this department? In this district?
5. What kind of orientation and/or support, if any, have you received as a new teacher in this school? in this district? Has the orientation/support been formal (e.g., an orientation program) or informal (e.g., colleagues giving advice)? How do you feel so far about the value of this orientation/support?
6. FOR MIDDLE SCHOOL/HIGH SCHOOL TEACHERS:
   a. Tell me about the different preparations/subjects you'll be teaching this semester.
   b. Please describe your teaching load and what's involved for each preparation. For each preparation:

   > What are your goals for this preparation?
   > What is the most important thing you hope students will learn in each preparation?
   > How are you thinking of organizing the class?
   > What is the curriculum you will follow?
   > Where does it come from?
   > What materials (textbooks, books, workbooks) will you be using? How did you select these materials?

   c. Tell me about the students in your classes. How will their characteristics affect your teaching decisions?
7. FOR ELEMENTARY TEACHERS:
   a. Tell me about your goals for this class. (After initial answer): What are your goals in the teaching of writing? What are your goals in the teaching of reading?
   b. What is the most important thing you hope your students will learn? (If not described, prompt for important Language Arts learning.)
   c. Tell me about the students in your class. How will their characteristics affect your teaching decisions?
   d. How are you thinking of organizing your class? What curriculum will you follow? Where does it come from? What kinds of structures will you

    use for teaching Language Arts (e.g., reading groups, literature-based reading: prompt for explanations of any labels [e.g., whole language, writing workshop, etc.])?
  e. What materials (texts, basals, tradebooks, programs) will you be using? How did you select these materials? (If they have any syllabi or written materials for their classes, be sure to collect.)
8. What's it like to have your own classroom now? How has being a first year teacher, as opposed to a student teacher, changed your approach to teaching? (Probe for teaching methods, curriculum, etc.)
9. What are some of the most important things you learned last year that you hope to incorporate into your classroom? How do you think they might show up in your teaching? (Probe for both student teaching and coursework as influence; probe for Language Arts instruction in particular, if not mentioned.)
10. As you look ahead to the school year, what do you feel most confident about? What do you feel least confident about? Tell me the things you most would like to learn about teaching English/Language Arts now that you're facing your own classroom. How do you think you might go about learning them?
11. Describe any professional development opportunities you'll have this year, both formal and informal (personal decision to join IRA/NCTE, join e-mail discussion, etc.). What do you think they'll provide for you?

During their first year of full-time teaching, the participants were observed in three or four observation cycles, depending on availability, that followed the same procedures as those during their student teaching, with the interview protocols adapted from the Year 1 questions. When possible, school-based mentors and administrators were interviewed and feedback sessions with the participant were recorded. Supplementary artifacts such as the state core curriculum and testing program were also included in this phase of the data collection. Additional artifacts from the participants' university programs (e.g., course syllabi and program descriptions) and teaching settings (e.g., curriculum materials and mission statements) provided a third data source for the purpose of corroboration.

Data Analysis

The data were analyzed during research apprenticeships. My approach to doctoral training interprets my department's requirement for each doctoral student to experience a research apprenticeship as a long-term, one-on-one effort to analyze data and produce manuscripts for presentation and publication, with the student sharing all authorial credit; when the participating teachers were available and interested, they were also recruited as coauthors of studies dedicated to their cases. In research apprenticeships, the student and I met for two 2-hour sessions each week for four semesters if they were my own doctoral advisees, or for two semesters if I worked with a student not under my advisement. Ideally one case could be completed in two semesters; some, however, required four.

Our approach was to collaboratively read and analyze all data from the focal case, using the Atlas.ti qualitative data analysis software to code each observation and interview. (The specific version of the software varied, depending on when a case was analyzed and which updates became available during the analysis.) The question of reliability through independent coding was thus addressed in that we discussed each coding decision until we agreed on how a quotation should be coded (see Smagorinsky, 2008, for a detailed rationale for this approach). This method enabled us to work flexibly with the coding system, adjusting it throughout the coding process, rather than predetermining the categories and applying them uniformly thereafter. Although some people claim that there is a "latent positivism" inherent in data coding (St. Pierre, 2014, p. 8), I reject this interpretation. Instead, I see coding as the manifestation of the study's motivating theory and thus an essential means of aligning theory with analysis. Given that the coding is continually discussed and refined across the data set, we viewed our work as constructivist and relational rather than "positivist," a term I have found people to use as a straw person designed to denigrate work that relies on categories, no matter how provisionally and developmentally they are offered.

The interviews and field notes were analyzed to identify the pedagogical tools that the focal participant employed, the ends toward which they were used, the source that the participant attributed in learning how to use it, the area of teaching in which it was used, and whether or not the tool was conceptual or practical. An example of coded text follows. During an interview in her first year of full-time teaching (Johnson, Smagorinsky, Thompson, & Fry, 2003), Leigh was asked,

[Q]: When you were teaching those two lessons—and you can either talk about them together or you can talk about them separately—what kind of concepts were you emphasizing?

Leigh: Well, as far as the essay I just wanted them to be familiar with the format of writing the five-paragraph essay, getting that down where they don't even have to—where [they] know exactly what they're supposed to be doing no matter what topic I give them, they're used to doing it. It will sort of come a lot easier for them.

In this quotation—Atlas.ti's term for a circumscribed segment of text—we discussed and identified the "tools" of *writing five-paragraph theme* and *teaching to state curriculum/ assessment*. Because they served immediate instructional purposes, we coded them both as *practical*. Leigh made an "attribution" to the state *mandate* that required her students to produce five-paragraph themes for the state writing assessment (in this case the attribution was made prior to this quotation). Two "areas" figured into her decision-making, *writing* and *assessment*. Leigh's instruction was designed to address two "problems": the mandate's role in the *context* of her teaching and her *students' learning* about how to succeed on this assessment.

Through this method of data collection and analysis, we had access to fundamental aspects of the participants' development of a conception of effective teaching. The tool codes enabled us to understand the primary means by which they taught, and the attribution codes allowed us to trace aspects of setting that influenced their decisions. The problem codes helped us understand which of the many teaching challenges available they attempted to address through their use of pedagogical tools and the areas of their teaching responsibilities to which they dedicated their attention.

Through our engagement with the data in this fashion, we were able to infer how the individual teachers who comprised our sample engaged with their environments over the course of one to two years and how those interactions helped to shape their emerging conceptions. The remainder of this book's chapters detail the findings of those case investigations and the conclusions that these studies afforded us in thinking about how people learn to teach the curricular strand of Language Arts at the elementary level and the discipline of English in secondary school.

3

The Apprenticeship of Observation, Updated, and Its Effects on Beginning Teachers' Evolving Pedagogical Conceptions

Lortie (1975), in his sociological study of the teaching profession, used the term *apprenticeship of observation* to describe the thousands of hours that people spend in classrooms as students. Through this lengthy informal exposure to teachers and teaching, they absorb a sense of what teaching ought to look like, even if they don't enjoy the experience. To Lortie, the twelve to fourteen years that people spend as students in preschool, kindergarten, primary, middle, and high school classes, along with what they experience in universities prior to enrolling in teacher education programs, suggest to prospective teachers how schooling should properly be conducted. With this deep acculturation to education as a conserving profession—one that is resistant to extensive change and that continually reinforces status quo values and practices across generations—people enter teaching with deeply rooted values about the conduct of school that are difficult to abandon in the relatively brief time that most people spend in teacher education programs. They then begin their careers in schools predisposed to embrace the values that attracted them to return to teaching for their careers in the first place, thus helping to contribute to the overall stability of schools as cautious, intransigent institutions whose constituent members are acculturated to maintaining the conventions and traditions that have long driven educational practice (Smagorinsky, 2010).

Lortie (1975) found that students see teachers "front stage and center like an audience viewing a play," thus learning about teaching in a manner that is "intuitive and imitative" rather than formal. This implicit, proleptic means of socialization stands in contrast to the "explicit and analytical" (p. 62) instruction they get in education programs, often in methods courses designed to de-center authority. Buchmann (1987) describes these conventional "folkways of teaching" as "ready-made recipes for action and interpretation that do not require testing or analysis while promising familiar, safe results" (p. 161). These "default options" provide a set of reliable strategies that teachers can fall back on, consciously or unconsciously, when they are uncertain about how to proceed pedagogically, because they are doing school the way they experienced it and thus teaching appropriately.

Lortie (1975) concluded that the apprenticeship of observation tends to weaken the effects of teacher education, which may emphasize instructional approaches from traditions (often those following from Deweyan progressivism) that are not widely practiced in schools and thus that lack sanction and verification in prospective teachers' assumptions about proper schooling. Lortie's findings suggest that beginning teachers may either resist, or may find it conceptually difficult to envision, teaching, or schooling more broadly speaking, in any way other than how they have experienced it. These experiences, in his study, typically involved lectures, authoritarian approaches to texts, disciplinary imperatives that place teachers and students in hierarchical roles, limited speaking roles for students, individualistic notions of competition as the basis for student positioning, and other formalist and authoritarian pedagogical roles for teachers.

The brief intervention of university faculty with alternative pedagogies has little chance of penetrating a consciousness so deeply socialized and oriented to authoritarian teaching. Practica and student teaching take place in the very institutions—schools—that have provided the lengthy indoctrination to these conventions. Beginning teachers are therefore frequently immersed in settings that reinforce the school's status quo, and they view university ideals and their accompanying practices as abstract and not relevant to the realities of classrooms. This perspective is often reinforced, in my experience, by MTs and other school-based faculty who speak dismissively of university teacher education as too theoretical and thus of limited practical value. University teacher education programs therefore often find themselves at odds with the very institutions they hope to prepare their students for, and often see their work weakened by the assimilative priority of schools once TCs begin to spend their time in classrooms.

Updating Lortie's Formulation

This predominant conception of the apprenticeship of observation views one's socialization to teaching through conservative schooling as fixed and impenetrable, and impervious to change. Using data from a different era, my colleagues and I have found that these assumptions are problematic when applied to the current era (Smagorinsky & Barnes, 2014). Lortie (1975) based his findings on surveys and interviews from the early 1960s. The enduring legacy of his study is to frame the apprenticeship of observation as one that fundamentally conserves extant school values, thus perpetuating them generation after generation in classrooms. In contrast to describing their teachers as exclusively authoritarian, however, the teachers in our study named a variety of teaching models from both the conservative and progressive pedagogical traditions. They reflected on and critiqued teachers from their past, often characterizing those from authoritarian traditions as harsh and uncaring. They projected visions of their own teaching and the associated identities they hoped to take on, and these images tended to follow constructivist principles. This research suggests that the apprenticeship of observation is more variable and less deterministic than is often associated with this period of development.

Mewborn and Tyminski (2006) concur, arguing from their study of preservice mathematics teachers that "Lortie's use of the term apprenticeship of observation seems to pertain to the general milieu of teaching, rather than to specific instances of teaching and learning" (p. 31). They are concerned that Lortie's (1975) effort to generalize across interviews and surveys led to a homogenization of inferences and helped contribute to the broad belief that learning to teach is a function of cultural transmission that takes place throughout childhood, adolescence, and early adulthood in classrooms.

Furthermore, as a Cold War era researcher, Lortie (1975) studied teachers with highly localized knowledge. With limited communication outside the costly prospect of attending academic conferences, teachers had access primarily to the teaching and learning conceptions available to them in their teacher education programs and in the schools in which they worked. Teachers entering the profession a half-century later have access to a far wider range of influences and resources through the internet and its many affordances. The teachers from their own educations attended schools in which process-oriented, constructivist approaches have been more widely embraced and emphasized, reinforced through professional organizations and their extensive networks, publication vehicles, online resources, in-service workshops and institutes, and meetings. Relying on Lortie's data from a half-century ago involves considerable faith in its currency. Yet the profession he described existed in a very different world from that experienced by twenty-first-century teachers.

Mewborn and Tyminski (2006) argue that relying on Lortie's (1975) account from the mid-twentieth century represents the fallacy of the *snark syndrome* or *snark effect*. Byrne (1993; cf. Wideen, Mayer-Smith, & Moon, 1998) coined this term to account for the ways in which an idea becomes widely accepted through repetition instead of empirical evidence. It is derived from Lewis Carroll's poem, *The Hunting of the Snark*, in which a claim thrice spoken grows in truth value. Lortie's conclusions have been repeated so often that they have become woven into the assumptions of teacher education. Mewborn and Tyminski present counterevidence that suggests that people learn a variety of approaches through their experiences as students, arguing that Lortie's own evidence supports this view. Indeed, Spangler (née Mewborn) told me that when she spoke to Lortie during the writing of her article with Tyminski, he said that he was not aware that people had latched on to that piece of the book and amplified its importance, and he was surprised to learn that his study had largely been reduced to a questionable interpretation.

An Updated Apprenticeship of Observation

I next summarize the findings of a study (Smagorinsky & Barnes, 2014) of TCs reflecting back on their own schooling to get a better sense of how schooling experiences shape teaching practices. It relies on data from the various teacher education programs described in Chapter 2. The interviews focused on the participants' positive and negative experiences with teachers, and the conceptions of teaching that they hoped to put into practice based on these apprenticeships of observation. Because the three programs studied had unique goals and structures, and because one concerned elementary school Language Arts and the other two focused on Secondary English/Language Arts, I present the findings by cohort.

If the participants' schooling had resembled that of Lortie's (1975) cohorts, the apprenticeship of observation would have had a conservative influence on beginning teachers, in terms of both the teaching methods employed and the manner in which schools conserve their values and practices over time. We would then assume that participants across programs would describe a preponderance of objectivist, teacher- and text-centered instruction across the span of their educations, given that such teaching has long been found to characterize school (e.g., Cuban, 2013; Goodlad, 1984; Harber, 2004).

This assumption, however, was disconfirmed repeatedly in the interviews. The education of the participants involved both conservative and progressive instruction and influences. Most of the instruction the participants characterized as exemplary and worth emulating in their own careers was progressive, constructivist, communal, rigorous, caring, and open-ended. To use a phrase from work I'm currently developing from a subsequent set of teachers involved in a longitudinal study, when speaking of the sort of teacher they hoped someday to become, they envisioned a *projected teacher identity*, that is, a sense of optimal developmental outcome for their own teleological pathways as a teacher. This finding suggests that such methods were widely practiced by the teachers who had taught our participants and that they served as part of the appeal of the teaching profession for them. Negative characterizations, in addition to being identified far less frequently, concerned teachers' rigid, authoritarian, harsh, and undemanding instructional approaches and were described by our participants as to be avoided in their own teaching. In general, then, the finding from Lortie (1975) that teachers inevitably gravitate toward authoritarian practices was contradicted by newer data suggesting that many teachers go into teaching to defy such approaches and conduct classes more oriented to cultivating student participation, drawing on their personal lives, and providing open-ended learning opportunities amenable to constructivist principles.

Distribution of Attributions across Grade Levels

Table 3.1 lists the totals of positive and negative teaching examples for each of four categories across cohorts: all teachers, Pre-K/elementary teachers, secondary school (middle and high school) teachers, and college professors. We assume that the data reflect a recency effect such that secondary school TCs tended to recall more from their secondary and college experiences than elementary TCs. From this point on, I will use pseudonyms that clearly distinguish the two university programs from one another.

Table provides data from *within* cohorts. The data suggest that members of the Southern Plains Elementary Language Arts cohort were much more likely to recall teachers from Pre-K and elementary school than were members of their university's Secondary English Education program. Meanwhile, the Atlantic Piedmont Secondary English Education cohort recalled more at each level, and with a more even distribution, which we assume to be a function of the kinds of activities engaged in by each separate cohort. The Southern Plains Elementary Language Arts program required that TCs reflect on their own elementary experiences, an emphasis that

Table 3.1 Distribution across Grade Levels of Attributions

	Southern Plains University Elementary	Southern Plains University Secondary	Atlantic Piedmont University Secondary	Total
		Positive		
All	19	3	38	60
Pre-K/Elem	20	8	35	63
Secondary	51	47	47	145
College	28	43	32	103
		Negative		
All	10	2	11	23
Pre-K/Elem	22	5	8	35
Secondary	13	25	23	61
College	15	22	21	58

Table 3.2 Percentages within Cohorts of Attributions across Grade Levels

Southern Plains Elementary Language Arts Program

	Positive (%)	Negative (%)	Total (%)
All	16	17	16
Pre-K/Elem	17	37	24
Secondary	43	22	36
College	24	25	24

Southern Plains Secondary English Education Program

	Positive (%)	Negative (%)	Total (%)
All	3	4	3
Pre-K/Elem	8	9	8
Secondary	47	46	46
College	43	41	42

Atlantic Piedmont Secondary English Education Program

	Positive (%)	Negative (%)	Total (%)
All	25	17	23
Pre-K/Elem	23	13	20
Secondary	31	37	33
College	21	33	25

undoubtedly made those older memories more accessible during the interviews than they were to their secondary education counterparts. The Southern Plains Secondary English Education cohort was what we have characterized as conceptually fragmented, with no two TCs taking the same course sequence from the same faculty and minimal formal reflection on schooling experiences through literacy memoirs and other vehicles. This fragmentation likely led to less agreement, given that their teacher education had less cohesion and thus less focus. The Atlantic Piedmont Secondary English Education program followed a cohort design that included extensive reflection on school experiences through such vehicles as a learner autobiography in which they reconstructed their development as a reader and writer.

The data suggest that a program's structure, focus, and process may affect the manner in which one's apprenticeship of observation overtly informs one's conception of teaching. Specific activities and experiences that encourage TCs to reflect may contribute to their reconstruction of their schooling experiences. These reflections may inform new experiences in deliberate ways, although they run the risk of having personal experiences with people of similar acculturation represent the learning processes of all, potentially producing deficit conceptions of students socialized in different sorts of homes and communities. This risk is great when White middle-class teachers—by far the dominant demographic nationally and in all three cohorts—instruct students of color, those from lower socioeconomic groups, immigrants, and others whose life trajectories depart from those that are inscribed in White TCs' autobiographical ruminations (Ballenger, 1999; Gay, 2000; Paris & Alim, 2017).

Further, I review each university program's interview analysis. I characterize each program, and then describe the positive and negative teaching models identified by participants in their interviews. Both universities were state namesake universities with Carnegie classifications of *very high research activity* and NCATE-approved programs. Each had a stand-alone College of Education in which all teacher education courses were taught. For all three programs, students enrolled for their first two years in general education content-area courses in the College of Arts and Sciences. For their third year, the students took a mix of courses in the College of Education (e.g., special education, foundations, educational technology, and educational psychology) and Arts and Sciences (for the Secondary English programs, primarily taking certification-required classes in the Department of English, for example, courses in Shakespeare and American Literature). Fourth-year students were heavily immersed in College of Education courses oriented to teaching methods, practica, and/or student teaching.

Southern Plains Elementary Education Program

Program structure and focus. The Southern Plains Elementary Education program was mostly taught by tenure-track faculty, with some classes taught by adjunct professors. Participants at times regarded these adjuncts more highly than they did some of their tenure-track professors. In the elementary program, in the final semester of their senior year, they took a set of five content-area methods classes from curriculum and instruction faculty, each accompanied by thirty hours of field experiences. In the fifth year, for graduate credit, they would do their student teaching and take an action research class during one semester and take electives during the other.

The faculty embraced Piagetian constructivism as the umbrella concept to guide their students' thinking about teaching, streaming its principles throughout all Elementary Education courses. TCs learned to contrast the program's notion of constructivism with what their faculty termed *traditional teaching*, which generally referred to authoritarian, teacher-centered instruction. According to the participants, the traditional-constructivist binary worked better in theory than in practice. Program faculty did not always teach according to constructivist principles. Some were notorious for lecturing about constructivism and giving objectivist tests on its tenets. Several of the negative examples of authoritarian teaching in the interviews referred to faculty who emphasized constructivism as a value. Even on those points of general agreement, various faculty interpreted the concept differently, consistent with the conundrum of defining a notion that itself represents multiple possibilities (Phillips, 1995).

Positive characterizations. The Southern Plains Elementary Education program TCs spoke positively of teachers who employed *constructivist teaching*, hardly a surprise given how it served to structure their orientation to teaching at the university, and given that the interviews took place in close proximity to their coursework. Manipulatives and play-oriented learning characterized their positive Pre-K through elementary school instruction. The secondary school teachers they hoped to emulate allowed choice in learning, had students dramatize literature, co-constructed curriculum with students, and employed other open-ended, activity-oriented, and participatory practices. College professors also provided open-ended teaching and discussion, student choice in learning, learning through exploration and activity, and opportunities for group projects, interpretive assignments, and the synthesis of learning in student work.

Other positive pedagogies not included in the constructivist category were compatible with constructivist principles. The TCs from this cohort spoke admiringly of teachers they viewed as interdisciplinary, thought-provoking, open to individual pacing, encouraging of critical thinking, and available for conferencing. Each of these practices stood in contrast to the "traditional" instruction they associated with rigid authoritarianism, suggesting that they had internalized their faculty's binary presentation of teaching possibilities.

At the same time, on some occasions participants did acknowledge the value of some authoritarian practices. One saw value in a teacher who had zero tolerance for errors and who required "close reading" of literature, a perspective associated with New Criticism, an interpretive school that emphasizes textual autonomy, the belief that meaning is inscribed in texts for readers to discern, with a reader's experiences muted to emphasize a text's presumed inherent meaning. (See Nystrand, 1986, for a critique of the doctrine of the autonomous text; Thomas, 2014, for a critical view of close reading's inscription in the Common Core State Standards; Hickman & McIntyre, 2012, for an effort to salvage and update New Criticism in light of its critical potential; and Shanahan, 2013, for a defense of New Criticism due to what he believes is the excessive infusion of readers' autobiographical knowledge into textual meaning.) These examples, however, constituted a distinct minority of practices that the TCs hoped to enact in their own teaching.

The TCs also admired certain demeanors in the teachers they had experienced. Teachers who held high expectations were consistently identified as exemplary, as were those exhibiting a temperament of respect, care, support for and belief in students, and the creation of a flexible, community-oriented environment that helps motivate students to learn. Such teachers valued students and their opinions, which became available in student interactions and collaborations that required patience and a disposition to mentor young people.

Negative characterizations. The TCs from this cohort spoke disparagingly of teachers who were rigid and objectivist, and who imposed rote learning through lockstep instruction. They also found some teachers incompetent, especially those who were disorganized and would get off track with their teaching, who were ignorant in their subject area, who were ambiguous about assessment criteria, who held students to low standards, and who paced their instruction poorly. These poor teaching practices, they reported, were accompanied by harsh dispositions such as being authoritarian, humiliating, manipulative, bullying, nagging, morale-crushing, and negative. I would add that not all teacher-centered or lecture-oriented teachers are so cruel and insensitive. These dispositions were, however, frequently associated with authoritarian teachers in the interviews, whose questions cued the participants to describe the teachers they had disliked and hoped to avoid becoming in their own careers.

Southern Plains University Secondary English Education Program

Program structure and focus. The five-year Southern Plains University Secondary English Education Program included both undergraduates majoring in education and M.A.T. students getting certified. We characterize the program as being *structurally fragmented* (Zeichner & Gore, 1990) because the students did not go through the program as a cohort; rather, they could take courses in any order. The same required course might be taught by different faculty, adjuncts, or teaching assistants, without articulation to provide consistency in focus and method. Without a cohort approach, two students could start and end their programs of study on the same dates without ever being in the same classes or taking the same instructors.

Prior to the methods class, students' coursework was concentrated on fifteen courses taken in the Department of English in the College of Arts and Sciences. Before student teaching, the students took one methods class, with roughly forty hours of accompanying field experiences required. Aside from the English methods class and a Theory of English Grammar course, TCs took no courses from faculty in the curriculum and instruction department. This disjointed approach left students without a sustained focus on a unified conception of teaching. The TCs could go through the program taking courses that were not in formal dialogue with one another about pedagogy. As a result, they did not engage in the kind of goal-directed, tool-mediated communal activity that gives an education program a particular culture and focus and that enables its students to develop a conceptually unified approach to teaching (Smagorinsky, Cook, & Johnson, 2003) and thus regard it as their *conceptual home base* (Smagorinsky, 2002). The interviews of the TCs in this program provided a clear contrast with those of the same university's Elementary Language Arts cohort, whose constructivist orientation was consistent and strong across all interviews.

Positive characterizations. The TCs from this program attributed 51 out of their 101 positive models to matters of *pedagogy*, 36 to *demeanor*, and 14 to *environment*. Without using the term, the TCs in Secondary English referenced what we labeled *constructivist* teaching often, accounting for twenty-one of the fifty-one positive pedagogy codes. The Secondary English students were far more likely to recall secondary and college teachers than Pre-K through elementary teachers, suggesting both a recency effect and a greater attention to secondary school experiences in coursework, although the latter is difficult to reconstruct, given the differential experiences of the students with their various instructors.

Like the Elementary Language Arts TCs, the Secondary English TCs hoped to emulate the teachers from their past who enacted open-ended, discussion-based, active, project-oriented, and life-related teaching practices. They identified other practices that were well-aligned with constructivist teaching: flexibility, creative teaching, interdisciplinary learning, thematic teaching, multiple perspectives, a personalized curriculum, and others. Only a few formalist qualities (associated with authoritarian teaching) were identified favorably: New Critical values for literary criticism, formal writing in genres, and dictionary speed drills.

The TCs from this program identified a host of positive demeanors, most of which involved being supportive, sensitive, personable, accessible, caring, and challenging. They also were impressed by teachers who viewed their teaching as occasions for learning, a reflective stance that insulates them from authoritarianism. One TC spoke admiringly of charismatic and highly confident college professors, and those with overt liberal and socialist political values. The TCs overall hoped to be like those teachers who had high expectations for students and who created environments that were positive and noncompetitive, were structured with boundaries, and were characterized by a "homey" feeling, one in which they felt comfortable, safe, and at ease.

Negative characterizations. The Southern Plains Secondary English TCs focused more on *demeanor* than *pedagogy* when discussing teachers who made a negative impact. They disliked teachers who had harsh and inflexible dispositions, narrow perspectives, low expectations for students, and indifferent and impersonal attitudes toward students. The same TC who valued liberal and socialist teachers, not surprisingly, found politically conservative teachers to be repellant.

Negative pedagogies fell into two areas. The TCs identified instructional incompetence such as unimaginative teaching, directionless teaching, ignorance about literature, and inappropriate content and process. They also disliked teachers they considered rigid in their emphasis on detail rather than meaning, erratic in grading that did not correspond to students' effort, and stifling in writing instruction predicated on formalist, structural requirements rather than meaningfulness.

Atlantic Piedmont University Secondary English Education Program

Program structure and focus. The Atlantic Piedmont University Secondary English Education Program employed a cohort approach that enrolled, at the time of the research, twenty students, including both undergraduate and M.A.T. students seeking certification. In the fall semester of their final year of study, the TCs took three courses—instructional planning, adolescent literature, and teacher research—that were team-taught by two English Education professors in consecutive time blocks, allowing the three courses to operate as a single integrated course and providing opportunities for extended, interrelated conversations to take place regularly. The TCs spent twelve hours a week in the classroom of their MT throughout the fall semester, and did their student teaching in the same classroom during the spring semester, when they simultaneously took a reading methods course and attended a seminar during which they discussed their student teaching experiences. In spite of the lengthy time they spent with their professors on campus, the program was heavily field-based, relying on the TCs' single MT for apprenticeship into the profession and for methods on how to teach in the setting of their practica.

The two English Education professors built their program around the theme of *making connections*. Course readings promoted a student-centered, process-oriented approach that stressed the importance of reflective practice. The course projects and activities were designed to help the preservice teachers learn more about and make connections with schools and students. These principles were in turn emphasized in practica and student teaching, although with varying degrees and in different ways, depending on the MT's school, values, and situation. The program thus had an assimilative approach, with socialization into existing school practices overseen by their MTs—a characteristic, I would argue, of field-based teacher education programs.

Positive characterizations. The positive models named by the TCs from this program directed 91 out of their 152 positive attributions to matters of *pedagogy*, 55 to *demeanor*, and 6 to *environment*. Without using the term, the TCs referenced constructivist teaching practices often, accounting for fifty-eight of the ninety-one codes. They characterized exemplary practices as collaborative, interactive, creative, activity-based, relevant, and project-based, and as designed to build on students' interests and learning pathways. The TCs also admired some pedagogies that they occasionally termed "traditional": mastery learning, direct and straightforward instruction, reading used as a way to moderate student behavior and settle classes down, and classes governed by order and predictability.

Positive demeanors included an engaging teaching style in which the teacher cared for, respected, supported, and believed in their students. They further spoke highly of teachers who had high expectations, were dedicated to teaching, and reflected on their practice. Some TCs also stated that elementary school learning environments that encouraged them to learn involved either incentives or competition, including rewards for a high volume of reading.

Negative characterizations. Of the sixty-three negative attributions made by the TCs, forty-eight were to *pedagogy*, fourteen to *demeanor*, and one to *environment*. The TCs disliked rote learning accompanied by an overemphasis on formality, direct grammar instruction, overly precise requirements for notebook maintenance, tedium, beating subjects to death, mono-disciplinary studies, lectures, an emphasis on coverage over depth, restrictive environments, vague and directionless classes, poorly run discussions, and exams that require excessive preparation, but little learning. They were discouraged by teachers who were harsh, who were negligent toward students and teaching, and who did not interact with students.

Discussion

The apprenticeship of observation data from this study contradict assumptions that follow from Lortie's (1975) classic sociology of teaching. In spite of the three programs' very different organizations and emphases, and in spite of the two very different locations of the universities and the teaching levels of the elementary and secondary programs, the TCs produced remarkably similar characterizations of teaching that they hoped to emulate and of teaching that they criticized as ineffective.

The timing of the interviews could have affected the beliefs about teaching that the TCs revealed. We talked to the students right after coursework that emphasized the sorts of values they reported, and prior to student teaching in which those values were put to the test in the unpredictable and contradictory world of the classroom. As subsequent chapters will report, the same students found that the context of teaching affected the degree to which they could teach toward their stated values and the manner in which their conceptions of teaching remained on the same track. At this point in their learning, however, the models that they named tended to reflect an idealistic belief in Deweyan progressivism, with a value on student-centered pedagogies, constructivist activities, and supportive demeanors and environments. Given that the TCs' exemplars had in fact been able to enact such practices, the idealism was firmly grounded in worldly experience and was thus reasonably available for emulation as a source of teaching possibilities.

Some might argue that Lortie's (1975) findings characterize what teachers feel in their bones, rather than what they can articulate consciously in interviews, as was available in the research reported here. One's immersion in school, they might say, acculturates them to conservative traditions proleptically, in ways that they cannot see or disengage from, and thus are more likely to replicate subliminally. Lortie's research, however, did not concern the subconscious. Rather, his method relied on self-reports and reconstructions of past experiences. Our findings thus, like Lortie's, cannot be dismissed on the grounds that powerful feelings that are difficult to articulate comprise the apprenticeship of observation, rather than accessible memories available through interviews.

Lortie's (1975) conclusions about the conservative nature of schooling could follow from the era in which he collected and analyzed his data. It is possible that in Lortie's era males dominated the concepts driving schools. The production of knowledge in universities, and the leadership in schools in spite of the preponderance of women in classrooms, was largely the province of men, who might be more prone to authoritarian and thus conservative schooling (American Association of University Women, 1992; Gilligan, 1982). Changes in the composition of people in professorial and leadership positions have resulted in women having a greater say and stake in the values of the profession. The largely White, female composition of the classroom teaching population is now better reflected in university teacher education programs, and in school administration, albeit with gender bias shaping perceptions of their efforts (Garn & Brown, 2008; Jean-Marie & Martinez, 2007).

Although schools are noted for their resistance to change, much knowledge in professional organizations and teacher education programs has been published since Lortie collected and analyzed his data in the 1960s and the 1970s. These typically progressive ideas have become much more widely available to teachers through the growth of the internet. Publication—along with nings, blogs, lesson and unit libraries, and other sources of ideas—has become more economically feasible, and faster to produce and distribute, often through the internet, enabling curriculum and instruction to adapt more quickly and easily than it did when documents were laboriously produced and shared in costly final print-and-mail form. The TCs we studied, and the teachers who had taught them, had a far wider range of possibilities to consider than did the more provincial teachers of Lortie's (1975) era.

Multiple traditions have always been at work in education (Applebee, 1974). Progressivism has played a role in US education since John Dewey's first faculty appointment in 1884 and his first book fifteen years later (Dewey, 1899). It was around well before Lortie was born. It has, however, become more widely practiced since the mid-1970s through a confluence of factors: greater emphasis in colleges of education, more widespread circulation through modern means of publication, new educational research identifying the effects of progressive methods on students' learning, and changes in school-based curriculum and instruction. Other sorts of research, at the same time, have reinforced hierarchical notions of race (Herrnstein & Murray, 1994), formalist assessments of reading (Pianta & Hamre, 2009), and other authoritarian perspectives on teaching and learning. Simply claiming a research base to support a belief, then, is complicated by the fact that different paradigms draw on different data and methods to investigate the same topic, often coming to opposing conclusions. These contradictory empirical arguments contribute to the general problem I address in this volume, that being the difficulty of thinking consistently and coherently within settings in which multiple perspectives are available.

The apprenticeship of observation, as taken up by the field based on Lortie's (1975) study, has relied too much on data from a distant era and, as a result, has overemphasized conservative influences. Schools have thus been cast as monochromatically "traditional" and stubbornly resistant to change. The new forces of "accountability" might be leading schools toward a conservative turn (Slater, 2015), and data over the forthcoming decade may well indicate more authoritarian models should this trend continue. That possibility, however, would not follow from the conservative nature of schools and the teachers they hire. Rather, it would follow from the increasing influence of neoliberalism, which embraces laissez-faire economic liberalism dedicated to privatization, austerity, deregulation, free trade, minimal government spending, and the elevation of the private sector in motivating the economy. Neoliberalism's accountability emphasis as applied to schools has had many consequences, including promoting privatization of education, commodifying instruction, and, paradoxically, increasing regulations in the form of assessments via multiple-choice tests that discourage open-ended teaching (Au & Ferrare, 2015).

Still, at least in this study from the beginning of the twenty-first century, we found that TCs have a wide range of exemplars to draw from, and have a clear preference for teaching that serves the personal and social growth of students. Rather than relying on a dated conception derived from Lortie (1975), no matter how foundational his study was a half-century ago, educational researchers should continue to investigate the phenomenon of the apprenticeship of observation and track its influences with newer generations of teachers in new eras of expectations to keep the construct fresh and relevant as schools continue to evolve. For the teachers in this study, the apprenticeship of observation provided a template upon which constructivist pedagogies could be established for their own teaching. In the next set of chapters, I look more closely at what sorts of experiences they had in their classes, their student teaching, and their first jobs, and how these experiences helped to shape their developing conceptions of how to teach effectively.

4

Concept Development in Teacher Education Coursework and Practica

This chapter looks at the effects of university coursework and initial practicum experiences on preservice teachers' development of concepts to guide their teaching (see Barnes & Smagorinsky, 2016). Drawing on interviews from the three programs reviewed in Chapter 3, I show how TCs' efforts to learn to teach in conceptually unified ways are compromised by their immersion in contradictory environments involving both schools and universities. Rather than representing two discrete, unified worlds, as suggested by the two-worlds pitfall metaphor proposed by Feiman-Nemser and Buchmann (1985), and extant in recent conceptions (e.g., Braaten, 2019 and others), each involves within-world contradictions that produce dissonance in TCs' efforts to teach in conceptually unified and satisfying ways (Smagorinsky, 2013).

The poet Walt Whitman, in *Leaves of Grass*, acknowledged inherent human contradiction in his verse from "Song of Myself" in 1892:

> Do I contradict myself?
> Very well then I contradict myself;
> (I am large, I contain multitudes.)

Whitman's multitudinous self suggests that the availability of conflicting means of mediation, and the resulting lack of conceptual clarity available to people, is inherent to being a social human being. This phenomenon has been convincingly identified by researchers in evolutionary biology. Dutton and Heath (2010) conclude that "multicultural individuals are able to shift between multiple cultural frames depending on which one is cued by their current situation. Interestingly, even monocultural American individuals shift their self-construals, value endorsements, and social judgments depending on situational cues" (Gardner, [Gabriel, & Lee], 1999, p. 60). Because environments cue thinking and action, and because environments are contradictory, finding comprehensive conceptual coherence of the sort idealized by Vygotsky (1987; see Chapter 1) is not possible in learning concepts when the concepts themselves are in dispute. Individuals might seek consistency, but to Dutton and Heath (2010), "it is computationally impossible for an individual to ensure complete coherence among any reasonable number of elements" (p. 61). Cultures, they argue, are always in flux, producing shifting environments that cue a variety of responses that may not be consistent with one another, no matter how principled a person might aspire to be.

This framework accommodates the Bakhtinian perspective that people's thinking is shaped by heteroglossia, the streams of discourse that infiltrate their minds and shape their thinking, and not always in harmonious ways. Bakhtin (1986; Wertsch, 1991) was fundamentally historical in his conception of speech genres, making it important not only to address the voices in their immediate sense but also to trace them back in time, to situate them within discursive traditions that in turn shape emerging perspectives. People ventriloquate—that is, they revoice ideas and expressions from prior utterances they have taken up—conceptions with cultural histories, and their immersion in social environments that are replete with competing traditions and associated values makes the emergence of a stable, consistent frame of mind difficult to achieve.

Teachers are no exception. They find themselves within such vast webs of contradiction that arriving at coherent conceptions undoubtedly is as computationally impossible for them as it is for anyone. Beginning teachers are affected by deliberate programmatic interventions in universities of the sort often studied by teacher education researchers: the epistemology of assigned readings (Pasternak et al., 2017; Smagorinsky & Whiting, 1995), the consequences of community-engagement experiences (Barnes, 2016), reflective writing during coursework (Florio-Ruane, 2001), service-learning opportunities (Kinloch & Smagorinsky, 2014), responsive mentorship during practica (Cherian, 2007), the integration of technology into teaching (Sang, Valcke, van Braak, & Tondeur, 2010), the use of experiential literary narratives to prepare teachers for multicultural teaching and to develop students' narrative imaginations (Phillion & He, 2009), and countless other factors available through coursework in ways that may or may not be consistent with one another. Each of these is embedded in a historical tradition that gives them authority and viability, even when they contradict each other.

Teachers' work is further shaped by nonprogrammatic factors such as the politics of school environments (Moore, 2012), the influence of students (Smagorinsky, Boggs, Jakubiak, & Wilson, 2010), implicit beliefs in such virtues as the Protestant work ethic (Cozzarelli, Wilkinson, & Tagler, 2002), federal policies (Cohen & Moffitt, 2010), state and local funding that may or may not provide sufficient resources (Biddle & Berliner, 2003), conflicting beliefs about what is involved in developing young people's character and how schools should promote character education (Smagorinsky & Taxel, 2005), the dispositions of students toward schoolwork (Kaufman, 2004; Sleeter, 2001), and other elements. Beginning teachers are often expected to become highly proficient instructors or even master teachers through one to two semesters of coursework and practica, and a semester of student teaching (see, for example, National Council for Accreditation of Teacher Education, 2008). Yet they are more likely to have fragmented understandings of how to teach due to their exposure to multiple conceptions of effective teaching that pull them in many different directions (Bickmore, Smagorinsky, & O'Donnell-Allen, 2005; Johnson, Smagorinsky, Thompson, & Fry, 2003; Smagorinsky, Cook, & Johnson, 2003; Smagorinsky, Wright, Augustine, O'Donnell-Allen, & Konopak, 2007). Longitudinal research I'm conducting with teachers as they move deeper into their careers finds that this fragmentation continues as their work is subject to pressures from multiple sources once they are beyond the formal purview of university professors.

This work complicates such binaries as the *two-worlds pitfall* (Feiman-Nemser & Buchmann, 1985), which positions conservative schools against progressive universities for novice teachers' attention, influence, and loyalty. This polarization suggests that each of these two worlds has internal conceptual unification that insulates them from one another and gives them a mutually exclusive character. Yet as this chapter will detail, this simple binary is too limiting to account for the many directions in which beginning (and veteran) teachers are pulled. Rather, beginning TCs experience a *multiple-worlds pitfall* (Smagorinsky, Rhym, & Moore, 2013), with neither schools nor teacher education programs necessarily providing unitary conceptions of teaching. Each, instead, includes competing beliefs about teaching available from a variety of stakeholders, supporting Walt Whitman's belief that he contains contradictory multitudes and evolutionary psychologists' view that the world is too complex and incongruous for individuals to hold consistent views in relation to their environments.

Background to the Study

This chapter draws on interviews conducted with volunteer TCs from the three pre-service programs reviewed in Chapter 3. These interviews took place just after the completion of their coursework and initial field experiences and prior to the beginning of their formal student teaching. The goal was to understand what the TCs learned about teaching and what they attributed their learning to during their teacher education programs, including both practica and coursework. To understand how their teaching conceptions were influenced by these experiences, the TCs responded to questions soliciting the following information and understandings:

1. What *pedagogical tools*—that is, the means by which instruction is carried out—did the TCs report learning about during their teacher education programs?
2. What *pedagogical areas*—that is, the responsibilities within a teacher's purview (e.g., assessment and planning)—did the TCs' pedagogical tool knowledge fall within?
3. To what *sources* did TCs attribute their knowledge about how to teach the English or Language Arts curriculum?
4. What did the TCs report that they did *not* learn from teacher education and practicum experiences?
5. In what manner did the TCs in each of the three programs, each with a unique structure, construct and describe their experiences? Overall, how were the characterizations of the three programs similar to and different from one another, as described in the participants' interviews?

With respect to this last question, the purpose was not to compare and contrast the three programs to identify the "best" program. Rather, it was to see if program structures, processes, and emphases produced different conceptions and different degrees of conceptual unity in relation to factors outside the program's control (school influences, other university coursework, policy contexts, etc.), and to draw inferences about program effects without determining a preference for any program design, each of which was in large part a function of the specific faculty members' preferences, personalities, and experiences in relation to state and university requirements for teacher education programs, and so was not replicable in other settings.

Pedagogical Concept Development amid Contradictory Means of Mediation

In the original research report on what TCs learn from teacher education programs and initial field experiences (Barnes & Smagorinsky, 2016), we found much to complicate the two-worlds pitfall pitting progressive universities against conservative schools (Feiman-Nemser & Buchmann, 1985). To report the findings, we relied on conventional tabulation of frequencies with which the research participants named and detailed their various influences. We found that approach useful in ways, but also a bit dry. To provide a more compelling way of conveying the swirling contradictions surrounding TCs prior to student teaching, we enlisted the talents of Michelle Zoss, a scholar-artist who had provided the cover illustrations during the editorial terms for two journals in our field, the Young Adult Literature journal *ALAN Review* and the teacher education journal *English Education*. We asked Michelle to create an illustration of a TC trying to find her direction amid a host of gravitational forces, each beckoning her in a different direction, with her head turned to depict her uncertainty amid multiple pathways and competing influences. Michelle came up with the drawing shown in Figure 4.1.

As complicated as this image seems, it does not fully capture the dynamic nature of the myriad factors influencing each individual TC's conception of teaching. Rather, we reduced the complexity to identify a set of categories within which competing influences may fall: the apprenticeship of observation (here, always in the back of the TC's mind), the university-based aspects of the teacher education program, the university-based liberal arts courses, the bureaucratic and policy-related aspects of education, the practicum and student teaching experiences, the community, and the teacher's personal life. Each of these factors influences and is influenced by the TC, and works in relation to the others, albeit often in contradictory ways. It is indeed "computationally impossible for [a teacher] to ensure complete coherence among any reasonable number of elements" (Dutton & Heath, 2010, p. 61) given this vortex of forces. To return to issues raised in Chapter 1, orchestrating these influences into a coherent understanding of the whole environment, as the orthogenetic principle postulates eventually happens, appears to be nearly impossible, given the scope and complexity of schooling amid roiling and contradictory social worlds.

For example, let's take a hypothetical TC in a university program, a composite of programs I have known. The Educational Psychology course might emphasize Piagetian constructivism in conjunction with information processing accounts of cognition, each of which emphasizes biological factors in learning and development, and minimizes social factors, and which views human development as a function

Figure 4.1 Teacher Candidate Trying to Find her Conceptual Way.

largely of age-based changes in cognitive capabilities. This class might rely on "brain-based" teaching (Jensen, 2008) that positions thinking solely within the skull. The TC might simultaneously be enrolled in a teaching methods class that takes a sociocultural perspective grounded in Vygotsky's (1987) notion of social mediation as the primary factor in thinking, speech, and human development and relies on a very different theory of constructivism more attentive to social factors than brain processes such that it emphasizes diversity rather than cognition as a universal set of processes (e.g., Smagorinsky, 2018a).

This same student might take English literature courses that emphasize the professor's reliance on an authoritative literary theory as the primary lens for interpreting texts; and at the same time take an English/Language Arts Education course in which the professor distributes interpretive authority among the students through book club discussions (see Addington, 2001, for just such a study). Within English Education alone, different professors might teach to their specialties that may not align well with one another. A tenured professor might lecture authoritatively on theory while eliding practice; a teaching assistant or clinical faculty member closer to the classroom might emphasize teaching practice apart from its motivating theory and suggest that theorists are out of touch with classroom realities. One professor might favor open-ended reader response theories of literary engagement, another might teach pedagogies for instructing students in explicit strategies for interpreting texts. All of these contradictions take place in one of the two worlds of Feiman-Nemser and Buchmann's (1985) pitfall, suggesting far less agreement in either world than is typically assumed.

Field experiences might simultaneously produce additional contradictory influences. One MT or other school-based colleague might emphasize the development of "life skills" among students who are less likely to attend college (Smagorinsky, Jakubiak, & Moore, 2008); another might grudgingly teach to prepare students to pass standardized district end-of-course tests no matter how dubious the knowledge tested (Smagorinsky, Lakly, & Johnson, 2002); yet another might see school as a character-building environment (Smagorinsky & Taxel, 2005); and another may respond to the specter of high-stakes writing examinations with formalist instruction (Johnson, Smagorinsky, Thompson, & Fry, 2003).

Schools in turn are situated within district, state, and national political landscapes whose values and imperatives provide endpoints for instruction that are often at odds with those emphasized in teacher education. There might be technology initiatives with a variety of tools and emphases, testing mandates (indeed, there will be testing mandates), school safety programs that both emphasize inclusion and encourage students to report each other's suspicious behavior, heavily bureaucratic teacher assessment programs that are time-consuming and that emphasize conduct that might be discouraged in universities, and much more. Schools also must respond to local community values, such as parental initiatives that assert their right to object to what they consider invasive teaching that questions their religious beliefs, values, and practices, and thus prohibits any sort of introspective or critical frames of mind, typically in opposition to what university professors believe should be cultivated in students (see Chapter 11).

Figure 4.1, then, while depicting the bewildering pathway surrounding TCs during university programs, is only partial. There are a host of other experiences, people, and places that influence novice teachers as they prepare to enter classrooms on their own. Rather than attempting to oversimplify the process of learning to teach by assuming that they are solely responsible for shaping beginning teachers' conceptions and practices, teacher education programs need to face the fact that a variety of factors outside their control contribute to the novice teachers' preparation for the classroom. I next document what the TCs in our research reported as affecting their teaching approaches before they began student teaching.

Program Effects

Regardless of which of the three programs the participants learned within, TCs referred to a wide range of factors affecting their pedagogical thinking. Even though they were explicitly asked what they learned during their teacher education programs and were not asked about other influences, their responses extended far outside their formal university education to include a broad range of knowledge gained from a wide variety of often-contradictory sources. Their interviews revealed that the two-worlds pitfall did indeed await TCs torn between campus and school values, in a broad sense. But each site included both authoritarian and progressive values and practices, often in conflict with one another, and each was responsive to contextual factors that complicated any binary thinking about schools and universities.

I review each program separately. Each section includes (1) the *concept map* produced by the collection of TCs interviewed for the research from each program; (2) tabulated accounts of the *knowledge sources* drawn on; (3) tabulated accounts of the specific aspects of the *educational landscape* described by the TCs; and (4) tabulated accounts of the *pedagogical concepts* they had learned about. The tables further identify what the TCs stated they did not learn during teacher education.

For the concept maps, each program's participants were asked to produce a collective concept map depicting their understanding of how to teach English/Language Arts (see Chapter 2 for the procedures). The discussions surrounding the concept map productions were recorded to get an understanding of why the TCs included each component of the maps. I next detail each program's TCs' conceptual orientations, based on these data sources.

Southern Plains Elementary Language Arts Education Program

This program's strong Piagetian constructivist emphasis (Piaget, 1954) and the faculty's unanimous endorsement, if not necessarily practice, of its principles was evident in the interviews. Compared with participants from the other two programs, TCs in the Southern Plains Elementary Language Arts Education program reported learning about constructivism—specifically, Piagetian stage theory—and general (i.e., not subject-specific) planning with the greatest frequency. Because this program's coursework was organized into five discipline-specific methods classes (math, social studies, science, reading, and Language Arts), it is not surprising that TCs would report learning about general planning more often than the other two programs, which were specifically dedicated to Secondary English Education.

The program's constructivist emphasis accounts for why TCs reported learning constructivist teaching methods with greater frequency than the TCs in the other programs. Given that this program had the most fully articulated theoretical conception behind its coursework among the three programs studied, this finding is not surprising, even as TCs from all three programs described beliefs and practices that could be considered constructivist.

Concept map. The TCs from this program were the only ones whose concept map named a theory, in this case, *constructivism*, which they placed at the top of their map as the basic principal for their teaching. All instruction flowed from this concept (see Figure 4.2). The TCs clustered each practice according to subconcepts such as *learning styles* and *multicultural education*.

Their category for *stages of development* included attention to both Piaget and Vygotsky because one TC, Penny, stated that she was more oriented to Vygotsky's socially mediated notion of human development than to Piaget's age-triggered conceptual growth. Bruner (1987) has observed that "for Vygotsky unlike Piaget, there is no 'stage' but only a progressive unfolding of the meaning inherent in language through the interaction of speech and thought. And as always with Vygotsky, it is a progression from outside in, with dialogue being an important part of the process" (p. 11). In contrast, Piaget described human development as a biological process responsive to age-based maturity, regardless of social context. The program faculty's Piagetian dedication provided the undergirding conception behind the notion of constructivism that the TCs learned in teacher education. Piagetian concepts were further embedded in coursework throughout the College of Education, helping to reinforce age-based, stage-oriented human development as an authoritative way of understanding human growth as subject to biological triggers more than socialization.

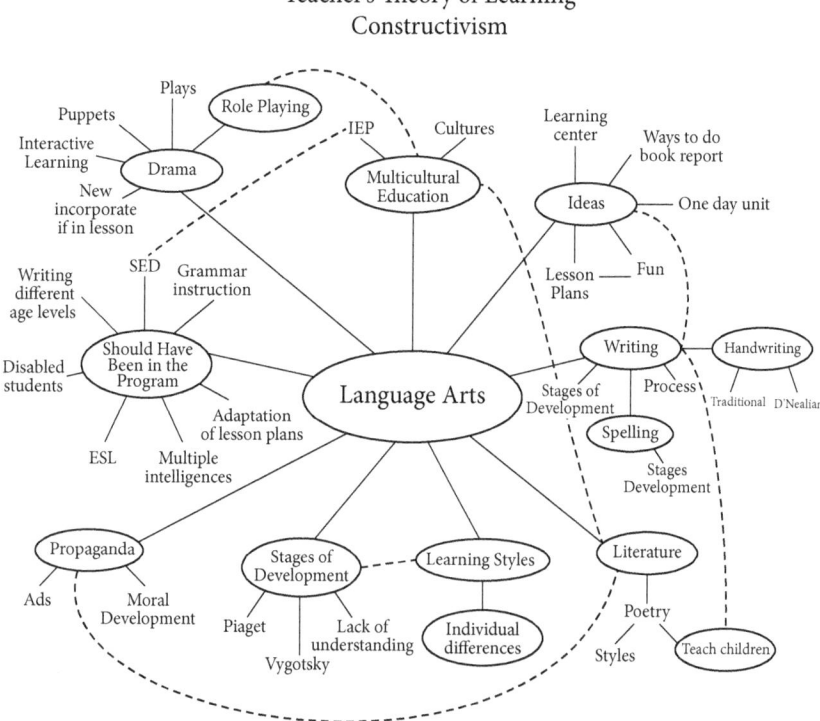

Figure 4.2 Southern Plains Elementary Language Arts Education Program: Concept Map.

The issue of constructivism's source and meaning came up during the concept map discussion, which included questions from the researcher:

> Q: I see you have got "stages of development, linked to Piaget." Is that what you all have in mind for the stages of development?
> Penny: I am more of a Vygotsky.... I see it as being more of a kind of explaining how it goes along and Vygotsky is more of an interactive type of [inaudible]. It is not strictly I am the teacher, I am going to tell you this. OK, I know more about this.... Piaget says OK at stages 0–18 months, we are doing this. [Inaudible] concrete. In 7th grade, it would be painted like this.... Piaget is more strict, this is your limit for this.... To Piaget this is how it is; and Vygotsky, this is what you can do with it.

Penny's summary of the two perspectives centered on what she considered the fixed nature of Piaget's stages and her understanding of Vygotsky as being more "interactive," which I interpret to mean more relational and social in how, when, and in what direction people grow conceptually. She also associates Vygotsky with children's potential more than with their limits within chronological stages. The other members of the cohort did not respond to her remarks about Vygotsky and Piaget, while including them in the concept map.

As the concept map shows, these TCs considered constructivism to be their umbrella concept, with the curricular strand of Language Arts, the research focus, then centered beneath it. As Penny said as they began co-authoring the concept map, constructivism should go "at the top with 'teacher' and then the arrow pointing down." Her preference for Vygotsky did not require a rejection of constructivist teaching practices that the others associated with Piaget. Sharon, another TC in the group, defined constructivism as

> your theory of teaching. I mean, that is like if you agree that kids have hands-on experience as opposed to you filling a cup. Everything you do [as a teacher] is going to have that here.... Constructivism is just allowing children to develop their own knowledge with your guidance. I mean, you're helping them kind of do some boundaries and kind of helping lead them to discover things for themselves, and in their own way, but also making sure they don't discover something in the wrong way, where they think they can tie their shoes by rolling them up or something. You kind of help them along but you let them discover for themselves instead of spoon-feeding them or just pouring knowledge into them.

The rest of the group agreed with this definition, with only Penny's addition that "we forget to feed ourselves in the learning process. I have constructive knowledge myself, so I see teachers as being learners too." This constructivist orientation served as the hub for a set of teaching considerations, including psychological factors (*stages of development* and *learning styles*), curricular strands (*writing, literature, drama,* and *propaganda*), *multicultural education*, and a general category of *ideas*. Several of these subcategories included a *stages of development* subcategory, suggesting a Piagetian dimension to the curriculum.

Knowledge sources. Table 4.1 lists the various knowledge sources identified by the TCs from this program during their individual interviews. The distribution of sources was divided roughly equally between field experiences (fifty-five) and university (sixty). With an emphasis in the research on studying the TCs' instruction in the Language Arts strand of the elementary curriculum, the interviews elicited more about their Language Arts and Reading methods classes than any others, although the TCs did make references to other methods classes on occasion, along with required classes for all teacher education students in Exceptional Learner, Learning and Cognition, and other general areas.

Educational landscape. Table 4.2 details more specifically what the TCs reported learning, regardless of knowledge source. The educational landscape codes suggest that field-based learning exposed TCs to concerns that may or may not have been covered in university courses, such as family issues that teachers ultimately address in classrooms, and how schools function politically and operationally. In schools, the TCs also came to terms with the general problem of the two-worlds pitfall, such as understanding the structural issues that make schools difficult places in which to practice a constructivist pedagogy. Not surprisingly, schools provided the setting in which TCs learned of the life behind the curtain to which they had not been privy as students: teacher conflicts, school politics, resource shortages, student diversity outside the rarified sorts of honors classes they themselves had been enrolled in, and more.

Table 4.1 Southern Plains Elementary Language Arts Education Program: Knowledge Source

Knowledge sources participants attributed their knowledge to	Frequencies in the interviews
Field Experience—School setting	28
Field Experience—Teacher	22
University courses—Methods Block	19
University courses—Methods: Language Arts	14
University courses—Methods: Reading	5
Field Experience—Students	4
University courses—(General)	4
University courses—Learning and Cognition	4
University courses—Methods: Mathematics	3
University courses—Child Development	3
University courses—Exceptional Learner	3
University courses—Media and Technology	3
University courses—School and American Culture	3
University courses—Methods: Science	2
Field Experience—The Act of Teaching	1
University courses—Methods: Social Studies	1
University courses—Teacher Education (General)	1

Table 4.2 Southern Plains Elementary Language Arts Education Program: Educational Landscape

Category	Frequencies in interviews
Community (Christian values are explicitly endorsed in some schools; knowing when to act *in loco parentis*; schools include diverse cultures, races, and learning styles; some students' home lives are difficult; parents can be violent/threatening; domestic abuse; school struggles may follow from home life)	11
School operation (chain of command for dealing with problems; counselors can provide perspective on kids; open-classroom environment, politics of; principals and teachers may have different philosophies; procedures for legal matters, school functions disrupt teaching and learning; urban schools are rule-oriented; each school operates differently)	10
Two-worlds pitfall (highly structured environments don't accommodate constructivist practices; schools and university occasionally aligned; university expectations inappropriate for kids in school; university expectations inappropriate for school resources; university theory must be negotiated to fit school classrooms,)	9
Policy (excessive standardized testing; policies require teaching against beliefs; standardized test scores can make teachers and schools look bad; test-driven priorities; teachers must accommodate to the school's expectations)	7
Curriculum (some elementary classes focus on worksheets; some teachers rely on showing movies; state curriculum's requirements; state curriculum may be pitched inappropriately for many kids' levels; curriculum-literacy skills are integrated, but separated for assessment)	6
Teacher education (different programs have different philosophies; professors don't always practice what they preach; teacher ed program limited opportunities to learn from students because of emphasis on learning from mentor teachers)	6
Professionalism (teacher conflict undermines student learning; teachers interfere and meddle with each other's business)	5
Resources (many schools are resource poor; availability of speech pathologist)	5

Pedagogical concepts. Schools also provided the setting in which university ideas could be put into practice. As Table 4.3 reports, the university's constructivist emphasis provided the lens through which they viewed their experiences in schools. The sorts of dispositions and practices identified in the interviews as constructivist map well onto the sorts of teaching that the TCs had experienced in their own schooling and hoped to incorporate into their own instruction as part of their projected teacher identities (see Chapter 3); the teaching they hoped to avoid fell into the other side of the binary, "traditional" instruction. They valued open-ended classrooms, caring teachers, personality-centered instruction, choice in learning, experiential learning, activity-based classrooms, and related pedagogies.

These preferences, however, came into conflict with test-oriented schools, worksheet-based instruction, the prevalence of basal readers, resistant or emotionally

Table 4.3 Southern Plains Elementary Language Arts Education Program: Pedagogical Concepts

Category	Frequencies in interviews
Language Arts Teaching Principles	
Constructivist methods (student interests guide learning inquiries; active learning; authentic books; multiple text modes; student choice in reading; use everyday texts; bridging prior knowledge to current knowledge)	10
Reading/Literature pedagogy (basals and workbooks go together; how to choose good books; how to use a basal reader; real books interest kids more than basals; use of multicultural literature)	6
Planning (integration of curriculum; skills can be taught out of context of usage; teacher guides learning rather than directing it)	3
Language pedagogy (teach grammar skills)	2
General Teaching Principles	
Constructivist (reading conferences; student choice; teacher learns from student; learning centers; student ownership of classroom; reading and writing workshops; authentic writing promotes kids' engagement; constructivist methods need to be instituted at the beginning of the year; personal writing can promote thinking; classroom arrangement should not be centered on the teacher; kids can learn from mistakes; student groupings should change; students want to learn; teachers should not always know or provide the answers; authentic learning experience; avoid worksheets; cooperative learning; creativity; discovery/exploratory learning; eschew memorization; experiential learning; focus on each student so they feel valued; hands-on learning, manipulatives, implementing group work, incorporating song; learning can be more engaging without textbooks; making learning fun; promote active learning; promote freedom of expression; self-guided exploratory learning; student-led class segments; students' self-assessment on learning; constructivism [with traditional as foil]; cooperative learning; discovery/exploratory learning)	53
Planning (aligning instruction with objectives; be creative; designing cross-curricular unit; diverse ways of teaching; employ variety of strategies; flexible pacing of lessons; good plans don't always work in practice; including real world examples and connections; integrating arts and literacy instruction; knowing disciplinary content; learning is social; preparation can make classrooms productive learning sites; providing print-rich environment and opportunities to read and write; teaching skills in context of usage; team teaching can produce disarray; thematic units; using mnemonics; using music to aid memory; variety of text types; writing lesson plans; centers can help integrate curriculum; teaching from workbooks does not guarantee learning; integrate and diversify curriculum; designing fair tests; not all students' work needs to be graded; seating arrangement must be aligned with pedagogy; adapt methods to needs of the setting; theory sometimes works in practice)	40
Disposition (be assertive; be open; being nonjudgmental allows teachers to become kids' confidants; caring attitude; cultivate kids' self-esteem; flexibility; support for kids; question own assumptions about exceptional learners; support students' success; teacher enthusiasm is contagious; teacher's self-assessment on teaching; set boundaries with students; developing self-esteem to cultivate experimentation; how to find things on your own; opportunities limited by convergent-question assessments; high expectations for kids)	20

Differentiation (individual pacing; individual pathways; provide for special needs; variation in kids calls for variation in teaching; knowing individual kids; individual rather than standardized assessment; immigrant students require greater attention; accounting for diverse learners)	11
Human Development (delight in kids' lightbulb moments; Piagetian and Vygotskian theories; stages of development allow for new types of instruction; developmentally appropriate instruction; Piagetian Stage Theory; Piagetian Theory in practice [practicum])	8
Control (behavior can be managed gently; classroom management; reward and punishment; contracts with students)	4
Technology (educational software; how to use classroom tech)	2

Not Learned in Practicum

Planning instruction (constructivist teaching; scaffolding student learning; authentic engagement with texts; learning from materials requires follow-up discussion)	4

Not Learned in Coursework

Planning (a range of theories; extreme constructivist teaching can leave kids floundering; kids' scientific background knowledge; questioning strategies; methods (not enough))	7
Classroom processes (how to deal with local tragedy; working with emotionally disturbed children; specific strategies for teaching; how to discuss race and religion in class)	4
Technology (using new technologies)	2
Parents' perspectives (exceptional children)	1

distressed students and their parents, and other factors that complicated the premises of a constructivist approach. In general, the two-worlds pitfall was evident in the interviews, with TCs describing problems of implementation in schools as a major challenge and oversight in their university courses when the theory met school realities.

Within these two worlds, however, there were contradictions that made them internally conflictual. The deep Piagetian structure of this program appeared to work against the implementation of a major stated goal of the College of Education, that being its emphasis on diversity and multicultural education. Piaget's own research was monocultural to the extreme; he primarily studied his own children to develop a biological theory of what happens at particular ages in terms of children's growth, producing a sampling error, that is, an identification of norms based on an unrepresentative population. This stage theory based on Eurocentric norms, and specifically those of Piaget's children, provided the backbone of the TCs' developmental understandings, Penny's dissensus aside.

Yet their general coursework emphasized human diversity without resolving the conundrum that many US children are raised quite differently than were Piaget's children or others who fit neatly with his schedule of biologically triggered developmental stages. The Southwestern state that hosted this program, for instance, had a large Native American population that promoted growth that was culturally quite different from the norms that drive Piaget's developmental stages (Four Arrows, 2013). Significantly, Penny claimed a Native American heritage, which Chapter 5 details as a major factor in her teaching. It also included African Americans whose norms are often found deficient when inappropriate stage theories are applied to them (Harris & Graham, 2007). When Piagetian developmental norms are applied to people whose cultures do not promote them, children and youth are prone to damaging interpretations of being developmentally behind, culturally deprived, lacking in intelligence, and other debilitating conclusions. The state in which this university was located included both university and schools whose mascots were the "Savages," with Native images associated with the mascot characters, suggesting a belief in their backwardness and a reduction of their culture to a cartoonish image oriented to violence and subhuman development.

Addressing race in classrooms was identified as an important issue in the interviews, yet is notoriously challenging for beginning teachers and is often presented in teacher education in questionable ways (Berchini, 2017). Navigating that tension between the College of Education championing of diversity and its own structural dedication to fixed developmental stages that produce deficit conceptions of those not following them was a major challenge. The TCs, for instance, often revealed frustrations with knowing how to teach classes that included mainstreamed special education students, themselves often diagnosed as being deficient according to their lack of alignment with developmental norms. The rejection of Piagetian norms is fundamental to Disability Studies in Education (e.g., Gabel, 2005), given how age-based developmental standards are used to classify students in ways damaging to their psychological growth, social status, and opportunities for learning in mainstream classes. The Piagetian undergirding of a program dedicated simultaneously to human diversity produced an irresolvable contradiction in this program's structure.

The diversity conundrum was further evident in the world of schools, all of which claimed to honor the diversity of their students. The TCs noted that many parents opposed diversity education, making it difficult to implement. Many in schools also taught and promoted Christian values that are often alien to Native students, whose religion is often more oriented to natural coexistence than worship of a single, all-powerful deity (Four Arrows, 2006; Smagorinsky, Anglin, & O'Donnell-Allen, 2012). Like universities, schools stated a commitment to diversity and multiculturalism, while at the same time operated according to the deep structure of schools: the institutionalized curriculum and assessment, dress codes, codes of conduct, approved speech genres and social languages, conventions for interaction, composition of administration and faculty, the physical arrangement of schools, the hidden curriculum, and other structural factors that organize the educational process according to a specific value system.

The schools provided another challenge in promoting diversity, that being what the TCs termed excessive standardized testing that established instructional priorities for teachers who were obligated to follow procedures and meet school-wide goals. The TCs noted that principals and teachers often had different priorities that were manifested in this contradiction. The uniform expectations of testing were not responsive to the home conditions that the TCs found their students living in, in some cases characterized by abuse and violence. Students' homes further promoted diverse cultures and learning styles. This set of within-world contradictions further complicated the two-worlds pitfall in that the university's constructivist emphasis did not provide enough tools for working with children and youth who were not socialized to self-directed academic learning or developing according to Piaget's stages, and schools often modeled more authoritarian teaching than the facilitative role emphasized on campus allowed.

In neither school nor university did the TCs find ways of negotiating this challenging aspect of teaching. Possibly complicating this problem on campus was the tendency of some faculty professing constructivism to rely on lectures and correct-answer exams to teach its points. The ideals thus were difficult to realize in practice, in part because schools and universities were out of alignment, but also because both schools and universities provided contradictory environments for learning to teach in a conceptually coherent way. Some TCs noted that the emphasis on constructivism, in spite of its coherence, limited their exposure to other theories that might have helped them navigate these environments more effectively. Undoubtedly the idealistic presentation of constructivism on campus, without sufficient practical tools for implementing it in schools, contributed to their view that Piagetian constructivism had limitations in preparing them for the classroom, and that other theories should have been available. It also appears that age-stage-based developmental theories do not help teachers work with diverse populations with differential means and ends of socialization, and thus different developmental trajectories and processes, requiring them all to be force-fit into a single schedule that produces deficit assumptions about those who do not fit its timetable.

The cohort's concept map included attention to Piaget's stages of development; yet these essential features of his theory rarely appeared in the TCs' interviews or observations, nor did other key elements of his perspective. For instance, Piaget's theory revolves around the notions of *accommodation* and *assimilation*. Assimilation occurs when an existing schema does not work, and it needs to be changed to deal with a new, discrepant experience. Assimilation involves a reconstruction of mental operations. Accommodation is directed outwardly and involves using an existing schema to deal with a new object or situation. The engine of development, in conjunction with age-triggered capabilities, is *equilibrium*, which occurs when schemata can incorporate most new information through assimilation; yet disequilibrium follows when the schemata do not fit with new information, producing frustration that leads to the restoration of balance and security via accommodation. This new state of equilibrium enables sufficiently robust new schemata for the process of assimilation to become possible for new experiences.

The TCs did not mention any of these functions during the research. Rather, they focused on teaching practices that were open-ended and allowed for self-directed pacing and production. Their appropriation of the concept of constructivism, then, appeared to be selective, and concerned what was applicable to classroom teaching as they understood it. From a Vygotskian perspective, their conception of constructivism as a group, then, was at the level of the complex or pseudoconcept, wherever one draws the line. From a Piagetian perspective, the TCs often had trouble assimilating Piagetian theory in its entirety into their schemata for teaching Language Arts, and as the chapters that follow relate, were often thwarted in their efforts at accommodation by the constraints of their environments.

Southern Plains Secondary English Education Program

TCs from the Southern Plains Secondary English Education program talked about influences that were evenly divided between field and campus, with thirty-eight coming from each. In addition, there was one reference to fellow teacher education students as a knowledge source. The TCs referred to learning about teaching from their practicum MTs for nearly a third of their attributions of teaching tools, in spite of a fiasco in the field placement office that delayed practicum placements until the very end of the semester, requiring highly compacted field observations in classes other than English where they had to meet a semester's worth of field experience hours in a few scrambled-together weeks.

The surprisingly large number of references to MTs, often in disciplines other than English, could be due to a variety of factors. The recency effect (Ebbinghaus, 1885/1913) of having done all of their field experiences just prior to the interviews could explain some of this phenomenon. At the same time, the program structure could have contributed to their reliance on the field for knowledge about how to teach. Prior to the methods class, TCs' coursework had a content-area emphasis, with roughly fifteen courses taken in the Department of English. Before student teaching, the students took one methods class as their program capstone course, with roughly forty hours of accompanying field experiences required. The methods class was taught by two professors, each quite differently, and TCs took whichever course was offered during the semester they signed up to take it. One professor emphasized unit design, the other taught the methods course as a poetry writing workshop. The Theory of English Grammar course was taught by either an English Education faculty member or a Department of English professor. The education professor emphasized linguistic variation and language pedagogy; and the English professor took a linguistic approach without a pedagogical emphasis.

In contrast to the single methods course in this program, in the same university's Elementary Education program, TCs took five methods courses, one per major subject area (science, mathematics, Language Arts, reading, and social studies); and in the Atlantic Piedmont English/Language Arts Education program reviewed next, TCs took four related courses from two professors who team-taught the entire program, with a minimum of eight courses in the Department of English. TCs in this program simply had less engagement with the English Education professors than those in the other two programs had with their pedagogical faculties, and more with faculty in Arts and Sciences emphasizing literary criticism.

The program structure assumed that a single teaching methods course would prepare TCs for the myriad responsibilities of teaching the English/Language Arts curriculum to diverse students in public schools, and would overcome all other influences on their conception of how to teach the discipline. The data suggest that it did not succeed in meeting this expectation, although struggles experienced by TCs from other programs suggest that teacher education programs, regardless of structure, can only do so much. This limitation, I would argue, is amplified when the program requires intensive and assimilative field experiences that may contradict what is taught on campus and may reinforce status quo approaches to curriculum and instruction, thus overwhelming what is emphasized by university professors who have no influence in schools' hiring and retention practices beyond the provision of reference letters and informal recommendations.

Concept map. This group's concept map (Figure 4.3) suggests that these TCs lacked any central conceptual driver in their thinking. Rather, they identified a set of teaching concerns that are common to most beginning English/Language Arts teachers and placed them on the drawing, and then included relevant subcategories when appropriate. The map appears more descriptive than conceptual. That is, the curriculum is divided into its traditional strands, and each strand is parsed by an instructional emphasis or classification of its genres, without a guiding theory or perspective such as constructivism or student-centeredness, as was more clearly evident in the other two programs' TCs' concept maps. Their concept map was largely oriented to identifying the range of responsibilities they anticipated meeting as teachers, serving more as a menu of responsibilities than as a conceptual approach to teaching secondary school English.

Knowledge sources. TCs from this program made thirty-eight references to school-based sources and thirty to university sources, most of which were to English Education faculty. With relatively little pedagogical coursework to draw on from campus, TCs possibly got more of their ideas from their MTs during practica, even with such problematic assignments from the field placement office, although the recency effect of the timing of the interviews on the heels of concentrated field experiences may explain some of their attributions.

Educational landscape. The TCs learned about the educational landscape of teaching in terms of how schools work in politics, operation, and other forms of

Table 4.4 Southern Plains Secondary English Education Program: Knowledge Sources

Knowledge sources participants attributed their knowledge to	Frequencies with which each code was identified in the interviews
Field Experience—Teacher	25
English Education faculty	23
Education courses—General	8
Field Experience—School setting	7
Field Experience—Students	6
University courses—Developmental Psychology	5
Fellow teacher ed students	1
University Course—History class	1
University courses—Drama	1

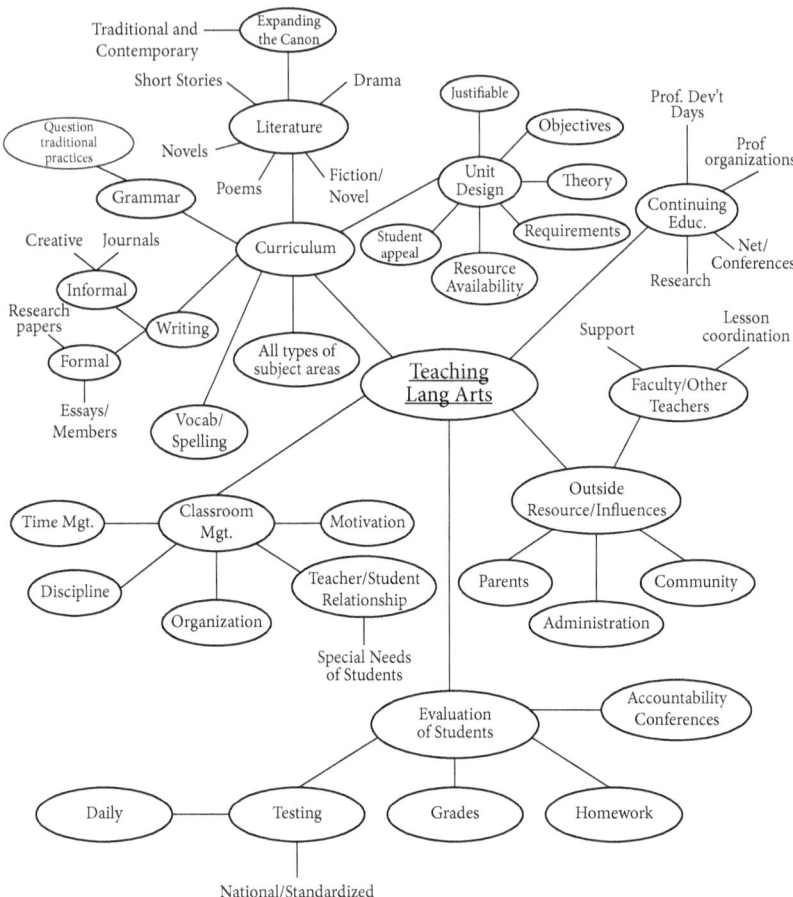

Figure 4.3 Southern Plains Secondary English Education Program: Concept Map.

social machinery. They began to see the curriculum as more than a collection of lessons and more as a broadly related set of experiences aligned with assessment demands that nonetheless allowed for some instructional freedom. They also learned about social issues not addressed in coursework, such as parental opposition to diversity education in a Bible Belt environment and how to conduct classes that included mainstreamed special education students. They further made the seemingly inevitable observation that schools and universities are divided in both values and practices, suggesting the presence of the two-worlds pitfall without attending to variation within those worlds.

Pedagogical concepts. In the area of discipline-specific and general teaching practices, the TCs aligned their interpretations of coursework and field experiences with the values they had stated in reflecting on their apprenticeships of observation (see Chapter 3 and Table 4.6). Although their program lacked a coherent vision, given the paucity of courses required of them in their subject area and hodge-podge organization in meeting the rest of their certification requirements, their preferences nonetheless gravitated toward what might be termed a generally Deweyan approach

Table 4.5 Southern Plains Secondary English Education Program: Educational Landscape

Category	Frequencies in interviews
School operation (how whole schools work; middle school team approach; old and limited technology limits teaching; open-classroom environments are distracting; politics of; schools operate by administrative routines; secondary school and primary school differ in structure; some teachers just punching in)	10
Curriculum (curriculum and assessment are aligned; each school develops its curriculum uniquely; English teachers at grade level do same work at same pace; some schools emphasize lessons more than whole curriculum; teachers have leeway in interpreting the curriculum)	6
Student pathways (mainstreaming challenges teachers)	6
Community (parental communication; parents oppose diversity education; schools include diverse cultures, races, and learning styles)	5
Teacher Education (English professors look down on education professors and students; disciplinary culture—Education/Arts and Sciences have different values; program integration—courses lack articulation)	3
Context (critical stance on educational issues; social and political issues surrounding schools)	2
Resources (many schools are resource poor)	2
Two-worlds pitfall (progressive theory doesn't always work in practice; sometimes schools don't follow research-based practices)	2

to education that emphasized unique developmental paths, activity-based learning, authentic literacy experiences, open-ended and discovery-oriented learning, an aversion to formalism, and related values that fit well with what the same university's Elementary Education program TCs called constructivist teaching, without the conceptual foundation provided by Piaget.

Their interviews placed a greater emphasis on instructional planning than did the Southern Plains Elementary Education program TCs. They spoke extensively about instructional planning, often built around themes, a major emphasis of the methods course taught by one of the two English Education professors. Their teaching thus was attentive to identifying clear learning objectives, and scaffolding instruction designed to help students meet them. Perhaps significantly, the TCs made more references to "other" educational courses than to their English Education courses, and the program's relatively limited exposure to their disciplinary faculty could serve as the primary reason for this ratio. Seventy-two references came to general education courses, and forty-five were attributed to English Education faculty. The two were often aligned, such as the emphasis on identifying learning objectives and scaffolding students' learning toward them.

The Piagetian emphasis of the TCs' general coursework, however, as outlined in the review of the Elementary Education program's structure, suggested a stage-based approach to human development that was counter-paradigmatic to the sociocultural perspective emphasized in the TCs' English Education coursework, producing a within-world conflict with considerable implications for teaching in relation to matters of human development. The College of Education's deep structure of Piagetian

Table 4.6 Southern Plains Secondary English Education Program: Pedagogical Concepts

Category	Frequencies in interviews
English/Language Arts Teaching Principles	
Planning (addressing culturally diverse learning styles; designing thematic units; engage students with creative thinking; planning for block schedule; rationale for instruction; relate literature to students' experiences; sequencing; theoretical grounding for planning; writing educational objectives; writing lesson plans; most teachers use textbooks cover to cover; pre- and post-instruction assessments; scaffolding)	17
Constructivist methods (involving students; learning by doing, not by instruction; student-centered teaching; teachers facilitate learning; connecting reading to real world)	9
Reading/Literature pedagogy (provide practice time; attend to multiple student interpretive perspectives; reading broadly; reading from author's perspective; reader response pedagogy)	5
Assessment (how to write a test; how to grade papers; students need papers returned promptly; teaching toward outcomes)	4
Curriculum (AP curriculum content; historical foundation; nontraditional writers; historical perspective on English curriculum)	4
Language pedagogy (perfect grammar is an illusion; teach grammar in conjunction with reading and writing)	3
Writing pedagogy (allow writing in many textual genres; provide practice time; high yet realistic expectations)	3
General Teaching Principles	
Constructivist methods (using technology; learning through play; projects; recapturing fun of elementary school in high school English; struggling students can have fun learning; summoning childhood memory as basis for writing; teachers can make learning interesting by moving beyond rote; teachers need to hook kids on instruction; enjoying learning; student choice; students take ownership of learning; motivational techniques; role of prior knowledge)	16
Planning (aligning instruction and assessment; making theory practical; making transparency/slide presentation; scaffolding; synthesizing knowledge from different courses into unit plans; writing and teaching toward objectives; there are creative ways to teach; writing lesson plans)	13
Disposition (uncomfortable with sexual topics; young teachers must differentiate selves from kids; overcoming performance anxiety; initial nervousness of getting up in front of people; flexibility; mutual respect for students; consistently firm; equitable treatment of diverse students; good grades can indicate good teaching; teachers want students to succeed)	11
Human development (exploring values; how children develop identities that shape adolescence; imaginatively project social futures; people are continual learners; phases of Adolescence, Piagetian developmental stages)	7
Control (classroom management; students take advantage of soft-spoken teachers)	6
Knowledge of students (cultures, home lives, diversity, readiness for learning, ability to "do school," dislike of rote teaching)	6

Differentiation (many students are less accomplished than novice teachers anticipate; recognize special needs; variation in kids calls for variation in materials)	4
Appropriate instruction (meeting needs of minority students; teaching mainstreamed classrooms)	3
Culture and diversity (navigating multicultural classrooms; race relations should be discussed in class; teachers should know and respond to their students' racial cultures)	3
Technology (how to use spreadsheet; making laminations)	3
Not Learned in Practicum	
Curriculum (knowing what to teach and leeway within guidelines)	1
Not Learned in Coursework	
Planning (how to write a lesson plan; how to teach; moving theory into practice; integrating mainstreamed SPED students into regular instruction; preparation to teach)	5
Technology (how to use sophisticated tech; secondary school applications; using new technologies)	5
Classroom processes (how to work with kids; classroom management; what classrooms are like)	4
What Not to Do with Kids	
Stick to plan even if students are bored; be mean, sarcastic, and racist; disregard offensive comments; favor the boys; let kids be mean, sarcastic, and racist	6

developmental psychology was at odds with the program-specific emphasis on culturally specific development that is not necessarily responsive to age-triggered cognitive advancements in Western thinking.

The discipline-specific emphasis on sociocultural rather than biological human development included constructivism in the TCs' growing conception of effective teaching. Vygotsky and Piaget were both considered developmentally oriented, constructivist psychologists, albeit with different conceptions of what mediates development, the environment, or the individual's biological maturation. The TCs thus referred to constructivist practices resembling those identified by the Southern Plains Elementary Education program TCs, without naming them as such. This teaching was oriented to activity- and choice-based learning, teachers facilitating more than lecturing, and other practices associated with Deweyan progressivism. They still found that these practices did not necessarily work well in the schools to which they had been assigned, positioning university values as not always relevant to school conduct.

Another within-world discrepancy noted by one TC concerned status differentials between faculty in disciplines and faculty in education. They reported what many College of Education faculty will attest to: Department of English professors look down on them and share their condescension with education students, by extension looking down on TCs themselves. In this program, the TCs took abundant courses in the Department of English and had one required English Education course, producing an overwhelming influence from faculty in Arts and Sciences as pedagogical models.

Departments of English have long been hierarchical, with literary critics at the top. Beneath them fall those whose work is more practical. Composition and Rhetoric faculty tend to be lower in status, no doubt because they do the practical work of teaching writing rather than talking literary theory. As Kinneavy (1971) once said:

> Composition is so clearly the stepchild of the English department that it is not a legitimate area of concern in graduate studies, it is not even recognized as a subdivision of the discipline of English in a recent manifesto put out by the major professional association (MLA) of college English teachers . . . in some universities is not a valid area of scholarship for advancement in rank, and is generally the teaching province of graduate assistants or fringe members of the department. (p. 1)

Those in teacher education tend to fall yet lower on the scale; not only are they involved with pedagogy but they also teach people who will work in schools rather than universities, and teachers are often blamed for incoming shortcomings of college students (e.g., Cherif, Adams, Movahedzadeh, Martyn, & Dunning, 2014) and thus are viewed as inferior. Within the university world, then, there are fissures that undermine the notion that it represents a unitary environment in opposition to that of schools.

Atlantic Piedmont Secondary English Education Program

The analysis found that this program, which was more tightly managed than its Southern Plains University counterpart, produced attention to teacher dispositions and knowledge of students at much higher rates than were available from interviews with TCs from the other two programs. The faculty in this program intentionally designed coursework to encourage TCs to draw connections between their university-based courses and their practicum experiences, claiming in their public documents that their design insured a "seamless" transition from program to school, a claim not substantiated by data reported here, or later in this volume. Further, the faculty's field-based approach amplified the effects of MTs for ground-level pedagogical ideas situated within particular school contexts.

This program's collaborative approach produced far greater cohesiveness in the campus world than did either of the other two programs studied. Undoubtedly, this absence of internal conflict followed from the fact that two professors team-taught the entire program for the TCs' year of certification coursework, spending two full days each week in class with them exclusively and doing much of their field supervision themselves. The TCs in this program also reported fewer disjunctures in the schools in which they did their practicum. What emerged from the interviews was the program's unity and coherence in within-world conceptions. Yet this coherence did not always extend to the schools and their values, suggesting a two-worlds problem that ran counter to the designed intentions of a program claiming a seamless transition between university and schools.

Concept map. The concept map (Figure 4.4) produced by the TCs from this program is quite telling in terms of how this program focused on students without necessarily providing teaching strategies for advancing their academic knowledge. When asked

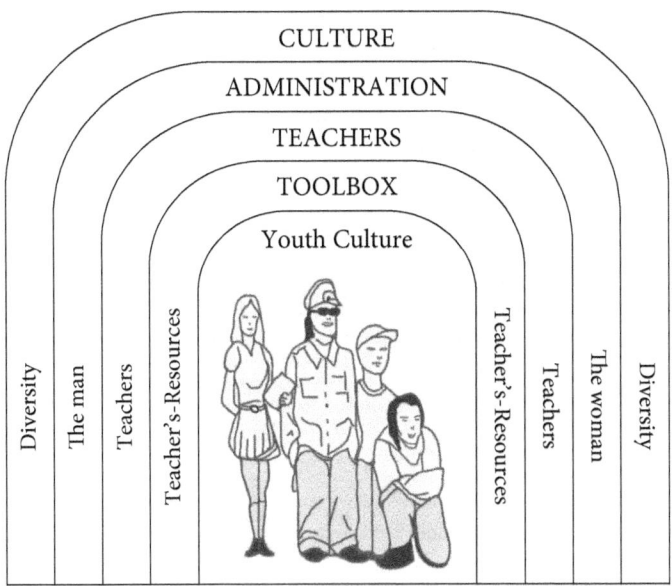

Figure 4.4 Atlantic Piedmont Secondary English Education Program: Concept Map.

to depict their conception of *teaching*, the TCs produced a drawing of *students* and the factors that surround them. They did not describe any pedagogical tools, focusing rather on youth and their environments. This activity was designed to enable a set of program participants to map out their conception of their discipline, and their interpretation was to depict the world of adolescence, with teachers among the spheres of influence surrounding them, in unspecified ways.

The task called for each participant to produce an individual concept map, after which the group produced a single map that coordinated their personal conceptions. Natalie summarized her individual map by saying, "the teacher program has taught me . . . to pay attention to your students and [the] need to make them the center of the classroom." When the participants produced their group map, they began with a group of students and above them drew a rainbow-like design, with each spectrum representing a key cultural influence: youth culture, the toolbox of teachers' resources, teachers themselves, administration, and culture marked by diversity. The decision to place students at the center of the drawing began about a third of the way through their discussion:

> Sharon: Most of us seem, you know—all of us, actually, seem to have focused around what we would use in the classroom. The classroom was the center, it seems, of everybody's. So wouldn't we want to make the classroom the center of our concept map?
> Steffi: Perhaps a student to represent the classroom student.
> Sharon: Okay, so student in the center?
> Steffi: Student in the center—

Sharon: Right. We all—anybody object to student in the center?
Abbie: We all endorse student in the center.
Randy: A student or more than one.
Sharon: I think I'd put more than one. I think I would put more than one because that's why we're looking at so many different tools—is because we're wanting to address more than one child. We're looking to meet the needs of—
Andrea: Well, I figure by putting the students in the middle we're putting everything that is student and student-oriented, in particular since we're putting multiple [students in the middle]. That's kind of the social interaction, what they're bringing into the classroom. They're the most important thing right in the middle. . . .
Steffi: We could put everything around the middle feeding into the student, using arrows perhaps.
Abbie: Yes.
Steffi: All the things—like the students are in the center and all the tools that we would use to affect the student feed into the student. So you have arrows all into the student.

The focus on students would presumably produce teaching methods that cultivated their potential, although no such methods were mentioned. Rather, the TCs had learned that the primary order of business for a teacher is to get to know students, and plan instruction from there.

Knowledge sources. The TCs from this program referred roughly evenly to university and school sources for their knowledge about how to teach (see Table 4.7): forty-four attributions went to school-based people, and forty-nine to university-based people, with ten more to their cohort members, whom I'm separating from these distinctive environments and positioning as hybrid influences. This last figure stands remarkably in contrast to the single reference by the Southern Plains Secondary English Education

Table 4.7 Atlantic Piedmont Secondary English Education Program: Knowledge Sources

Knowledge Sources	Frequencies
English Education Faculty	31
Students in Practicum	26
Mentor Teacher—Assigned	18
English Education Cohort (fellow students)	10
Assigned readings	9
University Courses (Ed psych, Foundations, Special Education, English department course in teaching Shakespeare)	9
Negative—Mentor Teacher/Practicum	7
Negative—Teacher Education Program	6
Self (Girl Scout Leader; parent; personal reflection; prior teaching)	6
Mentor Teacher—Informal (school colleagues; family members)	2

program TCs to fellow students as sources of learning, and zero such references in the Southern Plains Elementary Education program. I interpret this difference to be a function of the intensive cohort approach, one that was designed to include carpooling to school sites to promote discussion and the concentration of coursework in the hands of the same two professors working collaboratively.

The structural fragmentation of the Southern Plains University's Secondary English Education program produced highly divergent programs of study that appeared to affect the TCs' possibilities for learning from each other through their teaching experiences. Yet the Southern Plains Elementary Education program's TCs did not refer to one another at all as a source of learning, even with a cohort approach, suggesting that a cohort approach alone is not necessarily going to promote TC's learning from each other. The main difference appears to be the team-taught approach and the placement of multiple TCs in the same school, and the frequency of carpooling to intensify this effect. The two professors' joint control over all pedagogical coursework appeared to reduce any variation that might follow from having five subject-area specialists teaching the subject-specific methods course of the Southern Plains Elementary Education program.

This program's knowledge-source data were also anomalous in the high frequencies with which its TCs referred to students in their field placement as an influence on their teaching decisions, accounting for 22 percent of all references. Second only to the English Education faculty, students in the fall semester practicum were identified as the source of teaching ideas most frequently, with thirty-one references to the English Education faculty and twenty-six for students, far more than what they reported learning from their assigned MTs (eighteen attributions). One possible explanation is that the year-long placement in a single classroom beginning with the fall practicum provided familiarity with a single set of students, something not available in the more distributed nature of the practicum-heavy elementary program in this study, and something absent from the dysfunction of the Southern Plains Secondary English Education program where the field experiences all took place within a few weeks in placements in various subject areas, cobbled together at the last moment. With the faculty emphasizing making connections with students, several influences converged to account for this cohort's greater focus on students as sources of knowledge on how to teach well.

This program's TCs were the only group who referred to themselves as the source of their teaching ideas. One possible explanation could be the program's emphasis on reflective practice. TCs were encouraged to consider their university-based coursework in light of their practicum experiences. Such reflection could have encouraged TCs to engage in their own sense-making, contributing to a vision of themselves as knowledgeable about various teaching principles.

Educational landscape. Table 4.8 lists the educational landscape codes, which reflect issues reported by TCs from the other two programs. This program, however, did produce the greatest frequency of *two-worlds pitfall* codes, raising doubts about the faculty's claim of seamless integration of their work on campus with schools. The TCs' observations about *school operation* and about the sorts of politics and hidden agendas at work suggest that the school sites were not unified worlds, but environments where

Table 4.8 Atlantic Piedmont Secondary English Education Program: Educational Landscape

Category	Frequencies
School operation (politics of; hidden agendas; communication lines; administrative roles; teacher culture; types of schools; procedures for getting assistance; bureaucratic routines; teachers help one another; teachers share frustrations)	15
Two-worlds pitfall (classrooms are not ideal; schools and universities have different values; progressive theory doesn't always work in practice; synthesize school and university knowledge)	13
Student pathways (tracking and racial composition; social promotion; tracking is about socialization)	6
Community (diversity; parental intervention; White flight)	3
Policy (work with school board; work on standards projects; write research proposal)	3
Curriculum (accommodates styles and ability ranges [includes "disability"])	2
Long-term issues (educational history; cyclical nature of teaching styles)	2

predictable human conflicts are played out in the educational landscape, complicated by dissonance in the community about how to conduct school and factors such as tracking that, like White flight and other parental decisions, produced segregation at the expense of diversity ideals.

Pedagogical concepts. Table 4.9 details the specific concepts learned by the TCs in their teacher education program. In general, these concepts were oriented to student-centered teaching that emphasized learners' self-chosen pathways and teaching stances predicated on support, care, and facilitation. As the concept map would suggest, the TCs in their interviews placed students at the center of their attention, although with an eye toward the state curriculum and how it shaped their work in classrooms.

This program's COE did not include a dedication to Piaget's stage theory of human development, and so did not produce the sort of within-world contradiction evident in the Southwestern US university's two programs. Nor, however, did it include a sociocultural dimension. Rather than having human development serve as a program structural value, this program endorsed what might be termed a progressive vision that did not orient itself especially to cultural variation or theories of human development, instead focusing on the cultivation of individual students' potential in traveling their chosen pathways.

The absence of a cultural perspective was evident in the interviews with one African American TC. He was highly critical of the faculty's nondirective teaching philosophy, finding it more compatible with children well-socialized to schools' ways than those from families less oriented to White and middle-class formal learning environments. He was familiar with Delpit's (1995) work on the linguistic codes of power, and was assertive in demanding greater attention to the fact that not all students are school-ready in their socialization to conduct, communication genres, and other areas that are well-internalized by middle-class White students. This sort of critique has been directed at various constructivist approaches (e.g., Richardson, 2003) of the sort advanced in this program. The program, taught by two White middle-class women,

Table 4.9 Atlantic Piedmont Secondary English Education Program: Pedagogical Concepts

Category	Frequencies
English/Language Arts Teaching Principles	
Constructivist methods (journals; writing and reading workshops; portfolios; open-ended inquiry; student-centered teaching; peer editing; discussion; understanding is better than memorization; metacognition; teachers facilitate learning; attention to learning processes; exploratory learning)	17
Assessment (organization; alignment with instruction; portfolios; not necessary to grade everything; attention to state assessment; reasonable and appropriate goals)	7
Reading/Literature pedagogy (cultivate love and need for reading; choice in reading; Shakespeare; anthologies are limiting)	5
Sequencing (begin with accessible instruction; chunking longer readings; sequencing can be flexible)	4
Classroom logistics	2
Language pedagogy (theory of grammar instruction; formalism can be appropriate)	2
Writing pedagogy (how to research a topic; give students practice)	2
General Teaching Principles	
Dispositions (each style unique; personal life and experience affect teaching; teaching is a performance; there is always more to learn about teaching; teachers are learners/works in progress; teachers change over time; reflection promotes growth; manage much at once; tough job; it's okay to feel out of control; teachers are observers; teachers get ideas from multiple sources; teachers are resilient; teachers should risk failure with new ideas; teachers learn from failure; patience; resourcefulness; sense of humor; fairness; positive attitude; respect for kids; don't take things personally; exhibit professionalism; flexibility; teachers should keep relationships with students bounded)	46
Constructivist methods (ground abstract in concrete; relate new learning to prior knowledge; real world utility for school learning; publish student work; school can have a vocational purpose; kids often don't like subject matter; peer editing; collaborative learning; peer assessment; lesson planning; connections between students and curriculum; dialogic classroom; learning by doing; engaging kids is challenging; using technology; kids dislike academic reading)	24
Differentiation (multiple intelligences; kids have different learning styles; kids have different talents; groups respond differently to same instruction; variation in kids calls for variation in materials; not all kids like the same teaching; learning disabilities; low literacy levels)	16
Knowledge of students (teaching is responsive to students; incorporate student choice; kids different from teachers; kids today different from my generation; students don't see teachers as whole people; youth culture; adjusted to kids' levels; based on students' cultures and experiences)	16
Planning (organization; preparation; adjust lessons *in situ*; have a backup plan; interdisciplinary teaching; scaffolding; teaching within time constraints; kids expect to be told what to do)	12
Community (rapport with students; knowing and caring for students builds community; interpersonal relationships matter; kids' home lives present challenges to teachers)	9
Theory (theory changes in relation to new experiences; connecting personal and academic knowledge; education classes are too theoretical; theory doesn't always work in practice)	9

(*Continued*)

Table 4.9 Continued

Category	Frequencies
General Teaching Principles	
Culture and diversity (inclusive approach to diversity; Delpit's views on explicit teaching of codes of power; culture should be discussed in class; theories of race and education; students' cultures frame educational practices; race-based traits; racial performance disparities)	8
Control (kids can be manipulative; kids can be resistant; some kids like in-school suspension; classroom management; speaking with authority without condescension)	6
Human developmental ("natural" development; teachers can change kids' lives; moral development)	6
What Not to Do	
Curriculum and instruction (teach grammar; use process approach with kids who need direct instruction; emphasize quantity over quality; be disorganized)	7
With assessment (overmark with red ink; multiple-choice tests)	3
With kids (bore; alienate; be mean and sarcastic; disregard disengagement)	2
Not Learned in Coursework	
Planning (units; lessons; grammar instruction; alternatives to process method; integrating media and technology; moving theory into practice)	7
Classroom processes (classroom management; how to lead discussion, how to lecture)	5
Not Learned in Practicum	
Assessment	1
Classroom management	1
Integrate media and technology	1

reflected values of the White middle class and was unresponsive to critiques of the assumptions behind progressive methods from minoritized people.

TCs in this program reported learning far more general teaching methods than those specifically appropriate for English/Language Arts instruction, a surprise given that this was the only one among the three programs studied where the TCs enrolled in more than one English/Language Arts methods course, unless one counts the Southern Plains Elementary Education program's Reading course and the Southern Plains Secondary English Education program's Theory of English Grammar course when taught by an English Education professor. Here, the students spent full days twice a week with the same two tenured professors in their discipline yet reported that from their professors they learned 39 teaching ideas specific to their subject area and 152 ideas categorized as general. Andrea, one of the TCs from this program, described her professors' approach as follows:

> They try very hard to keep things general. Generally they want us to base education on experience. Generally they want us to create a diverse and accepting

classroom.... They are all very general ideals, and they try very hard not to tell us how to apply them, to give us opportunities to apply them for ourselves, but not to tell us how to, necessarily. They will show us examples, maybe, but all in all we have to draw some of our own conclusions.

Much of what they learned in English/Language Arts methods involved open-ended, student-directed learning: writing in journals, working in reading and writing workshops (choice-driven reading and writing with individualized trajectories and processes), portfolios, and related pedagogies that allow students to chart and direct their own learning. This program's TCs produced no statements about instructional planning specific to their subject area, in contrast to the other two programs studied. They did report learning general planning ideas, but also noted that instruction in planning was a program shortcoming. Rather than teaching methods of instructional planning, the approach emphasized by their English/Language Arts professors appears more oriented to creating environments in which students direct their own learning toward their own goals. The presence of abundant two-world pitfalls codes suggest that this approach did not fit well on the templates of the schools in which they were placed, in spite of extensive efforts to find good matches and thus a seamless transition from university to school.

Discussion

These findings suggest that the two-worlds pitfall is alive and well. The bifurcation into two distinct worlds, however, obscures internal contradictions within each of these worlds unless each is tightly controlled and exclusive in how, and from whom, TCs learn to teach. The interviews complicate a number of assumptions about learning to teach. First, teacher education programs cannot be overly confident that they provide what I have called the *conceptual home base* for understandings of teaching and learning (Smagorinsky, 2002). I know that such a thing is possible, because I developed this notion based on the remarkable community of teachers who attended the University of Chicago under George Hillocks, where I got my M.A.T. in 1977 in one of many cohorts he taught in English Education (see McCann, 2018).

Such a possibility is dependent, I would say, on two factors. First, it relies on a tightly controlled conceptual focus of the sort that I experienced at Chicago and that is evident in the Atlantic Piedmont Secondary English Education program's co-taught approach. Having one to two professors teach a whole program's pedagogical coursework provides TCs with a singular, coherent vision and a set of related practices that is amenable to conceptual cohesion. Pragmatically, however, it creates little space for other teaching for faculty with such a specific focus on preservice teacher education, such as the doctoral seminars often prized by research-university professors. Although other coursework elsewhere in teacher certification programs might contradict the approach imparted in tightly controlled coursework, as when the Southern Plains English Education program's single-course sociocultural emphasis conflicted with the COE's Piagetian foundation, having one to two professors continually reinforce a perspective across multiple courses and topics ought to produce a stronger conception of teaching than single courses that potentially get lost in a sea of contradictory ideas, agenda, paradigms, and other sources of conflict.

Second, that pedagogical approach needs to have practical value when road-tested with students. I know from experience that the Chicago program resonated with its TCs well into their careers, as attested to by the fact that we are still publishing work advocating for the teaching methods we learned decades after attendance (e.g., Smagorinsky, 2018a, 2018b; Kahn, Walter, & Johannessen, 2009; McCann, 2014; Wilhelm & Smith, 2017), those centered on the activity-based, collaborative, inductive learning of procedures for the writing and reading of texts following task and genre conventions and expectations. The Atlantic Piedmont Secondary English Education program's focus on adolescent worlds more than teaching methods appears to have provided fewer concrete pedagogical tools, if the two-worlds pitfall codes are an indication; it's hard to determine the impact of student-centeredness as a value based on the data reported in this chapter.

The data in general support the notion that each of the two worlds, in the absence of a tightly managed concentration of courses on campus, is more fragmented than the two-worlds pitfall metaphor suggests. TCs learn about teaching in a variety of settings that operate according to their own principals and are often are out of dialogue and in conflict with one another. Learning to teach is thus a function of a developmental conundrum in which TCs may be on multiple pathways simultaneously, each headed in different directions and following different rules. And this is before they ever teach classes on their own. The chapters in the following section detail how these processes become further complicated in student teaching, and ultimately in the TCs' own classes once they have graduated and been hired by school districts.

5

Cultures of Color and the Deep Structure of Schools

This chapter demonstrates how the deep structure of schools—defined in Chapter 4 as the institutionalized curriculum and assessment, dress codes, codes of conduct, approved speech genres and social languages, conventions for interaction, composition of administration and faculty, the physical arrangement of schools, the hidden curriculum, and other structural factors that organize the educational process according to a specific value system—can undermine its goals for educating diverse students equitably. I look at how a cultural mismatch between a TC of Native American ancestry and the site of her student teaching produced conflicts that are inevitable when uniformity and formalism govern how a school is organized, operated, and managed. I further compare and contrast her experience with that of a White TC from the same constructivist program, doing her student teaching in the same school, who experienced very similar frustrations. This analysis shows that TCs immersed in constructivist values in the same teacher education program may face similar obstacles when they work in highly regimented school settings. Yet these similarities mask cultural differences between the Native and White teachers in this research, which produce more deeply rooted epistemological differences that extend well beyond the two-worlds pitfall and into the cultural world in which learning to teach is embedded.

Calls for the diversification of the teaching force in both recruitment and retention are now routine in both scholarly and public essays. This effort to create polyracial faculties is motivated by a host of needs, including the following: to provide more culturally relevant teaching (Chiu, 2016), to give students of color own-race teachers to whom they can relate and look for exemplars (Egalite, Kisida, & Winter, 2015), to produce a more trustworthy teaching force for all students (Cherng & Helpin, 2016), to give people of color more opportunities in a profession that is overwhelmingly White (Madkins, 2011), to diversify faculties for broader perspectives and experiences (Wells, Fox, & Cordova-Cobo, 2016), and no doubt to serve many other ends. Teachers are roughly 85 percent White, while White students comprise under half of the school population (National Center for Educational Statistics, 2017a, 2017b), demonstrating a disproportionately White faculty teaching an increasingly racially diverse student population. Yet simply adding faculty of color to schools for diversity ignores the fact that race is not skin deep. Race, in contrast, embodies cultural values and practices that run deep to the bone. People of color do not always fit well within dominantly

White social institutions (Majors, 2015; Smagorinsky, 2017). Nor do they necessarily share what Lipsitz (2006) calls the *possessive investment in whiteness* that entrenches and perpetuates middle-class White cultural values and their attendant practices, and excludes others, often through devious and deceptive means (Wines, 2019). Adding diverse people without altering fundamental social and material structures that govern life in schools will change appearances and pockets of practice, but have little effect on the broader challenge of making schools more responsive to diversity in society and the teaching force, of teaching to sustain the home cultures of students from minoritized populations (Paris & Alim, 2017).

As I reviewed briefly in Chapter 4, the Atlantic Piedmont Secondary English Education program's research participants included a single African American TC. He left the program before completing his student teaching, however, and so the only data from him come from interviews and concept map contributions during his coursework and initial practicum experiences. As reported there, he was at odds with his faculty over matters of cultural-historical issues facing African American students. He rejected the faculty's generalized notion that getting to know students is the primary knowledge teachers need for effective instruction. He repudiated their broadly construed student-centered methods associated with whole language and progressive pedagogies, which he considered to be better suited to White students acculturated from birth to the social practices governing schools than to Black students who needed, he felt, more explicit direction in how to navigate school environments and academic expectations, per Delpit (1995).

This chapter focuses on two teachers, one White and one from a racial category that, remarkably, does not even register in a recent report (U.S. Department of Education, 2016) on the racial distribution of teachers in the United States: Native Americans. White teachers dominate the profession, with Black and Latin[1] Americans making up the bulk of the remaining 15 percent or so. Native Americans are included in the category of "Other," described in a footnote as comprising "the sum of Asian, Pacific Islander, American Indian or Alaska Native, and Two or more races" (p. 8). This group comprises about 0.5 percent of the teaching population: one out of every 200 teachers, distributed across four racial groups and people who identify as mixed-race. If recruiting more African Americans into the profession is regarded as a national priority by many, then it seems that including more Native people is also important, given the historical suppression in schools of Native culture and languages (Crawford, Cheadle, & Whitbeck, 2010) and the continued marginalization of indigenous ways in US schools and universities. Such practices, argue Native American scholars, conceivably could enrich educational practice and US society for all students, and specifically could make school a more welcoming and nurturing setting for Native students (Four Arrows, 2013; Jilot, 2016; Morgan, 2009).

---

[1] I use Latin to describe Mesoamerican- and South American-heritage people. Rather than using Latin@, which includes a gender binary, or Latinx, which suggests an orientation to one gendered group (the transsexual population), I simply avoid the suffix altogether and so remove gender from the identification of the people.

The two teachers were enrolled in the university program previously described in this volume: the South Plains Elementary Language Arts program, which featured a strong emphasis on Piagetian constructivism, both at the departmental and at the college-wide levels. Both TCs featured in this chapter felt very comfortable with constructivist values, which I again review here to set the stage for the issues in this chapter:

> The role of teachers is very important. Instead of giving a lecture the teachers in this theory function as facilitators whose role is to aid the student when it comes to their own understanding. This takes away focus from the teacher and lecture and puts it upon the student and their learning. The resources and lesson plans that must be initiated for this learning theory take a very different approach toward traditional learning as well. Instead of telling, the teacher must begin asking. Instead of answering questions that only align with their curriculum, the facilitator in this case must make it so that the student comes to the conclusions on their own instead of being told. Also, teachers are continually in conversation with the students, creating the learning experience that is open to new directions depending upon the needs of the student as the learning progresses. Teachers following Piaget's theory of constructivism must challenge the student by making them effective critical thinkers and not being merely a "teacher" but also a mentor, a consultant, and a coach. (teAchnology, n. d.)

This facilitative role, however, met a stern rebuke from the school in which the two focal TCs in this chapter did their student teaching. I next review the school setting of their student teaching and how it produced conceptual challenges to both TCs; and I then look more deeply at how the similarities between their struggles hid the more complex reasons for the mismatch between the school and the Native American TC. These more deeply rooted differences, I argue, may be extrapolated to help explain why the teaching profession may be more impervious to change than calls to diversity faculty through simple hiring practices can address. Instead, schools would require restructuring in order to accommodate diversity beyond slogans and appearances (cf. Gutiérrez, 2008).

School Site

"This is a very traditional school."

This statement was made by Rona, the MT for Penny, the Native American TC featured in this chapter, during an interview about her mentoring. By itself, it was unremarkable. However, the context of her remarks amplifies its importance in describing Warren G. Harding Elementary School. We were sitting in the corner of the school's capacious cafeteria. The only other person in the room was a cafeteria worker at the opposite end of the room, clanking dishes and well out of earshot. Yet when Rona described the school's reliance on basal readers and then characterized the school's traditional ethos, she dropped her voice to a whisper, not wanting to be overheard and viewed as possibly critical of this central value, even in a large and virtually unoccupied school space.

Harding Elementary's approach emphasized phonics and basal readers for reading instruction, and workbooks as the primary arena for student writing, teacher authority, and student discipline. Teachers emphasized "basic skills" as building blocks for literacy. The workbook activities required students to produce language in proper form in response to text-generated prompts and questions. Teachers occupied highly authoritative roles in the classroom, and students were tasked with mastering the information transmitted by teacher and text.

The school's "traditional" orientation was evident in interviews with Catherine, the MT of Sharon, the White TC featured in this chapter. Catherine was an experienced teacher in her town's school system and a figure of some authority within the school and district. She held the title of *head teacher* in her school, a position that made her in effect the school's assistant principal, a role that underscored the gravity of her values on the faculty. Catherine revealed her beliefs about the qualities she sought to develop in an early career teacher under her guidance, saying:

> I look for classroom management, rapport with the children, well prepared for her lessons, and it's not done at the last minute, the way she carries herself, I look for voice tone, I look for all those qualities. . . . If they're not well prepared, they don't have voice tone, they don't have rapport with the children, it doesn't matter how well they're prepared, the lesson's not going to be carried out. The same with classroom management. If she doesn't have control, the best lesson is lost.

Catherine's conception of good Language Arts teaching was consistent with Harding Elementary's reputation for promoting "traditional" instruction, as it was characterized by the university Elementary Education faculty and reinforced by Rona:

> I would place most of my emphasis on I would say structure. Because structure is going to cover any kind of expository writing, where you have, if the child can write a good sentence, then they've got some of the basic skills of capitalization and punctuation, complete thought, and I feel like by the time they leave third grade a good language arts basis for a child would be to be able to write that solid paragraph, and that's going to include spelling. . . . Language Arts starts with being able to write and know the basic skills, [i.e.,] to be able to have it correct, we've got to have all those other things in place. Spelling, and I also place a great emphasis on grammar, correct verb agreement.

She also endorsed "the old-fashioned diagramming of sentences." Her conception of good Language Arts teaching centered on providing a foundation in grammar: "I don't care if it's reading or writing, because all of your workbooks that go with your basals in reading, those aren't just comprehension skills, those are language skills." Teachers should model such formalist understandings, she felt, ideally learning grammar in the university teacher education program and then imparting that knowledge to students during classroom lessons.

Catherine's approach to mentoring Sharon in her third-grade classroom was in the *mimetic* tradition (Jackson, 1968). She assumed that Sharon would learn how to teach by imitating her methods as closely as possible. She said,

> A teacher learns to teach by first, observation. . . . Then I'd say the modeling by the teacher consultant [i.e., MT]. I can see myself in Sharon because she's taken on a lot of the classroom management skills I have. . . . When an intern first comes to you, they are trying to internalize I would say more classroom management skills because the university cannot teach that. That is by experience. Then as she tries her wings or his wings on different subjects with feedback from me, then things are corrected, things are added.

This perspective was consistent with Warren G. Harding Elementary School's reputation in the district for traditional instruction, both of students and in the training of beginning teachers. The notion of the two-worlds pitfall is predicated on disjunctures of the sort evident in the university's constructivist orientation and in the school's overtly authoritarian approach, as embodied in Catherine. Yet it masks the complexity that our interviews suggest is always present in intricate social settings, including in both schools and universities. Multiple worlds, rather than two, are always in play when beginning teachers navigate the transition from their formal learning in universities to the practical work that awaits them in schools. The next sections report on how two TCs of different cultural orientations experienced the tensions between their socialization as people and as prospective teachers, and the expectations for proper teacherly conduct in the setting of one school with a reputation for teaching according to "traditional" values associated with formalism and authoritarian instruction.

Sharon

I begin with Sharon, who in many ways typifies the general teacher education student population: White, middle-class, cisgender, heterosexual, and female. She was scheduled to graduate college four years after graduating high school, an accelerated pace for her university where seven years of attendance was the norm for graduation at the time of the research, and where the average undergraduate student was twenty-seven years old. This seven-year window was interpreted on the faculty as a consequence the difficulties that many students had in financing their education, and the frequent pauses they require to work and earn their next tuition investment. A second factor, in the view of faculty, was the decision to enter college late for women marrying young and beginning families rather than attending college out of high school. Sharon, in contrast, was planning her marriage for the summer after graduating, a common experience for students in her program. Like any individual, she experienced intersections with other demographic categories that complicate any effort at typicality. Yet she appeared to be a typical enough prospective elementary school TC to enable some possibilities for representativeness of the beginning elementary teacher population.

Background

Prior to college, Sharon had lived her whole life in the same state. She described her schooling as consisting of mostly "traditional" teachers. Following high school, Sharon attended one year of college as a business major in a neighboring state, then transferred back to her home state's namesake university, where she became an Elementary Education major. She was a highly regarded prospect by her professors, and classroom observations and interviews showed her to be conscientious, intelligent, and committed to teaching.

She also shared the program's orientation to constructivist principles. In spite of her socialization in what she described as traditional schools, Sharon said in an interview that her projected teacher identity cast her as a teacher who

> is supportive and cares about what the kids know. And more than anything that I'm driven more by the kids wanting to learn [than] what my classroom should look like or what I feel like my teaching role should be. . . . That's what I feel like a good teacher should be, always be open-minded [and] willing to change and willing to adapt to different kids' levels and different environments.

As reported in Chapter 4, she said during her cohort's concept map composition that the constructivist teacher should help "lead [students] to discover things for themselves, and in their own way, but also making sure they don't discover something in the wrong way." Sharon's acknowledgment that teachers should make sure "they don't discover something in the wrong way" suggests a conflict within progressive methods in general: students should be engaged in inquiry and discovery in order to construct their worlds, but those discoveries ultimately may need to conform to "right" ways of doing things. Even when on campus, she found a discrepancy within this cherished constructivist principle, one amplified in her student teaching where there were clear right and wrong ways to do things, particularly with respect to behavior and language use.

Her account of constructivism did not refer to age-based developmental stages, or the emphasis on assimilation and accommodation, staples of the conception she had learned on campus. I interpret her (and, based on other cases, her cohort's) selective use of constructivism as a theoretical compromise suggesting a complex or pseudoconcept. If unfettered individualism of the sort available through Piaget's study of his own children is cultivated through personal discovery that is mediated by processes of assimilation and accommodation in service of finding equilibrium, then the notion of doing things the right way is irrelevant. Yet the teachers needed to teach a fixed curriculum, and also taught diverse students who may not have conformed to Piaget's stages and processes. Eliding aspects of his theory thus appeared part of Sharon's process of adapting theory to practical demands, albeit in highly thwarted ways under Catherine's mentorship.

Conflicting Conceptions of Teaching

> "What I am concerned about is I think that throughout this semester, being with my [mentor] teacher as opposed to being at [the university], I just hope that I don't totally switch to her side."

Sharon made this remark one month into her student teaching over the lack of opportunity she had to teach according to the principles she'd learned in her pre-service program. This fear prompted her concern that she would eventually become the traditional teacher she had learned to critique at the university. If assimilation and accommodation are central aspects of Piagetian growth, and if they have salience for learning to teach at the cusp of adulthood, she had few opportunities for either during student teaching, and felt throughout that she was in a state of disequilibrium.

Catherine's values were well illustrated in the lessons observed during Sharon's student teaching, which had a common pattern in our observations. Sharon confirmed that these routines characterized the way in which Catherine required her to teach. In the typical Language Arts lesson, a story would be accompanied by a series of worksheets in the supplementary workbook, classified by curriculum strand or facet of reading. One worksheet on vocabulary required students to classify words; one on using new words had students match definitions with words and put words in blanks in a pre-written paragraph; and one on comprehension had students complete the summary of a selection by filling in facts from the story.

Each worksheet page also had a generative task at the bottom of the page. A typical such task might say, "On separate paper, write a paragraph about your favorite kind of music. Use three words from the box." Throughout the observations, whenever the students would come to the generative question at the bottom of the page, Sharon would say, "No bottoms"; that is, students were instructed *not* to do these open-ended tasks. Students would mark them out with large X's and move on to the next worksheet and its objectivist questions. Sharon verified that Catherine followed this procedure whenever the class used the workbooks, and that she was expected to mimic Catherine's lead in jettisoning worksheet items that encouraged personal or creative responses.

Sharon referred to her frustrations during the second concept map activity, conducted at the end of student teaching, when the cohort turned to the traditional/constructivist continuum:

> What traditional versus constructive is? She was head teacher. She is boss. [group laughter and remarks] Well, I'm serious. There is no way I would dare tell her she is doing something wrong. You've got to be kidding! . . . My teacher had taught for like 19 years in the same room, so I didn't dare even say that her bulletin boards looked crooked or anything. . . . Even if I had had the freedom to try out a lot of things, my 3rd grade, these kids didn't respond well to constructive learning. They went crazy. Because then if you had like open discussion or if you were having something that was not their norm or they raised their hand to respond, they just went berserk. . . . They couldn't handle not having their structure they were so used to.

Students' socialization to authoritarian teaching, then, reinforced the distance between university theory and classroom practice in this setting. Further, Catherine's mimetic approach to mentoring left little room for Sharon to practice constructivism, either as a teacher with her third-graders or as a learner about the practice of teaching. Sharon expressed this frustration during our interviews following her teaching. Toward the end of her student teaching, we talked about her experiences, where she said:

> I'm just not practicing anything that I learned in college. I mean, anything. . . . It's you do, ok, well you're finished reading this story, you go to workbook. And I feel like that's almost making me, making me not think. . . . I guess I'm jealous of the people that got [placed] at the schools with the teachers that are real original and real creative and want them to think about different things and ask them questions about, well why did you teach it this way? . . . And I feel [cheated]. . . . I think it's easy for people who just say that it would be easy to use whole language, but I think you have to practice with that. . . . She tests them out of the textbook, and their reading grade is worksheets. I mean that's their reading grade, across the board. Worksheets. Their language arts grade is worksheets and letters. . . . So I guess that's what I'm saying. That it would be easy for me my first year teaching to go over to the other side just because I'm afraid, just because I'm not confident enough in my abilities, you know, 'cause [inaudible] and I don't have, especially in a school that [is traditional]. I mean it's so much easier to say, I give up, I'm doing it just like you, and we're all going to be happy campers, and no parent will complain.

Sharon had little choice but to yield to Catherine's vision of effective teaching in order to preserve a positive relationship and receive a supportive evaluation. Catherine's imposing presence required her to abandon her prospects for enacting a constructivist pedagogy during student teaching. She summarized her dilemma by saying:

> I don't know if I am going to be able to [be a constructivist teacher] within this classroom. I don't know how much leeway she is going to give me. And I know not to step on her toes. She will definitely bop me back in line. That is pretty evident. She doesn't—I mean, she thinks that I should be there to learn from her and not to in any way take over her classroom. Which is fine.

This last statement suggests that Sharon's frustrations were significant, but not enough to discourage her from persisting with a teaching career. Her feelings of vexation followed from her preference for constructivist teaching, forged during her apprenticeship of observation and cloaked in conceptual vocabulary in her teacher education coursework. Yet as a product of what she acknowledged to be traditional classrooms herself, she was not fully out of sorts, not so deeply out of tune with the eminently traditional Harding Elementary that she could not grit her teeth, survive, and move on in hopes of better classroom days ahead. Penny, described next, had a similar feeling of disjuncture, even with far greater leeway under a less authoritarian mentor. Yet she experienced the dissonance differently, based on what I would call cultural dispositions that worked in opposition to the school's values.

Penny

Penny was in her late thirties at the time of her student teaching and was a single mother of daughters aged twenty-three years and eight years. She was about ten years older than Rona, her MT, a dynamic that undoubtedly gave her greater leverage than Sharon had with Catherine. Rona and Penny liked, admired, and spoke highly of one another, mitigating any serious problems that might have developed in the differences I enumerate next.

Background

Toward the end of her semester of student teaching, a fall placement, Penny asked me if I had any suggestions for how to decorate her room for the late fall season. I recommended what seemed normal to me, as a White US citizen, for that time of year: a Thanksgiving theme. "No," she said. "I don't do Thanksgiving." In response to my puzzled look, she clarified: "I'm an Indian." She did not specify a tribal orientation, rather identifying generally with Native American heritage. This acculturation, as I will argue, contributed to how she experienced Warren G. Harding Elementary School.

Like Sharon, Penny embraced constructivism, although not quite the version favored by her professors. During the same concept map activity that Sharon participated in to close the semester of student teaching, Penny insisted on including Vygotsky as well (see Chapter 4), without saying where she had learned of his sociocultural theory of human development. She was the only TC in her cohort who mentioned a developmental theorist other than Piaget. Penny's invocation of Vygotsky during the concept map activity indicates that she was less wedded to Piaget's age-triggered outline of children's conceptual development, and appeared dismissive of its explanatory potential for all children. Rather, she attended to how people interact with one another, and how those interactions shape the process and trajectory of human development. Although she never explicitly tied this more flexible perspective to her Native American heritage, it conceivably could have followed from her broader misalignment with the school, and with a key driver of the academic day, the pace and schedule of instruction.

Penny's Native orientation became a factor in her conception of time. She felt constrained by the school's ways and means, particularly in the manner that the school structure discouraged teaching that allowed for students to learn at a comfortable pace:

> Penny: The only thing that I don't like generally across the board, about how the lessons go or don't go, is I feel this really big time crunch thing coming around. I mean, it's like, "Okay, you've got 20 minutes to do this lesson," and I know it should take an hour or an hour and a half, so I don't know how to get all that worked in. Because my teaching style definitely doesn't fit that school, which is very structured and traditional, and I'm not. So it's like kind of I'm trying to work in a little bit of who I am—the structure so that I don't totally mess the class up, because I don't think it would be fair for me to go in and do completely what I think, because . . .

Q: What do you think the source of that time conflict is, is that a personal thing, or is there something else?

Penny: Well, yeah, because of who I am, I think well—I don't know if it's, I can't tell you the source, but I can tell you that I don't necessarily function like everyone else does, at 8:00 you do this at 10:00 you do this, at 9:00 you do this. Time is more of a—it's not, time is not just determined by what a clock says it is. I can look at my house and know that because every clock has a different time. I mean, because if it's close it's great, you know, it's not one of those things I worry so much about—the process of going through this time span is a lot more important than thinking, "I've got to get finished, I've got to start here and finish here and my product has to be done at 2:15 in the morning." That's not who I am. I know that culturally maybe there is something to be said to how I respond to time or how I respond, or wait time or those kind of things, which I think might be good in my class because I'm not so quick to get answers from the kids, that it's like I understand that you need to think about it. I know a lot of my professors want answers, instantaneously, now! With me it's like, no, I can't tell you now, let me think about it, process it, work with it that way. Time—there's like two different time spheres. I've got my time, and then there's this, well, what my brother calls it is "the White man's time." . . . He's like "Okay, you're coming over 7:00 White man's time or at 7:00 your time?" I was like "Well, it's Saturday, it may be 7:00 my time." . . . The time thing is that, you know, because the school is real structured and they have all these requirements for grades, I would have to fit in to what they're doing. You have to have two grades here, two grades here, two grades here, two grades here, two grades here, two grades here, so I'm looking at eleven grades. Well, if I taught the way I wanted to teach, I couldn't get the grades they expect to get. Okay, my grades would come from—well, assessment is a whole other ballgame, that goes against most what everybody else thinks too, so, I think I'm gonna get me a kitchen timer, I'm gonna time it, okay we've got ten minutes to do math, okay, we've got 15 minutes to write. Because I feel stressed and pressured to produce grades, which in the first grade, I mean, you know, all these kids are going to have wonderful grades for the next two weeks because, hey, I saw improvement. I mean, smiley face, that works, that's 100 in my book, so that's been something I had to think about.

In many ways Penny sounds like any other student from her cohort in describing the two-worlds pitfall. Yet her difficulties are compounded by a more fundamental difference in how to view time. Krueger (1989) discusses how Native American notions of time do not fit easily with Western scheduling:

> In the relief and pleasure of really being taken seriously as a human being, it is also easy to forget that at the very moment one is being helped to feel at ease, the healer may simultaneously be putting off someone else for whom she will then be "late." That kind of time consciousness includes time to be compassionate and human. Taking time and tuning in. . . .

> There are benefits to the highly structured time frame: predictability (which makes people feel safe, too); an order and harmony of its own; it can fit and function well in an eight-to-five world. But it does not create "knowing" and comfort. The more fluid time consciousness has its own benefits: making real human contact, creating ease, creating comfort through knowing an "other," and faith. This kind of time does not fit as readily into an eight-to-five structured world. (pp. 227–28)

This conception echoes Delpit's (1995) contention that African Americans tend to "believe teaching begins instead with the establishment of relationships between themselves and their students" (p. 139), and thus spend time cultivating rapport in ways that might violate the parameters of a tight schedule. Krueger's (1989) comments are remarkably applicable to the conceptions of time that I observed in the classroom of Rona and Penny. Penny's approach was based on a "fluid time consciousness" that provided opportunities for extended human contact and created an environment of comfort and ease. Lessons stretched out beyond their scheduled bounds and at times occupied the time allotted for another subject area. Librarians were occasionally kept waiting while Penny stretched a lesson so that students could complete it.

Her approach was hardly unique to Native Americans. Teachers who embrace process-oriented approaches to teaching and learning are likely to hold a fluid time consciousness, regardless of race or cultural background. Belgarde (1992) has shown as well that Native American identity exists along a continuum from efforts to fully assimilate with White middle-class culture to efforts to maintain a strong cultural and tribal identity, a range no doubt also applicable to most nondominant group members. Indeed, the faculty who taught Penny and Sharon included two women who claimed a Native American heritage, one of whom required that the TCs produce constructivist lesson plans, and then assessed the students at the end of the semester with an exam that involved five pages of fill-in-the-blank items. My reference to Krueger's (1989) account of time should not suggest stereotypical attitudes about Native American approaches to time, but should rather help explain Penny's own cultural account of her difficulties with Harding's structure, and I would argue, with the deep structure of schools, especially as they increasingly adopt business-model accountability systems for their operations that emphasize efficient, clock-driven time management and specific outcomes.

Rona

Rona, Penny's MT, was highly regarded as a teacher and mentor. Among her strengths was the sense of order and harmony that her efficiency brought to her teaching, a value that fit well within Harding, yet was at odds with Penny's fluid time conception. Her lessons moved along briskly in a classroom set up so that there were clear traffic lanes that allowed students to move from activity to activity easily and with little difficulty. Her students appeared to have great respect and admiration for her as a teacher and a person, and the university faculty valued her as an MT. Even with this good fit with Harding's emphasis on order, Rona was somewhat of a maverick within the school. She was working on a master's degree, and for her thesis was developing a reading program based on children's literature rather than basal readers, a departure from the "no bottoms" approach favored by Catherine in her reliance on commercial workbook assignments.

During one interview I mentioned that I had noticed the efficient quality of her teaching during lessons I had observed. I asked her to talk about it:

> Q: One thing I've noticed in the times when I've seen you teach is that you are very aware of your schedule and the time. You know, the lessons are very, I would say, crisp. You know, your management of the time. Could you talk a little bit about why that's a priority for you? Is that something within you or is that something . . .
>
> Rona: I think so. I'm always—I'm punctual. I mean, even outside of the school, I'm at places I need to be on time. And I guess that is—I've never really thought about it before, but that's something that must be important to me. And so I know that I need to end math by two o'clock so that we'll have five minutes to get ready to go to the library or to go to P.E. or to go to reading buddies. So, yeah. I am pretty crisp, probably.
>
> Q: Is that—and I've noticed Penny is less crisp, and is that something that you've talked to her about or does it matter?
>
> Rona: Yeah, because like when we do go to 4th grade reading buddies, they are sitting there waiting for us at 1:50. But I think the more as you teach, you get into that groove more because this is still all so new to a student teacher and you've probably never had to check. And I remember running over and being late when you first start teaching. That takes some time to get into the—you know, I've been here seven years, so I know the routine. And she hasn't. She's only been here a couple of months.
>
> Q: Let me ask this: I got a sense from what you said a moment ago, you kind of felt a sense of responsibility to other people in the building to be where you are expected so that they are not—their time isn't wasted. Is that something you would do—how can I ask this? Is that kind of the type of obligation you get when you have to work with people and see them the next day and the next year? Do you know what I mean?
>
> Rona: Probably. Yeah. Probably. And I told the students, you know, sometimes in school we have to stop. We may not be finished. That's okay. We can finish up tomorrow. I mean I always let them know there will be a time that we can finish if it's something that we haven't finished like a writing lesson or math lesson or social studies picture. Sometimes in school we have to stop because we have to go to 4th grade. They are waiting for us. And I think if you are up front with them and tell them—now that I think about it, that lets them know that time is—that's something I value. And I hadn't really thought about that before.

My review of Rona is not meant to suggest she shared Catherine's authoritarian stance and mentoring style. Rather, it is to demonstrate her understanding of the pacing and scheduling of the school day and of the civic duty of teachers to respect other people's schedules in relation to their own, and how that aspect of Rona's personality and values made her a good fit with the school in many ways, if not always with Penny. I next show how that conflict manifested itself during Penny's student teaching.

Illustrations of Conflict in Practice

Penny, as noted in the interview with Rona and corroborated by Penny, was not so "crisp" in her time management, a tendency illustrated next from the observational data and follow-up interview. Her lessons tended to overrun the time parameters established in Rona's planning book. Penny attributed these differences to her compatibility with the constructivist principles of her university program:

> Penny: I see this as being real constructivist in nature because the kids are all doing it, you know, they're not just copying something, they're not just memorizing something, they're creating it on their own. And I guess it's those kind of things that are my kind of philosophy, that if they construct it, they'll more likely remember it or use it or those kind of things.
> Q: Do you see a constructivist influence on the other language arts instruction you'll be doing over the next week?
> Penny: I hope so. I try to put it in wherever I can. I mean, I guess that's why I'm having such a hard time with the penmanship thing and the U paper [a lesson emphasizing the letter *U*]. Because I don't see it, I just see it as being traditional and not—I guess everything has its value, but for me I just feel uncomfortable with it. I'm not a traditional teacher.
> Q: Are there any other things that you can think of that might have influenced your planning for the teaching you'll do next week?
> Penny: Well, I think, you know, just about everything I learned at the university has led up to this, of the constructivist theory. I mean, I feel comfortable with that, I think the research supports how children learn, understanding the learning styles of the children . . . . I think that all of that goes into what I feel comfortable with, and what I don't feel comfortable with. So I think it has been an influence on who I am as a teacher.

Penny felt uncomfortable with much about the structure of Harding, feeling that it provided little opportunity for constructivist teaching. Her views about conforming to rules directly contradict Catherine's value on the primacy of correctness. Even working with Rona, who was among the most constructivist teachers in the school, Penny revealed that she felt handcuffed when given the opportunity to teach.

The following example occurred during a regular activity in Rona's class, the reading of a children's literature book to the class. In this routine Rona or Penny would gather the students before her on the floor at the front of the room and read to them a book from Rona's children's literature collection. On the day I observed Rona reading, the story was a book in the series about Arthur, an aardvark who confronts all manner of dilemmas that he and his friends must resolve: housebreaking a new dog, putting on a school play, and so on. Rona's approach was to read a page or so of the story and then ask a set of questions: How does Arthur feel? What does "triple" mean? If you've read a lot of other Arthur books, how would you describe Arthur's sister D.W.? After an answer or two, Rona would move along and read the next page, even if several children were still waving their hands to be called on. The lesson ended at precisely the minute it was scheduled to end. The pace for reading and discussing the story was thus determined by the schedule, and the lesson fit neatly within the demands of offering the whole of the first-grade curriculum.

Penny's reading followed a different beat; to paraphrase Henry David Thoreau, "If a woman does not keep pace with her companions, perhaps it is because she hears a different drummer. Let her step to the music which she hears, however measured or far away." The book Penny read during my observation was about Johnny Appleseed and his travails as a pioneer. My observational notes of the story time reading include the following:

> Penny stops, asks why a character wanted to have a tree-chopping contest. Lots of hands up, lots of answers. After hearing each answer she says, Those are all good ideas, let's read ahead and find out. Occasional questions from Penny—So what did he do? So why would the pioneers want to buy the trees? So they'll have shade, to have trees to pick apples, say the kids. What do you think they mean when they say they "exaggerate" a little bit? Penny tried to get them to see the traits of a tall tale: What do you think Johnny's doing here [showing a picture from the book]? Do you think that really happened? Meanwhile, eye on the clock, Rona got up at 1:12 and began preparing for the next lesson scheduled for 1:15, putting a paper cup at each student's desk. Penny continued with the reading and questioning. Story finished. Question: So thinking back on the story, what were some of the changes Johnnie and his family went through? His mom got divorced, said one girl. No, not quite. His father died, said another. He almost got bitten by a tiger, said another. Do you think that was real? asked Penny. No, said kids. He planted apple trees.

No matter how many children raised their hands in response to a question, Penny would call on every one, at times as many as ten of the eighteen students for a single question, no matter what the responses were or how long the process took. At a time when the reading was scheduled to end, Penny opened up a new line of questioning designed to get students to think about the story as a whole, again calling on every student whose hand was raised. The lesson ran over the scheduled time, even with Rona observing the class and helping to set up the next scheduled lesson as time expired. Penny's next lesson had to be cut short because she had allowed the reading to exceed its allotted time.

When asked how she thought the lesson had gone, Penny said that in spite of the fact that the lesson had run over,

> It was too rushed. There wasn't enough time and continuity from one aspect of the lesson to another aspect. I don't think you can just do something like tall tales at

15 minutes here and 15 minutes there over a week at a time and come out with a true understanding or grasp of what the concept was. . . . It is just real hard for me to kind of whip through these topics.

This theme recurred in our discussions: the brisk pacing resulted in lessons that lacked continuity. In Penny's view, the highly structured curriculum at Harding discouraged time for exploration, participation from multiple students and extended time for each, and opportunities for seizing teachable moments. In discussing the way in which spelling lessons were prescribed by a central curriculum, she said,

Yeah, this is what I've been finding out, that the spelling words are pre-ordained by the high priestess of spelling. So I mean, there's like, I just learned about the spelling words, it doesn't matter if it's related to anything you're doing. It's just planned out. A lot of things are just planned out, like you do short O's this week, that's what you do.

She preferred instead to teach more opportunistically and spontaneously in response to needs and interests that came up through more extended lessons.

Assuming that culture is a function of engaging in social practices through the use of cultural tools (Cole, 1996), Penny's troubles with Harding's curriculum and the time demands of the schedule followed from matters of acculturation. Penny offered the insight that the students, even in first grade, had been conditioned to regard school as a place where their thinking and learning processes were of secondary importance to the efficient functioning of the school system, just as, from Sharon's perspective, the students struggled with open-ended opportunities due to their socialization to following instructions:

Q: From what you just told me, what's difficult for the children is not what's cognitively challenging in the material or the assignments, but almost a social fit with the pacing or—
Penny: No, no, see, they're really good at that. It's unpacing them and unstructuring them is what's hard.
Q: Because of the structure that Rona has established earlier in the year?
Penny: Because this is first grade, they haven't been socialized. Most of them have been kindergarten, transition at Harding. So this is in actuality, for students this is their third year there, so I mean, you've got all this structure going on for three years, which is, gee, half their lives, so to then say what's unstructured, they're kinda like "what?" . . . Even in the first-grade level there was just so much structure in the poor kids' lives that they had been in kindergarten and transition and now in first grade. I mean that's two or three years they're getting this really traditional structure stuff, and so when I would come in and try to do creative kinds of things, they are like, "I don't know what you're trying to get at." I'm like, "Well use your imagination and like [inaudible]." That was real stressful.

Penny's reference to "transition" was to the school district's policy of allowing students to delay entry into first grade by attending a year of school between kindergarten and first grade to give them an extra year of maturity before their formal education began. The fact that many first-grade students had already been socialized for half of their lives into the traditional structure of Harding Elementary made it difficult for her to operate with a different pace, one that was less cost-effective but allowed for more exploration of ideas and personal construction of knowledge. Sharon's experiences under Catherine's mentorship suggest that the subordination of learning processes to lesson scheduling was well-established in students' acculturation to school, thus, making it increasingly difficult for a teacher like Penny to integrate curriculum and emphasize the process of learning.

From a Vygotskian (1978, 1987) perspective, the students' frameworks for thinking had been appropriated through their social practices of schooling. Even as early as first grade, the students believed that there was a right way of doing school, one available through their participation in the cultural routines emphasized at Harding Elementary. Not only did their acculturation to these schooling practices make it difficult for Sharon and Penny to enact constructivist teaching methods under the guidance of their MTs, it made it difficult for students to recognize constructivist teaching as worthwhile and respond appropriately to its more open-ended approach.

Discussion

This chapter has focused on a particular sort of disjuncture, one superficially explainable via the two-worlds pitfall metaphor, but one I argue is compellingly accounted for by a mismatch between Penny's Native American conception of time and the efficiency model practiced at Harding Elementary. The two worlds of university and school were in conflict for sure. However, Penny felt that Piagetian stage theory was too rigid and individualistic to account for human diversity, and she found this value at work both on campus and in the school. She valued the relational interactions more consistent with Vygotsky's sociocultural developmental theory as having greater salience to her stance as a cultural person and work as a teacher. This critique fit with her cultural outsider status as a Native American, first in higher education, second in the teaching force, and ultimately in Harding Elementary.

The university, then, was not the only world at odds with the school; and the school and university were aligned in structural ways. Penny's cultural world was a factor in her ill fit with Harding's rigid structure and schedule. Single cases make generalizations difficult, but perhaps it is not surprising that the next year Sharon married her college sweetheart and began teaching in a school more congenial to her values. Her coda, "which is fine," then, spoken in relation to her account of Catherine's dominant presence in her student teaching experience, might have signaled that she could endure the dissonance because she saw a future in teaching in spite of the oppressive mentorship she had. Penny, in contrast, had generous and supportive mentorship, yet did not teach the following year. She took master's degree courses, and then fell out to touch. I don't know if she ever sought or took a full-time teaching position; online searches never associated her name at the time of the research with a school faculty listing.

Whether she did teach or not, her case does help reveal a deep cultural mismatch for some prospective teachers of color who find themselves misaligned with schools, making their recruitment and retention precarious prospects for school administrators hoping to diversify their faculty without changing the school organization and processes. People have called for the recruitment of more Native teachers (e.g., Edwards, 2017). I would argue that simply issuing calls or changing the color of the teaching force does not promote sufficient diversity when schools themselves stand immutable and only want teachers of color who fit existing structures and routines.

Penny's experiences illustrate what McKinney (2017), in her study of postcolonial schooling in South Africa, calls the *Anglo-normativity* of educational institutions in nations colonized by Europeans. The Anglo-normative deep structure of schools is evident in how Penny, as a Native American, felt alienated by this value system and at odds with its linear time conception and clock-driven scheduling. It is likely, I would argue, that the Anglo-normativity of US schools helps maintain education's persistently White teaching force and creates conditions that make diversifying it largely possible only for those people of color whose socialization allows them to fit within its structures without altering them. Their congeniality helps to perpetuate educational structures and practices that favor those whose life experiences have normalized middle-class White ways of being as seemingly natural, and it helps administrators claim a degree of diversity without altering the process of schooling.

I clearly do not have the breadth of research participants to make a broad claim to this effect, but the value of case studies is getting beyond the surface of things and into their gritty details, if only with small samples that perhaps are "telling" (Mitchell, 1984) (and perhaps not, according to Andrews, 2017): those cases "in which the particular circumstances surrounding the case serve to make previously obscure theoretical relationships suddenly apparent" (Mitchell, p. 239). The particular circumstances of this case suggest that, for at least some teachers from historically excluded demographics, schools continue to marginalize them when they only absorb them without changing how they operate, and without accommodating a wide range of teaching and learning styles and processes. Teacher educators need to recognize this problem, although the problem of myopia is exacerbated when the teacher education population itself is largely White, at least from my eyeballing of the people in my profession; it's hard to get reliable demographic data on who teaches the teachers. But if general statistics on who gets doctorates suggest anything, US university faculties in general are largely White (National Center for Educational Statistics, 2017b), and presumably those taking positions in teacher education are too.

In relation to the potential of the Common Core State Standards (CCSS) to produce positive change in schools, Applebee (2013) saw the CCSS as a layer atop many well-established layers of the deep structure of schools. He used the metaphor of the *palimpsest*, a manuscript page from which the text has been removed so that the page may be used again, while inevitably bearing traces of the original writing. To Applebee, "the CCSS documents are a palimpsest, with deeply embedded traces of our ongoing professional and political debates about the nature of effective curriculum and instruction in the English language arts" (p. 25). The deep structures of schooling are difficult to dislodge, producing a situation where multiple conflicting paradigms and practices simultaneously inform and comprise curricula, instruction, assessment, and other key aspects of the machinery of schooling.

This problem is germane to my consideration of building a diverse workforce without changing the foundation on which it operates. To Applebee (2013), the entrenched permanence of each layer in the composition of schools makes them inherently contradictory, and unfortunately so, in that they get in one another's way. Taylor (1985) considers this presence of competing perspectives within a single outlook a "rotten compromise," entangling competing belief systems (p. 247). I would argue that it's simply an inevitable fact of living within long-standing institutions whose historical ideological and practical layering has produced contradictory environments.

A different layering metaphor that also contributes to this analysis is that of *laminations*, which,

> argued Holland and Leander (2004), help to explain how identities appear stable and yet are also multiple and, at times, conflicted. Laminations are constructed through the layering of identity positions one over the other; just as layers of varnish might stick or congeal, so do laminated identities. Moreover, just as one might see evidence of the layers of varnish on a piece of wood, so we might also see the layers of identity on a person. To play out the metaphor even further, those layers can be stripped away, reapplied, nicked, scratched, or even gouged. Thus, identity as layers of positions (i.e., as laminations) carries with it the histories (hence, the overlap with the concept of histories in person, or even possibly, of habitus) of past experiences. (Moje, Luke, & Street, 2009, p. 430)

I find the laminations metaphor a bit sticky. I've always thought that another layering metaphor, *lasagna gardening*, would make a better analogy for human identities, because its more organic, rather than inert, composition is closer to the conduct of vibrant human lives. The lasagna gardener places layers of paper, kitchen scraps, compost, and other decaying matter in the ground, with the assumption that worms and other natural processes will eventually work them together into a rich, fecund synthesis. Biologically, the individual elements will always be part of the soil composition, while also decomposing into the whole of the mix. The soil, no matter how thorough the blend, will always include measurable traces of the original components. Ideally, soil does not include elements that work against each other, as might happen in palimpsests or laminations; yet the earth and above-ground environment always include surprises, and chemical dumping may infiltrate a soil's mix. The soil does not choose its own composition.

I've both gardened and laminated furniture, and feel that lasagna gardening is more appropriate to human life than layering manufactured products in impenetrable strata onto inanimate surfaces. Yet lamination undoubtedly has more rhetorical snap than lasagna gardening, as well as more public familiarity than my niche analogy.

Whether one produces palimpsests, laminates, or lasagna gardens, the various layering metaphors help illuminate issues with discordant identities in the context of learning to teach, and represent the problem of diversifying a faculty at the surface without altering the deep structure of the institution. The palimpsest of the school curriculum and other structural factors rests on a foundation whose traces of prior coatings remain intact and in play. The multilayered laminations or compost materials of teachers' identities also include traces of old layers that may produce conflicts with newer strata. In these metaphors, the layers are more dynamic than they are in Applebee's (2013) notion of the curricular palimpsest. In schools, the new layers must always rest on the foundation of the old and thus produce contradictions that are difficult to displace. Identity work, including pedagogical concept development, also involves layering: from attendance in "traditional" schools to racialized identities to attendance in conceptually organized teacher education programs to practice in schools, and beyond. These identities do layer upon one another, but in more dynamic ways, such that they intermingle, without necessarily reaching the state of integrated fertility available in soil. In other words, fluid human identities rest upon more static school structures in ways that produce cacophonous experiences for teachers trying to work toward conceptual coherence in their work, especially when teachers' socialization provides an ill fit with the institutional structures they attempt to enter.

As long as the workforce in both schools and universities remains invested in Whiteness (Berchini & Tanner, 2019; Lipsitz, 2006) as a structural value, that dynamic is unlikely to change. Teacher educators have little chance of changing how schools function. What they can do is recognize the complexities of their own environments and those of schools as a way to help prepare TCs for the inevitable contradictions they find in their thinking, and not expect these incongruities to be resolved, given the computational impossibility of thinking coherently about complex social problems. They can further examine their own practices to see if their own socialization is best suited for people like themselves and is an ill fit for those of different acculturation. Typically, in my experience, problems and contradictions are papered over by flowery rhetoric, such as claiming that university-school transitions can be "seamless" or that diversity is to be "celebrated" rather than grappled with. I think that we are better served by more sober, reality-based attention to how hard this work is, and how to do it in ways responsive to the challenges it presents, an endeavor that requires reflection on how the deep structure of schools is more congenial to some than to others. This reflection in turn would require a willingness to examine the deep structure of schools and the commitment to making change well below the surface of appearances.

6

Fuzzy Concepts in Teacher Education and Their Consequences in the Classroom

This chapter focuses on two beginning teachers from Southern Plains University, Jimmy from the Secondary English Education program and Tracy from the Elementary Language Arts Education program. Both exhibited unconscious contradictions in their teaching during student teaching and in their first jobs. Rather than considering them to be two confused young people, I locate their inconsistencies in teaching Secondary English and Elementary Language Arts in their immersions in competing pedagogical traditions, each of which is grounded in broader philosophical debates. The simultaneous influence of contradictory paradigms on their teaching was exacerbated by either theoretical and pedagogical neglect in their teacher education programs (Jimmy) or inconsistent presentations of a guiding pedagogical theory in university coursework (Tracy). Their MTs themselves taught within contradictory epistemologies, and in their guidance of TCs, they modeled conceptually inconsistent teaching, and guided their mentees toward practices that vacillated among traditions. Once in their first jobs, Jimmy and Tracy were subject to the priorities of the schools in which contradictions were available in school and departmental practices, normalizing them in their practice and allowing for their incorporation into their instruction.

This analysis does not see the university programs and schools as distinctive and oppositional sites for learning, as the two worlds of the two-worlds pitfall. Rather, each was contradictory in ways that were complicit in the conceptual disunity, that is, the complexes or pseudoconcepts, evident in the two teachers' instruction. Chapter 4's analysis of the three teacher education programs in this research suggests that the Southern Plains Elementary Education program provided a governing constructivist orientation reinforced across methods courses; the group concept map suggests that its TCs were able to chart its conceptual flow and relationships well, if not entirely representing Piaget's developmental theory, and if not entirely embraced by all program TCs (see Chapter 5).

The same university's Secondary English Education program, in contrast, included a haphazard collection of courses with no specific theoretical approach and little opportunity for reinforcement, even if there had been one, given the paucity of courses taught by the program faculty. Yet as this chapter details, neither program produced in the TCs a coherent set of theoretical principles accompanied by articulated practices to produce conceptually unified teaching in schools. Providing a fuzzy conceptual understanding in teacher education appears then to have consequences for how teachers ultimately navigate school cultures.

We begin with Jimmy from the Secondary English Education program, then move to Tracy from the Elementary Education program. Because the issue of constructivism has been thoroughly accounted for in Chapter 5, in this chapter, I rely on that review to set the stage for Tracy's experiences. I provide greater description of Jimmy's context, including attention to the historical contexts in which he taught literature, a central demand of teaching secondary school English.

Jimmy

Jimmy was not a "typical" English Education TC. He was a male, he got credentialed at the graduate level, and he was in his mid-to late twenties. He was a native of his college town, as a youth having attended the school in which he ultimately did his student teaching. He began college at the Air Force Academy but transferred to and graduated from his state's namesake university. As an undergraduate, he had planned to go to law school, but during his senior year, decided to pursue a master's in English based on his positive experience in a class in the Department of English. "That made me think about wanting to teach," he said. "I just felt you can have more of an impact on peoples' lives in high school." He then earned a teaching certificate as part of his master's degree.

Jimmy's experiences in the discipline of English were heavily weighted toward the humanities and the values of literary criticism, given his deep immersion in the Department of English and his more fleeting involvement with COE coursework, especially in his teaching field. He therefore lacked extensive involvement in a pedagogical long-term conversation with other students and faculty in his area of concentration. I adapt this notion from Applebee (1996), who advocated for classrooms in schools to engage in deliberately undertaken "curricular conversations" that extend across a semester's or year's study, serving as an overarching medium for collaborative inquiry into a discipline's texts and themes. Such conversations allow TCs to participate in an exploration and development of a conceptual vocabulary for understanding, critiquing, and practicing instructional approaches. Structurally fragmented programs such as the one that Jimmy experienced do not provide this conceptually strong preparation for teaching. In his case, that fragmentation produced a theoretically eclectic approach to teaching literature that at times left him at odds with himself, an internal conflict that he did not always recognize as he invoked competing traditions in his teaching.

Conceptual Fuzziness in Teacher Education

Jimmy revealed his lack of coordinated preparation for teaching during an interview, saying,

> I'm thinking of having objectives for the classroom and maybe developing activities to meet those objectives, which is one thing I wish I would have had

more instruction on and more input on throughout my whole experience in the education program. And going from that point to developing lesson plans and the activities that were going to meet those objectives I think is one thing I would like more.... In my methods class I never had to write a unit for classrooms, which amazed me that I didn't have to do that. And it was in [the Theory of English Grammar class] that I actually wrote a unit, and I didn't have to do that. It was one of the options of projects that I could have done, so I chose to write a unit for that. So I could have conceivably gone all the way through my education program without writing a specific unit of instruction for an English classroom.

Jimmy's teaching methods class was taught as a poetry workshop rather than a class about pedagogy. He left it without a clear sense of how to plan instruction, outside what he had learned for teaching the language strand of the curriculum for his Theory of English Grammar class. In the absence of explicit attention to instructional planning, he was left to draw on his apprenticeship of observation in schools, his experiences with English faculty in the university, and the mentorship and collegiality of teachers in his practica, student teaching, and first job site. These contradictory sites and sources produced a mixed-bag pedagogical approach that lacked coherence, and that suggested that neither of the two worlds in the two-worlds pitfall provided conceptual consistency to inform his approach to teaching.

Tensions between Traditions, and Conceptual Disunity

Jimmy's teaching exhibited unresolved tensions between traditions when teaching the discipline of English/Language Arts. I use the term *tradition* very differently here than I have when referring to the Southern Plains Elementary Education program, in which the TCs had learned to use the term "traditional" to characterize authoritarian instruction, in contrast with "constructivist" or student-centered teaching. Rather, I rely on Applebee's (1974) notion of *pedagogical traditions*, which are historical ways of teaching a school subject. One such tradition is the "traditional" teaching used as a foil for constructivism in the Southern Plains Elementary Education program, one generally found to dominate school and university instruction (Cuban, 1993; Goodlad, 1984; Kahl & Venette, 2010; Schuh, 2004). Yet authoritarian instruction is one of many traditions available to teachers, including constructivism, critical pedagogy, and others.

Often, these various traditions are aggregated into a small set of competing epistemologies. Cuban (1993) has called these traditions *teacher-centered* and *student-centered* modes of instruction. Marshall, Smagorinsky, and Smith (1995) argue that teachers of literature are simultaneously influenced by two traditions: the *New Critical* method that focuses on the text itself and its critically accepted meaning (generally considered teacher-and-text-centered); and a *transactional* approach that foregrounds the reader's experiences in relation to reading (generally considered student-centered). Dixon's (1975) taxonomy includes three traditions. Two (what he called the *skills* and *cultural heritage* traditions) emphasize the acquisition of skills and knowledge (teacher-and-text-centered). What he calls the *personal growth model* focuses on developmental learning processes, the well-being of the learner, and the need for meaning to emerge through speech rather than being established through external authorities such as teachers and texts (student-centered).

These traditions are often pitted against one another as a forced choice for TCs, as indicated by the traditional versus constructivist dichotomy of the Southern Plains Elementary Education program. As Chapter 5 shows, however, the competition is often played out in teachers' minds as they work within settings in which multiple traditions are simultaneously in play and exerting influence. Like the two-worlds pitfall metaphor, the teacher-centered versus student-centered binary masks the fact that most settings are conceptually complex and absorb influences from many quarters, producing difficulties in teaching in wholly consistent ways.

Jimmy exhibited tensions between two competing traditions in his literature instruction. He is similar in some regards to Sharon from Chapter 5, who hoped to lead her primary school students "to discover things for themselves, and in their own way but also making sure they don't discover something in the wrong way." For teachers of literature, this contradiction obtains when traditions' oppositions are not resolved, such as when one tradition is concerned with getting it right according to historical norms, and one relies on personal constructions of meaning that are highly personal and idiosyncratic. Historically, literature instruction has been shaped by what is known as New Criticism (e.g., Ransom, 1941), an approach developed in the 1930s as a way to provide literary studies with status in the academy through the adoption of what were considered scientific means of analysis. Unlike the hard sciences, which study phenomena whose properties may be identified with at least temporary certainty (yet are also interpreted by scientists ideologically; see Latour & Woolgard, 1979), literature is written for ambiguity. New Criticism provides a set of analytic tools to help produce authoritative readings of canonical works through close reading of textual signs and codes, which can be transmitted via lectures. Some (e.g., Rejan, 2017) see reconciliation between New Criticism and approaches that allow for readers to instantiate meaning based on their life experiences, and no doubt many teachers seek some sort of middle ground between the two. New Criticism's stated principles and the opinions of people in policy positions, however, view the reader's personal life as a corrupting factor in their inscription of meaning in texts, a feature celebrated by proponents of the Common Core State Standards (Coleman & Pimentel, 2012; Shanahan, 2013).

New Criticism relies on a reader's grasp of a technical vocabulary (setting, denouement, metaphor, etc.). Under close New Critical analysis, the literary text exists independent of its author, and its meaning resides within its language itself. Readers should tune out contexts and intertexts, including their own lives, as urged by Coleman and Pimentel's (2012) in touting the CCSS claim that reading should proceed within the four corners of the text in detective-like manner. The text has a single correct meaning that is available to the astute reader; a work's meaning is inherent, rather than being constructed by readers. Readers avoid the "affective fallacy," the error of equating a work with its emotional effects upon an audience. Applebee (1993) and others have argued that by incorporating these values into textbooks and high-stakes assessments, educational institutions have established them in many teachers' minds as the most appropriate approach to teaching literature.

New Criticism's approach regimented the teaching of English so convincingly that it became the default approach to studying literature in schools and universities for many decades (Applebee, 1974, 1993). It provides a stable knowledge base that can be transmitted through lectures or shaped during discussions, and is amenable to testing because it produces "proper" readings that follow from its principles. New Criticism is not the only formalist approach available. The Chicago School (Crane, 1952), for instance, is synonymous with Neo-Aristotelianism because it relies on Aristotle's concepts of plot, character, and genre. Although some people have conflated Chicago's approach with New Criticism as formalist, they were in fact rival approaches. Chicago critics accused New Critics of being too subjective and of excessively valuing irony and figurative language. Chicago critics sought complete objectivity and a strong classical basis of evidence for criticism, and adopted the Aristotelian value of structure or form of a concrete, whole literary work rather than attending to the linguistic techniques at more atomistic levels, as did the New Critics. Both approaches are formalist, teaching student readers to break down texts in terms of technique to determine the author's inscribed meaning and the techniques through which it is embedded.

Other approaches, however, emphasized readers' subjectivities, at times radically so. Rosenblatt (1938 and subsequent editions) is credited with creating intellectual space for reader-oriented conceptions of the reading experience via "reader response" approaches that put readers and texts on roughly equal footing, emphasizing the texts that readers imagine in response to reading as the outcome of a fruitful textual engagement (see Smagorinsky, 2001). Texts are not to be parsed in detail in this approach but are to be used as a stimulus for a reader's response, which might not be analytic at all. Bleich (1975) and others took this perspective to its extreme, asserting that the text itself matters far less than what readers experience and what they make of it.

New Criticism and reader response approaches have dominated much discussion in English Education over how best to teach literature, producing the sort of teacher-centered versus student-centered dichotomies available in the "traditional" versus constructivist debate and other challenges to teachers. Yet other approaches remain available. Various critical perspectives, for instance, are less concerned with making meaning from texts, and focus instead on deconstructing the political and equity issues surrounding reading and writing, the production of texts, and related social questions that surround literacy. These approaches might not focus on meaning or readers at all, instead looking into such factors as the author's privileged position in writing about a topic and providing a perspective on it, the construction of gender in a text or in access to publishing, how racialized characters are constructed by authors of different cultural backgrounds, or other questions related to power inequities and the distribution of authority in society. These approaches might yield the insight that when White males dominate literary criticism, women's issues and texts written from other cultural perspectives get subordinated, and literature written by other sorts of authors are reduced in value (see Rabinowitz, 1987, himself a product of the Chicago School, yet in this case, undertaking a gendered critical analysis of canonicity).

Critical theories of this sort are among the many perspectives beyond the established binary of teacher-centered New Criticism and student-centered reader response theory. This set of polar extremes accounts for much of the tension within textbooks and anthologies and in teachers' practice, if not among many university literary theorists and occasional pedagogues (e.g., Appleman, 2015). The list of other lenses through which to undertake the formal study of literature includes, at the least, Moral Criticism and Dramatic Construction, Psychoanalytic Criticism and Jungian Criticism, Marxist Criticism, Structuralism/Semiotics, Post-Structuralism/Deconstruction, New Historicism/Cultural Studies, Post-Colonial Criticism, and Critical Disability Studies (Brizee, Tompkins, Chernouski, Boyle, & Williams, n.d.). This source lumps together New Criticism and Neo-Aristotelian (Chicago School) perspectives as structural, in spite of their clear rivalry, so I can only assume that these categories are broad and include competing critical understandings within categories.

My point with this brief and undoubtedly incomplete review is not to roil the debate over which approach best suits teachers, students, and schools. Rather, it's to establish the fact that there are multiple traditions at work in the teaching of literature, and that even those with a single orientation—formalism/structuralism, reader response, and critical theory—might be at odds, producing tensions between traditions in the teaching of literature.

Jimmy's example suggests that these tensions work simultaneously within individual teachers and their teaching of literature such that conceptually different approaches are enacted together, producing contradictions in how the subject is taught. Marshall et al. (1995) found this phenomenon at work in teachers they studied, calling it "doubleness": teachers were concurrently indebted to traditions that determine a proper reading and those yielding interpretive rights to students. These traditions run much deeper than locations within schools or universities, while concurrently residing in both. In universities, the distinction is often made between teacher-and-text-centered Department of English approaches and College of Education student-centered approaches (Addington, 2001). Yet English literature faculty are not so unitary, as the earlier list of possibilities indicates; and some COE faculty lecture on student-centered teaching, as Tracy's case demonstrates. Schools might include both teachers who rely on anthologies impressing New Critical values on instruction and teachers who view the reader's construction as the purpose of literary study and source of textual meaning.

Different traditions require different orientations to the subject matter. Each suggests a specific way to arrange class, relate to students, organize student activity, conceive of assessment, regard and encourage knowledge, consider the meaning of meaning, and otherwise orchestrate students' experiences in relation to the curriculum. Various traditions might be invoked by the same teacher in the same class without being melded into a single, consistent teaching approach. As Rejan (2017) argues, such a synthesis might be possible. If the examples of Marshall et al. (1995), Jimmy in this chapter, and others are representative of a subset of teachers, they may be more juxtaposed than integrated in both conception and practice. Many university teacher educators find this theoretical mashup to be a sign of a weak mind that resorts to Taylor's (1985) rotten compromise, and they wonder how their program graduates can so easily abandon progressive teaching ideas. My interpretation is that even the smartest, best-prepared teachers will inevitably find themselves conflicted in their teaching, perhaps unconsciously, because the social settings of their educational experiences and training themselves are inconsistent and contradictory.

These traditions are powerfully evident in classrooms, do not originate as strictly school-based or university-based, may be practiced in both similar and different ways in both universities (and their subunits such as education and English departmental cultures) and schools, and are evident in many areas of life outside formal education. It is common in the business world, for instance, to complain about graduates' lack of formal and structural knowledge of proper textual form (Casner-Lotto, 2006), because attention to the personally transformative possibilities of literary engagement or writing process is irrelevant in the world of commerce. As I write this book, there is political attention to the possibility of merging the US Departments of Education and Labor, suggesting that the purpose of education is to focus on the formalist demands of workforce preparation rather than student-centered human growth of the sort advanced by Dixon (1975) and other Deweyan progressives. The tension explored in this section thus falls well outside the two-worlds pitfall that considers teaching understandings as the province of only two worlds: distinctive and conceptually unified schools, and distinctive and conceptually unified universities. The tensions that influence instruction in contradictory ways have deep historical roots and current societal applications, and do not just beleaguer the teacher of literature.

Student Teaching

Jimmy did his student teaching in an Advanced Sophomore English class in a school in which college preparation was the primary driver of instruction. His MT, Kim, was one of the district's most highly admired teachers, a school "Teacher of the Year" and occasional instructor in the university English Education program Jimmy attended. She hoped Jimmy's instruction would involve

> respecting the students and building on student ideas and really introducing the theme before they go into the literature. And making literature real to the students . . . to make it come to life and help them to see more of what was happening and what was not written in the page, but some motivations that the author expects you as reader to come up with. We teach them to read more carefully and be more sophisticated readers.

Kim had the dual concern of caring for students and using their personal experiences as a critical means of engaging with the curriculum, and teaching them the close reading skills that are prized in New Criticism, which is insinuated into the fabric of schooling through its presence in teacher manuals and ancillary materials, and its long history of implementation in classrooms and university English classes. These dual values were reiterated when Kim identified the most important things that students could learn in her English class as "self-esteem" and "thinking skills," the first foregrounding affective experiences and the second concerned with technical approaches to reading and writing. Each of these dual values has historically played a role in both education and the teaching of English/Language Arts. The two have often been positioned in opposition to one another, with the teacher-centered/student-centered continuum often expressed as a binary. Yet as Kim's dual values suggest, they often do coexist, if not always with conceptual integration. I do not locate this as a problem in Kim, or teachers like her. Rather, I see her, like most teachers, as manifesting the conflictual environments in which they have learned to teach in their articulation of theoretically incompatible values and practices.

The teaching of literature occupied a great deal of Jimmy's instruction. Under Kim's guidance, and in the absence of explicit instruction in the university program in how to plan units, Jimmy designed instruction conceived to (1) enable students to make personal sense of the curriculum and (2) lead students toward particular preferred interpretations of the literature. Like Sharon, then, he hoped to allow students "to discover things for themselves, and in their own way but also making sure they don't discover something in the wrong way," exhibiting the "doubleness" identified by Marshall et al. (1995) and being embodied in Kim's supportive and much-appreciated mentorship.

Kim's student-centered influence on Jimmy's teaching was evident in how she talked about her own instructional values. Her goals for her students included the abilities to make personal connections to literary themes, to write about those connections, to participate in interpretive activities such as small-group discussions and presentations, and to learn strategies for engaging in interpretive projects independent of her direct influence. By developing competence and confidence in these capacities in relation to challenging literature and with the assistance of instructional scaffolding, students could elevate their self-esteem as they demonstrated competence in reading and responding to challenging works of literature.

Jimmy believed that student-centered activities enabled him to honor students' "learning styles," an idea to which he had been exposed in his university coursework, one that, he said, "makes sense to me on a gut level." Students, he said, might be able to interpret literature "artistically in pictures," an approach through which students can "show a lot of understanding about what they mean by a novel, a short story." Jimmy's recognition that students learn in diverse ways contributed to his comfort level with Kim's tutelage and with the general student-centered pedagogies learned on campus, such as designing introductory activities (in the Theory of English Grammar course), writing found poems, asking authentic questions (i.e., those that are open-ended and grounded in students' inquiries), and producing a student newspaper.

Jimmy's teaching also included instruction from the tradition variously known as teacher-centered, cultural heritage, objective, formalist, and other names denoting the emphasis on learning and analyzing a formal body of knowledge. Kim helped to direct his teaching toward seemingly contradictory ends. After engaging in constructivist activities during the unit on courageous action, for instance, Kim assigned the students a five-paragraph theme (see Chapter 7), which in the minds of many is the epitome of the formalist tradition in that it is entirely dedicated to paragraph form and sequence, right down to sentence construction (see Johnson, Smagorinsky, Thompson, & Fry, 2003) without necessarily making logical sense in its content (Hillocks, 2002). Jimmy remarked that "I think they had already learned how to [write five-paragraph themes] . . . . most of them knew what she was talking about," suggesting its institutionalization in the school curriculum.

Jimmy invoked the New Critical tradition, a complementary means of instructional formalism, in his own teaching when leading discussions of literature. He led his students in discussions of *A Separate Peace* after preparing "discussion questions about things I thought were important to the development of the novel and the characters. . . . I was kind of geared towards leading them a certain direction." Jimmy referred the students to specific passages from the text and displayed seven questions on a screen, which students were to respond to in complete sentences in notebooks, with volunteers reading their responses. Jimmy said he wanted students to "hit on the key elements in the story and relate the significance of maybe a metaphor or some symbolism . . . . Or even stuff like character development." This instruction was designed to prepare them for a unit exam in which they had to support interpretive claims with textual evidence, a key New Critical task: "Having them support that with a quotation, also, that makes them find evidence for what they say. Which I think is important, especially when they have their test later, they are going to have to do another test. They are going to have to support what they say with evidence from their story." Jimmy also gave quizzes and assignments that required fixed answers, including identifying both basic factual plot developments (e.g., "How is Finny injured as a result of falling from the tree?") and responding to seemingly interpretive questions that likely had preferred answers ("Where is the Devon school located in regards to the rivers, and what is significant about this location?"), the sort of question found in new critically informed student support texts such as *Cliff's Notes*.[1]

Jimmy's formalist teaching appears grounded in many settings, reflected in both his and Kim's consciousness in teaching both literary study and writing about literature. Its source is difficult to ascertain with confidence, but appears to have been located in formalism's systemic integration into the domain's cultural practices in schools and universities so as to be central to teachers' own experiences as students. Taking a methods course that involved writing poetry instead of learning instructional planning undoubtedly affected his conceptual knowledge of the field, leaving him subject to the influence of the site of his student teaching in which both progressive and formalist teaching values obtained in what appears to be an uneasy alliance. When teaching in the constructivist tradition, Jimmy designed instructional sequences that scaffolded students' ability to work independent of his influence by teaching them learning strategies for their literary inquiries. His New Critical and formalist writing instruction involved his consideration of the meaning of a text and his construction of questions that led students toward that interpretation. The approaches appear less a hybrid and more an unintegrated juxtaposition of progressive and formalist values and practices: he taught in New Critical ways on some occasions and constructivist ways on others, sometimes within the same class period and toward very different ends.

First Year of Full-Time Teaching

Jimmy's first job was at Pullman City High School (PCHS) in a nearby suburban setting. He also coached football,[2] a demanding extracurricular position occupying

---

[1] See https://www.cliffsnotes.com/literature/s/a-separate-peace/summary-and-analysis/chapter-6
[2] That is, US football, not the game known as futball or soccer.

most of the fall semester that no doubt constrained his available planning time and made it an attractive option to default to local norms that accommodated his division of labor and attention. The school district required that teachers cover specific content and skills. Jimmy reported that "the curriculum guide is pretty specific. They have certain works that I'm supposed to teach, certain concepts that I'm supposed to go over for each one," each in the formalist tradition: "The literary terms that would go with [the literature], like plot and things. Then there would be a section of drama and you have to teach *Romeo and Juliet* . . . . heroic couplet, blank verse were some of the literary terms that had to go with that." He also had to teach the research paper and a set of grammar skills.

Jimmy felt that this curriculum provided good support: "That's been pretty helpful though for me just starting out. . . . If you follow the curriculum guide for what you're supposed to be teaching and what literary terms they are supposed to know, material and stuff, you usually don't have any trouble meeting those." The curriculum guide strongly influenced his teaching:

> They had [the curriculum] broken down into categories that you would teach and the literary terms or concepts they were supposed to learn along with those. I found that it's affected the way I've taught in the fact that I tend to go by categories. Like we started out with short stories, so we'd read short stories. I'd give them activities where they either do some creative writing stuff or they'd write their own short stories . . . and then have to incorporate the terms as far as like having direct characterization and things like that. So, I find myself teaching by those chunks. . . . I don't know that I necessarily like teaching that way.

He acknowledged that this approach was not consistent with what his few classes in pedagogy had stressed at the university, yet he also acknowledged that "it's more convenient" for a teacher at the beginning of his career. He hoped "to do more of a thematic type teaching" in his second year after he'd gotten a year of experience under his belt; this research, however, did not extend beyond his first year at PCHS. His teaching illustrates a conundrum described by Grossman and Thompson (2008), who found that beginning teachers rely heavily on curriculum materials for support, and that these materials "powerfully shape their ideas about teaching language arts as well as their classroom practice [and] that new and aspiring teachers need opportunities to analyze and critique curriculum materials, beginning during teacher education and continuing in the company of their more experienced colleagues" (p. 2014). This conclusion requires the availability of experienced colleagues who share university critical dispositions and values, a sort of colleague not available to Jimmy. He had this opportunity neither at the university nor in his initial teaching, leaving him to rely on the curriculum for support without a critical perspective beyond his gut feeling.

Jimmy's main influences during his first year at PCHS were the curriculum and his colleagues, who included teachers from his own secondary school education whom he contacted for teaching ideas on occasion. At PCHS, teacher-and-text-centered teaching methods predominated and were the measure of excellence for English teachers. Jimmy reported that he planned his lessons by "look[ing] up the materials I have to teach that day [according to the curriculum] and deciding how to break it up and into what materials in there, developing objectives for that particular activity.... There's daily objectives about—okay, by the end of this day you should know what a heroic couplet is or what an iambic pentameter is." Jimmy said that his instruction in short stories focused on plot, character, and other elements of literature required by his curriculum, which embodied New Critical values. Field notes described his teaching in this setting as follows:

> Jimmy writes on the board: exposition; rising action, climax, falling action, resolution. Jimmy draws a diagram. "What in your opinion is the climax?" Student: "When Romeo kills Tibalt." Jimmy discusses the student's answer. Jimmy explains exposition (Romeo). Jimmy: "When we meet Romeo for the first time, how does he feel about Rosalyn? That tells us about his character. What else is exposition?" Jimmy begins to discuss rising action. Student: "Romeo and Juliet get married." Jimmy: "What's something else we can put down?" Student: "Tibalt kills Mercutio."

His teaching at PCHS included occasional student-centered instruction, such as a research project in relation to a thematic unit featuring *The Odyssey*, a required text that Jimmy taught in the context of the theme of the journey. This theme was manifested in the writing he assigned, to write about "why they're on their journey. They've written a narrative essay on some places they've gone to and what they've learned or experienced on that trip. Just looking at the journey as a theme for life." Jimmy had done the project as a high school student, and contacted his former teacher for the activity when he learned that he was required to teach *The Odyssey* at PCHS. For the project,

> They pick a place they'd like to go to and research not only some information about that particular destination, but also they need to plan it out to the minute. If they had to take a plane there, they had to call the airlines and figure out what planes are going where, how much tickets are, and basically come up with a budget as well as an itinerary.

The budget needed to cover food, travel, lodgings, and other expenses incurred during the trip, each calculated in terms of the type of car being driven and the number of people taking the trip. They also had to write a formal business letter requesting information from a Chamber of Commerce or other organization about the site being visited. Students worked individually on their projects, but, said Jimmy, "I might have them work in groups or cooperate on things like an editing stage." Although this writing included formalist elements, the choice of topic and details placed the assignment in the progressive tradition of engaging students in open-ended problems without single, clear-cut solutions, if not necessarily forms.

Summary

Jimmy's teaching gravitated toward the norms of PCHS as he moved away from campus and then Kim's mixed-tradition tutelage, and into the largely formalist school setting.

Jimmy's autumn coaching responsibilities often extended into evening commitments that required him to attend opponents' games to scout their schemes and personnel, and to do other duties associated with preparing his team for practice and competition. These obligations cut into the time he had for instructional planning. To compensate, he availed himself of his colleagues' lesson plans, which appeared to work within the teacher-and-text-centered pedagogical tradition and to incorporate principles of New Criticism, consistent with what was engrained in textbooks and high-stakes assessments.

Jimmy's case illustrates the difficulties that beginning teachers have of teaching in conceptually unified ways, unless they rely wholesale on formalist conceptions as their guiding and abiding approach, which enables them to fit well within the bounds of schools and their dominant traditions and curricula, and broader mandates that are authoritarian in conception and design. His conceptual conflicts do not appear to have been a problem solely of school versus university. Both paradigms were available in each, no doubt contributing to their easy availability, if not synthesis, in his teaching.

Jimmy taught comfortably within conflicting paradigms without appearing to recognize that they represented different visions and conceptions. His university program was too diffuse and random to provide conceptual continuity for him and his classmates sufficient for developing a strong, consistent vision to guide their teaching, especially those whose methods course had been a poetry writing workshop. Kim mentored Jimmy with a foundation of relating students' lives to their literary experiences, considering the world from students' perspectives, and planning activities that enabled them to engage with literary themes on their own terms; and at the same time, attending to formalist requirements in their own writing. His instruction at PCHS leaned much more heavily toward the teacher-and-text-centered tradition, even as he expressed reservations about it and hoped to teach more thematically after he'd gotten settled.

At PCHS, Jimmy taught all new courses, experienced time management problems because of his coaching duties, and felt cut off from his colleagues by the school schedule. He relied on a small group of kindly colleagues, trustworthy former teachers, and the curriculum materials to help him prepare for his classes. Most of this help, offered by teachers who themselves had little free time, came through access to lessons in file cabinets, rather than the close and careful mentoring available through Kim or urged by Grossman and Thompson (2008) among colleagues. He taught these lessons with a trial-and-error approach, hoping that with further experience, he would know which ones worked best for him. Like the curriculum itself, these lessons embodied the teacher-and-text-centered pedagogical tradition, one generally at odds with the student-centered teaching approach modeled, if unevenly, by Kim during student teaching.

The experienced, exemplary teachers studied by Marshall et al. (1995) and many other highly regarded teachers are similarly ensconced in these two apparently contradictory philosophical worlds. Jimmy, I should stress, had a great rapport with his students during all of our observations, and would be embraced on just about any secondary school English faculty as an excellent teacher and good citizen. Kim, as I've reviewed, was among her district's most valued faculty members. My identification of their conceptual disunity is not a critique of their professionalism, ability, dedication, knowledge, or value as teachers. Rather, it highlights a critical challenge of teacher education: how to prepare teachers for the inevitable conflicts they face when enacting instruction in schools in which multiple traditions are at work, and in which the principal center of gravity and measure of excellence leans toward formalistic, teacher-and-text-centered instruction. "Doubleness," as described in Marshall et al. (1995), bordered on being a character flaw or intellectual shortcoming. Here I position it as an inevitable, if not satisfying, consequence of teachers' immersion throughout their schooling and engagement with broader social life in multiple paradigms, both in university programs and in schools, that resist reconciliation and wholly consistent pedagogical practice, especially when the university teacher education program presents concepts initially in fuzzy ways with little practical application.

Tracy

Jimmy's case demonstrates how a single teacher may embody, depending on the circumstances, different conceptions of teaching without clearly recognizing their discrepant assumptions or fitting them comfortably within a unified approach. Tracy's case reveals a related sort of problem, that of a teacher attempting to implement a constructivist, student-centered approach in schools that provided accommodating settings, yet having difficulty employing constructivist practices toward genuinely constructivist ends. Like Jimmy, she was a highly regarded TC in her state's most competitive university. She was described by her university supervisor as being "first or second in her class" in terms of accomplishment.

Tracy thus makes a good case to consider when confronting problems of conceptual disunity, because she herself, like Jimmy, cannot be considered to be a dim, confused young person incapable of resolving discrepancies. Rather, she was immersed in settings that produced conceptual contradictions, which in turn appeared to produce inconsistencies in how she implemented a constructivist pedagogy. Although I focus on her struggles in this chapter, I must emphasize that her faculty at the university regarded her as one of the very best students in a large teacher education program that had the most competitive admissions requirements of any university in its state. In her teaching, she received excellent evaluations from all who reviewed her work in the field. Her excellence in the classroom, both as a student and as a teacher, provides a compelling reason to focus on her vicissitudes in understanding and putting into practice the concept of constructivism.

Tracy enrolled in the Southern Plains Elementary Education program, described in Chapter 4, in which Piagetian constructivism was presented as the optimal and sole theoretical lens through which to understand teaching and learning. Yet the definition of constructivism, she found, was amorphous, being inconsistently articulated by different professors in her university courses and erratically practiced by some in their assessments. She was further daunted by the possibilities for enacting constructivism in schools. She completed a field experience in a child development facility where she saw preschool children "running around doing everything" such that "little lights go on" when the kids, through self-guided adventures, engaged in continual discoveries.

Schools, however, seemed difficult sites in which to provide a constructivist pedagogy that fostered a delight in discovery. The thought of ten-year-olds running around a classroom shrieking for joy upon learning a new concept did not seem realistic to her inside public schools. Tracy wondered, "How could you do this? . . . Would your school support you?" She accepted the idea of "controlled chaos" as an analogy for what she envisioned taking place in her future classroom, but doubted whether she could become a full-fledged constructivist teacher in the sorts of schools she visited and taught in, where classes were highly structured and authoritarian. Children were typically seat-bound, and teachers would direct their learning through such vehicles as reading comprehension cards.

Tracy illustrates the struggle that novice teachers have in appropriating concepts about teaching, especially when they are ambiguously presented, as constructivism was on campus, in spite of its general utility as a pedagogical approach. When asked how she envisioned herself as a teacher, she responded, "I guess I kind of want to be a constructivist teacher." Her phrasing hints at the uncertainty she felt about the conceptual tool that provided the overarching theme of her teacher education program.

In Vygotsky's (1987) account of concept development, people move gradually, if sporadically and nonlinearly, through a series of general stages that move thinking toward conceptual unity. This synthesis is informed by both worldly experience and formal academic knowledge that enables abstraction and application to new contexts. Along the way they pass through stages that increasingly refine understandings to eliminate discrepant elements (see Chapter 1). My own critique of his conception (Smagorinsky, 2013) finds his reliance on firmly established biological examples to mask the impossibility of arriving at a unified understanding of a *social concept* such as constructivism, given that there is no universal agreement on what it includes. This problem was evident on the Southern Plains Elementary Education faculty itself. As Phillips (1995) has demonstrated, defining constructivism remains a murky endeavor in the broader field of education. Falling short of social conceptualizations is not, I have argued, a fault or failure. It is a function of being a social human being who is surrounded by myriad inconsistencies that are computationally impossible to resolve into coherency (Dutton & Heath, 2010).

Participant

Tracy was a White middle-class woman from the US southwest. Both of her parents were teachers in the school system she had attended, which Tracy described, consistent with her teacher education faculty, as "traditional." At the elementary level, students were confined to "sitting in desks the whole time," reading out of basals, and doing extensive grammar work, including the diagramming of sentences. Tracy viewed her own middle school experiences positively, citing some of her favorite teachers from those years as being the most nontraditional, that is, interactive, engaging, and hands-on. Tracy also did well in high school, after which she enrolled in her state's namesake university, where she was originally a journalism major, then a computer science major, and finally, after struggling with mathematics, an Elementary Education major in the Southern Plains Elementary Education program featured in this research.

Confusion about Constructivism on Campus

Tracy described her understanding of constructivism with ambiguity and ambivalence. During an interview she said,

> Well, I mean, I believe, you know, the children do construct their own knowledge. But it's not totally constructivism because you sit there and you say, well here is the materials that they can use to construct this knowledge. So you actually provide the materials for them that they have to construct from the knowledge, so I couldn't really say that that's true. I mean in a sense it is constructivism, but in another sense it's not really. I don't know. It's just hard to say what exactly it is. I don't know. I believe I will keep expanding on my term forever and ever. I don't think anyone knows exactly what constructivism is. . . . In my education here [at the university], everyone is like, well, you know, they have to construct their own knowledge, and that means constructivism. And I was just like—so if you say construct their knowledge, that means they're like, well, no. And then when we're done we sit there and say, this is kind of [inaudible]. You know, its kind of like letting them find their own way and find their own knowledge and do this and do this and do this. . . . And so I can't really say that I am a strong believer in constructivism, because I don't know what it is.

Tracy implied a desire to be provided with a clear and consistent definition of constructivism that she never got, instead being left to construct her own definition based on her experiences within a constructivist framework, offered inconsistently in her many and varied education courses. She believed that her understanding of the term would continue to grow, but expressed frustration over the coherence of the conception that provided the foundation for her understanding, especially given the contradictory ways in which she was taught about constructivism on campus. In her Language Arts methods class, she said, the professor would say,

> This is how you should do it, and here is the book, you know. This is a great lesson, blah, blah, blah, blah, blah. But read chapters 1 through 9, and you're going to have a test on it in two weeks and memorize this, this, this, and this so you come down, you have a test and it's all listing. You know, list the six characteristics of blah, blah, blah, and so you had to sit there and list and explain. And so we had pages and pages and pages of tests. So her tests did not follow her philosophy necessarily, and so it was just kind of frustrating, because you're like, well, you're telling me to teach this way, you know, and we're sitting here saying, well you don't necessarily have tests. But they have to memorize, you know, do not have a test that they memorize things. And then what does she do? She has this stuff memorized everything for, you know. I mean it was just kind of—I thought it was kind of humorous just because that's how a lot of the classes were.

During one of this cohort's concept map activities, the subject of professorial inconsistency came up as rather a sore subject among the TCs, summarized by one as "do as I say and not as I do." Not only was it not practiced as preached but it was also preached and practiced inconsistently, as Tracy said in an interview: the faculty "constructed their own knowledge about it so no one really knows exactly what it is and I don't think every one will ever really know what it is. . . . Everyone's version is totally different from everyone else's." This uncertainty inevitably produced problems of implementation in the TCs' classrooms. Jimmy had learned no governing principles in his program; Tracy learned about one, but not in ways she found clear or consistent. In both cases, the fuzziness of the concepts in teacher education produced conceptually shifting practices in their classrooms.

Student Teaching

Tracy's MT during student teaching was Sarah, like Tracy, a White middle-class woman. Her classroom layout reflected her creativity and her stated priority that students "feel really good about themselves, [which] helps them to be more successful in the long run." She believed that her school allowed "freedom about whole language and really trying new ideas." Sarah encouraged students to use the various spaces created for quiet reading when they were finished with their work, and lessons were structured around learning centers: self-contained areas in the classroom where students engage in independent or collaborative, and usually self-directed, learning activities within a given amount of time, after which they move to the next center to work on new projects. Sarah used the term *whole language* in more or less the same way that constructivism was used on campus to describe literature-based (rather than basal-and-workbook) reading instruction and open-ended writing opportunities. Sarah viewed her own teaching as a hybrid of both traditional (authoritarian and formalist) and whole language (constructivist) approaches, saying, "When I went to college, it was more the traditional approach. And it's been a while but I have managed to, I feel like, use both, the basals and the traditional approach and the whole language using different grade books and chapter books." Sarah's remarks suggest her recognition of competing traditions that required juxtaposition, if not integration, for teaching in the setting of schools governed more broadly by authoritarian and formalist values.

De-centering the Classroom

To illustrate a fuzzy concept's consequences for classroom practice, I focus on one dimension of Tracy's teaching: *de-centering* the classroom to allow students to have greater agency in directing their own learning. When asked to describe her Language Arts methods class professor's image of a good teacher, she said:

> I'm really not sure. Let's see, to have a lot of creative ideas. To have a lot of authentic books and bring a lot of writing or plays or other types of things to where children can be active in their classroom—not just sit there and [inaudible] read a book.

You know how silent reading or whatever, but they can go all over the room and, you know, lay in the bathtub if you have one in your classroom or whatever, you know. Read whatever they want to read. You know, pull in things from outside of the school—not necessarily just from inside—you know, like from their own environment. You know, you could even go outside in the playground and read or you could bring in other things like newspapers, magazines, you know, other things from everywhere, and just have the children learn from what they read. . . . So [Sarah], you know, just kind of had the children again construct their own knowledge, but have tools ready for them to use.

Sarah's classroom actually did have a bathtub in it, so no, that is not a typographical error. Tracy embraced the principle that learners should construct their own knowledge, independent of the authoritative views of the teacher. The teacher provides a rich environment replete with tools and materials that students can draw on in their individual constructions of knowledge. In this de-centered classroom, the teacher, the texts, and the curriculum no longer dictate the daily schedule. Rather, each child develops a unique focus and pursues personal goals related to that focus using available classroom resources. The center of the classroom thus becomes the individual students themselves and their work in a variety of learning centers, and shifts in relation to the child's unfolding interests and constructions.

Tracy's efforts to de-center her classroom were compromised by both the immediate and surrounding contexts of her teaching, complicated by the fuzziness of her understanding of constructivism based on contradictory and ambiguous definitions of the construct in her coursework. The data indicate a continued value on physically de-centering the classroom through reading and writing centers and the use of various devices to provide students opportunities for activity. Yet although her class had the *physical* appearance of being de-centered, the *content of the instruction* did not provide for the kind of *social de-centering of authority* essential to a constructivist pedagogy.

Prior to student teaching, Tracy contrasted her own education with the ideal way in which she would set up a classroom, saying that when she was in school "each desk was in a row. . . . I have a variety of different ways that I would like to, you know, have my classroom—maybe in a circle, you know. Not necessarily have any one, you know, as the important person in the room." Her description of constructivist classrooms consistently referred to alternatives to traditional organizations that kept students seated in rows, with their attention focused on the teacher and prescribed curriculum. Instead, she described arrangements that enabled greater activity and multiple directions for students to move in. During a field experience, she rearranged the desks for social interaction, in contrast with her host teacher's row-based organization, to shift the focus of students' attention away from herself and toward one another.

She described the ways in which this physical de-centering worked in service of social de-centering to redistribute authority across students. In contrast with teachers from her own schooling, who provided all answers and directed all activity, she said, "I learned that you shouldn't always give the students the answer. I don't even think you should give them the answer. Just go well, you know, what do you think? And if they don't get it, you know, what you consider the right answer? You can kind of lead them back, but not necessarily give them the answer." As a student in school, Tracy had been a very active child whose teachers had imposed a passive role on her, one she found stifling. As a teacher she declared a commitment to de-centering her classroom in order to encourage students' curiosity and knowledge construction.

Some of Tracy's field experiences enabled her to view classrooms with distributed authority and direction in action. In a laboratory kindergarten affiliated with the university that she described as "wonderful," the room was set up with centers, books were everywhere, and the children responded actively to their learning opportunities because

> it was their room. It wasn't the teacher's room. I mean their stuff, all their papers and everything were all over the wall, you know, and they got to pick where they put it so they could put it on the chalk board if they wanted so she never used the chalk board. . . . They were just always going, always learning something. . . . They had their lights come on.

Sarah's second grade classroom during Tracy's student teaching fit well with her ideals. A couch for independent reading was tucked away in the corner, with bookshelves providing selections to choose from and areas where they could work out their reader's theater performances. Desks were arranged in clusters of four, and there were several centers throughout the room: a computer, a masterpiece theater, and two horseshoe-shaped tables filled with scissors, glue, and markers. And a bathtub.

Tracy described the ways in which she and Sarah used the classroom arrangement for their teaching. Tracy's account suggested significant student choice and activity across the classrooms affordances, with occasional formalist tasks such as answering questions at the end of a story:

> Sometimes we don't go back by the couch. We go up in the front, and they use the chalkboard. We just move them around. . . . We've been trying to get them on schedules, you know, like we'll put up on the board "Things to Do." And then during the day they have to do their DEARs [Drop Everything and Read] and after they're done with that they have to—like they read in that book. Like read page blah, blah, blah, and answer the questions at the end. And so they also do their own independent work. And then we have purple folders which is their individualized reading. They're all in different books. So they're all answering different questions. . . . They can read to me and we can discuss, you know, kind of have a conference about what they're reading. . . . We also have the centers. . . . They have a math center and it's not hard. They're not hard activities at all, but they get to work together because we have activities where they have to—cooperative groups where they have to produce one thing, and that's really hard for them. But it's not like pressure. If they get it done, they get it done, and we're happy. If they don't get it done, then okay. It doesn't really matter, but you all learn that you each have to compromise.

When asked if she would teach with this approach, Tracy said, "I would probably use this format. I have seen it all semester and it works wonderfully." The generally constructivist arrangement and intent manifested in the physical de-centering of the classroom did not always distribute authority and remove the teacher and curriculum from the students' focus, however. Even with choice in what they would read and where they would read it, the students were evaluated according to commercially prepared worksheets; and the evaluation of the cooperative work done in the centers counted less toward the students' grades than the worksheets. During student teaching, Tracy's notion of de-centering was realized physically in the arrangement and many of the activities, but not in terms of the means of assessment. For the most part the students' activity was teacher-directed and was assessed according to conventional and standardized vehicles.

I do not make this observation harshly. Sarah was an outstanding mentor and did an admirable job of including constructivist principles in her teaching. From the standpoint of developing a conception of constructivist teaching, however, the student teaching experience reinforced the difficulties of appropriating a concept that is learned through incongruous instruction and then modeled in uneven ways. This inconsistency suggests the ways that the deep structure of schools can provide obstacles to teaching according to the progressive values often emphasized in teacher education courses and valued by many practicing teachers. They further illustrate the manner in which the two worlds of school and university both represent conceptually conflicted settings, rather than being distinctively whole and oppositional sites for learning to teach.

First Job

Tracy secured her first teaching job at Lakewood Elementary School in one of the state's largest cities, far from campus. The school had a 51 percent poverty rate, with the student body being 66 percent European American, 17 percent Native American, and 17 percent African American. The principal considered her school to be an "inner city" school, and said that the teachers were faced with great challenges over the increasing urbanization and poverty among the students. Instructionally, the faculty was caught in the Reading Wars pitting phonics against whole language instruction—a battle still raging (Castles, Rastle, & Nation, 2018)—with the school principal siding with phonics as the basis of literacy. Tracy reported that the majority of other teachers "want me to teach phonics" in her kindergarten first-grade class to provide a foundation for reading and writing so that "whenever they get [the students], they [can teach] whole language," a term used at Lakewood to refer to the constructivist practices Tracy had learned on campus.

At Lakewood Elementary, Tracy had less support for enacting the constructivist classroom she had envisioned prior to student teaching, even as her classroom appeared to be modeled on Sarah's, minus the bathtub. Field notes refer to a physical organization that, in the best of all possible worlds, ought to promote students' self-directed learning:

> There are four computers in a corner. A movable bulletin board, various buckets of cubes and crayons. Behind Tracy's desk there is a shelf that contains teacher

editions of basals and social studies books. There are two large boxes: 1) Celebrate Reading, a learning system for kids who need more reading support; 2) Phonics Manipulatives Kit. There is a poster of the students and their reading buddies. The desks are grouped in 3's, with larger tables together (coloring area?).

There are two areas that have children's books.

2:05PM: Some students are going to a Writing Center. There is . . . a list of words. The students copy the words. There is a Reading Center, a make-a-paper-plate Santa, and cut-and-paste shape center. The students at the Reading Center are listening to a tape with their book. The writing is to learn spelling words. Tracy walks around the room going from center to center checking on students' progress. When students are done, they can go to work on the computers. There is a word program (*First Letter Fun*). The student chooses the beginning letter of a picture on the screen. The other program is *Primetime Initial Consonants*. The student is shown a letter and must choose between 3 pictures for the correct answer.

Tracy physically de-centered the class through flexible seating for group work and for reading and writing centers. Students' work in these centers, however, was directed by the prescribed school curriculum, which emphasized phonics in the first grade. Throughout her teacher education program, Tracy had had no experience with first graders, no background in emergent reading, and no training in phonics instruction. At Lakewood, she had no scholarly resources to assist her with her teaching of the curriculum. She thus relied on a commercial textbook that the school had reviewed yet not adopted, with the review copy available for her to consult. During an interview she said,

> I found these [books], and I thought well, I have to have a spelling test. And for spelling, I mean they've already done cat, hat, you know, all the easy words, so they know how to spell those. And we did the color words even though they still don't really know how to spell them. We did the number words up to ten, and so stuff around the room that they can see every day, but then I was like, "Okay, I'm running out of words." I did the easy words, c and a, and so, for me, I just looked in there and thought, this [textbook] is just from heaven because I had no idea what first graders were supposed to know.

In the absence of any guidance beyond the general imperative to teach phonics and the availability of a review-copy textbook, Tracy relied on a directive approach to teaching. She reported that she "did do some whole language with it. This week I did—last week I did all whole language. I kind of rotate weeks." She went on to say that "I think they really need phonics," yet "I don't know how to teach phonics. . . . With [the university program] I really didn't see any phonics anyway." At the level of initial decoding, she had neither the background nor the resources to teach letter-sound correspondence through constructivist means. She wished to "make it fun somehow, and right now I really can't make it fun" because of her inexperience with teaching phonics, a curricular demand that is more amenable to authoritarian than constructivist approaches.

Summary

By the end of her first year of full-time teaching, Tracy appeared to have developed a complex or pseudoconcept for the notion of constructivist teaching. Her classroom at Lakewood had all of the physical appearances of a constructivist classroom with its interdisciplinary instruction and physical de-centering. Yet the instruction was not motivated by student choice, and the physical arrangement did not socially de-center classroom authority. Constructivism had been an amorphous concept during her university program, was practiced by Sarah in both faithful and inconsistent ways under the district's term of whole language, and had become a remote influence in her first year of teaching when there was no theoretical reinforcement of the concept and where she ran into instructional challenges such as the imperative to teach phonics. This primary responsibility defied a constructivist approach beyond the notion of invented spellings—spelling unfamiliar words based on the writer's existing phonetic knowledge—which were not on the table at Lakewood.

Tracy was left to make whatever connections were available, for example, that whole language is equivalent to constructivism, and that arranging the classrooms with centers made her classroom a constructivist workshop. Without a cohesive conception of constructivism to work from, and with a deep structure that supported what she considered "traditional" instruction, a complex or pseudoconcept best served her situation: she maintained a constructivist-looking classroom that masked a teacher-and-text-centered curriculum. The problem was not that the school's curriculum overpowered the philosophy, but that her understanding of the philosophy was not well enough conceptualized to broker the curriculum in constructivist ways. Thus, the de-centered appearance remained, which the settings of the schools allowed; yet she did not socially or intellectually de-center the classroom, which the settings discouraged.

Tracy was predisposed to embrace a constructivist philosophy. Her reflections on her own schooling demonstrate her recognition and appreciation for constructivist teaching practices, even as they remained nebulous to her given constructivism's commitment to idiosyncratic constructions of knowledge and meaning, and her professors' inconsistent accounts of it and of discrepancies between what they preached and what they practiced. If Tracy exhibited a complex or pseudoconcept in understanding constructivism, that fragmented understanding originated in her course work and its conflictual presentation and practice on campus, and was then mediated in dissonant ways in schools, constructivist in many ways and appearances, and authoritarian in others. As a top student and TC, she struggled to implement the principal emphasis of her teacher education program, not due to personal shortcomings, but in response to its fuzzy conceptual presentation on campus and to school settings that valued formalist assessment in spite of constructivist appearances.

Discussion

This chapter has detailed two teachers from different programs within the same university, each problematic in its own way and each conceptually inadequate in preparing its graduates, as illustrated by these cases, for coherent teaching approaches. The programs themselves cannot, I believe, carry the whole burden of blame. Rather, they embodied conflicts in which they were situated historically. The general idea of student-centeredness was contradicted in Jimmy's university English literature courses and in the authoritarian instruction in some of Tracy's teaching methods classes. The schools themselves in turn provided environments in which conceptual and pedagogical inconsistencies were never addressed or resolved. Perhaps a coherent teacher education program could have at least allowed for critical reflection on the difficulties of enacting constructivist teaching in schools that include formalist assessments, but neither appeared to have had such opportunities on campus. Nor did the schools provide the critically aware and reflective MTs that Grossman and Thompson (2008) hope for, in spite of the general excellence of the guidance and modeling that both Jimmy and Tracy received.

I focus here on Jimmy and Tracy, and Kim and Sarah, because they were so highly regarded in their schools and on campus. Their difficulties with teaching in conceptually coherent ways speak to the challenges of working within conceptually conflicted settings, and of learning pedagogical concepts, either not at all or erratically in coursework. I reject the idea that the teachers featured in this chapter and, throughout this volume, call for more selective teacher education admissions standards and thus smarter teachers, as argued by Levine (2006). The people featured in this chapter were respected, lauded, and rewarded for their teaching excellence, without always meeting university ideals. Perhaps we need realistic teacher educators more than we need ideal mentors and TCs, and a greater recognition that taking courses on campus cannot provide the full-blown conceptual unity that few teachers ever practice. In this chapter I have not even addressed the challenges presented by mandates that impose formalism and high-stakes consequences for not teaching the right and wrong of the curriculum. I take that matter up in the next chapter, in which I look at how curriculum and assessment mandates produce frustrations and frank discouragement for teachers whose ideals get crushed by the weight of the testing apparatus that teachers and schools increasingly face.

7

Policy, Practice, and Disruptions in Concept Development

In this chapter, I focus on one teacher from each of the two Secondary English Education programs featured in this volume, both of whom landed jobs in schools that were subject to external mandates. At the district level, Andrea from Atlantic Piedmont University was required to teach a curriculum that was centrally established and subject to a common district-wide test. At the state level, Leigh from Southern Plains University taught eighth grade in a state in which all eighth-graders had to pass a writing test for which the rubric specified a five-paragraph theme. Their teaching needed to work within the contours provided by these high-stakes assessment vehicles, and Andrea's teaching had to follow a script so that each ninth-grade class in a large and economically diverse district got the same instruction.

The cases unfolded quite differently, and the sources of variation might involve a combination of personal dispositions and school experiences, university training, and comfort levels with the specific mandates responded to. Both were highly regarded by their teacher education faculty and received outstanding ratings from the schools in which they taught. Both took jobs in affluent, comfortable communities and schools with, in many ways, enviable work conditions. The mandate-driven curriculum and instruction produced different effects on them, however. Andrea was far more frustrated with her teaching than was Leigh, for whom the formulaic five-paragraph theme was not the restrictive influence on her instruction that many attribute to it. Had they changed places, it's hard to say whether or not Leigh might have been the one grinding her teeth on a regular basis under Andreas's district's scripted curriculum.

These cases allow a look at how teaching in the context of mandates affects teachers' concept development, without coming to generalizable conclusions. They feature two top TCs from their states' namesake, and thus most competitive, public universities, teaching in affluent suburban school districts where the students were largely college-bound. These seemingly cushy destinations, however, did not necessarily provide them with opportunities to put into practice what they understood to be their best teaching, particularly in Andrea's case.

As is always the case, arguing from small samples has its perils. At the same time, in-depth studies of individual cases allow for intensive looks into processes whose revelation might inform discussions of how such curricular impositions as standardized curricula and assessments work at the classroom level and within teachers' conceptions of their work. I, thus, am not making broad, definitive claims based on this close look at two teachers. Instead, I'm offering their cases as examples of how curriculum and assessment mandates can affect practice and attendant thinking in terms of pedagogical concepts, with the understanding that they could not possibly represent all beginning teachers working in such contexts, even as they might represent the experiences of a certain type of teacher in certain sorts of settings.

Andrea: Teaching within a Prescribed District Curriculum

Andrea had grown up in prosperous suburbs in the US Southeast, attending schools with test scores much higher than national and state averages, and with national recognition for excellence. Ninety-four percent of students in her school system continued their education after high school, 87 percent of whom enrolled in colleges or universities. Andrea was a high achiever who took enrichment and gifted courses throughout high school. She described her education as "traditional" or "old school," which she said she had "admired as a student because I worked well under it. It is very direct, very straightforward. It allows the student and teacher to feel as if there is a great deal of control involved in the process of education."

Her undergraduate college education was similarly authoritarian. An English major, she fit well with the department's canonical orientation and reliance on lectures, a method that met Andrea's expectations:

> I feel that when you come to college you have accepted a certain path of education, saying you are more willing now to be a receptacle and more independent. When I showed up to those classes I got and expected lectures. . . . The student at that point chooses to study a subject that they are better able to study, and therefore they can deal with the fact that it is not presented to them in an easy, or not an easier format, but isn't tailored to striving to help them understand it.

Her writing in her major consisted entirely of literary criticism, which she "never felt attached to," yet wrote "well enough so that I was never really asked to rewrite it or to think about it."

She decided to teach after graduating and enrolled in a master's program at the same university, one that certified her to teach. Her education classes were mostly populated by undergraduate education majors and a smaller number of other master's students. She entered her certification program with expectations based on her own formalist education to that point:

> I was just bound and determined, I wrote on my application, "I am going to teach grammar. I am going to teach diagramming." I don't know why that didn't make them throw me out to start with. . . . I had an argument with my mentor teacher. I said that people were too soft on grammar and that more hard grammar needed to be taught, and I had arguments with anybody who would stand still long enough for me to debate the issue with them. I sat on those front steps and cried because

somebody challenged my ideas. And then finally after four months of resistance to the inevitable conclusion, I went ahead and decided it was true. They didn't need that kind of grammar, and it just broke my heart because I was so ready to give it to them. That was definitely one of the most painful ideas for me to give up.

The Atlantic Piedmont University English Education program has been documented in prior chapters. The conflicts she recounted in abandoning her views on grammar followed from the student-centered emphasis of her university program and its rejection of her own formalist orientation. Conventional understandings of the apprenticeship of observation would predict that, once in schools, she would be fated to default willingly and easily to her authoritarian schooling, especially if those values were present in her sites of teaching and shaped her practice. Yet she wholeheartedly embraced the program's values to the point where teaching in accordance with a prescribed curriculum oriented to right-answer district exams became a difficult task for her once she was in her own classroom.

Andrea recognized that the student-centered education emphasized in her certification program was at odds with her own education, describing her program as promoting "progressive, liberal education," one that, she said,

> I now realize that [is what] most of the world needs. [An education] that doesn't necessarily let you feel like you are in control, because in real life you are not. It allows for more exploration, connection of education with experience and building scaffolding of various concepts. . . . A lot of times by trying to structure and direct, you sort of get in the way of what would naturally have happened and have been more beneficial for them if you would have let it happen the way that it was going to happen for them. I feel like in a classroom where you are not trying to constantly interfere with each student, students of different levels of ability could naturally coexist and feel challenged in one classroom.

Andrea recognized that "there is not just a class of little me's somewhere. [Formalist teaching] would work if it was just a class of little me's." Rather, she began to shift away from being authoritarian and toward an emphasis on personal connections with learning, abandoning her faith in the value of the detached analysis of texts. Her account of progressive education included a belief that teachers should not get in the way of "natural" processes, mirroring her university professors' lack of direct instruction in teaching methods. Rather, her professors relied on TCs to work out for themselves how to implement the general student-centered values they advocated for in their campus classes, without getting in their way. Yet much that happened in her teaching sites indeed got in the way of anything "natural" that might have unfolded in a world unencumbered by structure and guidance of the sort envisioned on campus.

Student Teaching

Andrea did her student teaching in a small, rural high school in an agrarian county where about 90 percent of the students were White and 10 percent Black. Andrea taught both the "general" (i.e., lowest) track seniors and an Advanced Placement class. Andrea said, "I would say that there is a wide difference between what is viewed as a good teacher [at the university] and what is view as a good teacher" at the school. Her MT, Stella, said that "theory is good if it would work [the way her professors believed], but it doesn't," suggesting less seamlessness between the teacher education program faculty and their group of MTs in schools than Andrea's professors believed or acknowledged. Andrea's professors, for instance, impressed on her "the theory that maybe you should have students write each day in the classroom. Stella would say, 'But, they don't like to write. They get frustrated. They don't like my topics. I don't have time to grade all that.'"

Andrea often felt handcuffed by requirements and at odds with the curriculum she was required to teach, even though she had unusual liberties. Stella's mother was quite ill during Andrea's student teaching and was frequently absent, and Andrea's university supervisor made rare and unhelpful visits, leaving the research observations and interviews as her principal opportunities for reflection on her teaching. During one of these visits, she described Stella's instruction as lacking strong curricular integration: "I feel like they're getting a potluck teaching approach, kind of a little bit of this and a little bit of that, which I just—I don't know what to do, to be honest, to remedy that." In contrast, her first job provided such a thoroughgoing straightjacket that she felt frustrated by the ways in which the curriculum and assessment largely effaced her perspective, planning, and judgment from her instruction.

First Job

Andrea accepted a position at the palatial Deer Creek High School (DCHS), one of twelve high schools, and seventy-five schools in total, in a large and diverse district in a major metropolitan area. DCHS was a *U.S. News and World Report* Outstanding American High School, a National Blue Ribbon School, one of *Newsweek*'s top 500 schools in the nation, and a [State] School of Excellence. Its students and faculty, along with the school's School Parents, Teachers, Students Association, had won many state and national competitions. DCHS had high enrollment in gifted programs (23.2 percent compared to the district's 10.6 percent and state's 6.5 percent) and had little evidence of poverty, as indicated by:

- Low numbers of students eligible for free/reduced lunches (0.7 percent, compared to the district's 32.9 percent and state's 43.4 percent)
- A low dropout rate (1.3 percent compared to the district's 6.5 percent and state's 6.5 percent)
- Low enrollment in vocational labs (39.6 percent compared to the district's 47 percent and state's 55.5 percent)
- Low enrollment (4.2 percent of its students) in special education.
- No Title I program, no ESOL program, and no students enrolled in remedial education

The district as a whole, however, was large and diverse, and included urban schools with greater poverty and cultural diversity among the students. The county school system's administrators were concerned that students at schools like Deer Creek were getting a more demanding curriculum than those in less advantaged communities. In order to avoid creating disparities in expectations for the district's less advantaged students, the curriculum developers were asked to prepare a centralized, standard curriculum for all students. Assuming that low-performing schools' poor test scores followed from low expectations, the administrators strove toward equity in the form of what it called a "tightly held" curriculum designed by county teachers.

This curriculum specified the instructional and assessment materials, and their pacing and sequencing, for each course in the district. Each teacher got a binder that scripted the teaching for each English/Language Arts course in grades 9–12 so that all teachers for each grade level throughout the district would assign the same literature on approximately the same day, ask the same questions, and use the same assessments. This curriculum was tied to standardized county-wide tests that assessed students after each unit, requiring teachers to follow the curriculum guide faithfully. These tests mirrored the format for the SAT, whose test scores helped account for DCHS's reputation for excellence and whose specter in part shaped the school culture. The school instituted "PSAT Week" during which, Andrea said:

> We have to all wear a t-shirt on Monday that encourages them to study for the PSATs. Every student in every class, okay? English and Math has to—on Monday has to spend their whole class period administering a test for it. And every single class period has to spend a minimum of twenty minutes doing prep exercises for the SATs for the rest of the week.

Test-taking hints were included in the daily announcements. Freshmen were required to participate in PSAT week to prepare them for their sophomore year, and the district covered their costs.

Andrea's first-year assignment consisted of five classes of regular-track ninth-grade English. The "potluck" ninth-grade curriculum itself was organized in a seemingly random sequence. Andrea felt that many of the prescribed literature selections were unappealing: "I find myself very frustrated because this curriculum does not resemble what I want to do in my classroom.... The awful part is that the curriculum is boring in addition to everything else. The stories are mostly unchallenging. The students don't connect with them . . . this curriculum does not care if the students have a love of reading." Andrea felt that the curriculum was distant from the interests of the students, making it difficult for her to establish the kinds of connections that she'd learned to value in her university coursework.

Andrea's Teaching within a Prescribed Curriculum

Andrea approached her teaching of the tightly held curriculum with three different stances, none satisfying:

- Acquiescence (acceptance of, compliance with, or submission to the curriculum)
- Accommodation (a grudging effort to reconcile personal beliefs about teaching with the values of the curriculum)
- Resistance (opposition to the curriculum, either overtly or subversively).

Andrea was not alone in disliking the curriculum, saying, "The faculty think the curriculum's ridiculous. Everybody thinks it's ridiculous. It's amazing to me that basically the county office can say you must teach naked every Thursday and I think everybody would come to school naked on Thursday and just say, don't worry, this will wear off." Andrea was discouraged by her colleagues' compliance with the curriculum, even as she continually accommodated her beliefs about good teaching to its requirements. She described the university's "ideal classroom" that provides an "organic environment" where teachers "have individual goals for your students, particularly tailored to their strengths and weaknesses and something that they could even apply within their own self-motivated assignments." At Deer Creek, she said, "I don't have that kind of classroom, and I'm not under the illusion that I do. So I think one of the most dangerous things that I see is that there's this hybrid classroom being created that does not achieve the goal of either school of teaching. And so ends up someplace in between," in conceptual and practical limbo.

This unsatisfying hybrid produced a strain in her teaching of Audre Lorde's poem "Hanging Fire." Prior to reading, to prepare them for a poem centered on a fourteen-year-old's life dilemmas, Andrea asked the students about their interests and concerns. She then began an activity in which the students were given words from the poem and asked to work with a partner to come up with connotations. These pre-reading activities provided the grist for a discussion about what the poem might be about. After they read it, Andrea led a discussion about the poem's meaning, and then had the students reread the poem, followed by another discussion focused more on details of poetic language. Following this discussion Andrea had the students return to their partners to come up with an interpretation of the poem.

Andrea's class appeared to embody the student-centered ideals valorized in her pre-service courses. Yet she found it unsatisfying. She said that she had chosen the poem "because it's the poem that they ask the county questions about on the test . . . and I wanted our discussion of it to be fresh in their minds as they sat down to take the test. So I left it to the day before the test." Andrea then acknowledged that her role in the discussion was more directive than it first appeared: "The county questions will ask a question and will give an answer that I don't necessarily agree with. But in the course of the instruction I will attempt to purposely convince them all to believe that this would be the answer to this kind of question." On the most recent district test, for instance, there had been a question about the Constantine P. Cavafy poem "Ithaka," taught in relation to a unit on Homer's *The Odyssey*. Andrea said,

> One of the questions asked, What values—or what themes does this poem emphasize? And the answer that they wanted you to choose from the multiple choice questions was Odysseus's—or the importance of home and family. And—but in the process of reading the poem, the poem really talked a lot more about the value of the journey. And so I thought—oh, I really hated that that was the answer to that question. But in the course of the discussion I attempted to convince the students that were they ever asked that, they should answer that it was the importance of home and family. Pretty pathetic, I know. Sorry. What else am I supposed to do?

Andrea's accommodation to the district curriculum led to the hybrid classroom that she found so frustrating: at once both student-centered, in her effort to help the students make personal connections to the poem's themes as she understood them, and test-centered to help students do well on the district test.

Andrea's MT at Deer Creek, Janet, believed that "Andrea's a very gifted, natural teacher. She has presence. . . . Morally and ethically she was really ready to be a teacher." Andrea had a strong identity as a teacher (see Alsup, 2006), one that provided her with a sense of self so strong and consuming that she found any compromise to her beliefs to be a betrayal of principle. This integrity came into play during acts of resistance, when she undertook subterfuge against mandates that constrained her efforts to teach a student-centered curriculum. In November, she reflected on how she had accommodated her view of the ideal classroom she'd learned at the university to survive at Deer Creek. She said, "I appreciate the fact that what they were teaching me in the program was a certain ideal that I may not attain this year or next year or the year after. That part of what you do is try to incorporate as much of that ideal as you can into what the current educational reality is." She still wished to

> come back to fighting for room for the student in the classroom, student voice and choice and direction of their education, as well as just keeping them interested instead of subjecting them to their own education. So that's sort of what I think of as my philosophy of education. You know, consider the student. . . . Sometimes you think that maybe people don't notice that there are students in the classroom.

This effort was difficult for Andrea within the confines of the district curriculum. She admitted that

> The only way I got through the first few months of teaching was saying, well, I'm going to quit next year, so just have to make it through this year. And I think now I'm feeling a little bit more like okay, well, I don't really want to quit. I just want to, you know, rewrite the curriculum, which may not really be an option either. But at least I can—I am beginning to feel like well, I can have some influence and I can practice some rebellion, and I can see what I can shake up.

Here Andrea reveals a transition from accommodation to resistance, if not yet overtly or loudly. For her unit on the dystopian novel *Fahrenheit 451*, she gave students four genres—art, video, drama, and music—for producing collaborative interpretations of the novel, and said, "They seemed to really enjoy it, a lot more than they enjoyed reading the book actually. They hated the book, but they enjoyed doing the project. I got a lot of neat video projects that ended up being really fun. And several musical interpretations. One group even brought their whole band over." When asked whether these projects were part of the district curriculum, Andrea replied, "No. They sure weren't. . . . I just did it. And curriculum be damned." For the next required unit in the curriculum on The Family, she intended to teach Paul Zindel's adolescent novel *The Pigman*. Asked whether the book came with the prescribed curriculum, she said, "It didn't, no. It was one of the books lying around discarded in the book room. And it's basically not even on the list. So [whispering] I just did it."

Resistance allowed Andrea to use instructional practices that met her goals for teaching in ways that engaged students with the curriculum and made their interests and interpretations come alive. These occasions of resistance came when other priorities with high-stakes consequences, such as district test preparation and its demands for correct interpretation, were not compromised. By accommodating the competing goals of meeting formalist testing demands and building knowledge from students' lives and experiences, Andrea created a hybrid classroom that provided a full commitment to neither and a sense of frustration in her own assessment of her teaching.

By late March, Andrea felt frustrated at the teacher she had become. She said,

> I never feel like what's supposed to be happening is happening. It's making me feel bad, and I'm not doing a good job, and lots of times I don't really like who I am in the classroom very much. I feel very controlling and authoritarian. And when the kids say they don't want to do it, and they're bored, and it's obvious, and I just feel the same way. I would just rather say, okay, you're right, let's not do this. Let's do something else. I have to be constantly telling them no, don't do that, stop talking, listen to me, turn around, sit down, hush. I have just been bitching at these kids all day and I'm tired of bitching. I feel like a big grump.

Her feelings of frustration led to occasional feelings of acquiescence, much like those that she had criticized in her colleagues earlier in the year:

> My dad said at the beginning you were just so distraught, and you seem still upset, but not as if you're just crazy anymore. And I was like, well, you know, if somebody just keeps hitting you and keeps hitting you day after day, you just get to the point where you're not surprised anymore. It still hurts but, you know, you're not offended.

This acquiescence came at a cost. By year's end she said, "I'm not a good teacher. I'm an awful teacher. But I'm also not allowed to try to be a good teacher, so there you go. But now at this point I'm feeling so frustrated that I don't even know if I could be a good teacher if they gave me the freedom to try." Some teachers would have been very happy to have worked under this system, because it removed from their lives the demanding task of instructional planning and the need for professional growth. Teaching is, to them, a job. For Andrea, teaching was her identity of the sort that Alsup (2006) concludes should predict a dedication to a teaching career. The frustration that she felt was that the curriculum took over the role of planning and *did not let her work enough*. As a result she did not like the teacher she often had to be, and felt fearful of the teacher she might become.

In Andrea's case, then, the requirement to teach within a prescribed curriculum leading to a district-wide test produced frustration and difficulty in enacting the sort of generalized student-centered approach she had grown, grudgingly at first but ultimately wholeheartedly, to appreciate on campus. Her belief in the value of student-centered teaching became an ideal that was difficult to realize within the confines of DCHS's county's tightly held curriculum, and its effort to provide an equitable education to students across its many and varied schools. Practicing her university professors' values and using them as the template for her own conception of effective teaching proved to be impossible in this setting, no matter how attractive the teaching job might appear based on the school's abundant resources and school-ready students. Although small acts of resistance were available to Andrea when the stakes were low, she acquiesced and accommodated for the most part in her teaching practice to the demands of the curriculum and the preparation of students for its assessment.

Her experiences illustrate a phenomenon identified by Scribner (1997) in her study of a milk factory production line. Presumably, such work would be rote and strictly repetitive, and on the surface it undoubtedly is. Similarly, teaching according to a scripted curriculum is often described as mindless (Milner, 2013), zombie-like (Demko, 2010), and other terms that assume that going through someone else's motions involves no thought or originality. Scribner, however, found that within these routines, milk factory workers are continually making judgments and thinking creatively within the contours of the repetitive motions.

Andrea was hardly thoughtless as she enacted the scripted curriculum in coordination with the other teachers in her district. As a teacher, she thought about a great many things over the course of every period and school day. In addition, she fought against the curriculum script she was required to follow faithfully and, when available, undertook subversive actions to teach in ways she felt appropriate. A scripted curriculum is surely a straightjacket of sorts. Yet within its limitations, teachers can resist and create when the consequences of their actions do not work against students' performance on the assessments that drive the curriculum and instruction script.

Andrea's conception of effective teaching thus got a rude welcome at one of her state's most admired schools, leaving her wondering if she was fit for the profession and its formalist demands, in spite of how well such an education had worked for her in her own K–12 and undergraduate experiences. After a year of full-time teaching, which marked the end of the research period, her practice appeared to embody what Vygotsky (1987) would call a complex or pseudoconcept, although not because of her own conceptual confusion. Rather, her teaching exhibited a strain resulting from a conflict between her values and the demands of her teaching setting, one in which the goals of neither the student-centered nor teacher-centered traditions could be met wholeheartedly. For Andrea, the mandated curriculum, instruction, and assessment thwarted her ability to realize in practice the ideals she had developed on campus, leaving her frustrated and wondering about her future in the classroom.

Leigh

Leigh got credentialed through the Southern Plains Secondary English Education program and taught in middle schools for both student teaching and her first job.

As a first-year teacher, she spent a good bit of instructional time having her students write five-paragraph themes. This formulaic essay gets harsh treatment from many teachers, theorists, and researchers who find it more stifling than useful. The model that students are instructed to imitate includes five paragraphs: an introduction, three body paragraphs, and a conclusion that restates the introduction in light of the topics of the body paragraphs. Often, the structure of individual paragraphs is specified as well, such as the imperative to begin each body paragraph with a topic sentence, followed by five to eight supporting statements that include examples supporting the topic sentence, around which the paragraph must cohere with unity.

Kennedy (1998) characterized the five-paragraph theme as the paradigmatic exemplar of the "formalist ideal" (p. 37). Hillocks (1986) argues that instruction that relies on the imitation of models "leads some students to the notion that they must sit down and produce a finished essay without the necessary intervening processes" (p. 228), with the five-paragraph model the most common exemplar to imitate in schools. It is often specified in rubrics used on high-stakes writing tests, even those requiring, strangely enough, narratives (Hillocks, 2002). Given its dodgy reputation among writing experts, it's important to understand its persistence in English classes. In prior work upon this account of Leigh is based (Johnson, Smagorinsky, Thompson, & Fry, 2003), my colleagues and I speculated on this phenomenon, and identified a set of reasons for its durability in classrooms, as articulated in scholarship on the topic:

Acculturation to traditions of schooling: The apprenticeship of observation often produces the replication of practices experienced during one's own education, especially in the absence of alternatives in teacher education and other sources of knowledge of writing pedagogy. If beginning teachers did well with five-paragraph theme instruction themselves as students, it could conceivably serve as their fallback pedagogy when they are called upon to teach writing, especially if their preservice program, like Leigh's, did not include a course in writing instruction, instead packing all preparation to teach in a single methods course of a semester's duration.

Limitations of teacher education programs: English Education programs have often been faulted for emphasizing literature instruction at the expense of writing instruction (Kiuhara, Graham, & Hawken, 2009; Lillge, 2019; Morgan & Pytash, 2014; Tremmel, 2001; Zuidema & Fredricksen, 2016). Language (mainly grammar) instruction in teacher education does not even show up in internet searches, perhaps because discrete grammar instruction has shown quite poorly in research in either improving writing or improving grammar (Hillocks, 1986 and many other reviews) and is frowned upon in academia, if not schools and their testing demands. (Chapter 10 focuses on learning to teach grammar.) In the absence of attention to writing pedagogy, beginning teachers may rely on what they know from experience for the writing strand of the curriculum; and what they know from experience often emerges from formalist traditions.

Shortcomings of teachers: Emig (1971) believed that teachers do not read or write very much and thus have limited knowledge or vision to guide their teaching, and so teach five-paragraph themes because of "teacher illiteracy" (p. 98) and "neurosis" (p. 99). To Wesley (2000), "teachers of the five paragraph theme . . . have become complacent in their acceptance of a tool that purports to nurture but, in fact, stunts the growth of human minds" (p. 57), although this claim has no factual basis. Ignorant, lazy, careless, unreflective, mentally disturbed teachers are the culprit to these critics, relying on formulas in the absence of thoughtful, principled practice.

Poor work conditions: Lott (1996) sees poor work conditions—too many students, too little planning time, too few resources, too imposing a bureaucracy, and other burdens and limitations—driving teachers to take shortcuts. Nunnally (1991) finds that "as a response to the task of instructing multiple sections of over-enrolled classes, the explicitness of the five-paragraph theme—the discreteness of its parts and their functions—makes it practical to teach as well as eminently gradable" (p. 68). From this perspective, the five-paragraph theme provides an easily teachable, learnable form for teachers overwhelmed with too many students and too little time for planning and grading, making formulaic instruction an appealing fallback for teachers.

Institutional pressures: Wiley (2000) believes that formulaic writing is "easy to teach, easy for students to grasp and apply, easy to produce prompt results in raising students' standardized test scores" (p. 61) and "replicates what is found in high scoring essays on district-wide tests and AP exams" (p. 61) through which they are held accountable. With schools often evaluated on their students' test scores, schools may pressure teachers to teach to high-stakes, mass-administered tests, including those evaluating writing, no matter how ignorantly constructed they might be (Hillocks, 2002).

Potential as a genre: Dean (2000) argues that the five-paragraph theme can be a useful "genre" when teachers "see beyond the limitations of the form to what else it could be" (p. 54). She asserts that form-oriented writing instruction can provide students with a structure for generating and expressing ideas. Others might question this claim because it attends largely to formal features of a text, whereas sophisticated genre theories emphasize social action and communicative purposes that respond to the discursive and ideological expectations of communities of practice (Bawarshi & Reiff, 2010), and not such surface features as the placement of a topic sentence, a staple of five-paragraph theme instruction.

In the case of Leigh, I would rule out shortcomings of teachers, given that she was a highly regarded student in her state's namesake university, getting certified in a master's degree program after earning outstanding grades as an undergraduate. Her work conditions were quite favorable, ruling out that interpretation. I next review the specifics of her case and consider the most viable interpretations in light of the most common explanations for the persistence of the five-paragraph theme in schools: that she had little training in teaching writing, defaulted to five-paragraph theme instruction because it had served her own education well, and found herself teaching to a state writing test that used a five-paragraph theme rubric to evaluate her students and, by implication, her teaching. She did so in the absence of severe institutional pressure to do so, although her colleagues did apply peer pressure to meet high pass rates on the exam.

Background to the Study

Leigh had grown up in a prosperous small city in the same state as her namesake university. She had earned a BA in psychology at the same university in which she then took her teacher certification course work as part of her master's degree. She hoped to be like a teacher from her own background who had been on "a personal level with us. She didn't just stand up there and lecture. She was willing to work with us one on one." Leigh aspired to find "creative ways to engage the students to have them relate what we're studying to maybe their personal life experiences . . . . At least it makes students feel like they're a little more in tune with what they're studying." She said that her memories of what she felt like as a student strongly influenced her approach to teaching: "The thing I draw on most is probably trying to remember back when I was in eighth grade." Her apprenticeship of observation, then, provided a very student-centered model toward which she aspired as a teacher, a value very much in tune with her orientation as an undergraduate psychology major interested in human development and school engagement. It also included formalist instruction in five-paragraph themes, with which she had succeeded in her own schooling, giving her a high comfort level with such a pedagogy. As this research consistently demonstrates, then, the two-worlds pitfall rarely involves discrete settings, with schools conservative and authoritarian and universities progressive and student-centered. Rather, each involves complex webs of experience that straddle multiple pedagogical traditions.

Leigh's experiences in the university program followed from its structural fragmentation and absence of a course in writing pedagogy. With little formal training in the teaching of writing, she was left with two primary sources of knowledge to guide her instruction: her apprenticeship of observation, and her colleagues in her student teaching site and first full-time teaching appointment.

Student Teaching at Walt Whitman Middle School

Leigh did her student teaching in a sixth-grade class in Walt Whitman Middle School in her college town. Her mentor during her student teaching was Mrs. Hoover, who allowed in an interview that "I never really thought I wanted a student teacher because I'm one of these control people. I like having control over my classes." As I will detail, her control-oriented personality was manifested in her formulaic approach to teaching writing and strict adherence to rules governing the compositional product.

Mrs. Hoover's writing instruction for her sixth-graders focused on writing paragraphs and addressing grammar. She stressed the *five-sentence paragraph* that included, Leigh said, "a topic sentence and then three supporting sentences and a clincher sentence." Mrs. Hoover evaluated paragraphs for what she called *content* and the *mechanics* of grammar and usage. Content, she said, "is if they follow directions. Do they have a right and left hand margin? Did they indent for each paragraph? Do they have five sentences per paragraph?" Mrs. Hoover served as Leigh's primary source of writing instruction. Her university supervisor visited infrequently and offered little useful advice, and her university coursework included attention to writing pedagogy as one facet of unit planning in her single methods course.

Under Mrs. Hoover's mentorship, even that staple of the student-centered toolkit, journal writing, became a vehicle for formalist instruction. Vocabulary lessons involved pretests, memorizing word meanings, and then testing, after which, said Leigh, "we have them write journal exercises using their spelling words." The process-oriented approach of drafting their paragraphs also served formalist ends. Students were required to show that they had "clustered"—that is, produced a nonlinear outline—and written a first draft before a final draft of a paragraph could be graded. Students who turned in paragraphs without the cluster or first draft were sent back to produce these preliminary stages, generating the outline, generally assumed to be a planning device, after the fact of writing the composition (or in this case, the paragraph). Leigh explained to Mrs. Hoover her response to a student named Lou, who turned in a paragraph without the steps that had led to it:

> Lou was wanting to turn his in, and I said, "No, you're going to have to go back." Plus he only had like maybe four sentences per paragraph, and I told him that's not—he's not going to get a good grade if he doesn't follow the directions. Because I told him to start over. . . . He could use [paragraphs previously written] as his rough draft, but the clustering, I told him to go back and do the clustering for each of those paragraphs that he wrote.

Mrs. Hoover's guidance provided the primary setting in which Leigh learned a writing pedagogy, apprenticing Leigh into a formalist perspective heavily reliant on rigid teacher direction and assessment according to textual features and specified processes. These practices were at odds with the engaging instruction that she said that she valued and hoped to provide her students with. Like Andrea, she appeared to be at conceptual and practical odds with herself in response to the contexts that shaped her understanding of how to teach writing, without the levels of self-awareness exhibited by Andrea. This is less a criticism of Leigh than an observation that she felt reasonably comfortable enough with formalism, and had been taught few alternatives during teacher education, leading to a perspective that included little doubt or resistance to an emphasis on structure as the primary basis for writing instruction.

First Job at Sequoyah Middle School

Leigh's first job was in Sequoyah Middle School (Sequoyah MS) in a homogeneous and relatively affluent suburban community with award-winning schools and students. Sequoyah had impressed her when she interviewed, leading her to say in retrospect, "This was about the only one I came out thinking, 'I would just die to have this job.'" Her primary administrator, Dara, was a former English teacher with an MA in English Education. Dara liked a "noisy classroom. . . . When I hear a certain level of noise, I know . . . that's the sound of learning." Leigh also had a mentor, Katherine, who observed her class occasionally and met with her weekly, primarily for support. Leigh was a member of one of three teaching teams for the eighth grade, whom she relied on particularly for management matters: "The team helped probably just as far as dealing with individual students, but not really with my actual lessons or anything like that I was teaching."

She also sought advice from other English teachers for pedagogical or curricular assistance, saying that these colleagues "gave me a lot of ideas. A lot of the units I did I took from them." These colleagues greatly influenced Leigh's decisions about how to teach writing. Leigh's administration was highly supportive. Her principal led the faculty in book clubs where they read novels and met monthly; he also formed student book clubs that included guest visits from noted authors, including Gary Paulson. The school administration and faculty placed a great value on literature, and they tried to establish a climate in which reading was valued and rewarded. This unusual relationship made Sequoyah MS a comfortable, supportive place for Leigh to establish her teaching career.

Leigh's teaching was affected by two state mandates. The state English/Language Arts curriculum required what Leigh described as "Narrative, descriptive, expository, and persuasive paragraphs, and longer compositions that establish and support a central idea with a topic sentence; supporting paragraphs with facts, details, explanations or examples; and a concluding paragraph that summarizes the points." These specifications suggested five-paragraph themes in accordance with the rubric used for the state writing test that her eighth-grade students were required to take and, for the sake of Leigh's job security and the school's reputation, pass.

At Sequoyah, there were multiple motives and values in the key settings in which Leigh learned to teach writing. Her administration encouraged Leigh to teach in noisy, open-ended, and experimental ways, with near indifference toward the state mandate requiring preparation for a five-paragraph theme to test their writing proficiency. Her colleagues, however, influenced her to teach more restrictively in preparation for the writing assessment.

Leigh's use of the five-paragraph model clashed with other values she expressed regarding the need for students to connect with their education. Leigh's psychology major had emphasized information processing, through which she had learned about the critical role of *prior knowledge* in students' connections between their personal worlds and the texts they read and wrote in school: "I keep trying to draw on things they've learned. There's a word, schema and prior schema. I like for them to draw on what they know. And I also find myself trying to relate as much [as possible] this literature and what we're doing to their lives."

Leigh embraced student- or response-centered approach to teaching, filtered through the potentially restrictive five-paragraph form. She continually referred to her prior instruction that year in the five-paragraph theme, with the expectation that students could build on previous lessons to improve their performance on new efforts. For this instruction, she relied on a series of handouts provided to her by her colleagues, who applied pressure on her to emphasize the five-paragraph format to increase her students' pass rates on the state writing test, even as her administration viewed test preparation with less urgency.

One observation illustrates how she taught the model. Before having the students begin their writing, she led a discussion in which the students generated content for their essays, similar to how Hillocks (1995) advocates for generating ideas in conversation prior to writing so that students begin with material to work from. She also included attention to the process for generating the various paragraphs, reinforcing procedural knowledge from prior lessons in how to write the essays. In December of her first year at Sequoyah, field notes recorded the following:

> Leigh asked them to take out their 5 paragraph essay handout on "The Pearl" [by John Steinbeck]. She said, last week we practiced writing an essay, not worrying

about grammar but focusing on the format. What we're going to do now is work on an essay about Tom Sawyer so we can get more and more practice. Look at your essays and the comments I made on your comments. Look for the star where I made my second round of comments. Use those comments to help you on the next essay. Before we get started, what do we need to do? Prewrite, say the kids. What else? Pick a topic. Think about things to write about, she said. Give me some ideas. [Kids suggest issues from *Tom Sawyer*.] Let's talk about writing the essay, said Leigh. We have five paragraphs. What are they? A kid said, an Introduction, a body, a conclusion. Tell me about the intro paragraph. What do you put in your first sentence? A thesis, said a kid. Good said Leigh. What else do you include in the intro paragraph? You tell how you support it with your three reasons, and put a transition sentence. Paragraph #2, what goes in this? Reason #1, said a kid. Good, said Leigh. What about paragraphs 3 and 4? Reasons 2 and 3. Remember to stay on topic, she reminded them. If you are writing about superstition, and your first one is warts, make sure you only write about warts. . . . Concluding paragraph, some of you struggled with this in your career papers. Mike, read your concluding paragraph. Mike read. OK, said Leigh, he had an introductory sentence. Then what did he do? He restated his three reasons. Then what? He restated his thesis. Leigh wrote this on the board and stressed that this is how they needed to write their concluding paragraphs. What paragraph does this resemble? The introductory paragraph, she said. Now, what do you need to do? Write, said a kid. What do you need to do first? Pick a topic, he said. What do you write first? Your intro, said a kid. Leigh said, once you write your intro, you're set. You're going to have to look through your books, through the handouts—those are summaries of each chapter. These are tools for you to use. This essay will require a rough draft and a final copy—last time we only wrote a rough draft.

This instruction was almost exclusively formalist, reinforcing to the students the features they would need to include. She relied on students to provide the class with the proper elements of the theme, suggesting that this drill was well-rehearsed from prior lessons.

Early in the second semester, one week before the state writing test, Leigh led the students through practice on two different five-paragraph themes. One was a new essay that they began in response to the prompt Leigh provided from a previous state writing assessment. She told the students that the assessors looked for evidence that the students had revised their essays, so she focused on revision for the second theme, with special attention to their introductory paragraphs. She emphasized the form expected by state writing assessment evaluators and how the content of their ideas could fit into this form. Leigh's writing instruction was thus heavily influenced by the state writing test and, while including attention to content generation, focused on what assessors would look for in their essays.

Dara, recognizing Leigh's anxiety about the state writing test, did not discourage her from teaching the five-paragraph theme, yet also encouraged her to see beyond its limitations. When Leigh told Dara that she was "worried about this writing test," Dara replied that the school's 99 percent pass rate on the test should temper her concerns, yet "by teaching them a real formula kind of writing that they can access when they need it, which is when they'll need that, that's the best you can do. . . . On the other hand, I don't want them to think that's the only way to write." Dara downplayed the importance of the five-paragraph theme on other occasions as well, encouraging teachers to give reminders in outlining and identifying "kernel points" to teach "the real basics of a five-paragraph essay without writing a five-paragraph essay."

Leigh, however, remained concerned that "they are going to be taking this writing test. They are going be going on to ninth grade. If I don't do my job at this point, they are going to be hurting." MT Katherine approved of how Leigh prepared them to write five-paragraph themes:

> I know that she has done an excellent job of teaching writing skills because in my class I have my eighth graders do three assignments that involve writing a formal five-paragraph essay. And I always have my kids tell me what team they're on, and the students that have had her for English do a super job in writing paragraphs and writing five-paragraph essays. So I know she's done a really good job of teaching writing skills.

Leigh revealed the kind of guidance provided by her colleagues when discussing her instruction in the five-paragraph theme:

> That's something that I've talked a lot to the other two eighth-grade English teachers about, and so they've helped me on that. But they just said, "Give them lots of practice. Have them practice writing this essay as much as possible" . . . because that's kind of the structure they look for when people grade these writing samples that they have to give.

The setting of Sequoyah MS thus produced conflicting guidance in how to teach writing. Her colleagues' attention to the state writing test, and Leigh's success in teaching toward its rubric, led her to be constructed as an excellent teacher of writing. Her administrators no doubt appreciated her focus on this mandate, given how it reflected on their own performance. Yet Dara recognized that students from affluent communities like theirs usually passed the tests no matter what sort of instruction they received and thus encouraged, if not convincingly enough, Leigh to explore more creative approaches to writing.

Leigh's acquiescence to the formalist demands of the curriculum appeared to come without the sort of rueful accommodation and efforts at resistance that accompanied Andrea's teaching of her restrictive "closely held" curriculum toward district tests. Teaching toward the state test, seemingly without question or concern, appeared to be a dutiful response to a curricular demand that left her conceptually untroubled. Yet in relation to the state test, she often referred to *pressure* and *stress*, a psychological state she perceived in her colleagues and experienced herself. In late September she said that her students needed

> to learn to write because eighth grade takes that writing test in the spring and that's a big thing with this writing test which all the teachers stress about. . . . I want them

to focus on being able to write an essay. You know, giving me a thesis statement and backing up your thesis statement, and just your basic old boring essay. . . . I think more and more I'm focusing on structure so that they can write that.

In January, weeks before the state writing test, Leigh felt the stress weighing on her, saying,

> I don't feel like I can spend any other time on any other type of writing [than the five-paragraph theme] right now. I have all these other things I want to do as far as writing, but up until they take this test, I don't feel like I can do anything else. . . . I'm just trying to get them ready for this test. And I've told them a hundred times that's my goal, and we need to work on this. . . . I feel like I can't do as many fun activities and different activities. And maybe once I've, like I've said before, maybe once I have some more teaching experience and know what to expect with this writing test a little more and know what works and what doesn't as far as helping them write, then I can vary a little bit. But I think definitely because just like I said, I'm going to let them do some more creative projects in writing after this writing assessment test is over. Right now I feel like I'm just pounding it into them. It kind of stresses me out. This whole writing test stuff.

Much of the stress she experienced came from pressure applied by her colleagues. Leigh said, "I've never heard like if they do awful, that you're going to be fired or anything like that, but I've heard it reflects on you. . . . One teacher commented to me, she said, 'Well, you're lucky you have honors kids because your tests will be higher than mine.'" Dara had assured her that her students would pass without intensive preparation, yet Leigh's colleagues emphasized the precipitous nature of the test scores in terms of their reputations as teachers. Leigh meanwhile worried that "I'm not even sure what I would do for another type of essay" because of her limited preparation to teach writing.

Several years later, Leigh was asked about her teaching of the five-paragraph theme. She wrote,

> During my 3 years of teaching 8th grade English I was extremely stressed about the 8th grade writing test/writing the 5 paragraph essay. Although we practiced it a great deal, I was still stressed until the tests were turned in. I became less anxious as the next 2 years passed. The students seemed to have a firm grasp on what was expected and seemed to be able to write good essays in trial situations. . . . I did really feel pressure to teach to the test, but I could manipulate each essay assignment or relate it to our current novel, so it didn't become too repetitive. We also did continue to work on 5 paragraph essays along with other types of essays . . . after the test was over. That way they would not forget that method of writing; however, we also used it to compare to other types of writing.

Leigh's remarks during her fourth year of teaching suggest that the test was still foremost in her planning of writing instruction. Rather than providing greater variety, she would continue to work on five-paragraph essays even "after the test was over" lest they forget the form. She explained why the five-paragraph theme still dominated her instruction:

> The pressure of the writing test mainly came from my 8th grade English colleagues. I think they explained to me how important this was so I naturally assumed the stress. The scores . . . are reflected through the school as the results are published annually through the city newspaper. Our school has a history of doing extremely well in the writing test so that was always a nice reward to see the 98-99% passage rates. . . . My colleagues also taught the same writing method—there are 3 8th grade English teachers at our school. They all felt the same pressure I'm sure. I didn't feel much pressure from the administration. . . . I'm not sure I ever discussed it with them [though] I did discuss it with Dara my first year.

Leigh was affected by forces acting collectively on Sequoyah's teachers to uphold the standards of their school and maintain the high passage rates the community had come to expect. The surrounding pressure from the state and community to teach to the test influenced the eighth-grade English teachers to emphasize the five-paragraph theme to the exclusion of other writing, and Leigh gravitated to these norms. The combined pressures of state writing test, community values on high test scores, and faculty response to those influences appeared to supersede the effects of administration's encouragement to teach writing in more creative ways and diverse genres. University theorists might find her pedagogical reliance on this form to be a disturbing indication of her competence, but within her school, it made her a valued member of the faculty.

The five-paragraph theme's durability in classrooms has been attributed to acculturation to normative teaching practices, limitations of teacher education programs, personal shortcomings of teachers, poor work conditions in schools, institutional pressures from without, and/or a belief that it may serve as a useful genre. One, personal shortcomings, does not account for Leigh's instruction. Leigh was viewed as an outstanding prospect in one of the nation's select Blue Ribbon schools; in Dara's words, "Leigh's about an eight [on a scale of ten]. She's really got it together. . . . She's very poised and articulate and confident." Leigh also did not work under poor conditions. At Sequoyah, she had a sensitive and supportive administration that promoted literacy instruction, an outstanding facility, high-achieving students, supportive parents, competitive salaries, and other attributes.

The other four reasons appeared to be at work. Leigh's own positive experiences with writing five-paragraph themes as a student predisposed her to accepting the state's mandate as reasonable and fitting. Her teacher education program's single methods course had emphasized the teaching of literature and had involved no articulation with other courses, leaving her with little conceptual framework for critiquing the five-paragraph theme or developing a rationale for teaching writing in other ways.

Mrs. Hoover's mentorship at Walt Whitman had encouraged Leigh to emphasize the form of writing individual paragraphs, and at Sequoyah, her colleagues pressured her to teach toward the state writing assessment. Leigh learned in these settings that the five-paragraph theme was as an important and necessary tool for teaching writing to promote a high pass rate among her students. In taking her colleagues' advice to "give them lots of practice" with the format for the state writing test and by using the handouts that they had prepared for their own instruction, Leigh grew more secure as a member of her English department, becoming the "team player" her colleagues and administrators appreciated.

Reputations were at stake, including Leigh's within her department, Sequoyah's within the competitive district, and the district's relative to other similar communities in the metro area and around the state. Along with her deeper belief that the form was a useful instructional tool, it is no wonder that Leigh focused on teaching the five-paragraph theme and considered it a useful genre, if pass rates on the state writing test are the measure of a good writing teacher.

Discussion

This chapter has featured the cases of two beginning secondary school English teachers who taught under the pressure of formalist demands in the assessment of their students and, by implication, themselves, their schools, and their communities. Carrying the weight of those expectations in response to those mandates shaped their practice and thus their evolving conceptions of being good teachers. One common criticism of case studies is that they may be idiosyncratic, and thus not amenable to generalization (Stoeker, 1991). I do not offer these cases as proof of a point. They do, however, demonstrate how some beginning teachers, who undoubtedly represent a subset of other cases, experience mandates in their development of a conception of effective teaching of literature (Andrea) and writing (Leigh).

These cases suggest that concept development is subject to many factors, including those omitted from beginning teachers' education programs, such as learning how to teach writing in university programs. Yet Andrea's generally student-centered program lacked specific ideas about how to teach in student-centered ways, instead relying on her to figure out how to teach from students' interests or on colleagues to serve as pedagogical mentors, without attention to how school settings might mitigate against that possibility. Andrea found herself frustrated by her inability to circumvent the scripted curriculum and the sorts of answers to questions asked on the district test. Leigh appeared to share congruence with the value of the five-paragraph rubric, yet felt stressful pressure in doing it well.

Leigh appeared to be growing toward a formalist understanding of how to teach writing, and so it developed rather smoothly into the conception valued in her setting, if not without anxiety about how well she was doing it. She managed this growth without appearing conflicted, perhaps because she was able to work in strategies for generating content for the form. She illustrates a developmental conundrum embodied in the question, *Development toward what*? The teleological end toward which Leigh developed involved practices that worked well and were routinely and consistently mediated in one setting (the school). Yet these same practices and the end toward which they are directed violated many tenets of writing instruction favored by most theorists and many pedagogues, aside from Dean (2000) and those who share her confidence in five-paragraph theme instruction. If conceptual unity and acceptance within a community of practice are the measures of success, then she developed a sound concept. Yet that same approach is much reviled in other settings. To return to points articulated earlier in this book and posed in Smagorinsky (2013), social concepts are never clear and thus are difficult to conceptualize in the midst of contradiction. Judging Leigh's teaching, if that is the game here, thus becomes a very local matter, one impervious to a single logic or set of values.

Andrea's experiences left her feeling far more conflicted, given that her program of study had provided her with a core set of beliefs, if not practices, to serve as the basis for her teaching, even if they violated the values she had developed through her own schooling. The apprenticeship of observation in her case is less deterministic—in fact, not at all—than often is the case when Lortie's (1975) foundational study is invoked. The program's intensive and relentless focus on students, I infer, helped to shape her perspective on the most appropriate form of schooling, one centered on students' interests. Yet her teaching was consistently thwarted in practicing a student-centered pedagogy that met her own standards, with the district's scripted instruction and closed-ended test warping her teaching and leaving it, conceptually and practically, swirling in contradiction. She recognized and understood these contradictions and felt great internal disjointedness when preparing her students for tests she did not believe in and whose answers she often found wrong-minded. Unlike Leigh, who was shepherded toward formalistic writing instruction as a desirable norm, Andrea experienced greater dissonance in finding ways to teach that matched her emerging value on student-oriented instruction.

Mandates, then, can affect teachers' concept development in important ways. They are idiosyncratic in relation to personality, formative experiences, university preparation, institutional values and pressures, personal relationships within institutions, students' response to instruction, and many other factors. Teasing out the mandate as a solitary variable would require more sophisticated analytic tools than are available to me, especially when the mandates themselves are dissimilar. Yet overlooking them as factors in teachers' concept development appears untenable as they affect what is possible for teachers to enact in their classrooms.

8

School Settings and Course Assignments in Shaping Conceptions of Curriculum and Instruction

Does what you teach, and whom you teach, affect how you teach? In this chapter I make the case that a teacher's assigned course load and the traits of the students enrolled, situated within school settings, shapes both the practice and the conceptions of effective teaching. I draw on case studies focused on teachers whose student teaching took place in English/Language Arts classes designed for students taking a vocational curriculum, or in classes whose students were described by the teachers as having similar characteristics. In addition to conventional English emphases on literature and writing, vocational English classes have a workplace readiness emphasis that assumes that students above all need socialization to a specific sort of workplace. This assumption is based on the premise that the students lack basic courtesies and social skills, from knowledge of how to shake hands to an understanding of propriety and compliance. Their engagement with the subject of English/Language Arts, then, becomes embedded in a broader effort to direct their conduct so that they may fit well within vocational contours that may not represent the sort of work they aspire to do upon graduation. This focus affects how teachers construct students and their purposes for being in school, in turn shaping their development of a conception of pedagogy.

Jackson (1968), in describing the hidden curriculum, exposed the intangible, systemic forces that help to shape the behavior of people within schools. This aspect of the deep structure of schools promotes a deferential stance through the structure of the curriculum, the assumptions made by the teacher, the respect accorded to texts, and other factors that place students in a subservient position. The hidden curriculum includes "subtle or not-so subtle messages that are not part of the intended curriculum" (Nieto, 2000, p. 28). To use Cole's (1996) term, it is *proleptic* (Cole, 1996): adults' assumptions about the social futures of children implicitly shape their present action to bring about those very futures. It is also teleologically motivated (Wertsch, 2000): that is, activity is directed toward an optimal outcome presumed of participants, in this case, the workplace, narrowly and specifically defined. These factors suggest the need for educators to consider whose values become institutionalized in the school structure, how teachers' understandings of their work are shaped, what social futures are projected for students, and how teachers help to bring about those futures.

The hidden curriculum is thus engrained in schools at many levels (Kentli, 2009). Jackson (1968), McCutcheon (1988), and others find the classroom to manifest it most clearly. Meighan (1981) locates classrooms in the broader construct of the school. Apple and King (1977) argue that schools always instantiate values that they inherit historically such that they "embody collective traditions and human intentions which, in turn, are the products of identifiable social and economic ideologies.... The curriculum in schools responds to and represents ideological and cultural resources that come from somewhere" (p. 343). These sources, in spite of their generally old age, have enduring value in accounting for how schools undertake the process of socializing students to ideologies and the conduct that supports and promotes them. Relatedly, they account for how teachers develop conceptions of how to teach in the setting of schools.

The hidden curriculum works differently for students of different socioeconomic backgrounds in anticipation of different social futures (Anyon, 1980), with students from working-class families shepherded toward obedient roles low in workplace hierarchies, and children from executive backgrounds encouraged to show initiative and assertiveness. The reproduction of the social division of labor (Williams, 1977) is thus stratified in school structure and tracking systems (Sadovnik & Semel, 2010) that provide both different curricula and different roles for students in anticipation of their life trajectories. The assumption of these social futures is accompanied by assumptions about the students' acculturation and dispositions. Smagorinsky and Taxel (2004, 2005) found that character education has often been viewed as especially important for those students who come from lower socioeconomic backgrounds, who are from immigrant families, and who otherwise tend to be found in lower and vocational tracks in a school curriculum. These students are assumed to lack a good work ethic, an understanding of proper conduct, and the qualities that serve the machinery of commerce well, including punctuality, respect for authority, effort and investment with unpleasant work, thriftiness, and other traits that Weber (1930) ascribed to Protestants and their progress toward prosperity and heaven.

These values were present in the instruction of three teachers participating in the research drawn on for this book in their work with students in vocational tracks and regular tracks enrolling similar sorts of students. In spite of university training emphasizing the student's personal interests and needs, they found that in these teaching assignments, they could not rely on students to construct personal learning trajectories unencumbered by a teacher's imposition of standards or values. This chapter is not designed to judge whether or not the students were responsible for the instructional lockdown on student freedom, or whether or not the teachers' work within the curriculum and broader value systems was responsible for their disengagement. Rather, these cases illustrate how teaching assignments can shape teaching conceptions in relation to students' degrees of affiliation with school, engagement with the prescribed curriculum, goals for being educated, plans following graduation, and other factors that contribute to instruction that they find worth investing their time and attention in.

Three Beginning Teachers and Their Working-Class Students

All three teachers taught either vocational-track classes or working-class students resembling those enrolled in the vocational classes. Two of the teachers taught a vocational English class that had a character curriculum built into its workforce education curriculum. The other provided a de facto character curriculum for her rural, working-class students in a nonvocational English class as a way to improve their work habits. All three attended the Atlantic Piedmont Secondary English Education program that emphasized students at the center of the classroom, with instruction driven by their needs and interests. Yet in all three cases, the students' interests were jettisoned in service of instruction designed to prepare them for entry-level office jobs. Their needs were assumed rather than solicited, imposed rather than cultivated, and in turn were directed through a combination of curricular design and teacher choice situated within broader contours, including MT apprenticeship and the school's social order.

Prior to student teaching, each of the three teachers expressed a resistance to authoritarian teaching methods such as top-down management, formalism, and other ways of positioning teachers in judgmental roles and texts as magisterial accounts of culture and history (see Chapters 3 and 4). Once in their teaching assignments, however, they abandoned this student-centered epistemology, replacing it with an assumption that the students were not taking advantage of their educational opportunities because they lacked fundamental dispositions required of a strong work ethic.

The Teachers

I next profile the three teachers. Joni and Samantha were assigned vocational-track courses that emphasized both the domain of English and the workforce readiness. Brandy taught working-class students who were in nonvocational English.

Joni. Joni did her student teaching in the only high school in a rural county of roughly 46,000 residents, locally described as socially and politically conservative. Joni taught Applied Communications II, which primarily enrolled twelfth-graders and was classified in the lowest of the school's four tracks. Her MT said that

> Applied Communications [enrolls] students who are hopefully tech[nical] school bound, maybe someday. Probably the majority of them, though, will go into the work force next year, so we try to spend a lot of time [on workforce preparation], and I think it's real important for them to be ready for that. So [we teach] all kinds of communications skills. . . . [The students] are all vocational because applied communications doesn't count [toward graduation] for the college prep students. . . . The main concept they're supposed to get in the class is how important communication is . . . in life and the workplace. And they do that through learning about negotiation skills, good customer service.

Joni's first job was in one of fourteen high schools in a large metro-area district where she taught a sophomore course in the vocational Applied Communications curriculum that included fifteen students classified with behavior disorders, attention deficit disorder, and other special needs requiring Individualized Education Programs. Joni said that the curriculum was focused on workplace skills:

> They need to know things such as how to fill out—they're going to learn how to fill out résumés, fill out job applications, you know, write technical—technical writing, different things like that.... We're going to do the reading, writing, and thinking, but we're also going to add in the things you need to know for the workplace, since most of them are going probably directly into the workplace.

Joni thus began teaching with consecutive-year assignments in vocational English classes, teaching noncollege-bound students through a curriculum designed to socialize them to their presumed destination as entry-level workers in blue collar jobs.

Samantha. Samantha did her student teaching in a rural town in which 8 percent of families and 9.7 percent of the population lived below the poverty line, including 12.3 percent of those eighteen years old or younger. In this chapter, the analytic emphasis is on her student teaching. She is also featured in Chapter 11 in a much different setting for her first job, where her teaching took on a far different cast. In the site of her student teaching, the lower income students tended to end up in vocational classes, according to Samantha: "We have a lot of kids who come from families on welfare. We have a lot of kids who just have a hard time.... A lot of my kids... read between a second or third grade reading level." They often enrolled in Applied 1, the lower of the two vocational English courses and the one Samantha taught. Samantha's MT, Jude, said that

> We take the literature and their writing and gear it all towards workplace communication. And so just to help them make it in the world, to be a constructive citizen. When they get a job to be a leader on that job, to be a good worker.... [Applied 1 is] a hands-on course, sort of work-related a lot of the time. You know, career-focused.... [The students are] not planning on going to a four-year college. [They learn] basic life skills. This is how you write a letter. This is, you know, these kids are targeted because of low socioeconomic, low reading skills, writing skills, that sort of thing.

Samantha added,

> A lot of them have no plans on going to college, and Jude told me the sad fact is a lot of the ninth graders will drop out. So, I am looking at my kids, and I'm knowing that some of these kids could very well drop out as soon as they hit sixteen [because they] are just not highly motivated.... A lot of them have jobs, after school jobs, or girlfriends, or activities, [or babies, and they] put homework on the low end [of their priorities].

Brandy. Brandy did her student teaching and took her first job at the same school, one that enrolled 1,400 students and served the most rural and least affluent of the county's three school districts. Brandy's first year of full-time teaching is also treated in Chapter 10, centered on the teaching of grammar. The US Census Bureau reports that county residents in the site of her student teaching earned on average 16 percent less per capita than people throughout the rest of the state, and this number was even lower for the 12 percent of the total population who were African American. Sixty-eight percent of adults in the county were high school graduates, and 7.5 percent had graduated college. Her school data were not disaggregated from the county data; presumably the poverty and low graduation figures were amplified among the families in the school in which she taught, given its low ranking in demographic categories.

Brandy taught eleventh-grade Honors American Literature during student teaching and both ninth-grade "regular" track students and ninth-grade Honors students in her first year of full-time teaching. She often expressed concerns about her students' lack of motivation and commitment to academics, and how it affected her teaching, regardless of track. Before an observation, for instance, she cautioned the researcher that

> When you observe me, it is not me, because I have found that I have got to be so stern with this class. We really cannot have fun because the minute we start to have fun, they take it and they run.... I have to be so very controlling in this class, and it's really frustrating because it's not me. I think learning should be fun. Should not be one task after another after another with no discussion. Discussion techniques do not work in this class. A lecture does not work. I haven't figured out what works.

The Character Curriculum at Work

All three teachers emphasized a set of character traits in their teaching, each designed to prepare students for a specific sort of workplace and particular roles within it. The curriculum—and by extension the teachers—assumed that the students had less of an affinity for school than the university teacher education program's ideals would suggest. These ideals featured progressive, student-centered pedagogies that assumed that all students will engage with schooling enthusiastically if they are granted control over their own learning, an ideal thwarted in the classrooms of these teachers. Their presumed character shortcomings needed reform, in the eyes of the teachers and the vocational curriculum, in order for them to work effectively in entry-level roles in the service economy, with curriculum and instruction designed to enhance their entry into and trajectories within those bounds. I next review how the curriculum, and the students enrolled in these teaching assignments, shifted the conceptual trajectories of these three teachers from one grounded in romantic ideals of intrinsically motivated youth undertaking personal inquiries avidly in order to govern their own destinies, to one reliant on externally imposed structures designed to teach character traits, such as discipline, more than the English/Language Arts curriculum.

Work ethic, discipline, and control. The Protestant work ethic was a central value in the classrooms observed for this research, with instruction designed to improve both the students' work ethic and their motivation for performing assigned tasks. To Samantha, the root cause for her vocational students' lackadaisical approach to school assignments was their unhealthy resistance to work: "It all ties back into work ethics. It all ties back into their attitude and the way that they're doing things." These attitudes, she believed, led to behavioral problems, failure to complete assignments, incidences of cheating, and other forms of noncompliance in relation to school tasks, with the assumption that disengagement in school indicated a lack of a work ethic, a fundamental value of US character education initiatives (Smagorinsky & Taxel, 2004, 2005). Her formative teaching experience prior to enrolling in the Atlantic Piedmont Secondary English Education program had been as an assistant in a Montessori school where teachers supported the "natural" development of children and allowed them autonomy to define and undertake their own learning experiences. This conception provided a good fit for her coursework on campus.

Her vocational students, however, did not share this disposition for self-motivation in relation to schoolwork, leading Samantha to institute rules and consequences to enforce their compliance with academic responsibilities. In the absence of a work ethic that would produce volitional cooperation, regardless of the perceived value of the task, Samantha imposed an external disciplinary structure compatible with her MT's interpretation of both the students and the curriculum. The agreement of her MT, handpicked by the university faculty for her compatibility with their values, with this unromantic view of the students belied the "seamless" claims of her student-centered professors about the ideal relationship between school-based colleagues and the university program.

Brandy lamented the poor work ethic of both her Honors and "average" track students, of whom she said,

> They won't even pay attention in class. . . . The kids don't think much of [the textbook]. But I've about decided these kids don't think much of anything. . . . They just do not seem to want to put forth the effort, and they want to write sentences like "See Jack run." . . . It makes me wonder if they have not been socially passed [i.e., passed to the next grade level regardless of classroom performance] and are now expecting it. . . . They're in for a very rude awakening. . . . If you ask them to get out a pencil and paper and write something, their body language, they throw themselves around in their desks and, "Oh, I don't believe you're going to make me write two words." It is just—their attitudes need a lot of adjustment. . . . I'll sit down and I'll say, "What a good idea," plan something, and then it flops. And so far I haven't had any success with very much in this class. It's so depressing.

Her solution was to lay down the disciplinary law as a way to promote a stronger work ethic, to impose structure and consequences, in violation of the progressive values she had learned on campus and had espoused prior to student teaching. To get students to complete an assignment, for instance, she provided a draconian due date, and then relented and extended the deadline. She later acknowledged that she had never intended for the original due date to be enforced, but rather had imposed it in the hopes that it would motivate her students to work diligently in class. On another occasion, when students' responses in class suggested that they had not read an assigned novel, she warned them that "there will be an exam. You better read." Her stern approach was designed as "a wake-up call because I wouldn't—I will be honest. I was really mad. So

I kind of met them at the door and said, 'You will need your *Huck Finn* book and you will need about ten pieces of paper.'"

Brandy's punitive approach was administered around the time of Parents' Night, where she told the parents that their kids were not taking school seriously. She did so out of frustration and in hopes that the parents would get the message; and the parents "went home and chewed them out, and they realized, 'I'd better straighten my act out.'" In the days that followed, said Brandy, the students "were actually interacting for a change and not sitting there like a lump on a log. And even their essays looked so much better this time. . . . The entire week they were angels, and they really put their noses to the grindstone and started working."

The students' compliance thus came in response to threats from their parents and Brandy. Their motivation, she initially assumed, would be intrinsic, as her professors on campus believed. In relation to the tasks of the English curriculum, however, she found them unwilling to engage. Their reluctance to do assignments left punishment as Brandy's primary vehicle for getting students to endure and complete work they found tedious and irrelevant. This belief about students' disengagement from school and the need for punitive consequences for noncompliance produced a conviction that students needed accountability measures to get them to complete assignments.

Joni, for instance, said that "I tried to be the liberated new teacher who wasn't going to have quizzes all the time and stuff, and found out very quickly that you have to give them quizzes, even though I didn't want to." She experienced frustration in trying to enact an interesting curriculum for students who, she found, resisted her instruction:

> I just try to make any sort of connection, something kind of interesting for them to hope they'll grasp onto it. . . . They all hate English . . . and they hate to read. So it's really hard for me to get them interested in anything. And unfortunately a lot of the stories in the books are not too interesting. . . . I thought they'd really get into [the Reginald Rose drama] *Twelve Angry Men*. Some of them did, but I almost think it's a worthless battle, me trying to search around and hunt for things, because they don't get into anything.

The students' dislike of reading, she felt, rendered much of her university training otiose and idealistic:

> We learned a lot of really neat things in the classes at [the university]. But I think a lot of them could only be used in certain settings with the students. And my students are not to that point. Maybe my seniors would be. But a lot of neat and innovative ideas, my students cannot handle them right now. I've tried to do things that make things interesting and neat, and they still don't respond.

Samantha similarly lamented her students' dispositions: "They're just not highly motivated. [My MT] and I are still kind of working on how to deal with that. So it takes a lot of hooking and prodding[1] to kind of get them to complete things sometimes."

---

[1] "Hooking and prodding" is a rug-making technique requiring meticulous patience.

Samantha used assessments to help students stay on task, saying, "I can assess them to see if they can follow directions.... Another assessment I might be able to get from it is sort of a motivation, how motivated are they, how—and staying on task, those sorts of things I can kind of assess." All three teachers, along with their mentors and colleagues, interpreted the students' indifference to school to be a lack of work ethic, requiring the inculcation of better work habits and punitive consequences for those who remained resistant.

Cultural conventions. The teachers emphasized a range of cultural conventions that they believed the students would need to succeed in their jobs. Joni said that the Applied Communications curriculum sought to teach students behaviors, rituals, and expectations for workplace success through such activities as mock job interviews conducted by people from local businesses. Joni said, "The people they interview with are going to actually have like a check sheet sort of thing telling us how they do. It'll have a thing like how they dressed, how they spoke, correct grammar, all those types of things," including how they filled out job applications. The students got feedback on "how they dressed, how they spoke, how they answered questions." She said, "We'll probably talk more about body language. And one thing we need to work on is the handshake," one requiring a particular approach, posture, and grasp.

The cultural conventions imparted through this part of the curriculum envisioned a specific sort of workplace, the business office, and was dedicated to preparing the students for entering it and acting appropriately within it. Other sorts of workplaces where people get dirty, speak in colloquial ways, work within other sorts of hierarchies, and in general do not follow the rules of business office propriety were not considered among the students' vocational trajectories. I've argued (Smagorinsky, 2018b) that ignoring such contexts can miss the mark of students' actual lives and purposes. The school curriculum envisioned either a college destination for some students or an office environment for the rest, ignoring the many other ways of earning a living available to the students in these teachers' classes. This assumption in turn helped to shape the teachers' conceptions of how to prepare their students for life beyond school.

Respect, relationships, and discipline. Joni reported that her students had "more problems with respecting each other than they do respecting me. I know we need to work on respecting each other" for school, work, and personal relationships. Samantha explicitly built instruction in peer respect into her teaching to address relational problems she found among her students:

> I'm starting to feel like we need more of a community building kind of thing because people are going to have to learn how to work together in this class.... Part of the whole Applied I philosophy is learning how to deal with other people and communication in the workplace.... I'm going to try to design with them a contract that we can all live by. And then [do] some more community trust-building kinds of things.

The Applied Communications curriculum's character education modules were dedicated to topics such as interpersonal conflict, which Samantha could choose to accompany the literature curriculum. She chose a module on Communicating to Solve

Interpersonal Conflict because "some of them are somewhat abrasive, and some of them dislike working with anyone who's not their best friend. . . . They really need to kind of learn how to work with people, especially the work environment when you can't choose [your partners]. . . . One of the sections they did today talked about looking at things from a different point of view" to help them learn conflict avoidance and resolution.

These interventions were designed in relation to the broader problem of disrespect for authority shown by their students. Brandy reported that she had "a lot of behavior problems. . . . This is a class that has no respect for authority. As a teacher, I am told by this class over and over and over, 'You can't do that.' And I just look at them and say, 'Watch me.'" They would "just have to learn the hard way" who was in control of the classroom. Brandy herself had learned "the hard way" to abandon romanticized views of her students: when the school library couldn't lend books to students due to a computer glitch, Brandy checked out books for them, and four students neither returned them nor repaid her, costing her over $120. Adjusted for inflation, this total would amount to $180 in 2019 dollars, a substantial amount for a beginning teacher in a state with a low salary scale relative to the national average.

Brandy attributed her students' "horrible, horrible test scores" to the issue that they "have absolutely no self-discipline and cannot establish their own reading schedule, and they just decide it's not important to read. . . . [It] falls into any teacher's realm to teach them self-discipline and the importance of following through. This seems to be their biggest weakness." Joni drew a similar conclusion, tied to the issues of disrespect that she found to undergird their conduct in class:

> They're taking advantage of some of the situations in the classroom [such as] the constant talking when I'm talking. We talked about respect today. . . . I said, "We have a lot of discipline problems in this room. I think we need to talk about it, and you could help me decide, or we could all decide what the problems are." We listed them on the board and what we think the consequences should be.

Samantha said that in response to unruly behavior, she and her MT had come up with a variety of solutions, including establishing a seating chart and such measures as "detention and parent call. . . . I hate doing stuff like that. But I'm getting to the point where it's going to be necessary." Another solution she resorted to was to eliminate dead time. She said,

> I want to keep them busy. I want to keep them so busy that they don't have time to talk to each other and don't have time to play practical jokes, like turn the heat up to 90 or erase things off the board that I've written. . . . They just do the whole screwing around thing, and it's just really annoying. . . . I've got just lots of stuff planned, and my goal is to keep them busy so that they don't have time to do this stuff. . . . I purchased a timer and I've been setting it more often for activities so that when it dings . . . I say, okay, time to move on to something else.

Samantha described instruction on the Middle Ages and its literary figures, for which student groups made factual presentations. Following the presentations, said Samantha,

> I wrote up a little paragraph about the Middle Ages, leaving out key words that were in the notes, and that was on their test. So and I'm going to let them know. It will be the same thing when we do the Restoration test. I will just—you know, I'll do the same thing. I'll write up a paragraph, leave out key words, as long as you study your notes, you'll be fine.

Samantha acknowledged that her students related poorly to literature of the Middle Ages. She noted that many of her students did not do homework, leaving her to read aloud in class and test students on their attentiveness. Her students, she said, would tell her,

> "I won't read it. I won't read it if you tell me to do it for homework. I just won't." . . . That's the reason I'm having the quiz on Thursday, is to find out who did read. Part of what I think is going on is—part of it is that they're not taking me seriously. Oh, she's a student teacher, you don't have to listen to her. . . . I'm trying to get them interested in the Restoration, but I'm still also trying to keep them busy and keep them engaged so that I don't have to give anybody detention.

Keeping students busy, she felt, would help to address the discipline problems that interfered with the learning she hoped to encourage through the curriculum featuring archaic literature, in conjunction with the character education designed to teach them respect, responsibility, and other qualities. Presumably these character traits would get the students to complete assignments related to literature of the Middle Ages and Restoration periods of Great Britain, if not enthusiastically, then at least dutifully.

Perseverance. Joni described the absence of such character traits as perseverance in her students' difficulties doing assignments related to Lois Lowry's dystopian young adult novel *The Giver*, which is centered on themes of individuality, the emotional quality of life, and other elements of life in society. The novel's themes have been provocative for many English classes (Gross & Schulten, 2014), yet it did not engage Joni's students. She wondered, "Can they stay on task, which we're having a hard time with . . . . The quizzes help assess if they can stay on task. . . . If they turn in extra credit, you know they have some ambition," presumably a sign of good character. In the context of the Applied Communications curriculum, literary study served to promote dispositions such as the willingness and acquiescence to complete tasks, a sign of perseverance indicating strong character. The students, according to Joni, did not like the novel: "I fought them tooth and nail to read it. . . . It's just getting them to read is the hardest part. And I had to learn that I have to do quizzes. I didn't want to do quizzes, but I have to do them" to insure they would read it, even as it was a struggle

> just to get them to care about it and get them interested. A lot of them are probably repeating in the class. I hate to be all negative about it, but that's kind of just the facts, I guess. And we have a huge problem with absenteeism at this school. . . .

That's been my main struggle with them, is just to get them to care and to do the work. So I have to adjust my teaching likewise, I guess. I try to take up as many grades as possible because if I don't take something up, they most likely won't turn it in or won't do it. So I have to collect almost everything they do and stress to them that it does count.

Joni's instruction in relation to the Reginald Rose drama *Twelve Angry Men* about a jury deliberating about a crime that the defendant likely did not commit, and one juror's steadfast commitment to a fair trial, stressed the trait of perseverance in her students. Joni described how the worksheet she used promoted this disposition in her students:

I like this worksheet a lot because [it helped to] remind them if they didn't remember what protagonist and antagonist was. It also made them go back through the story and find examples of it. So not only did it help them, you know, back up the protagonist and antagonist [inaudible] for that, but also made them go back through and reread if they weren't paying attention the first time.... They won't go back through and find things. They'll just sit there [and say], "I don't know, I don't know how to do it." But they did really well with that one. I was really excited.... They went back and found the things they needed, the examples, without too much discussion or argument about it. And most of them got the right answers, too.

I cannot judge whether the students were as disengaged as Joni contends, or whether other sorts of teaching might have elicited their interest in these standard readings in English/Language Arts classes, each a possible source of discussion and reflection on important themes in human development and social cohesion. What is evident is how the students' disengagement with school as a whole manifested itself in Joni's class, and in the classes of Brandy and Samantha, and in turn shaped their conceptions of how to teach. On the university campus, middle and high school students were assumed to be naturally motivated to learn about life, literature, and literacy. In the classes they taught, however, the students were resistance to authority and schoolwork, and the teachers' recourse was to revert to formalism as a vehicle for promoting their work ethic, often against their own stated wishes and intentions.

Joni, for instance, tried to instill in her students a sense of compliance with her authority as a teacher, grading vocabulary presentations according to whether they "understood what they were supposed to do or not, especially following directions for the presentation. That was the main part of it, so I can see . . . if they follow the directions, and if they can get up in front and talk with people and work in groups." Following directions, she said, was the "main part" of the assessment. The content of the lessons thus became of secondary importance to the compliance of following instructions, conceived as a character trait that would serve the students beyond the lesson itself. What mattered was not learning vocabulary words, but learning how to take directions, presumed to be a valuable school and workplace disposition.

The teachers thus had to reconceptualize their understanding of good teaching in relation to the perceived habits of mind exemplified by their students' resistance to their teaching. Their recourse was to teach in accordance with the curriculum and the guidance of their MTs, shifting away from a progressive emphasis on students and their interests, and toward a regimen designed to enculturate them to a particular sort of disciplined mind and body that would serve them well in school and the workplace envisioned by the curriculum.

Time management. Samantha considered time management to be an important dimension of her students' work ethic. She gave an example of a typical occasion that revealed students' difficulty in organizing and spending their time wisely, and then staying on the assigned task: "Something I'm really hoping to pursue on Monday, the whole work ethics, wasting time. It takes us so long to get just certain small things done that we don't get to do everything that we have scheduled. . . . It's a work ethics issue definitely." Samantha said that when her students were assigned discussion questions, "they'd start talking about their boyfriends or something. So that—it goes back to the work ethics. I mean, it all ties in. It's really affecting what they're learning because I'm pulling teeth—I don't—I haven't found the right carrot to put in front of the horse."

Brandy too remarked that her eleventh-grade students had problems with time management, concluding the following: "Let's teach them time management. But how do you teach time management? You can give them the tools. You can't force them to use them. And I think that's . . . their biggest downfall. . . . They haven't figured out how to organize things, how to prioritize things." Among her solutions was to employ a timer to keep lessons moving briskly. Better time management would, she felt, help with other dispositions that the instruction was designed to promote, such as discipline, staying on task, and other attributes in both school and work.

Discussion

This chapter has focused on how teaching assignments help shape teachers' conceptions of effective instruction. The Atlantic Piedmont English Education program attended by all three had emphasized the students and their interests, encouraging the TCs to trust students to identify and develop what mattered to them as learners. It had further promised a "seamless" transition to schools, where handpicked MTs faithfully promoted the progressive pedagogies emphasized on campus. Yet during student teaching, the assignments placed the TCs in classrooms with students either in low vocational tracks or in regular track classes in which the students were described as disaffected from school and resistant to the curriculum. These assignments led to instruction based on formalist principles emphasizing right answers and correct form, the need to instill a work ethic in students so that they would complete tasks regardless of their investment in them, and external means of disciplinary enforcement to manage their behavior and require them to complete their assignments. The teaching they enacted, then, was shaped by their teaching assignments in ways that contradicted virtually every pedagogical principle learned on campus.

The vocational curriculum was designed for students headed to jobs requiring only a high school education or less. The students learned interviewing skills, including how to shake hands properly, dress appropriately, and so on. Students were instructed in responsibility, effective time management, and other character traits grounded in the Protestant work ethic to improve their prospects for success in the workplace, or at least the workplace built into the curriculum, one requiring office-style decorum for service-level jobs for which students needed to learn whole new ways of dressing and behaving.

Joni, for instance, was reported in the field notes to have said, "Guys need to wear a tie this year. [One student] wants to know what color of shoes he should wear with his pants. . . . [Joni] cautions them not to put that they couldn't get along as a reason for leaving" a prior position. The mock interviews were followed by "a check sheet sort of thing telling us how they do. It'll have a thing like how they dressed, how they spoke, correct grammar, all those types of things." Students typically, however, regarded such preparation as irrelevant to the job destinations they envisioned for themselves. Many already held jobs of the sort that their friends and family members regarded as career work: in auto shops, on construction sites, on farms, and in other lines of work where ties and proper handshakes were not required.

Joni taught her students the codes, practices, and rituals of jobs that required résumés, formal interviews, well-shined shoes, ties, and other routines and accoutrements that the students themselves believed were irrelevant to the kinds of jobs they sought and the ways they got them. Many of these students had already gotten jobs through informal, personal networks: connections through friends and family, familiarity through social relationships and common interests, frequent appearance at job sites, and other strategies more likely in working-class communities than white collar environments. Joni believed that the students did not "understand the seriousness of the résumé and the job application. So we're trying to emphasize that and what you need to be able to do it to get a good job." Her notion of "good job," embedded in the curriculum, was not the sort of job her students often aspired to, however, leading to complaints that were interpreted as signs of poor character.

The vocational curricula's character emphasis was designed, it appeared, to disrupt the reproduction of the social division of labor (Williams, 1977): the ways in which succeeding generations tend to replicate the economic patterns and status of their families of origin. Rather, however, than illustrating the Marxist critique that these patterns are manipulated by those who control capital, the desire for social reproduction came from within. Working-class students rejected the effort to redirect their life trajectories toward office environments and its assumptions that wearing a tie and firmly pressed trousers will lead to better lives.

The sort of instruction that served these ends required discipline more than creative or open-ended thinking. When Joni taught *Twelve Angry Men*, she was happy and excited that the students completed a worksheet successfully, demonstrating their perseverance with the task. This play potentially provokes discussions about social inequity, the merits and problems of the US judicial system, the role of the individual in a democracy, and other "big ideas." In contrast, the students' role was to find and label characters as protagonist or antagonist, eliding more complex questions that might invite more committed or emotional responses (cf. Berchini, 2016, for an example of how this phenomenon is reinforced by curriculum materials and teacher manuals regardless of academic track). The emphasis on staying busy and completing tasks requiring low-level fact-finding and recall created more orderly classrooms in which literary themes that might have engaged students' attention—as emphasized on campus—were not explored.

In identifying these patterns, I am not trying to villainize the teachers or even critique their instruction. Rather, I am trying to understand their concept development, which proceeded much differently from how their university program faculty's rhetoric and design would assume and encourage. Each teacher reported student disaffection, shenanigans, testing of behavioral boundaries, lack of commitment to academic assignments, and other behaviors that they and their MTs met with authoritarian measures to hold their noses to the curricular grindstone. All spoke of entering their first classrooms with somewhat idealistic notions of students' motivation to learn, and then having to clamp down with accountability measures when the students abused the assumption that they wanted to learn what was assigned.

At the same time, some observations suggested that the students had a lot to say about current and challenging social issues that came up in their literary reading. In Joni's first year of full-time teaching, for instance, she taught a low-track class in which the assigned reading was John Steinbeck's *Of Mice and Men*, which includes frequent use of the word "n*****." A number of students, both Black and White, complained about having to read it. Joni discouraged the discussion by explaining that the book was a literary masterpiece and that Steinbeck employed his characters to use the word ironically as a way to reveal its insensitivity. Students had much to say on race relations, yet Joni emphasized the literary value of the work, and then moved on to a formalist analysis of plot facts and vocabulary words.

This study suggests the difficulty of the transition that beginning teachers experience moving from their university programs into their first jobs, even when that transition is mediated by extensive field experiences in the classrooms of handpicked MTs who have input into the conduct of the program, as the university faculty claimed on behalf of their program design. All of the sixteen teachers in this research experienced dissonance of some sort, often based on school value systems that ran counter to their stated beliefs upon emerging from idealistic university coursework. The university programs' emphasis on some version of student-centered or progressive teaching came in conflict with the schools' emphasis on conformity to established norms: the alignment of curriculum and instruction with standardized testing mandates, the emphasis on conventional literary interpretations over student-initiated responses, the suppression of students' constructivist engagement with the curriculum in favor of the memorization of textbook-delivered information, exclusive instruction in formulaic writing such as five-paragraph themes on assigned topics at the expense of open-ended writing, and vocational curricula designed to instill work habits at the expense of thematic learning. As I have argued throughout this book, the superficial binary of conservative school and progressive university cannot account for these disjunctures; each is embedded in broader systems of epistemology and practice.

The teachers were agents of the school rather than individuals acting on their own. The curriculum itself assumed a lack of character in the two vocational classes featured in this chapter. Administrators are known to look down on teachers with behavioral management challenges and are not likely to hire or retain them, a profound concern of student teachers. The schools as a whole were assessed according to academic measures in the form of test scores and not on the quality of literary discussions, human growth, or students' preparation for jobs they wanted in lines of work they valued. Although a hidden curriculum may be manifest in individual teachers and classrooms, it does not occur in isolation. Joni and Samantha implemented vocational curricula that were replete with assumptions about lower-track students and their social futures. Brandy arrived at similar conclusions about her students without the formal structure of a vocational curriculum. The deep structure of the schools, and within schooling in general, helped to shape their beliefs about the need for students to develop character traits in tune with the Protestant work ethic as prerequisite to their developing into responsible students and adults.

In this sense, the two-worlds pitfall is evident in this chapter's illustrations, particularly as those worlds are more broadly situated, and as the world of school includes not only authoritarian adults but also resistant and disengaged students. Firmly opposing values were established in the two sites, or at least in the curricular tracks available for this research. Perhaps the two-worlds pitfall is most evident in low tracks where discipline and task completion serve as signs of academic achievement; we did not have access to other classrooms for a broader view of the school sites and how faithfully they manifested formalist and progressive values in ways that might complicate the simple binary between university and school. Yet the program's claims of seamless collaboration with teachers and schools suggests that rhetoric can never overcome profound epistemological differences that permeate these different locations for learning to teach, and that students' lack of enculturation to school, often through processes spanning many years, cannot be effaced by student teachers enacting progressive pedagogies in their short terms in school classrooms.

Constructing these teachers as poor candidates for the profession due to their negative construction of their students thus overlooks the difficulties that even accomplished TCs can have in learning to teach within multiple and conflicting settings, particularly those involving teaching assignments in the lower-track courses to which beginning teachers are often assigned (Kelly, 2009). These cases do illustrate what happens in classrooms in which ideals come in conflict with the orientations of students and with the curricula designed to change their course. Teaching assignments can channel beginning teachers into situations where the interests of neither teachers nor students are well-met. The settings described in this chapter were guided by limiting assumptions about the students and a curriculum that emphasized their assimilation to a specific set of norms for which they found little useful application in their social and work worlds. These cases illustrate the formative effect of the vocational assignments on the three teachers' early career development of a conception of appropriate and effective instruction, one that emphasized character education in the form of teaching students a set of qualities associated with the Protestant work ethic as antecedent to performing acceptably in either school or their anticipated work destinations.

Unlike Andrea in the previous chapter, they did not resist this characterization, but concordantly worked to use the curriculum to redirect their students' trajectories toward one that both they and the curriculum found suitable.

Consistent with how I have argued throughout this volume, I conclude here that learning to teach is not a linear process, but one that follows a twisting path (Smagorinsky, Cook, & Johnson, 2003; Vygotsky, 1987). Each of these teachers followed the immediate center of gravity, embracing progressivism on campus and formalism, discipline, and the need for a work ethic in their teaching assignments. Longitudinal data beyond the following year were not available to follow this path, which in other work (Smagorinsky, 2013) I have argued lacks a clear destination and thus is mediated over time by a multitude of often-conflicting values, requirements, and other factors. Running a progressive teacher education program does not guarantee producing progressive teachers; as these case studies show, those values can be jettisoned very quickly in the presence of other mediational means. Understanding these acculturative processes in the complex environments of learning to teach can help teacher educators take a modest view of what they potentially can accomplish with their programs and establish realistic expectations for their graduates and themselves in preparing new generations of teachers.

9

Competing Centers of Gravity within Settings of Learning to Teach

Among my main questions in these chapters is the extent to which the two-worlds pitfall, with universities providing progressive and innovative ideas and schools enforcing status quo formalism and mimetic learning, represents the realities of learning to teach. I've contested this notion, working from an assumption that the pitfalls involve multiple worlds that are complex in both the school and university environments. This chapter focuses on one student teacher, Anita, whose experiences illustrate how the two-worlds pitfall provides a very general distinction between universities and schools, but does not capture variations within each or similarities between the two.

Anita had grown up in a planned suburban community outside a major U S city. After attending a regional college for her first two years, she enrolled in the Atlantic Piedmont Secondary Education program featured in this volume, graduating from college four years after completing high school. Anita's field experiences and student teaching all took place in Ebenezer County High School (ECHS), situated in a county undergoing a transition from a sparsely populated rural community to a larger, more affluent, and more suburban county. Her classrooms represented the county's demographics: 90 percent White, 6 percent Black, and 3 percent Latin. About 6 percent of the total population lived below the poverty line. Anita's MT during her year-long placement was Will, a twelve-year teaching veteran who frequently mentored student teachers as part of the university program's handpicked MT cohort.

In this chapter, I focus on what I've called *competing centers of gravity* in Anita's learning to teach. This metaphor focuses less on individuals and their influence—for example, the influence of a MT—and situates each influence more broadly in epistemological traditions that amplify their gravitational effects. Anita's case illustrates how these competing centers of gravity are available within both schools and universities, rather than unilaterally positioning the two against one another, and how arriving at a consistent conception of how to teach can be complicated by the expectations, practices, and purposes of education suggested or explicitly required by each. Anita's development as a teacher further provides confounding problems to those who view growth as teleological, that is, toward an optimal outcome. With an explicitly student-centered teacher education program providing her epistemological foundation, rather than becoming increasingly student-centered as she gained experience in schools, she became more authoritarian over the course of the year in which she participated in the research.

This trajectory fit the mediational contours of ECHS and its socialization of youth. Yet it violated every tenet of her university teacher education program, if not her overall university experience. If human development represents growth, and if a TC changes in ways that are viewed by their university faculty as regressive, how is that teacher's trajectory to be interpreted?

From a sociocultural perspective, judgments of this sort do not comprise the theoretical task, which is to account for human development rather than to critique it. University teacher education faculty have long lamented their graduates' turn away from progressive values and their socialization toward authoritarian values; indeed, that problem provided the impetus for the CELA research I rely on for this volume. Yet school-based faculty and administrators often find progressivism to be romantic and theoretical, and see young teachers' pragmatic turn as appropriate and a positive direction for their conceptual and practical growth (Labaree, 2004). That tension was played out in Anita's experience, in spite of claims of ideal, seamless alignment between school and university made by her university professors.

The following sections review Anita's developmental pathway, beginning with her reflections on her apprenticeship of observation (see Chapter 3), including both school and university experiences, and following her through her teacher education program (see Chapter 4) and student teaching.

Apprenticeship of Observation

Anita's values were compatible with the other TCs from all three of the programs featured in this volume in valuing constructivist, hands-on, student-centered, activity-oriented teachers, and disliking authoritarian, formalist, impersonal teaching. The following sections detail how she described the good and bad teachers from her school and university experiences.

Good Teaching

Anita valued teachers who motivated students to learn through a disposition to care, encourage, nurture, and push students by engaging them in creative, activity-based, hands-on, personalized, meaningful, and expressive instruction through which diverse learners could succeed academically. She valued teachers who pushed her intellectually by emphasizing ideas rather than form and who, she said, taught her how to think. Anita described her tenth-grade English teacher's interactive methods as "just wonderful." When the class read *To Kill a Mockingbird*, the class divided into small groups, and each group was responsible for teaching three chapters of the novel, an activity that she said "was what made me know that I wanted to be one of those hands-on people." This teacher's activity-based class involved creative writing, writing in response to nature walks, and other open-ended means of expression. This instruction often included high levels of interaction that engaged students with one another, the teacher, and the material such that the class was enjoyable and promoted learning at the same time.

Anita, like many teachers in these studies, appreciated teachers who imposed high expectations on their students, those who were "very, very hard on me and really expected a lot." Her junior year English teacher, she said, "really pushed me to work hard in English, 'cause she knew it was something I was good at. . . . She always pushed me to speak in class. She pushed me to express my ideas. She pushed me to take risks when I wrote papers [and] not do the general, you know, reiterate what the teacher says." This notion of pushing students to perform at higher levels did not correspond to the nose-to-the-grindstone labor reported in Chapter 8, where low-track students were pushed to work hard on irrelevant tasks requiring persistent effort as a sign of a strong work ethic and thus high character. Rather, consistent with progressive ideals, this effort was invested to generate new thinking. To reiterate points from Chapter 8 with respect to the hidden curriculum, tracking systems can produce different identities among students, with low-track students learning to conform and high-track students learning to think and lead. This conclusion from long ago by Anyon (1980) appears to be alive and well in classrooms from a generation later and beyond, accounting well for Anita's teachers' high standards for independent thinking at high levels for students enrolled in high-track classes and presumed to have great potential.

In this vein, Anita preferred teachers who were primarily interested in the quality of the ideas that she generated in class, and who encouraged risk-taking as a way to promote thinking. The vocational classes of Chapter 8 emphasized correctness; Anita valued teachers who found errors acceptable when they followed from risk-taking. Anita "got the most from" a teacher who "encourages you to come up with your own ideas rather than simply restating what [the teacher] said, because that's what you think is the most important." These teachers, she said, "led me there and then allowed me to look for myself or try to figure out for myself, and then came back and talked about it with me." These experiences took place in schools, positioned by the two-worlds binary as inevitably authoritarian and formalist. Yet Anita drew on their modeling to envision a *projected teacher identity*, her sense of optimal developmental outcome for her own pathway as a teacher. She said, "I want to teach my students to think for themselves. I want them to analyze. I want them to look deeper. . . . If they can do that with a piece of literature, they can do that in life."

This practice of projecting a teacher identity serves a critical role in concept development (see Chapter 1). A working concept may enhance a learner's ability to anticipate how future action will unfold under circumstances that share enough traits with the contexts of learning to find application in newly developing situations (Smagorinsky, 2011). This conceptual knowledge helps teachers work deliberately and not by trial and error, both at the daily planning level and in their overall career trajectories. No one can *predict* the future. But teachers with a strong conceptual grounding can plan according to principles that enable them to *anticipate* processes and outcomes, with the caution that self-fulfilling prophesies might enter their thinking, especially in relation to situations and demographic groups whose cultural practices they do not know or understand, as Hyland (2005) and many others have found is often the case.

Anita's examples of good teaching in the progressive tradition came from her high school teachers and not her university professors. These teachers produced the images that helped her construct her projected teacher identity. As I report next, she found formalism in both sites, complicating the two-worlds dichotomy between school and university, and suggesting that the two sites are difficult to sort into two mutually exclusive categories.

Bad Teaching

Anita disliked teachers who were apathetic and disengaged from students, and who instructed through lectures, memorization, worksheets, and tests designed to promote students' learning of authoritative interpretations by memorizing single, correct answers and interpretations and reporting them back on tests. These tests required her to "cram," as she said, rather than explore and learn thoughtfully. One university English professor, she said, "didn't want you to understand. He wanted you to memorize. He wanted you to understand what he thought was important, not necessarily discuss what you thought was important."

Classes that predicated assessment on memorization involved little interaction, because the teacher did most of the talking, leaving students in a primarily receptive role. Authoritarian teachers, she said, "don't really teach you . . . . They're so into what they are talking about they've forgotten that you're teaching it to somebody." This lack of interaction prevented, she said, teachers from developing caring connections with students. They might be knowledgeable about their domain, but not interested in what students make of it on their own terms and through their own experiences.

Such teachers were available in K-12 schools, she said, although with different agendas and practices from what she found in university professors. In schools, rather than having such a commitment to their own literary interpretations that they dedicated their instruction to lecturing on them, authoritarian K-12 teachers "don't care, they don't want to be there, they don't want to teach you. They just want to give you a worksheet, they want you to be quiet, they don't want to give you a chance to talk, and they don't want to listen to your opinions." Schools thus provided Anita with models for both progressive and authoritarian pedagogical models, with her personal disposition leading her to value open-ended, risk-worthy inquiries over what she found to be tedious and unstimulating memorization and repetition, even of high literary theory.

Pedagogical Teachers at the University

Anita, like others from her Atlantic Piedmont University program, felt that her English Education professors were more theoretical than practical. She said that "the books we've read this quarter are just so much about the philosophy instead of the practicality." In Chapter 6, I refer to the "fuzzy concepts" available in the two Southern Plains University teacher education programs, and the Atlantic Piedmont English Education program's idealistic, student-centered emphasis that elided attention to specific practices would qualify for inclusion in this category as well. Anita's English

Education professors, according to the TCs participating in the research, were reluctant to teach specific instructional methods, preferring instead to present a general student-centered framework within which TCs would find its practical application either in their imaginations or under the guidance of a school-based MT theoretically selected for alignment with university values. "Most of what I've used in my school," she said of her initial teaching experiences, "has been what I've thought about myself in the beginning." Aside from occasional ideas such as writing literacy autobiographies, which she and her classmates were required to do by their professors for a course assignment, she found most of her campus classes to have little practical application.

Other required education courses emphasized diversity among learners. Her Educational Psychology class introduced her to "learning styles and the different theories about how people learn." Her Special Education course taught her "about the different types of learning disabilities or physical disabilities that are things that I'm going to be faced with as a teacher." Anita's teacher education program, then, emphasized understanding diverse, individual learners without providing concrete teaching ideas. This attention to diversity, at least as reported by the case study participants from this program, did not include attention to cultural issues such as race, gender, socioeconomic class, and other categories. Rather, the faculty validated a conception of diversity oriented to individual biographies, biological points of difference such as learning disabilities, and individual differences in learning styles. The students, as they are in most university programs, were primarily White and female, as were the professors. Their individual biographies were grounded in the White middle-class experience, suggesting limitations of personal reflection in teaching effectively with populations from outside the teacher's personal experience.

Student Teaching

Anita's year-long placement at ECHS was accompanied by the team-taught courses on campus in the fall semester. Anita did not refer to these university classes during her gateway interview, suggesting the prominence of the school site in her thinking about teaching. This influence of the school might be interpreted in different ways. To Cibulka (2009) in his role with the National Council for Accreditation of Teacher Education and its practice-based values, education classes involve mere "seat work," and programs should be more field-based. Yet field-based programs may produce field-based values that diminish the importance of campus-based learning, and programs heavily dependent on schools and MTs may undermine the importance of their own programs' coursework. Further, when schools do the hiring, the school experience will always matter more to TCs than what their university professors think, because university faculty have little concrete influence on job placements beyond issuing grades and writing recommendations. However the phenomenon is interpreted, in Anita's case her attention was firmly on the school and not the university program when discussing her learning about how to teach. The following sections detail how Anita's teaching was shaped within the contours of her student teaching at ECHS under the guidance of her MT Will.

Curricular Strands

Anita's instruction during research observations focused on the teaching of literature, primarily of Shakespeare's *Romeo and Juliet* and Golding's *Lord of the Flies*. The students' writing was largely related to their literary study, in particular their writing of journal entries about the role of literary elements in a given work; they also wrote Shakespearean insults, a eulogy for a literary character, and an essay. Each of these writing occasions followed from the provision of a prompt rather from any sort of instruction in how to write within the expected genre. Anita did not teach composing procedures that would help her students produce the genre assigned, which perhaps is not surprising given that her program had elided specific instructional ideas in favor of theory and ideals, and did not include a course in the teaching of writing. Anita's instruction in the language strand occurred once within the parameters of the research, and involved the discrete study of grammatical concepts from a grammar and composition textbook.

Anita's distribution of instruction across the three traditional strands of the English curriculum suggests that she was influenced by historically dominant approaches to teaching the discipline of English. English classes have long emphasized literature more than writing and language, a phenomenon reflected in the emphases of English teacher education programs (see Applebee (1974) and Willinsky (1991) for this school-based value; and Tremmel (2001) for the issue in English teacher education). Anita's balance of instruction appears typical of early career teachers who enter the profession with greater preparation for teaching literature than for teaching the remainder of the domain of English. The data suggest that the gravity of the dominant literary tradition of the discipline heavily influenced Anita's instructional emphases.

Pedagogical Tools

Anita's teaching included four pedagogical tools:

- Those that managed student *behavior*;
- Those that involved *closed-ended teaching*, that is, instruction that centered on specific correct answers;
- Those that were associated with *open-ended teaching*, that is, instruction that allowed for multiple possible avenues and student-directed exploratory learning;
- Those that involved *planning* to fit her particular teaching decisions in with larger instructional considerations.

Anita's pattern of tool usage followed a sequence that recalls the developmental processes of the teachers of vocational and low-track students reported in Chapter 8. She began with open-ended instruction that drew on planning in terms of literary themes. Her concerns about student behavior within this latitude led her to shift her emphasis to student behavior and the development of character traits that would contribute to more acceptable conduct. She ultimately relied on closed-ended instruction that required less creative planning and examinations on technical aspects of literary reading (identifying metaphors, etc.). Interpreting this pattern has its perils. She might have attempted open-ended teaching based on the influence of her university professors in conjunction with her preferred models from her own schooling, and then abandoned them when her students did not take advantage of her instructional latitude. She might have increasingly fallen under the influence of her MT and his more authoritarian guidance. In any case, the pattern suggests that an authoritarian pedagogy quickly surpassed her own stated values and the projected teacher identity she had established for herself prior to student teaching.

Anita's initial instruction was designed to make her students' learning fun and relevant through group work, multiple modes of expression, and open-ended interpretive work, aligned with her initial vision of teaching. Her students' management of these open-ended opportunities, along with Will's mentorship toward disciplinary control, led her to focus more intently on behavioral problems during the second observation cycle, with open-ended teaching virtually disappearing from her instruction while disciplinary means increased. This move toward greater control was evident in her instruction in the third observation cycle, where she taught almost exclusively with closed-ended practices, gravitating over the course of the semester toward behavioral and pedagogical means of controlling student conduct and restricting their learning opportunities to those assignments and assessments that had clear and unambiguous answers.

Attributions of Influence

The coding scheme (see Chapter 2) included the identification of each *attribution* Anita provided for the sources of the *pedagogical tools* she employed. The most frequently identified factor in her teaching was Will, her mentor. She also relied on the counsel of other teachers at ECHS for her teaching ideas. The Atlantic Piedmont program's field-intensive design gave the MTs great authority in instructing TCs in teaching methods, effectively making theory and ideals the province of the university professors, with practical matters outsourced to MTs. As a consequence, what she learned on campus, for the most part, stayed on campus.

Earlier, when she engaged in open-ended teaching, Anita's primary source of attribution was herself. When asked where she'd gotten an idea from, she said that she had thought it up on her own, perhaps a consequence of the teacher education faculty's reluctance to provide explicit instruction in teaching methods. Whether she produced these ideas from scratch is difficult to ascertain, given that from a dialogic perspective emphasizing intertextuality and the historical continuity of ideas (Bakhtin, 1986), no idea springs wholly from an individual, but rather is derived from prior engagement with others. No matter how her self-attributions at the outset of the semester might be interpreted, they declined as her teaching became increasingly focused on behavior and then on worksheets, tests, and other rote tools for instruction oriented to controlling student conduct and limiting their academic thinking to low-level memorization.

Anita's attributions to *students* as the impetus for her decisions might appear aligned with her professors' student-centered emphasis. However, like the students reported in Chapter 8, her students influenced her by resisting her instruction, not by embracing personal inquiry as an academic value. Only 10.8 percent of her attributions went to her teacher education program and her university supervisor combined, suggesting that attending to students might not have been linked to her professors' student-centered values. Further, student attributions more than tripled from the first to the second observation cycle, when Anita began to address behavioral issues in response to their classroom conduct. She continued to refer to the students for her decisions to engage in closed-ended teaching in the third observation cycle. Her attention to students as the source of pedagogical decisions, then, was not a function of making connections with them, as emphasized in her teacher education courses. Rather, she focused on students as a response to their behavior, which made it difficult for her to teach according to the projected progressive and student-centered teacher identity she had cultivated on campus. Instead, she increasingly exhibited a more authoritarian persona during student teaching.

Mentor Teacher

During the second observation cycle of the research, Will provided an interview on his teaching and mentoring. His perspective in these interviews focused on (1) the constraints imposed by the *block schedule* and the ways in which the schedule affected his teaching decisions; (2) his view of the role of *character education* as a way of inculcating in his students a disposition to learn; and (3) his belief in *developmentally appropriate teaching* with respect to his *behavioral expectations* for students and the *curriculum sequence* he constructed to meet their developmental needs.

Will frequently referred to the "time squeeze" that he faced in the school's block schedule. The rationale for block scheduling often promotes the benefits of improved relationships, more time for activity-based learning, advanced student achievement, and increased learning time, depending on how they are put into practice by teachers (Zepeda & Mayers, 2006). To Will, however, the block schedule imposed limits on his teaching. His teaching was not activity-based, for instance, and he did not adjust his teaching style when the district moved to a block schedule. Simply changing the schedule without helping teachers reconceptualize their teaching only produced longer classes involving the same approach. Instead of having the block schedule increase learning time, he found that the block scheduled *reduced* class time: "If I have to lose this [instruction] and jettison this two-week unit, I was willing to let it go. I could squeeze poetry down to a one-week unit instead of two if I had to." This "squeeze" limited Anita's choices, in terms of both the number of texts and units she could teach and the time she could devote to them. Her choices were shaped by Will's guidance to cut texts and instructional time, and therefore to reduce attention to learning processes and students' constructive activity.

The block schedule was accompanied by a departmental pacing chart that provided the schedule for what should be taught at each point of the semester. This pragmatic need to accommodate teaching decisions to the school organization—a problem faced by Penny in the highly ordered elementary school where she did her student teaching (see Chapter 5)—constrained her decisions to those that the schedule permitted. The schedule of the pacing chart possibly led to her gravitation to *closed-ended* instruction by the end of her student teaching. It is conceivable, and I would say likely, that no single factor influenced her gradual shift from progressive to authoritarian teaching. Rather, the schedule, the fuzzy concepts of the university program, the perception that the students lacked investment in school learning, the mentorship of Will, and perhaps other influences shaped her practice away from the values she had asserted at the beginning of the semester and toward those she had claimed had limited her own learning in school.

Will employed the sort of implied character curriculum described in Chapter 8 to produce habits of good character such as responsibility, unselfishness, and good study habits. Even though his students were not low track, like the students of the teachers in Chapter 8, he found that their habits of mind were inadequate to becoming engaged students, leading him to seek to shape the students' dispositions so that they conducted themselves appropriately, which he believed was prerequisite to being a good student. Disorderly student conduct was not in evidence during the classes observed for the research; their behavioral problems' documentation came instead from remarks by Will and Anita during interviews. Unlike the vocational students subjected to explicit character education in Chapter 8, Will's students at ECHS were relatively affluent and homogeneous, and had a public image of presenting minor behavioral challenges to teachers. Their character was found wanting in ways consistent with Anyon's (1980) work on the hidden curriculum, as flaws that would hold them back from the sort of success that awaited privileged people like them, in contrast with the vocational students being groomed for entry-level office work suited to people with only a high school education.

Will's values were aligned with those of the Protestant work ethic (Weber, 1930). When asked to describe the most important thing he wanted his students to learn, he emphasized how students' "study habits and your responsibility toward the steps I'm making now will, on down the line, have an effect. You add them all up, and all the steps are going to wind up putting you . . . in a positive direction." Will was concerned that his students, like those of society as a whole, exhibited "a very, very broad streak of selfishness, me-first attitude" that he hoped to address through his teaching. "It doesn't necessarily have anything to do with education. It's more of a moral approach," he said. Will found society's excessive emphasis on individuality to be counterproductive in developing responsible, other-oriented citizens. His effort to instill a sense of social responsibility appeared to be at odds with the value on individual uniqueness that characterized Anita's student-centered university program, one of many departures that upset claims to a seamless transition from university to school.

The notion of character emphasized by Will is difficult to characterize as either authoritarian or progressive. Will felt that he was teaching habits of mind that would be enabling in the students' participation in society, suggesting a liberatory intention. Some might find it an imposition to instill values like responsibility and respect, and might characterize such efforts as authoritarian. Perhaps the process and consequences would determine the value system, rather than simply the presence of an implied character curriculum. Situating the need for what Will called a "moral" dimension to teaching solely within schools and not in universities or other sites, however, would be a mistake, assuming that Weber's ideas were intended for broad application.

Anita's and Will's students, however, were not the only ones subjected to moral oversight. Her teacher education program had been given a state mandate that required teacher education programs to remediate at their own expense any graduates found wanting by school districts. The program responded by requiring each TC to sign a contract that effectively stipulated a moral code of conduct for teachers, including matters of punctuality, responsibility, respect, and other traits similar to what Will hoped to inculcate in his high school students. If Anita's case illustrates a two-worlds pitfall at times, it also documents the complications of assuming that those two worlds are entirely discrete.

Will described the curriculum in developmental terms consistent with Piagetian age-based stage theories (see Chapter 4). At certain ages, he felt, youth should have developed particular capacities such as "the proper use of language and composition strategies." Ninth graders, he felt, benefit from learning "what literature teaches us about life," and "what [literature] reveals about human nature and the fact that language and our proper use of language is important in any area of life." These understandings, he said, should serve as "a gateway level for further development" for ninth graders, suggesting a belief that the curricular sequence works in accordance with age-triggered biological stages that adolescents go through in their learning and growth. The developmental role served by the curriculum fell in two areas: (1) the students' gravitation toward institutional behavioral expectations, and (2) the ordering of the curriculum to meet students' academic preparedness.

Will sought to find the intersection of the students' age-based maturity and the expectations for appropriate behavior in school. He said, "Even though I'm much more of a disciplinarian than I used to be when I first started, I still tend to be [more] easy-going about things in the classroom." He felt that Anita lacked confidence in her authority with students and responded by being overly strict. He hoped to enable her to find her disciplinary persona in less confrontational ways as she got more comfortable in the classroom, so that the students could learn to regulate their own behavior within school propriety. He built his teaching on the assumption that the students needed to learn how to regulate their thinking and actions so that they could behave appropriately in group settings. Their development of proper character traits thus followed from his students' adoption of moral qualities that enabled them to act within the behavioral parameters he set on behalf of what he considered a cohesive society.

Will considered Anita to be overly strict during student teaching; simultaneously, Anita considered Will to be "very straightlaced" as a teacher. Will was "not as group-oriented, I guess, as I am, and he's more of a person who can stand up there and lecture. And I'm not." Anita reported that the two of them "squabble a lot about the fact that he says I try to make things too fun," with the squabbles being amicable and respectful rather than antagonistic. Will sought "not to make [learning] fun but to teach them something," said Anita. She defended her approach by emphasizing that she wanted to "make it interesting" rather than simply "fun."

Will, then, initially embodied some of the aspects of what Anita characterized as bad teaching in terms of preferring to lecture and emphasize content knowledge over high-interest activities. Yet she did not believe he was a bad teacher, only that he relied on practices she had rejected prior to student teaching. She ultimately gravitated toward those practices herself, with the stance and demeanor accompanying them. She struggled to manage students' behavior under open-ended instruction, and so moved toward greater control, first behaviorally and then instructionally. Anita's teaching became more authoritarian, in opposition to her initial goal of becoming a hands-on teacher.

In her first interview for the study, Anita described how her students affected her understanding of how to teach, informed by the assumption that "what works on paper doesn't necessarily work in the classroom," a dilemma that ultimately turned her away from university ideals. The teaching ideas she read about in pedagogical texts during coursework might work "in that classroom, but in another classroom they're not necessarily going to work." She believed that "each group of students is different. . . . My ideal of a student, you know, who sits there and takes notes and listens to me is not going to be a reality."

Although her studies had not acquainted her with a sociocultural theory, in this case, she professed to have a situated view of teaching practice, one consistent with the perspective motivating my own research. She also mounted a critique of teacher education programs that were theoretical at the expense of providing specific pedagogical practices and directing attention to which settings might enable their productive use, thus serving the goal of concept development. The assumption that appeared to motivate this program decision to avoid instruction in teaching methods was that skilled, well-aligned teachers in the field would mentor TCs in practice and thus round out their conception of how to teach. Yet such an outcome could only follow from practices aligned with theory, which was only occasionally available to Anita and other volunteer participants in the research. Under Will's guidance, she moved far from her university courses' theoretical depiction of avid, self-motivated learners, and taught in ways opposing its principles.

Anita and others from her cohort had learned on campus to place students at the center of a youth culture that influenced them in largely healthy and productive ways, with teachers' attention to this orientation setting the stage for instruction sensitive to their personal and academic needs. Anita's attributions to students as the source of her decisions pointed to their unruliness more than their learning inquiries, creating a conundrum in her developing conception of how to teach effectively, especially when it came to progressive assumptions. On campus, individual students and their immersion in youth culture served as the impetus for instruction. In ECHS, Will felt that students took this emphasis on individual paths of fulfilled exploration and abused it by behaving selfishly and disrespectfully, including their treatment of Anita as a beginning teacher. Anita resolved this discrepancy between idealized and actual youth by imposing a more restrictive environment, both behaviorally and academically, a shift that Will felt did not grant them sufficient leeway to find their own means of self-regulation within appropriate expectations.

Self in Curricular Context

Anita tended to identify herself as the source of a teaching decision with much greater frequency early in the semester than later. She reported that her personal monitoring of the students' learning led her to make choices about how to help them relate more easily to the characters of the novel as a way to help with their engagement with its action. After an early observation, she said,

> I've been trying to emphasize looking to [*Lord of the Flies*] specifically for a rationale of what we're doing. For the beast, and the same situation, try to relate it in some way to themselves. Yesterday I related it more personally. Today I didn't necessarily, but I did allow them opportunity to use their own opinions [and] try to relate it specifically to them, because they're having such problems in hating this book so much, which is fine, you know. Not everybody's going to love it.

Her initial open-ended approach, not confined by pacing charts or other structures, allowed her to think about the novel from her students' point of view, with its primary symbols providing themes tied to adolescent developmental conflicts that students could explore through the novel. Yet she reported that they hated the novel itself, making these connections less achievable than they appeared when written in a lesson plan book or theorized according to ideals. Personalizing the curriculum did not include choice of reading, and the reading prescribed in the curriculum did not appeal to them, making building instruction on their engagement a challenge.

This sort of reference to herself as the source of her teaching ideas occurred only once during the second observation cycle and four times in the third. Her dependence on her students for teaching possibilities became compromised by their disengaged response to her teaching of the curriculum. Anita was required to teach a robust curriculum within a set time period, one that included a focus on grammar toward the end of her student teaching, as required by the school's pacing chart. She felt the time squeeze that Will experienced on a block schedule, saying that she included the grammar lessons "because I felt like I had three weeks left, and I wanted to do something with grammar, because since we have so much to cover in a very short amount of time."

This section illustrates how multiple and competing beliefs pull at an individual teacher at all times and in all directions. Anita felt the pull of the university's core values at first, but they were discarded over the course of the semester in relation to her generally privileged students' disengagement from school, a curriculum that specified teaching novels such as *Lord of the Flies* that students disliked, the implicit character curriculum that viewed their disaffection from the curriculum as a problem of moral training, an MT who was personally supportive but provided a model of teaching that ran counter to her stated values, a curriculum with a formalist orientation with language study, and a pacing chart that specified that material must be covered, including grammar, a curricular strand given only marginal treatment in university coursework, a situation found by Pasternak et al. (2017) to be common in Secondary English Education programs generally. By the end, and not unwillingly, she had adopted and practiced the values of teaching that her projected teacher identity at the beginning of the research had rejected.

Curriculum Materials and External Mandates

Curriculum materials often provide a primary means of support for new teachers (Grossman & Thompson, 2008). In Anita's case, they also provided constraints on her teaching. She selected the two novels from the department's list of approved texts, *Lord of the Flies* and *To Kill a Mockingbird*, along with *Romeo and Juliet*. These choices fell within the ninth-grade curriculum and its canonical orientation. Her teaching of *Lord of the Flies* was guided by a teacher in the department who gave her access to his file cabinet of teaching materials. File-cabinet teaching typically involves handouts, assignments, and other formalist means of teaching in alignment with the department's cultural heritage approach to teaching literature, one oriented to textual authority more than student interest. During the semester these materials appeared in her teaching more often than university program influences. She did borrow from her professors' practical recommendations when she used a discussion web while teaching *Lord of the Flies*; that is, a graphic organizer designed to identify opposing perspectives on a single issue as a way to set up oppositions for argumentation. She also used a folklore unit developed on campus, but otherwise reported or exhibited little campus influence on her teaching.

Anita rarely referred to her Clare, her university supervisor, as an influence during student teaching. Clare said that her supervision of Anita was focused on encouraging her to provide individualized instruction without intruding excessively on the students' chosen pathways for learning, consistent with her university professors' method of providing broad guidance without specific teaching ideas. The consequence of this hands-off approach was that Anita's instruction began to resemble Will's under his more specific, omnipresent, and immediate guidance during student teaching.

Discussion

According to faculty documentation, the teacher education program provided a "seamless" connection between university and schools designed to provide a highly aligned experience for its TCs, a claim made by other teacher educators in describing their relationships with schools (e.g., Kahle & Kronebusch, 2003; Schoon & Sandoval, 1997). The competing centers of gravity affecting Anita's teaching, however, suggest that she was not immersed in a unified universe following a single set of gravitational laws bent toward campus values. Instead, Anita experienced dissonance not only between school and university but also within the school site, and between English and Education on campus. She negotiated her differences with Will over instructional emphasis and disciplinary posture, ultimately gravitating to his value system and teaching practices, and abandoning the core values of her campus professors. She found students to be less amenable to learning opportunities than she had initially assumed, and taught a packed curriculum within the time squeeze of the block schedule that limited the constructivist possibilities that she had entered student teaching with.

Over the course of the semester, Anita moved from a student-centered conception to one predicated on taming her students' behavior and centered on examinations of established, received knowledge. The hands-on emphasis promoted on campus withered as she became the teacher she had initially described disapprovingly. Anita's concept development thus took her in a direction completely opposite from what she and her professors had initially intended. She went on this course in spite of the supervision of Clare as the agent of her professors' values; opportunities to debrief, discuss, and reflect with others in the cohort during the student teaching seminar; and a course in reading during student teaching that presumably aligned with program values. Anita never spontaneously referred to any campus-based influences during the semester. Her attention rather was focused on her students and MT in making instructional decisions. This most immediate center of gravity grew in size and pull as the semester unfolded, exerting daily, pragmatic pressure on Anita to assimilate, as might be expected of field-based programs that outsource the practicalities of teaching to school-based mentors acculturated to authoritarianism, in spite of their selection for alignment.

With the field serving as the immediate and most prominent influence on her teaching, the fuzzy concepts of campus classes faded in her vision of how to teach. The field-based design of the teacher education program appeared to play a strong role in Anita's developmental path away from the teacher she had initially hoped to become. Relationships with the MTs were designed for a seamless continuity with campus values, yet in this case and others from the research, they worked in opposition to what her professors advocated. Field-based programs are embraced by many powerful influences in teacher education, from accreditation agencies (Cibulka, 2009) to major research efforts (Levine, 2006). It appears, however, that when the field is dominant in beginning teachers' developing conceptions, it impresses a pragmatic formalism and teacher-and-text-centeredness that instills the values of cultural heritage and authoritarianism. Extensive field experiences, if this research has generalization potential, appear to undermine efforts to produce change in schools, instead shaping beginning teachers to fit in with their established practices, to assimilate themselves to schools they had learned to critique in university programs.

Anita's progressive orientation was stopped in its tracks shortly after her student teaching experience began—a casualty of mentoring, school scheduling and pacing, student disaffection, a culture of authoritarianism, and the absence of the practical applications of student-centered pedagogies on campus or in university supervision. From a sociocultural standpoint, the mediated trajectory of her development of a broad teaching conception took a U-turn away from its charted destination and toward something altogether different when the school became her primary pedagogical influence. Understanding Vygotsky's (1987) notion of concept development as a process of goal-directed, socially situated, and tool-mediated action helps to explain how this sort of pathway leads to teachers' socialization to school norms. If campus is to contribute to the pathways taken by teachers, their ideals need to be clearly related to concrete activity so that theory unaccompanied by pedagogical tools does not decline in the midst of competing value systems and practices. That is, they should emphasize concepts rather than theory, requiring theory and practice to be integrated in ways that are responsive to the challenges offered by schools and those who populate them within the influences of historical and outside forces that shape them.

Anita's case provides an instance of typicality that many teacher educators can recognize easily: the highly regarded TC who before long begins to teach like most other teachers, in violation of progressive ideals emphasized in teacher education. Her trajectory confounds the idea that a teacher education program's ideals can be offered theoretically without practical application, and that TCs will figure out how to implement them regardless of the school structures, curricular organization and materials, school mentorship, student dispositions, and other factors that tend to shape teaching in authoritarian ways. If *Development toward what?* is the question, and if development is assumed to be a more or less good thing toward a positive destination, then Anita's case—which I believe is more typical than not—upends assumptions about concept development grounded in College of Education beliefs and values.

From the standpoint of the school and its developmental assumptions, Anita was able to shake the ungrounded ideals of campus coursework and become the authoritarian pragmatist that thrives in a suburban school setting. Her development in that sense went in the right direction, a conundrum that teacher educators need to recognize and address in their programs. Without attention to this fundamental reality of mediated development, they will continue to complain that their idealistic progressivism is being violated; or they might simply ignore the reality that their programs are not seamlessly related to the schools and continue to claim that they are; or might be oblivious to what happens once TCs hit the field and leave their studies behind, allowing them to claim victory without paying attention to the real consequences of their program assumptions and outcomes. Concept development is complicated in any case, and the contradictory environments of learning to teach, illustrated in Anita's student teaching, work against developing unified conceptions aligned with progressive values.

Further, if colleges of education hope to reform schools in the progressive vision, then field-based programs appear to work more in terms of assimilation than change, especially when part of the campus experience—for English teachers, lengthy exposure to lecture-oriented literary critics in required English courses—suggests that authoritarian teaching is intellectually viable, practiced at the highest level of the discipline. Finally, Anita's case illustrates the dilemmas that await any teacher education program that trumpets ideals without attending to the difficulties of implementing them in nonideal settings like schools. School environments—and university environments—are inherently contradictory and provide competing conceptions of effective teaching and worthwhile learning. Ignoring those complications to promote simplistic narratives of progressive idealism and seamless transitions appears only to make the challenging task of learning to teach even more forbidding.

10

Learning to Teach Grammar at the Intersection of Formalism and Flexibility

This chapter explores a common tension experienced by beginning English/Language Arts teachers: whether and how to teach the "language" strand of the discipline of English. Traditionally, English/Language Arts teachers have been responsible for teaching literature (and now, a broader range of textual forms and genres); composition (historically writing, but now including texts using multiple sign systems); and language (historically grammatical form as specified in textbooks, but occasionally more nuanced understandings of language variation and situational propriety).

As I've outlined in Chapter 7, when looking at Leigh's instruction in writing the five-paragraph theme, English Education programs have historically had an overwhelming emphasis on literature and how to teach it, reinforced by Departments of English where TCs are required to take roughly eight to fifteen content-area courses, and their own literary bias that often attracts them to the teaching profession. Writing tends to be assigned but not taught in English literature classes, which are dedicated to the content of literary criticism (Addington, 2001), and where writing competence is presumed rather than instructed. Composition and rhetoric faculty comprise the "toad in the garden" of literary studies (Crowley, 1998, p. 19), positioned lower on the status ladder than literary critics, often in the role of overseeing writing courses taught by teaching assistants and part time instructors (Carpini, 2004) where grammar instruction may or may not be covered beyond the correction of errors.

These classes are targeted to first-year students and are dedicated to improving student writing across the curriculum more than advancing pedagogical knowledge among prospective English/Language Arts teachers. Indeed, it's hard to know who will become an English Education major, given that career aspirations at the point of college entry do not necessarily predict college majors at the point of declaration and admission (Freedman, 2013). First-year composition is thus designed to help students write across the curriculum (Coffin, Curry, Goodman, Hewings, Lillis, & Swann, 2003), with teaching approaches assimilated from practice by aspiring teachers, rather than taught specifically in writing pedagogy courses.

And then there's the language strand, ignored by just about everyone instructionally, attended to largely when students' papers get graded and the red pen is unleashed. As argued by Ray (2015), "rhetoric and composition scholars have developed an aversion to grammar since the 1980s" (p. 103), influenced by over a century of research reviews (to be reviewed shortly) that have almost universally found the teaching of grammar as a discrete topic to be futile in teaching rules or improving speaking or writing. Composition and rhetoric instructors would not be expected to include grammar pedagogy in their courses, regardless of what particular teachers believe about correctness in their teaching and assessment of student writing.

English Education faculty are the only people who might assume responsibility for helping beginning teachers learn how to teach grammar, yet they have rarely included a grammatical pedagogy as part of preparation for teaching. Pasternak et al. (2017), for instance, in their detailed study of how universities prepare English/Language Arts teachers, found that 2 to 3 percent of bachelor's/master's programs in the United States require a specific methods course focused on grammar only. These courses are not necessarily pedagogical, and may be dedicated to topics like History of the English Language, linguistics independent of pedagogy, and other noninstructional foci. If grammar pedagogy is covered in the other 97 to 98 percent of programs, it happens within the confines of general methods classes or writing pedagogy classes, each with a full slate of topics to cover before grammar instruction is addressed.

All signs point to a glaring hole in English/Language Arts teachers' university education when it comes to teaching the language strand of the curriculum. As a result, beginning English/Language Arts teachers may begin their careers with an inadequate understanding of either grammar itself or how to teach it. Yet grammar instruction is part of what they are required to provide in their classes. Even if they have learned in universities to reject the idea that teaching grammar is a good investment of instructional time, beginning teachers are often appalled by the quality of student writing, especially if they have gone through school enrolled in high-track courses and have not mingled with the sort of student who populates the lower and middle tracks. It is common for TCs, such as the teachers featured in this chapter, who themselves are high achievers, to find student writing to be difficult to read and to wonder how to improve students' grammatical formation of sentences, among a host of infelicities available in student compositions.

This conundrum, I believe, cannot be attributed to the two-worlds pitfall. To be sure, university English Education faculty members and first-year composition instructors often reject the teaching of grammar as inherently ineffectual, and schools tend to require grammar instruction, reinforcing the idea that there is a clean break between the two types of institutions. Yet I locate the issues more broadly in a host of factors surrounding English/Language Arts teachers:

- Their personal beliefs about the nature of their work, situated within broader belief systems about linguistic purity, linguistic diversity across a host of demographic groups, the role of English as a matter of national heritage, expectations for how an educated person speaks, and many more epistemological traditions;
- Their experiences as students, particularly if they have gone through school in exclusive academic tracks and assume that everyone shares their fluency with textbook English;
- Their engagement with the domain of literary criticism and its formalist dimension, in both high school and college English classes;

- Their acculturation in university English literature classes to linguistic values on precision and conventional usages, a value that often affects how college-prep high school English teachers view their responsibilities;
- Broader societal pressures to produce students who can communicate through textbook English, and critiques from both higher education and the business world for any shortcomings of their graduates;
- The tendency to believe that one's own grammatical infelicities are acceptable, but that other people's violations are not;
- Inconsistencies in style and form books used in both schools and universities about what is acceptable and what is not;
- Misunderstandings about different meanings of "grammar" and which ones should be foregrounded instructionally;
- Formalist versus processual conceptions of teaching and learning;
- The overwhelming Whiteness of the teaching profession, including teacher educators, producing the assumption that textbook English has greater validity and status than versions spoken by minoritized people, residents of rural communities, working-class people, and others not enculturated to the speech practices of the dominant culture;
- And other factors that don't fit neatly into the two-worlds dichotomy of university and school.

I next review issues surrounding the teaching and learning of English grammar, which has historically comprised the language strand of the English/Language Arts curriculum, and then present how the tensions were played out with one research participant from the Southern Plains English Education program and one from the Atlantic Piedmont English Education program.

The Enduring Dilemma of Whether, and How, to Teach Grammar

Grammar and grammar instruction are very unpopular. I just ran a Google search on "hate grammar" that turned up 47,100,000 hits. "Hate Martin Shkreli," known as the Most Hated Man in America for jacking up life-saving prescription drug costs, produced only 150,000 hits. "Hate lima beans" turned up 510,000 hits, "hate Osama bin Laden" yielded 4,270,000, and "hate Justin Bieber" found 24,300,000. This grammar thing is just plain despised out there, nearly twice as loathed as Justin Bieber. I next review the research base that finds the teaching of grammar to be somewhere between futile and counterproductive, and then summarize the reasons it persists in schools.

The Research Base

English Education faculty have, for many years, pushed back against the whole idea of teaching grammar, backed by an extensive and comprehensive research base. This research has also provided university composition and rhetoric faculty with ammunition against teaching the often-tedious and difficult issues surrounding grammatical understanding and usage. Reviews of research on writing and grammar instruction by Braddock, Lloyd-Jones, and Schauer (1963), Hillocks (1986), Weaver (1996), and Graham and Perrin (2007) have concluded emphatically and without reservation that the teaching of grammar in isolation does not improve writing. If anything, dedicating instructional time to grammar *may adversely affect students' writing* because of the tremendous allocations of time it consumes at the expense of instruction in actual writing. These reviews have armed English Education faculty with a strong rationale for eschewing grammar instruction altogether, both in their own pedagogical teaching and in their TCs' classrooms.

From a research standpoint, few studies have even been conducted following the publication of Hillocks's (1986) review, even as they persisted following Braddock et al.'s (1963) withering critique of the idea that teaching grammar can improve students' writing. The contributors to my own follow-up twenty-year review of writing research (Smagorinsky, 2006) found little evidence that the teaching of grammar held researchers' interest, given the paucity of studies included in their summaries. Applebee and Langer's (2009) preliminary report based on NAEP data concerning the teaching of writing in schools over a thirty-year period included a single reference to attention to grammar, and then only as a proofreading afterthought. Graham and Perrin's (2007) meta-analysis did identify some studies of traditional grammar instruction, yet like Hillocks and others reviewing the topic, they found that the approach's "effect was negative. This negative effect was small, but it was statistically significant, indicating that traditional grammar instruction is unlikely to help improve the quality of students' writing" (p. 21).

The case, it appears, has been considered closed for some time now: teaching grammar is a waste of time and should be ignored or discouraged in both first-year composition and teacher education programs, and ultimately in schools, at least until students submit their papers and find them marked for their errors by professors who expect college students' writing to meet an accepted standard (e.g., Laser, 2015).

The Persistence of Grammar Instruction in Schools

If grammar instruction doesn't work as widely practiced—that is, as a discrete lesson unrelated to writing—why is it such a staple of the secondary school English/Language Arts curriculum? I consider this question next as a way of introducing how two beginning English/Language Arts teachers managed the tensions surrounding if and how to teach grammar. Chapter 7's attention to the five-paragraph theme identifies common explanations for the persistence of formalist staples of the curriculum in spite of university rejection of their value. Here I adapt those explanations to the question of why English/Language Arts teachers continue to teach grammar when university theorists and researchers have concluded that it is futile and inimical to writing development:

- *Teachers' enculturation to the traditions of schooling through their apprenticeships of observation*, which include grammar instruction as an essential part of the English/Language Arts curriculum;
- *The limitations of literature-based teacher education programs*, coupled with first-year composition programs that may de-emphasize grammar; and in contrast, literature professors immersed in belletristic values and elitist notions of proper language use that include textbook expectations, creating conflictual practices in Departments of English;
- *Shortcomings of teachers*, who undertake disembodied grammar instruction in spite of students' annual inability to learn it and a powerful research base that concludes that it is deleterious in effect;
- *Poor work conditions* (too many students, too little planning time, and so on) that limit teachers' ability to keep up with research or to conduct their own; to which I would add that teachers often distrust university research and researchers, and so may find their findings to be distant from their needs and realities (Hemsley-Brown & Sharp, 2003);
- *Institutional pressures* such as testing mandates that include assessments of grammar knowledge and usage (Ehrenhaft, 2018);
- *The five-paragraph theme's potential as a useful genre* to learn and reapply to new situations. This value might be extrapolated to refer to the ways in which grammar instruction is thought to exercise a "mental muscle" that strengthens structural thinking across the board and that allows grammar study to be "transferred" and applied to new contexts (Larsen-Freeman, 2000, p. 178).

Parallels between these two formalist demands of teaching English/Language Arts help to help explain the dogged perseverance of traditional grammar instruction in most US schools. If TCs were taught either formal grammar in school or no grammar at all in schools or universities, they have few options available to teach grammar when required by schools to do so, a challenge that encompasses the first two reasons listed earlier. The third explanation, that teachers are dim, is difficult to substantiate; it's not idiotic to think that students' writing ought to be comprehensible, and the decision to teach grammar might be made at the curricular, not the individual level. Poor work conditions undoubtedly limit the time teachers have to critique a curricular strand that has been historically foundational to the discipline of English/Language Arts (Applebee, 1974) and identify robust alternatives. These work conditions also often include curricular requirements and what is available in approved textbooks for teaching grammar, with formalism the dominant value of most such vehicles (Hillocks, 1995). With institutional pressures implicated in these latter influences, many forces appear to collude to produce the final issue: that grammar instruction might be understood as the means to sturdy, transferable knowledge about linguistic structure and usage, no matter what evidence students might present to the contrary. As a consequence, when the pacing chart dictates that it's time to teach the gerund, many English/Language Arts teachers ditch their reservations and teach it anyhow.

The problems are compounded by the presence of widespread disagreement on the purposes of language instruction, both in the staffroom and in the general population. These disagreements are embedded in broader disagreements about the purpose of education altogether (Phi Delta Kappa, 2016), both across the public and within school faculties. Language purists writing in the public domain such as Safire (1984) argue that there is a pristine version of the English language, violations of which degrade the individual and society. Stotsky (1999) believes that "we" are "losing our language" when words and means of expression are sourced from outside the Greek and Latin roots of European romance languages, and that society is in peril when the language is adulterated by corrupting forces from outside this heritage. African American scholar Delpit (1995) acknowledges colloquial versions of English, including African American English, yet asserts that students must learn the *codes of power* associated with textbook English that give them access to the benefits of the economy. Smitherman (2006) in contrast finds the notion of Standard English to be discriminatory and insensitive to the internal grammatical coherence of African American English, which she asserts is a legitimate form of expression that needn't conform to textbook standards. Noguchi (1991) takes the position that errors carry different degrees of status for their users, and that language instruction should help students eliminate errors that well-educated readers find most egregious (e.g., subject-verb disagreement). Williams (1981) finds grammatical rules to be so arbitrary and situationally contradictory that he wonders why they inflame such passions among composition teachers and scholars. Shaughnessy (1977), through her experiences with open-admissions city colleges in New York and students not exhibiting historically accepted fluency with speech conventions, found that deviations from textbook English are developmental and suggest that they indicate when writers are taking risks that should be encouraged. Hymes (1974) argues that all language use is situational and that the key for speakers is to develop *communicative competence* in order to engage appropriately in a variety of contexts, rather than for all to speak a "standard" version in all situations. García and Wei (2014) argue that people fruitfully engage in *translanguaging*, the deployment of a speaker's full linguistic repertoire irrespective of official language structures and conventions, often involving a mash of different national languages or ethnic/racialized speech. All of these views, and no doubt others, may be in play in any staffroom or university department, as well as in public discourse concerned with linguistic competence, complicating the idea that schools are inherently conservative and universities unwaveringly progressive. These tensions surround beginning English/Language Arts teachers both on the job and in their immersion in the broader culture.

Regardless of how these issues roil the environment, English/Language Arts teachers face the inevitable demand to teach textbook standards to their students. If the CCSS (2018a) are representative of what is expected in schools, then formalism is the name of the game, as evidenced in their outline of language standards reproduced in Box 10.1.

> **Box 10.1 Conventions of Standard English in Common Core State Standards**
>
> CCSS.ELA-LITERACY.L.9-10.1
>
> Demonstrate command of the conventions of Standard English grammar and usage when writing or speaking.
>
> CCSS.ELA-LITERACY.L.9-10.1.A
>
> Use parallel structure.*
>
> CCSS.ELA-LITERACY.L.9-10.1.B
>
> Use various types of phrases (noun, verb, adjectival, adverbial, participial, prepositional, absolute) and clauses (independent, dependent; noun, relative, adverbial) to convey specific meanings and add variety and interest to writing or presentations.
>
> CCSS.ELA-LITERACY.L.9-10.2
>
> Demonstrate command of the conventions of Standard English capitalization, punctuation, and spelling when writing.
>
> CCSS.ELA-LITERACY.L.9-10.2.A
>
> Use a semicolon (and perhaps a conjunctive adverb) to link two or more closely related independent clauses.
>
> CCSS.ELA-LITERACY.L.9-10.2.B
>
> Use a colon to introduce a list or quotation.
>
> CCSS.ELA-LITERACY.L.9-10.2.C
>
> Spell correctly.
>
> **Knowledge of Language**
>
> CCSS.ELA-LITERACY.L.9-10.3
>
> Apply knowledge of language to understand how language functions in different contexts, to make effective choices for meaning or style, and to comprehend more fully when reading or listening.
>
> CCSS.ELA-LITERACY.L.9-10.3.A
>
> Write and edit work so that it conforms to the guidelines in a style manual (e.g., *MLA Handbook*, *Turabian's Manual for Writers*) appropriate for the discipline and writing type.
>
> Source: http://www.corestandards.org/ELA-Literacy/L/9-10/

Significantly, the CCSS (2018b) only specify outcomes, not teaching methods:

> By emphasizing required achievements, the Standards leave room for teachers, curriculum developers, and states to determine how those goals should be reached and what additional topics should be addressed. Thus, the Standards do not mandate such things as a particular writing process or the full range of metacognitive strategies that students may need to monitor and direct their

thinking and learning. Teachers are thus free to provide students with whatever tools and knowledge their professional judgment and experience identify as most helpful for meeting the goals set out in the Standards. (http://www.corestandards.org/ELA-Literacy/introduction/key-design-consideration/)

Teachers are required to teach formalist dimensions of language use without being guided in how to do so, being constructed here as "free" to use their judgment and preferred tools. However, they are surrounded by multiple and competing judgments about language use and instruction in schools, universities, workplace critiques, and the general public. They are not free in their decision-making by any stretch of the imagination for the most part. If they have attended a typical teacher education program, they have been provided few if any tools for teaching the language strand, and if they have gone through a typical first-year composition program, they have not been exposed to a grammar pedagogy and may have been discouraged from thinking that teaching grammar is a good idea. Yet in schools, they are likely to face imperatives to teach it for a variety of reasons: to satisfy what are accepted as essentials of their disciplinary heritage, to prepare students for standardized tests, to prepare students for college expectations, to meet staffroom expectations for teaching their curriculum, to replicate their own schooling experiences that emphasize grammar as part of the US cultural heritage, to respond to workforce complaints that graduates can't speak or write properly, to prepare students for writing in other school disciplines in which the faculty expect proper English without having to teach it themselves, and so on.

Without concrete methods for teaching grammar, and with very concrete demands for teaching it, beginning English/Language Arts teachers appear likely to default to what is available: the school's grammar and composition textbook and its formalist orientation designed to teach grammar as a discrete and testable form of knowledge. In the absence of prior pedagogical knowledge of grammar from their own schooling beyond the use of the grammar text, and robust knowledge of how to teach it in their university programs, beginning teachers often rely on the curriculum material that the school makes available, in this case, the inevitably formalist textbook.

Or, like the teachers featured next, they seek other means of teaching grammar, both to satisfy external demands and to teach their students what they themselves believe to be good communication skills. Their cases demonstrate the tensions they experienced. They also reveal the efforts they made to make grammar instruction as interesting as possible, and to give students some degree of control in mastering formal requirements from outside their own linguistic repertoires. My purpose in reporting these cases—the only two from the high school research participants who emphasized grammar in their teaching—is to position these beginning teachers within tensions created by competing demands originating from multiple points not easily reducible to the two worlds of school and university. If grammar instruction serves as a fulcrum from which to consider the enduring opposition between process and product, student-centered and teacher-centered pedagogies, formalism and constructivism, then their experiences can be instructive in considering how people develop conceptions of how to teach formal knowledge within traditions that suggest opposing methods and values. The conflictual settings make it difficult to think in terms of linear paths of concept development, and to raise questions about what human development might mean when TCs' and beginning teachers' conceptions take directions that their university faculty find distressing.

The research included two beginning teachers who focused on grammar instruction during student teaching or their first year of teaching, finding themselves caught between tensions that complicated their efforts to teach in conceptually unified ways. Both Laura and Brandy embraced the progressive principles of their university programs, albeit in relation to very different program structures and course requirements. Both by choice and by requirement, they taught their students proper language use during their early career teaching. I next explore the tensions they experienced as they worked within conceptions of teaching that involved competing assumptions. The poles of this dichotomy included formalist and authoritarian principles at one extreme, and relational, engagement-driven, and open-ended teaching and learning at the other. Like most binaries, however, this one was insensitive to the vast range of possibilities in between.

Teaching Grammar within Oppositional Epistemologies

In what follows, I detail how Laura from the Southern Plains Secondary English Education program and Brandy from the Atlantic Piedmont Secondary English Education program taught the language strand of the English/Language Arts curriculum during student teaching and their first jobs. Of the many participants in the research, they were the only ones whose teaching involved a sustained grammatical focus. I first treat them independently, then try to make sense of their experiences as a whole.

Laura

Laura got credentialed in the Southern Plains Secondary English Education program, characterized earlier in this book as *structurally fragmented* because of its lack of coherence in structure, process, and orientation. She had grown up in a small rural town in the Southwestern United States, which was populated by about 5,000 people at the time of Laura's high school graduation, 88 percent of whom were European American and 8 percent Native American, according to census data. She graduated from college four years after graduating from high school, and she got married the summer after graduation, a union that led to several moves over the course of the research.

Projected teacher identity. A projected teacher identity is the image that beginning teachers (or teachers at any career stage) have of the teacher they want to become. In terms of concept development, this image represents the ideal, the teleological end, toward which they hope to develop. This anticipated future self is key to concept development in that it synthesizes what a person believes and knows, and uses that understanding to establish a personal trajectory based on the ideology and social practices suggested by that ideal.

Laura hoped to become a teacher whose students enjoyed learning in her classroom. She emphasized that her classes needed to be interesting for her students. She applied her interest in providing her students with an engaging and enjoyable education to her instruction in grammar, generally experienced as tedious and wasteful by students and frustrating by teachers (Petruzzella, 1996). Laura, according to her MT Mary Ford,

> easily built rapport with the students, and . . . is very creative and adept at planning lessons that are concrete yet challenging for the regular students. . . . Laura's teaching was naturally fun and creative. . . . She excelled at . . . helping kids understand why they were learning, what they were learning, and its importance in their lives, especially with teaching grammar.

Laura resembled most of the beginning teachers in the research in that she positioned herself against the drab, authoritarian experiences she'd had as a student; embraced teaching and learning that were predicated on activity and hands-on, constructivist, engaging, and participatory learning; was a top student at her state's most selective public university; and had bad memories of the formalist grammar and writing instruction she'd experienced in school. The projected teacher identity she established thus followed from a combination of the sorts of school experiences she had both appreciated and disliked, and the academic knowledge from her university Theory of English Grammar course taught in the College of Education that helped her to justify her preferences. As a combination of both spontaneous (everyday) and scientific (academic) concepts (see Chapter 1), this vision served as a useful conceptual foundation on which to envision and then build her own approach to teaching.

Preparation for teaching grammar. In her own education, Laura had primarily experienced formalist instruction. In one journal entry, she allowed that she "never really thought about the possibility that [formalism] was only one of many ways to teach English." Teachers she observed during practica taught grammar in the formalist tradition, leading her to write in a journal, "I never realized how unproductive that was until reading this chapter [from an assignment in the Theory of English Grammar course], then observing it in a real situation. It was horrible." Her own disposition and developing conception favored making classes fun and interesting, yet the language strand in the form of grammar instruction awaited her in the curricula she had to teach. The apprenticeship of observation is typically viewed as a formative experience in prospective teachers' enculturation to their discipline, with school experiences providing the default assumptions and practices for teachers to replicate in their own classrooms. Yet Laura's experiences as a student created an aversion to grammar instruction that she hoped never to replicate with her own students. This experience was then reinforced in her practicum observations when formalist grammar instruction had a deadly effect on students' possibilities for experiencing the curriculum in enjoyable, educational ways.

The Theory of English Grammar course included readings emphasizing the futility of teaching textbook English as a discrete skill. They advocated instead treating linguistic variety as both a fact and value. The readings discouraged instruction that positioned textbook usage as the sole acceptable dialect of the English language. Composition and grammar textbooks tend to treat textbook English as the one best version of the language, and other forms as dialects, even as "standard" English itself is a dialect that is appropriate in some, but not all, social situations. The course texts cautioned readers to avoid using textbook or worksheet exercises designed to enforce the textbook dialect on all speaking situations. They urged readers to avoid using exercises oriented to labeling parts of speech in given clauses and phrases, choosing a correct word to use in a given sentence (e.g., between or among), correctly identifying whether a collection of words is a phrase or clause, correctly parsing the language into its component parts, and in general treating language as a rule-bound system with a single correct version that should be used on all occasions, and doing so on workbook exercises independent of authentic usage. This instruction tends to be provided under the assumption that students will intuitively develop procedures for using language according to textbook rules in their own speech and writing, a foundational belief that all of the major research reviews covering over a century have found to be specious.

In contrast, the readings endorsed teaching grammar and usage in the context of student writing, respecting multiple vernaculars rather than insisting on a single "standard" version of English, encouraging generative approaches to language study that directly serve writing development, viewing students' linguistic knowledge and practices as resources to build upon in language study, embedding linguistic knowledge into writing that students value, avoiding approaches that restrict grammatical study to exercises and tests, interpreting "errors" as consequences of risk-taking and thus as signs of growth, and seeing written and spoken speech as vehicles for communicating appropriately in social contexts based on situational expectations and practices.

Although her textbooks offered valuable critiques of traditional grammar instruction, they offered less in terms of sound, concrete methods for teaching grammar effectively. The main generative approach they learned was sentence-combining, a method with roots dating to over a century ago (Rose, 1983) that builds syntactic complexity and maturity by having students combine given clauses and phrases into longer sentences. Laura was never observed using this method in her teaching, and she never referred to it in interviews, suggesting that the course provided her with a general ethos and theory and not with specific practices that she used in place of grammar exercises. I next review her management of the tensions she experienced in teaching a curriculum strand often found dull (Watson, 2018) through means designed to promote student engagement.

Student teaching. Laura did her student teaching at Willa Cather Mid-High, which included ninth and tenth grades in the city's unusual school structure. Her university supervisor made few appearances during her student teaching, and provided little feedback on her teaching on those occasions when she did observe, leading Laura to characterize her as "worthless" and devoid of "constructive advice." Laura's mentorship from Mary Ford thus served as a primary influence in her development of an approach to teaching. Mary herself was responsive to state, district, and school pressures to teach grammar through formalist means, and so was not exercising entirely free will with her guidance. Laura's instruction in grammar was shaped in part by testing mandates that required her students to label parts of speech in given sentences. Test scores could affect real estate values, and often were used to evaluate administrators' and teachers' competence, making teaching to the test part of life in the classroom as it is situated within broader ideological systems.

Mary encouraged Laura to cover grammar by having groups of students teach their classmates particular grammatical concepts. She had developed this method because she herself had only learned grammar when her career required her to teach it. She assumed that having students collaboratively study, discuss, learn, and teach a specific concept would promote their learning, as would being taught a range of concepts by their classmates. Yet the effects of this method were uneven in the classes during which Laura was observed.

Laura embedded the students-teaching-students activity within a diagnostic method that she had learned through a measurement course at the university. She began with a pretest on grammatical concepts that identified areas of strength and weakness. She then identified grammatical concepts for students to teach one another based on the results of the pretest. Some student groups taught their grammatical concepts with apparent effectiveness. The students appeared to enjoy playing the role of teacher, playing the role of students in relation to their peers' instruction, and playing with language in doing the exercises. Students taught one another through enjoyable activities: they made up songs, incorporated grammar knowledge into a *Jeopardy* game, used a *Schoolhouse Rock* videotape, and played musical chairs in response to grammar terms. The activity, when it worked, appeared to be successful in terms of teaching a dreaded subject in ways that the students enjoyed. At the very least, the students in these successful teaching groups learned a grammatical concept well enough to teach it.

However, some groups produced animated and creative activities that provided misinformation about the concepts at hand. Some groups did not learn properly what they were trying to teach, and authoritatively taught their classmates information that was wrong. According to field notes,

> One boy from the group announced that they were "doing verbs" and began by reading a definition and an example of a transitive verb to the class. Next, a girl from the group followed the same procedure in defining linking verbs (which are always intransitive) and helping (auxiliary) verbs. When one student said he didn't understand "the transitive thing," the girl explained (incorrectly) that all action verbs were transitive while all linking verbs were intransitive. . . . Throughout the lesson, students continually offered incorrect definitions and examples of transitive verbs.

Laura experienced tensions between teaching grammar through an enjoyable activity and teaching grammar so that students got the concepts right, the knowledge on which they would be assessed during standardized testing. The students participated enthusiastically in the activity, yet what they learned was at times wrong. Perhaps their poor learning was no worse than what might have happened if she'd used worksheets, assuming her students were more or less like those studied in over a century of research. Laura, in spite of these problems, felt that the benefits outweighed the negatives, saying, "I didn't really think that they would give that much misinformation. But I still think that a small portion of the class learns more by doing it than they would if I were standing up there" explaining sentence elements and assigning worksheets. Using constructivist activities to promote fixed formalist knowledge, then, had mixed results, producing enjoyment yet at times fallacious understandings of the material.

Following the activity, Laura gave a posttest that allowed her to link students' performance on specific grammatical concepts to particular student presentations:

> I will have to go back and cross-reference how they did on which sections and pretest and how they did on the post-test. To see if it was the lessons that helped or if they were just staying constant with what they knew.... If I go back and compare their scores on this test to the pre-test scores, then I can try and determine if they just still know what they knew before, [or if] they have learned something. And if they have learned something, then I can go back and look at, OK, what group taught that subject in that class, and what were their activities? And why did those things work? Or maybe it is just an easier concept.... I need to go back and see if any class has improved and maybe look at why or why not. Compare scores then, and see who taught it, and think about what they did.

Her use of this diagnostic procedure revealed an impressive grasp of the assessment procedure, one that she employed in service of a systematic approach to reflective practice.

Laura's teaching of grammar during student teaching, then, was influenced by a host of factors, including

- Experiences as a student that led her to reject dull and authoritarian teaching and to project an identity as a practitioner of a pedagogy of engagement, which helped her to resonate with Mary's approach to teaching grammar;
- The Theory of English Grammar course that reinforced the personal beliefs she'd developed as a student, without providing her with applications beyond the sentence-combining method that she never used;
- Practicum experiences in which she observed how students experienced workbook-based language instruction as tedious and counterproductive to useful learning;
- The testing mandate that required instruction in parts of speech;
- Mary's influence through her suggestion of having students teach one another syntactic structures;
- Her university course work, albeit not in English Education, through which she learned the assessment procedure.

These factors suggest the inadequacy of locating knowledge about how to teach in two incommensurate and distinct worlds of university and school. Both sites included multiple traditions that Laura orchestrated into a teaching approach that met her disposition, experiences, and theoretical understandings derived from both formal and informal sources. The approach of having students teach students avoided the tedium that had characterized her own experiences with learning grammar and that had been evident in the classes she had observed. It also produced misconceptions following from students' confusion about what they were trying to teach, a problem documented by a research observer and made evident through Laura's diagnostic method. Yet the partial success of the activity left Laura feeling that it was no worse than the formalist alternative, and at the very least had made the language strand more enjoyable to experience for her and her students.

First job: The summer after graduating from college, Laura and her new husband moved to Jacobsville, a city in another part of the state. Jacobsville was a prosperous community of 35,000 residents whose demographics included 82 percent European American, 7 percent Native American, 3 percent African American, 3 percent Latin American, 1 percent Asian American, and 4 percent other. The graduation rate was over 98 percent, and of these graduates, 65 percent entered four-year colleges and 9 percent more enrolled in postsecondary institutions of various kinds. Jacobsville was an affluent, politically conservative community that was "very supportive of education," according to Laura, and academic excellence.

The curriculum at Jacobsville High School (JHS), which served eleventh and twelfth grades only, did not require explicit instruction in grammar, according to Laura: "The only way I 'taught' grammar at Jacobsville was through essay edits, literature analysis, and journals/bell work. . . . It was more inclusion. I also taught a bit of grammar when we looked at poetry through discussion of word choices in particular poems. Other than that there was no grammar in my daily lessons." The absence of a policy mandate requiring isolated grammar lessons enabled Laura to teach in ways recommended in her Theory of English Grammar class. Given that this instruction was not visible during observations, and only available via her testimonies, it can't be documented here.

Second job: Rolling Hills Middle School. Following another career move by her husband to a suburb of a nearby city in the same state, Laura left JHS after three years and found a job teaching English at Rolling Hills Middle School (RHMS), where she taught for one year before taking a maternity leave from which she never returned. Rolling Hills did not provide Laura a great range of latitude to teach what she felt was important. Her assignment was divided into separate preparations for classes in Language (grammar and spelling) and Literature. She reported that

> My weekly instruction was divided by spelling, writing, and language. I gave a journal assignment each day to begin: freewrites, riddles, grammar questions, etc. On Mondays my language classes were responsible for completing their spelling assignment. We had spelling textbooks, so I had them work the lessons from the books. . . . I also had available extra credit worksheets they could complete in their "spare time."

Tuesdays and Wednesdays were "writing days" that focused on a specific form (e.g., descriptive, expository, narrative). Students would produce a draft, and then peer edit using a rubric she provided, after which they turned in a final draft that she graded and that they included in writing portfolios. Ideally, she said, "At the end of each writing unit they were to go to their portfolio and choose their favorite piece from the unit to be revised one more time for a unit grade, [but] this never worked since their papers never found their way to the portfolios."

Thursdays, she said, "were grammar days." For these she relied on a textbook that specified a topic of the day. To make things interesting, she said, "We often worked the lessons as a class—answering the questions aloud—sometimes for prizes, sometimes as a competition, sometimes just because," after which they did an exercise from the book. Fridays included a spelling test, which "sometimes was multiple choice, sometimes traditional out-loud tests. After the spelling tests we would work on the grammar lessons from the day before—either grading or completing."

Laura's teaching at RHMS appeared less constructivist than what she did during student teaching, and less situated than what she did at JHS. Her instruction began to resemble the sort of grammar instruction that she'd hoped to avoid earlier in her career: formalist, textbook-based instruction. Although she tried to relate their writing to language use and grammar, the fragmented curriculum discouraged such integration. Laura said about her teaching at RHMS, "I adapted my style as best I could given the parameters of the new environment; however, the student group and the policies and standards of the district caused me to shift my pedagogical model from the ideal." She did relate the grammar lessons to the students' writing, encouraging them to "explore expression and meaning, word choice, and overall effect of what they wrote." The context, however, constrained her choices:

> Even with all of this effort, I was an island in the middle of their educational ocean. I was trying to teach 7th grade students a new way to function in a classroom. That alone is enough to make a person want to run screaming at the end of each day. In my moments of frustration I came to understand how easy it could be to get into the rut that I worried about in my college journals. It took a great deal of ingenuity and planning to keep myself and my students engaged while still adhering to the standards and policies of the position I had accepted.

In the highly restrictive setting of RHMS, Laura tried to apply understandings from both her university teacher preparation and the settings of her first two teaching experiences. The curriculum required that she approach her subject in isolation, both from writing and from literature. She attempted to include the communicative dimensions emphasized in her university program, and to introduce activities as she had done during student teaching.

On the surface, it might appear that she had regressed as a progressive pedagogue, yet the Vygotskian lens (see Chapter 1) suggests more of a twisting path of concept development in relation to the mediation of different settings. The problem with that metaphor is that it assumes a clear final destination, and the different settings of Laura's learning to teach grammar pointed her in different directions. The university had suggested a process-oriented, activity-centered, generative approach to language teaching and learning; student teaching had emphasized formalist knowledge taught through constructivist means; Jacobsville had allowed free rein that enabled Laura to teach language in the context of communicative competence; and Rolling Hills had made a curricular distinction between grammar/vocabulary and the other English/Language Arts strands and positioned it as formalist knowledge.

Each setting provided different definitions of good teaching, requiring adaptations to practice that were at times out of synch with what Laura believed to be appropriate. With her departure from the profession at a relatively early age to dedicate herself to motherhood and family, her conception of how to teach grammar remained a work in progress and incomplete as her ideals met the demands and assumptions of the curriculum at RHMS, her last stop on her teaching journey.

Brandy

Brandy was an older student who, after graduating from a small rural high school, worked for twelve years as a zone manager for a local newspaper, during which time she got married and had children. She attended a two-year college before enrolling in the Atlantic Piedmont Secondary English Education program featured in this research. Her teaching of an implied character curriculum with working-class students is documented in Chapter 8, which provides additional details about her background.

Projected teacher identity. Brandy distinguished between "inquiry" and "control" approaches to instruction. An "inquiry" approach, she said, enabled students to take the lead and develop a sense of agency to direct their own learning. "Control" involved instruction in service of correct answers. She hoped to cede control to her students, as advocated by the two English Education professors. Prior to student teaching, she said that she admired teachers who allowed students to "let us do our own interpretations" without specifying "what you will get out of it." Her "favorite English teacher of all time" took an open-ended approach in which "she didn't do the 'I'm the teacher, I stand up here and talk and you listen.' . . . She was the first teacher that ever said, 'You know, I don't have all the answers. Just because I see it this way doesn't mean you have to see it this way.'" Such teachers, she said, "weren't pushy. . . . They kind of still left control to the kids. They never forced it on them."

Brandy hoped to import this philosophy to her teaching at Clinton County Comprehensive High School, the site of both her student teaching and her first full-time job. In anticipating how she would teach—that is, in articulating her projected teaching identity—she said that

> Good teaching is letting the students lead . . . because they might see things that I have never seen and take me somewhere new and interesting, just as I can take them someplace. Maybe it's a joint discovery. So I see a lot of interaction with good teaching, a lot of give and take on both sides.

Student teaching. Throughout her student teaching, Brandy taught "college-bound" students in an Advanced eleventh-grade American Literature class, in a school that operated according to a block schedule. Even with the "advanced" designation, the students had little motivation for schoolwork, according to Brandy, and their writing skills needed considerable development.

The codes for Brandy's student teaching are revealing in terms of how she focused her instructional attention, and what she drew on to inform it. During student teaching she only mentioned grammar twice, even with students she considered to have difficulty forming comprehensible sentences. Her attention to her students' writing processes came about because simply providing assignments—her initial approach to handling writing instruction in the absence of a writing pedagogy course at the university—resulted in student confusion. Brandy's solution was to backtrack and provide *post hoc* scaffolding of the processes that would help the students complete the assignments. To account for where she got her teaching ideas from, she referred four times to her university coursework and twice to others from her cohort, suggesting minimal influence from campus, especially when compared to thirty references to school-based influences, and thirty-two references to herself as the source of her ideas.

Her trial-and-error, assign-and-repair approach was evident when she taught Nathaniel Hawthorne's short story "Young Goodman Brown." Brandy gave the following writing assignment: "Decide if [Goodman Brown] has undergone a tentative, uncompleted, [or] decisive initiation." After issuing this assignment, she gave students time to produce a draft. Students, however, floundered with only an assignment and no procedural instruction on how to do the writing. She backfilled with some procedural instruction, starting with a suggestion that the students brainstorm for ideas, and then gave them the five-paragraph structure to fit them in (see Chapter 7). To help them launch these essays, she explained what goes into a thesis statement.

She followed this brief attention to general writing procedures—brainstorming for providing a school-specific form in which to slot their ideas—with a discrete lesson on parts of speech and their proper use in the context of a vocabulary lesson. The other occasion during student teaching on which she covered grammar involved a lesson on using note cards and the style guidelines provided by the Modern Language Association (MLA) (Gibaldi, 2003) for research papers they were writing.

The assign-and-repair approach also occurred when Brandy taught comparison and contrast essays. After assigning the form and finding that the students had no procedural understanding of how to write the papers, she had them compare and contrast familiar, tangible items—an apple and a pear—and had them fit their ideas into the five-paragraph template. The assign-and-repair approach worked well within the mentorship of Laverne, whose style involved allowing Brandy to engage in trial-and-error teaching and then, when she failed, to help her identify how the teaching had gone wrong. Brandy's preparation in her university coursework, which I've characterized as providing fuzzy student-centered concepts without practical applications, provided little foundation for developing a conceptually grounded approach for teaching writing and grammar, a gap that became apparent during the instruction observed for the research. Her campus coursework did not include a course in writing pedagogy and it appeared to elide grammar instruction altogether; the field-based emphasis of the program relied on the MTs to provide instructional support, according to their own style and knowledge. Her MT's approach was nondirective, leading Brandy to engage in trial and error, primarily in the form of assigning tasks and then having students not understand what to do, leading to a regrouping and more scaffolded approach reliant on formalism as embodied by the five-paragraph theme structure.

Brandy's teaching of writing and grammar is perhaps typical of many novice teachers in terms of preparation to teach these strands. She initially had envisioned herself as part of a new breed of teachers whose student-centered, progressive methods would transform the profession. On campus, she was provided with ideals but little practical knowledge for applying them. The field-based program outsourced the pedagogical dimension to MTs, with claims to a seamless alignment that was not evident in our study. The mentorship itself provided direction only after she assigned tasks without providing procedural instruction, and the students floundered, and then she was guided toward formalism such as the use of a five-paragraph theme template. Brandy gravitated to these norms pragmatically, in the absence of campus-based ideas on how to teach writing or grammar. She was then hired by the same school in which she had done her student teaching, suggesting that her approach received positive evaluations from the school-based faculty and administration. I next review how she taught the grammar strand during her first year on the job.

First year of full-time teaching. Brandy taught two ninth-grade preparations, one with two classes of English enhancement classes designed for "struggling readers" and one designated as an "average" English course. During the second half of the year, these courses changed, and Brandy taught two ninth-grade English classes designated as "advanced" (not Advanced Placement) and one listed as an "average" English class. Although Laverne, her student teaching mentor, was assigned to mentor Brandy during her first year of full-time teaching, Brandy made only five references to her in the three observation cycles, suggesting that Brandy was left for the most part to interpret her job for herself.

Brandy, like Leigh in Chapter 7, felt pressure to teach to the state writing test, albeit in a different state. When asked which concepts were most important for students to learn, Brandy replied,

> How to write. That is probably the single most important concept. They haven't learned like paragraph organization, how to stick to one idea per paragraph. And you may end up with five topic sentences in a single paragraph. So I think writing has been the most—it is the most stressed concept that they need to learn in order to pass the [State] writing test.

Brandy's attention to students' writing was thus shaped by the mandate of the exam and its formalist requirements, her stated belief in paragraph organization (and by implication, textual form) as a fundamental requirement for knowing how to write, and her own observations of her students and their response to her instruction. Compared to student teaching, Brandy gave far greater attention to grammar instruction (coded twice during student teaching, and twenty times during the first full-time year); individualized or self-paced instruction (three during student teaching and twenty-two in her first full-time year); and instruction based on what Brandy considered to be students' age-appropriate needs (zero during student teaching and ten in her first year of full-time teaching). She also gave far less writing process attention (from twenty-two instances to thirteen), which during student teaching had come after the trial-and-error stage in which students had struggled with simply being assigned a paper, and which provided retroactive scaffolding of the processes. Each of these factors, along with the differences in teaching assignments in each semester of her teaching, helped to shape Brandy's grammar and writing instruction in her first year of full-time teaching.

Brandy also made relatively few references to the influence on her teaching from her university coursework. She made a total of seven attributions from either preservice or graduate coursework (including a course she took while full-time teaching), seven references to ideas from students from her university cohort, fifty-four attributions to school-based influences, and twenty-three attributions to herself for her teaching ideas. Self-attributions can be difficult to trace to a source, assuming that all ideas come from somewhere and don't spring wholesale from individuals' minds. What seems clear is that they didn't come from the student-centered ideals on campus. Her teaching assignments in the lower tracks, and the writing fluency of the students enrolled in those tracks, undoubtedly helped to shape her conception of formalism as an instructional emphasis.

First observation cycle: An emphasis on form. As reported earlier, Brandy felt that she wasn't herself when observed for the research. At least, she was not fulfilling the projected teacher identity she had envisioned prior to her classroom experience. When the students didn't respond well to student-centered methods—open-ended discussion and attention to learning processes—she shifted from process to product, emphasizing formalism in her teaching under the belief that formal knowledge is prerequisite to inquiry and exploration of ideas. She struggled with issues of control with open-ended teaching, and her solution was to focus on behavioral rules, both to curtail student mischief and to remediate their language use toward the textbook standard.

Brandy's formalist shift was evident across the strands of the curriculum. With respect to grammar, because the students' writing included subject-verb disagreements, she taught a lesson on prepositions. After providing them a list of sixty-eight prepositions, she had them identify prepositions in sentences so that they would be better able to identify objects of prepositions and eliminate them as possible subjects of sentences. Brandy next provided four sentences in which the students were to underline the object of each preposition, using a timer to demarcate their time limit for the exercise. After reviewing the correct answers, Brandy gave a homework assignment to write each of the first twenty prepositions from the list of sixty-eight five times each.

Brandy told the students they could work on their poetry portfolios, generally conceived of as a pedagogical tool in the constructivist tradition. However, her teaching of poetry emphasized, as she said, "more identification rather than production." Initially, she

> was looking at having them produce their own poetry. [Yet] I've done a total 180-degree turn into abandoning the production of poetry and just recognizing the devices used, because it seems ninth-graders are having a hard time grasping these poetical devices much less being able to produce them.... This year it's more important that they be able to at least identify than to produce.

This formalist orientation shifted her use of portfolios away from its processual intention and toward demonstrations of their understanding of formal poetry elements. She had the students "find poems that use the different devices and identify the device used and how it affects the poem," a skill she taught through "worksheets and practice in identifying similes." The students' use of a poetry portfolio was tied to their grammatical studies: they were instructed to write what she called "a parts of speech poem, which I was using to tie in our grammar studies that we've been doing. With each part of speech you just write down like, you know, two nouns followed by three adjectives followed by two more nouns followed by adverbs." This knowledge led to the production of a five-paragraph theme on how poetry is different from prose, designed to have students explain the ways in which "the punctuation is different, capitalization is different, the structure is different, paragraphs you indent, poetry you do not, poetry has stanzas where prose does not, that sort of differences." Brandy had the students grade one another's work with a focus on their knowledge of subject-verb agreement, capitalization, and punctuation; and on their fulfillment of the requirements of the assignment.

The state writing test undoubtedly led in part to her formalist instruction. Yet her struggles with open-ended, constructivist approaches helped align her own values with those of the curriculum and assessment requirements, encouraged during student teaching by Laverne. Her own judgment about what her students needed was paramount in her explanations of why she chose to teach grammar as a structural issue in both what they read and what they wrote. With the university's influence fading in the face of what she saw as her students' lack of fluency with written speech, Brandy taught in relation to the imperative to have her students perform well on the state writing test, in which infelicities of form reduced scores, and her own belief that their grammar needed to be repaired as a prerequisite to their being able to communicate clearly through writing. Without a strong background in writing pedagogy or grammar instruction, either from coursework or student teaching experience, Brandy was left to make decisions based on the best available information and support, often her own judgment about her students' literacy needs and how to provide them with the proper foundation.

One feature of a strong concept is that it provides a road-tested, generalizable framework through which to anticipate future actions and developments (see Chapter 1). Brandy's trial-and-error approach suggests that her teacher education program's fuzzy conceptual grounding gave her few concrete tools through which to enact student-centered teaching with her rural school students. She responded by abandoning the idealistic values she had learned to appreciate on campus, and—still at the trial-and-error level, given that she had few models or pedagogical knowledge for teaching form—taught according to teacher-and-text-centered formalistic emphases. Without a conceptual background providing either specific pedagogical tools or strategies for working with nonideal student populations (i.e., virtually all student populations), she taught through a method of trying something, diagnosing what went wrong, and attempting something else.

Second observation cycle: Agency in learning about form. Later in the semester, Brandy had an epiphany that left her feeling elated and newly confident in her teaching. She came across a pedagogical tool for teaching the form of language in ways over which students had a degree of control, giving her formalist instruction a degree of student-centered autonomy. This tool involved a computer program that allowed the students to pace their own progress with formal textbook language knowledge and determine when they had achieved a satisfactory level of success, thus individualizing their learning in ways that appeared to reduce their resistance to Brandy as an authority figure and give them a degree of control over their proficiency as writers, pace of learning, and use of language in the context of school.

Brandy did attempt to include open-ended opportunities for the students outside the bounds of formal instruction. She would open class, setting a time for eight minutes or so to limit the activity, with a writing prompt such as "Your teacher has asked for the homework you were supposed to complete last night. You didn't do it. Make up a brief excuse so dramatic or so funny or so outrageous that you might be allowed to make it up tonight." She based her choice of topics on her reading of the students' moods and dispositions as they entered class.

Her teaching otherwise remained centered on form. Students' essays on *Romeo and Juliet* emphasized

> what can they infer from things and of course, you know, their grammar. Show me that they're utilizing what we've been studying in grammar. And have a central controlling theme for their whole paper as well as each topic—does each paragraph have a topic sentence and are they sticking with this topic sentence? . . . Even though I know all of the statistics that say direct grammar instruction does not work, that's what I'm doing, is direct grammar instruction. . . . They're just not going to pass the [State] graduation test if I don't focus more exclusively on their writing skills. And unfortunately, if you don't know grammar, it's really hard to write. . . . [The unit ends with] a major unit test, which is multiple choice, which I know is not the best assessment tool, but I'm required to have at least one multiple choice [test as preparation for the state graduation test].

Brandy's rationale for formalist teaching was thus embedded in external testing mandates and requirements for how to prepare students to succeed on it, and came in knowing opposition to what she had learned about the futility of formal, discrete grammar instruction as a way of improving usage in speech and writing. She taught this way not only to prepare her students for mandated tests, however. When asked what influenced her decisions, she said the major impetus was "the student work. I cringe when I read it. They cannot write. . . . There's a mental block of 90 percent of these kids because they cannot even write like they speak. So they will have these sentences that make absolutely no sense." Her view of her students' writing as deficient led her to abandon a unit on Homer's *The Odyssey* in order to create three weeks dedicated exclusively to writing, with an emphasis on proper form.

This focus got a boost when she discovered computer software that included sections on developing writing style and sharpening grammar skills. Brandy stated that this computer program, which focused on teaching the eight parts of speech,

> lets them retake these tests over and over and over until they get it right. . . . With that kind of control in their hands, they're more open to [the grammar exercises].

> And they're beginning to see they really do control all of their grade. . . . I'm really in love with this computer program. . . . Their whole attitudes have been a 360-degree turn. . . . They're coming in after school to play on the program. They come in before school if they have, you know, dead time in class because we're working on projects right now. And so like one will say, "Well, my partners aren't here. Can I just do my language lab instead?" So this program is motivating them.

She attributed the students' more positive attitudes to "the fact that I said I'm not taking this grade unless that's what you want me to take. It made them feel more in control, and I think it's that control issue with these kids. If they feel in control they're more likely to do what you want them to do." Her students' positive view of their grammar studies, she said, helped to relax her own stance with them. "Last Friday," she said,

> I was so impressed that they worked hard for two entire weeks. And third period is just not known for their effort. But they had really kept their noses to the grindstone for two full weeks. So last Friday we got to the part where Romeo and Juliet were getting married. I brought in a cake and drinks and we celebrated the wedding. . . . They were just like, oh my god, I can't believe she's doing this. . . . I may have actually tapped into what makes this group tick. . . . I really have to think that it's the [software] program and the fact that I relinquished control. . . . I realized these kids needed more control. . . . If I give more control to them, and I kind of stand back, maybe they'll teach each other a little bit better."

By yielding control of instruction to her students, Brandy indicated, their disposition toward her class changed, which led Brandy to seek additional ways to cede control. Her descriptions of her students changed along with her recognition of the consequences of surrendering control. Her language regarding—and presumably her view of—her students changed from the language of resistance and tension to that of approval and support, suggesting that she found her work to be more satisfying. Although the focus remained on form, she reported that both she and her students were pleased with her decision to allow them to regulate their own individual pace of learning, with noses gladly to the grindstone of learning correct form on grammar lessons.

Third observation cycle: Applying principles of agency to a new preparation. The spring observations found Brandy teaching an "advanced" rather than vocational class for ninth graders. She nonetheless found that her students exhibited "low motivation, but they're capable. It really frustrates me." Brandy continued to emphasize form in students' writing while allowing greater choice in their topics and personal directions. The students' scores on the state graduation test had dropped, leading the school board and administration to move away from "holistic writing" instruction because it "didn't give them a strong enough foundation. . . . Before you can go holistic they have to understand that there really is a formula behind everything. You know, sentences do have a structure. . . . But we never taught them that structure" such as paragraph form and "pulling all that grammar together and showing them how to integrate it. Why is it important that you know these different parts of speech?" she inquired from the students' point of view.

Brandy began the sequence with a pronoun lesson, using a blank overhead transparency on which she wrote down pronouns that the students offered. She next put up a prepared overhead involving pronouns in compound constructions, then another on pronouns and antecedents. Students then identified the personal pronoun and its antecedent in five given sentences, and Brandy reviewed their answers.

After attending to a writing assignment, Brandy took out a crate of clothespins and distributed six to each student. She wrote the parts of speech on the board, and a student wrote a sentence on the board, which Brandy felt lent authenticity to the activity because the sentence was not from a textbook. Each student was required to identify the part of speech of each word in the sentence. A correct answer enabled them to take a clothespin from a classmate; an incorrect answer required them to forfeit a clothespin to Brandy. The students wrote increasingly long and complex sentences over the course of the activity to enhance their chances of foiling their classmates and winning the game.

Like Laura, then, Brandy found ways to teach grammar in ways that the students didn't resist, and in some cases found enjoyable. Both taught the most formal part of the curriculum, the grammar and writing strand emphasizing correct form of sentences and compositions, in ways that allowed students to play and have agency in what they learned. The research did not study student learning, and so conclusions about the effectiveness of their methods is only available through observations and testimonials. At the very least, both felt better about their teaching after finding a way to teach a reviled aspect of the curriculum in ways that they felt produced student engagement, enjoyment, and investment.

Discussion

Cuban's (1993) outline of student-centered and teacher-centered instruction has provided the field with a binary that maps well onto other dichotomous conceptions of teaching, including the two-worlds pitfall described by Feiman-Nemser and Buchmann (1985), a metaphor that has reached the level of a truism in educational discourse. Although Cuban speaks of a continuum, the distinctions tend to be discussed as mutually exclusive possibilities in educational theory. In more recent work, Cuban (2009) has concluded that most teachers "have hugged the middle of the continuum of two teaching traditions, combining teacher-centered and student-centered practices into hybrids of progressivism" (p. 62) rather than teaching according to a consistent set of principles.

If my studies have any generalizability, the idea that teachers hug the middle of the continuum isn't accurate. Rather, teachers adapt to settings in ways that typically incorporate aspects of both teacher-centeredness and student-centeredness. Finding student writing to be unreadable, and teaching students to express themselves more clearly, is neither teacher-centered nor student-centered. Rather, the readability of written communication is centered. The two teachers in this chapter resolved the problem by recognizing that students whose written syntax is a jumble will have a hard time communicating in writing with other people, and trying to find ways to help them be clear in their expression in relation to their readers' and listeners' anticipations for language use. Formalism, they believed, cannot be ignored, and needs to be taught to help students manage their lives well.

One might disagree with some of their instruction: memorizing lists of prepositions, teaching concepts incorrectly yet having a good time doing so, requiring five-paragraph themes, and other requirements and restraints. Some of these decisions appeared to be solely the teachers'; others were undertaken in response to situational factors such as MT guidance, impending state tests, curricular requirements, a sense of responsibility to students and their families to prepare them for life in and beyond school, and others. Brandy exhibited growth in her ability to teach formal grammar in ways students didn't resist; Laura zigzagged in relation to demands and affordances of her environments, leaving the profession at a point where her setting required a highly formal approach to the language strand of the curriculum. Their examples illustrate the role of settings in developing conceptions of how to teach and, in Laura's case, to demonstrate how one's practice may have little relation to one's conception of effective teaching.

Hugging the middle of a binary/continuum, then, seems to miss the point in that it reduces the problem to how an individual operates between two possibilities, irrespective of contextual factors and imperatives. Rather, teachers respond to their environments in ways that may require them to draw on multiple traditions at once, leading to theoretical and often practical inconsistency. States and districts may require tests on grammatical knowledge. Students may write in ways that others have trouble reading. Teachers may have conflicting notions of if, when, and how textbook language should be deployed in speech and writing. Mentors and supervisors may place different degrees of value on fun and engagement in classroom activities, or for that matter, on whether students should be seated and quiet or active and interactive. Curriculum materials may be available providing a range of instructional means; or mentors or other colleagues may provide access to their ample file cabinets or may suggest activities they have developed that have worked for them. Parents and other community stakeholders may place different values on textbook speech and other dialects and may demand that teachers instruct their values and no others. University professors may shake their heads at schools' resistance to their values, in turn giving teachers reason to reject university professors as out of touch, which they surely are if they believe that ideals are sufficient and that teachers have unencumbered free will in deciding what and how to teach.

Teachers are caught in the middle of this chaos. Not, however, as Cuban (2009) presents the issue, because there is no single continuum that teachers hug the center of. Rather, there many shifting centers, each responding to different gravitational forces, all making demands on teachers and their instruction in ways that make conceptually coherent teaching difficult, if not impossible. In the midst of it all, teachers try to satisfy competing demands in relation to their personal values, all within a system of priorities about what is best for their students, their teaching, and their careers when administrators have the final say in who stays and who goes on their faculty.

11

Community Contexts and Their Societal Settings, and How They Shape Practice

This chapter focuses on a setting that may be overlooked in understanding how teachers' concept development is mediated: the broader local contexts in which schools are set, those provided by communities beyond the school walls, and the institutions with which those communities are affiliated and to which they are indebted. I'll open by providing a document that one of my master's degree students gave me when I taught a writing pedagogy course at the University of Oklahoma in the mid-1990s. After a month or so of classes devoted to writing instruction predicated on student interest, open-ended inquiry, exploratory writing, and other constructivist ideas, one of the students who taught in a middle school in a politically and socially conservative community said something like, "I sorry, but I couldn't do a single thing we've talked about here in my school."

The next week she brought in the following document, which parents in her community were provided by an advocacy group. They used this document to pressure the school administration to teach in literal, nonreflexive ways so as not to disrupt or question the values imparted through the Holy Bible and its stature as their families' and faith communities' primary, and perhaps sole, source of wisdom and knowledge:

> I am the parent of _____ who attends _____ School. Under U. S. legislation and court decisions, parents have the primary responsibility for their children's education, and pupils have certain rights which the schools may not deny. Parents have the right to assure that their children's beliefs and moral values are not undermined by the schools. Pupils have the right to have and to hold their values and moral standards without direct or indirect manipulation by the schools through curricula, textbooks, audio-visual materials, or supplementary assignments.
>
> Accordingly, I hereby request that my child be involved in NO school activities or materials listed below unless I have first reviewed all the relevant materials and have given my written consent for their use:
>
> - Psychological and psychiatric examinations, tests, or surveys that are designed to elicit information about attitudes, habits, traits, opinions, beliefs, or feelings of an individual or group;

- Psychological and psychiatric treatment that is designed to affect behavioral, emotional, or attitudinal characteristics of an individual or group;
- Values clarification, use of moral dilemmas, discussion of religious or moral standards, role-playing or open-ended discussions of situations involving moral issues, and survival games including life/death decision exercises; death education, including abortion, euthanasia, suicide, use of violence, and discussions of death and dying;
- Curricula pertaining to alcohol and drugs;
- Instruction in nuclear war, nuclear policy, and nuclear classroom games;
- Anti-nationalistic, one-world government or globalism curricula;
- Discussion and testing on inter-personal relationships; discussions of attitudes toward parents and parenting;
- Education in human sexuality, including premarital sex; extra-marital sex, contraception, abortion, homosexuality, group sex and marriages; prostitution, incest, masturbation, bestiality, divorce, population control, and roles of males and females; sex behavior and attitudes of student and family;
- Pornography and any materials containing profanity and/or sexual explicitness;
- Guided fantasy techniques; hypnotic techniques; imagery and suggestology;
- Organic evolution, including the idea that man has developed from previous or lower types of living things;
- Discussions of witchcraft, occultism, the supernatural, and Eastern mysticism;
- Political affiliations and beliefs of student and family; personal religious beliefs and practices;
- Mental and psychological problems and self-incriminating behavior potentially embarrassing to the student or family;
- Critical appraisals of other individuals with whom the child has family relationships;
- Legally recognized privilege and analogous relationships, such as those of lawyers, physicians, and ministers;
- Income, including the student's role in family activities and finances;
- Non-academic personality tests; questionnaires on personal and family life and attitudes;
- Autobiography assignments; log books, diaries, and personal journals;
- Contrived incidents for self-revelation; sensitivity training, group encounter sessions, talk-ins, magic circle techniques, self-evaluation and auto-criticism, strategies designed for self-disclosure (e.g., zig-zag);
- Sociograms; sociodrama; psychodrama; blindfold walks; isolation techniques.

The purpose of this letter is to preserve my child's rights under the Protection of Pupil Rights Amendment (the Hatch Amendment) to the General Education Provisions act, and under its regulations as published in the Federal Register of Sept. 6, 1984, which became effective Nov. 12, 1984. These regulations provide a procedure for filing complaints first at the local level, and then with the U. S. Department of Education. If a voluntary remedy fails, federal funds can be withdrawn from those in violation of the laws. I respectfully ask you to send me a substantive response

> to this letter attaching a copy of your policy statement on procedures for parental permission requirements, to notify all my child's teachers, and to keep a copy of this letter in my child's permanent file. Thank you for your cooperation.
> Sincerely, _____
> Copy to: School Principal
> Child's Teachers

Although the document may be a couple of decades old, the current political climate makes it likely that little has changed in families and communities where it was distributed back then. I include it here to demonstrate how school values are often shaped from well outside their own administrative jurisdiction, in this case by parents, churches, lawyers, lawmakers, the political donors who influence lawmakers, the electorate that puts politicians in office, and the broader, historically situated belief systems and institutions through which their views have developed.

I don't present this letter to mock the people who present it to their schools. I open with this anecdote, document, and reflection from outside the bounds of the research to illustrate how schools are not at the opposite end of a two-worlds binary, positioned against universities. Rather, schools are situated within communities and their value systems in ways that shape how teachers conduct their classes, their extracurricular activities, and in many cases, their personal lives. For example, in a story reported as far away as New Zealand,[1] a teacher who graduated from my university's teacher education program lost her job when she posted a photograph on a Facebook page protected by "high" privacy settings, showing her on a European vacation with a beer mug and glass of wine. Where she taught, posing with alcohol was considered immoral and below the standards of their faculty. Her firing was widely ridiculed in the internet, which did not change the setting in which that district's teachers taught. There are thus many worlds out there beyond school and university that help to shape how teachers go about their work.

I focus in this chapter on two teachers, one of whom taught in what I have characterized as a "corporate" community adhering to neoliberal conceptions of school and society (see Cuban, 2019), and one of whom taught in a far less restrictive environment that made "eupraxis" possible. *Eupraxia* (εὐπραξία) comes from Aristotle (350 BCE), who emphasized the need for disciplined reflection upon practice so as to understand it and improve it in future iterations. Praxis refers to a cyclical process of experiential learning through which reflection may transform practice. Eupraxia is available when teachers have agency to act upon their reflections. It characterizes what is available to people who are free to choose, a condition that is rarely available, thus serving as an ideal toward which to strive rather than an achievable state in a complex social environment.

I feature these two teachers because of the remarkable contrast they provide in how broader settings shape teaching contexts and possibilities. Natalie taught in a community that boasted of corporate values that in turn provided the contours for

---

[1] https://www.iol.co.za/news/world/teacher-fired-over-facebook-pic-1023313

teaching, learning, and assessment in restrictive ways that eliminated the possibility for teachers to engage in eupraxis. Samantha, whose student teaching is reported in Chapter 8, is featured here in her first year of teaching in a less restrictive environment, one that provided her with agency in decision-making, based on her own reflections on the effects of her teaching.

The purpose of the comparison is to take two teachers from the same Atlantic Piedmont University English Education program whose careers took them to large suburban school districts within an hour or so of each other. Their cases illustrate how their community settings produced different conceptions of schooling that shaped what was available to them pedagogically. In the case of Natalie, her teaching was at odds with her conception of effective instruction. What people do in classrooms is not what they necessarily believe they should do, suggesting that concept development cannot always be evident on the basis of actions, which may be at odds with conceptual thinking. In the case of Samantha, the setting allowed her to teach in relation to what she observed in her students in terms of their socialization to school and classroom expectations, and in terms of their engagement with the curriculum. Although I tend to avoid working in binaries, the contrast here is useful in looking at how two extremely different contexts shape instructional practice, student performance, and teachers' affective experience in carrying out their work.

Natalie

Natalie grew up in what she described as a "very small, small town" in a county classified as 95 percent rural, served by a single high school. The community was homogeneous, with 92 percent of the residents White and 7.5 percent African American, with the primary religion being Baptist. Natalie fit easily within the dominant demographic. Her projected teacher identity followed from teachers who had provided her with positive experiences with reading and writing. "The good ones," she said, "were more interested in their students." I next briefly describe Natalie's student teaching in a school very similar to the one she had attended, then follow her through her first and second jobs, each providing very different settings for her teaching, along with different levels of affiliation and satisfaction.

Student Teaching

Natalie's student teaching took place at a small rural high school under the mentorship of Leila, who was chair of the English department and a respected senior citizen of the faculty. Natalie taught tenth-grade general students who, like most students from this community, were agrarian or working-class Whites who had no plans to go on to college. In spite of Leila's membership in good standing with the student-centered Southern Plains English Education program and its emphasis on connections, including those between school and university, she relied heavily on worksheets and other formalist tools for her mentorship of Natalie. Leila's teaching relied almost exclusively on what

Natalie described as "All those file cabinets in Leila's room . . . they're just jam-packed with stuff she's collected over 28 years." These file cabinets provided the materials, largely worksheets and assignments from the formalist tradition, that Leila used to support Natalie's development as a student teacher.

Natalie used such worksheets as an exercise on "Using Modifiers" that included a fill-in-the-blank section on sentence completion (e.g., "Graham crackers taste [delicious, deliciously] with a glass of cold milk") and a multiple-choice section in which students chose the correct modifier for given sentences (e.g., "The jackal seems [ferociouser, more ferocious, ferociousest, most ferocious] than the hyena"). Natalie also used a worksheet from the file cabinet on *The Diary of Anne Frank* that consisted entirely of a series of correct-answer questions (e.g., When was Anne born? When did Anne and her family go into hiding? Where was the hiding place? Who kissed Anne? Who found Anne's diary?). Leila said that she used these materials

> To prepare the students for eleventh and twelfth grade, to get them ready for the [state] graduation test. But most of all is to get them to be able to go out into the world after they leave high school and have the skills they need as [inaudible] college, technical schools, but also for the students who may not necessarily go to school to be able to communicate effectively, be able to read and just to survive in the world.

Leila considered herself student-centered, a disposition she traced to the tragic death of her own son as a high school student, an event that led her to increase her care for students as individuals and to help prepare them for entering the work force with the greatest array of life skills and personal qualities possible. Yet she guided Natalie toward classroom processes and assessments that were highly restricted and text-based, allowing for little personal connection between life and classroom activities. Her file cabinet provided students, and Natalie, with concrete, measurable assignments that relied on their ability to complete tasks as expected. As Natalie explained on one occasion,

> She handed me a whole folder of like tests and quizzes for *To Kill a Mockingbird*. . . . It's about two inches thick. And I really tried not to use those. She wanted me to resort to it . . . I was going through, and I was retyping it, and I was going to use parts of it, and then I was like, I'm not doing this, I'm not doing this. So I went back and came up with my own. . . . I said, "Leila, I just really think that some parts of it are just real tricky and just nit-picky." And some of it's true/false, and I absolutely hate true/false questions.

Natalie was thus able to negotiate differences with Leila in order to include what she considered more student-centered instruction. She discussed her symbol instruction for a unit on *To Kill a Mockingbird* by saying,

> They're going to be doing a symbols activity. We're talking about the symbols in *To Kill a Mockingbird*. . . . We've already read tomorrow the chapters where they find

a lot of the things in the tree in *To Kill a Mockingbird*, and a lot of those symbolize different things in the book, the objects in the tree. And we did an activity at [the university] that I'm actually taking this from, where you watch the beginning of *To Kill a Mockingbird* and the intro to the film. And it has—it shows all these symbols in a box, and they break into groups, and they try to figure—list all the symbols on there and then what the importance of each is. And then they're going to try to come up with their own personal symbols, symbols for themselves. And they'll have to come up with three and write a paragraph on each and why that symbolizes them. . . . I really want it to be meaningful for themselves. I really try to talk about, you know, how they can relate to this, because Scout is so much—her growing up and the things that she does are so much like our own growing up.

The next day Natalie ran the activity to mixed results. She had the students work in small groups, and they struggled, apparently never having done group work before. They also had difficulty interpreting the novel as assigned, having been acculturated in Leila's class, and likely others before, to single-answer, objectivist questions. Natalie ended up offering her own interpretations of the symbols in this opening segment of the film. She often had to accommodate her own goals for teaching with Leila's more literal approach: "I really just want them to enjoy the book, and I don't think that can be done with all the quizzes that I'm having to give and the nit-picky details that they're having to remember." Yet her students appeared to have learned to follow the patterns established with Leila's restricted approach, making it difficult to shift to what Natalie hoped was a more student-centered literary experience.

Natalie's student teaching was often frustrating. She either used Leila's formalist worksheets or struggled to implement constructivist activities with students who had been conditioned to authoritarian schooling and who felt more comfortable with "nit-picky details" than open-ended inquiries, reminiscent of Penny's efforts to implement constructivist practices in a school with an authoritarian culture (see Chapter 5). She thus entered her first job with teaching experiences that did not reinforce either her prior beliefs about good teaching or the general student-centered conception emphasized on campus. Leila's mentorship did not provide the seamless relation between campus and school claimed in program rhetoric, indeed seeming to embody its opposing ideology, leaving Natalie holding to a belief in student-centered methods, but providing her with few methods with which she had experienced success. The outsourcing of practical teaching ideas to MTs in this field-based program provided a disjuncture that belied the program's claims to careful alignment between university and schools.

First Job

Natalie's first job was at Flannery O'Connor Middle School (O'Connor MS), one of seventeen middle schools in the state's largest school district. The district prided itself on its reputation for academic excellence, documented with state and national awards and with high test scores. The district took a corporate approach to education, as indicated by a letter from a school board member to district constituents that stated, "You are stockholders in the [County] Public School System. Your [County] property taxes dedicated to the public school system qualify you for stockholder status.... Moody's Investor's Service recently upgraded to AAA (Triple A) its bond rating for [County] Public Schools—the highest bond rating available" (emphasis in original).

The county's corporate outlook was evident in its emphasis on accountability. To avoid what the district's website called "social promotion," the district developed an extensive curriculum that was tied to what it called "a results-based evaluation system." Tests were administered in fourth, fifth, seventh, and eighth grades, and they served as "gateways" to the following year of school. Those who failed the test, *regardless of their grades in classes*, were required to repeat the grade level. Additional tests in tenth and eleventh grades determined whether a student graduated with a regular county diploma or what amounted to a certificate of attendance. The curriculum was aligned with a variety of standardized assessments, including the Stanford-9, SAT I, ACT, and the state standards, themselves aligned with the [State] High School Graduation Test and the Criterion Referenced Competency Tests. These test scores informed the district "stockholders" of the value of their educational portfolio, and thus became the primary drivers of instructional practice.

Natalie's opportunities for using a student-centered approach were limited in this setting, which institutionalized and mandated the skills-oriented curriculum favored by Leila during student teaching. The district website reported that the curriculum and assessment system provided "the standards for academic excellence for all students in [the County] Public Schools. They are what teachers are to teach and students are to learn. In every [County] classroom, instruction and assessment are tailored so that all students learn" the skills specified in the curriculum, which was tied to high-stakes assessments that determined a student's promotion to the next grade. This interdependent relation between curriculum and assessment was developed in response to the district mission "*to pursue excellence in academic knowledge, skills, and behavior for each student resulting in measured improvement against local, national, and world-class standards*" (emphasis in original).

The curriculum's institutionalization made it difficult to interpret and implement flexibly and with agency, particularly for vulnerable early career teachers like Natalie. During student teaching, Natalie could discuss disagreements personally with Leila and reach a compromise in the setting of the rural school district, its small schools, and the absence of a corporate mentality in serving students assumed to be headed to blue collar jobs, farm work, or marriage and family. The district that housed O'Connor MS, however, was controlled by a large bureaucracy whose administrators were invested in promoting the assessment system as a central means of validating the county's status among the state's elite school districts. The curriculum's required objectives and assessments were impervious to negotiation for the district's young and vulnerable teachers, and for any faculty whose competence could be evaluated and compared according to test results. The district's website asserted that "because the [standards] detail exactly what a child is expected to learn, teachers can tailor the classroom experience to meet a child's individual needs," a possibility that Natalie struggled with as a teacher of eighth-graders facing the district writing test in the spring, the failure of which would deny their promotion to high school, and would further affect her reputation with her administration and department.

I next review some of Natalie's experiences teaching within the corporate accountability system of her district. The instruction detailed in the three observation cycles, as might be expected, was focused on preparing for both the knowledge anticipated on tests and the methods used for assessment, neither of which matched Natalie's hopes for teaching in open-ended, student-centered ways.

Observation cycle #1. On the first day of observations, Natalie began with a Daily Oral Language (D.O.L.) lesson during which students corrected passages that included errors in capitalization and punctuation. She next led students in a review of an analogy worksheet tied to the standards and assessment, then conducted a vocabulary lesson in which students presented "SAT words" and their definitions to the class. The students were evaluated on their correct provision of the word, its part of speech, its definition, an illustration and explanation, the word used correctly in a sentence, the presentation, and neatness.

Later in the observation cycle she had students write on prompts related to what they would later be assessed on: "They've got *Writing to Tell a Story*, they've got *Research* and *Writing to Inform* and *Writing to Persuade*, which are all in the [standards and assessment]. That's all the writing that we're going to cover this year." During this observation cycle Natalie focused all of her instruction on curricular standards that would be tested, with some efforts to connect the lessons to students' lives, such as when the students' writing in response to prompts allowed creativity and a personal voice in the topic. These efforts were severely constrained by the restrictions of the curriculum.

Observation cycle #2. Natalie began class with a D.O.L. lesson, then led the students through another analogy sheet. The remainder of the class was dedicated to small-group preparation of vocabulary projects in which each group had a particular sentence formation (simple, compound, compound/complex, etc.) that they would teach to the class, an approach similar to that used by Laura in Chapter 10, except focused on sentence structure rather than parts of speech. The presentations included examples of the particular kind of sentence featured and a test or quiz, often in the form of a worksheet.

After making their presentations the next day, the students were assigned an analogy worksheet and were given time to study for a spelling quiz, neither of which was related to the vocabulary and sentence-structure presentations. Natalie said that she had planned the presentations as a

> hands-on activity, I guess, and getting involved with it and making it their own project and just having it be their own. And, of course, I've taught [in order to] emphasize sentences. That's the major grammar concept. And the reason for that is to try to help them score better with—sentence formation is one of the areas that they score on that writing test they have to pass.

Natalie identified three main purposes for her instruction: teaching students "to take responsibility for their own actions and for their work . . . preparing them for college. . . . And then, of course, I'm pushed by the [standards] concepts." Students' playful engagement during the vocabulary presentations was accompanied by worksheets and quizzes, suggesting an awkward juxtaposition of different traditions in their mimicking of teachers as they performed the role with their classmates.

Observation cycle #3. Natalie began class with a review of homework questions on Dorothy M. Johnson's "Too Soon a Woman," a story about pioneer life on the Oregon Trail. She posed additional questions about the story, and asked questions about the students' lives in relation to the difficulties faced by the pioneer women. The students then did peer edits on persuasive essays they had begun several weeks before, first with drafting, then library research for factual support of claims, then revisions based on informal conferencing with Natalie.

The next day, the students worked individually on revisions of these papers, relying on the peer critiques. During class, Natalie circulated and conducted conferences with individual students. On the board, she had provided laminated sheets with curricular objectives that provided grading criteria: "[Standard] #26—edit for spelling, fragments, and run-on sentences, [Standard] #35—write to persuade classmates of an opinion, [Standard] #39—write, combine and vary sentences to match purposes and audience."

Natalie described this instruction as a "writing workshop." Ideally, according to publications often used to guide teachers through this pedagogy, a writing workshop "invites and supports writing process. . . . Writers need Giacobbe's three basics of time, ownership, and response" (Atwell, 1987, p. 54). Natalie's planning included response opportunities from both peers and herself within time constraints. These limitations made the allowance of a student-determined writing process—the provision of which is an article of faith among writing workshop advocates—difficult to achieve. Natalie described this constraint as coming both from students' acculturation to school practices and her own eye on the pacing chart:

> The first question out of their mouth [is], When is this due? And they don't want to take the time to sit down and work at it and really draft their writing and work on their writing. . . . Some days I'm not careful, and I'll just sit there, and I find myself just giving them some of the answers when I know I shouldn't be. And sometimes that's for time's sake because I feel like I'm having to rush to get through all their papers and read all their papers. And when I really want to spend longer on it. But then we just don't have the time.

The focus of the workshop ended up attending to the curriculum objectives more than students' meaning-making or writing processes. Natalie described her evaluation of students' workshop writing as follows:

> I'm going to go over the five areas, the content organization and style and mechanics and usage and sentence formation. And we're going to talk about all those. And then I might save sentence formation, talk about it last because then I will—after we do the parts of speech I'm going to go into sentences and putting together sentences and subject and predicate and all that. Verbs. [inaudible] verbs and parts of speech. . . . I've tried to set up my scoring scale and the way I've weighted it similar to the writing test. And we've gone over the areas that they

look for, that they score under. Content organization, mechanics, usage, sentence formation, and style.

These five assessment areas were oriented to form rather than meaning. Natalie's implementation of a writing workshop format demonstrated a disjunction between her student-oriented values and the pressures of the curriculum mandates and assessment system. Faced with an extensive set of curriculum objectives to cover, she attempted to teach them in the context of methods such as writing workshop that she'd learned at the university that theoretically would help students make connections with their schooling. The imperative to assess form and mechanics, however, shifted the writing workshop's emphasis away from student-oriented qualities and toward the sort of "nit-picky details" that Natalie had found so objectionable under Leila's tutelage.

Summary. During the year in which she was observed and interviewed at O'Connor MS, Natalie emphasized formal aspects of language use, a pedagogy shaped by the corporate climate of the school district and its accountability system based on standardized test scores and punitive approach to test failure. Within that curriculum and assessment system, she undertook instruction—presentations, group work, projects, writing workshop—customarily regarded as tools in the student-centered teacher's toolkit. In her own view, however, the heavy focus on form and mechanics and the degree of coverage expected resulted in a pace and emphasis that made it difficult for her to teach in a whole-heartedly student-centered way. At the beginning of the next school year, Natalie wrote,

> I don't like what appears to be the future of education, middle school education in particular, either. I don't believe in single tests that claim to determine a child's performance and improvement over an entire year. I don't believe my salary should be determined by that single test. . . . I already don't have enough hours in a day to do the things I am required and need to do.

Natalie left O'Connor after her second year, settling later in a rural school that provided a better match for her backgrounds and beliefs. The corporate mentality of her first two years of teaching relied on a view of accountability that required continual testing of students according to predetermined skills amenable to measurement through either standardized tests or writing assessments that focused exclusively on form. She attempted to include playful opportunities within the restrictions of the curriculum, yet such play was limited by her concurrent effort to meet the district's standards for correctness.

Natalie's growth as a teacher was affected by the strict requirements of the curriculum. With limited opportunity to teach beyond the formalism emphasized in assessment, she left her job and temporarily left the profession before settling at the rural school. Natalie found O'Conner's dedication to a corporate structure to inhibit her efforts to teach in a student-centered manner. She instead settled in the smaller, more rural, relatively impoverished district where she could establish strong relationships and accompany them with teaching practices in which she believed. The epilogue she wrote for the published study is worth excerpting here:

Natalie's Epilogue

I taught two years at O'Connor Middle School and I was pretty much miserable the whole time. I felt very out of my element and not comfortable with what I was doing at all. I was very used to being successful at most things I attempted, and I just never could feel as if I was doing a good job teaching. Most days I felt like a total failure. I was terrified that my students weren't going to learn anything to take with them to high school, and that once they got there someone was going to let out my secret; I was nothing but a phony! I usually felt as if I was playing a role I was not prepared for and hoping no one would figure that out. I felt very isolated.

I said earlier that I was overwhelmed with planning. . . . I had no idea where to begin. [The first county I taught in] has their own curriculum in addition to the state's [Curriculum]. It combines [state] objectives and standardized test objectives. I was supposed to teach the reading *and* Language Arts curriculum in one daily 50-minute class period. It was an insane amount of material to cover. I have learned since coming to [my current county school system] that it would actually take something like 25 years to teach [the state's] curriculum! And in [my current] County they have categorized the state's curriculum into essential, important, and minimal strands. They have done what I could not do for myself during my first two years teaching. It was just too much to wade through. Especially considering I was supposed to spend even more time preparing my students for the high-stakes writing test in the spring and a battery of other standardized tests, the CRCT, ITBS test, Stanford Achievement tests, etc. In [the] County where I currently teach, we only prepare for one standardized test, the CRCT, [the] state mandated standardized test. I still feel sometimes that I am teaching to the test, but I feel much more organized. I still wonder if the students are learning, and many times I think they are not. . . .

In [the first county I taught in] I felt that no one was giving me those strategies to try. I felt that my planning time was eaten up with *useless*, I can't stress that enough, meetings. . . . We often had meetings or staff development courses four out of the five days a week. Thank goodness my current administrators work to protect our planning time! And because we prepare for fewer standardized tests I feel as though I actually have time in my classes to try the new strategies I've been given. I feel as though I actually have time to practice being a teacher, to become good at what I've chosen to do.

I am also happier now because I am in a school system that is much more like the one I attended growing up. It is much more rural. The students are much more grateful and respectful and appreciative. I have had nothing but support from my [students'] parents, and this is another tremendous difference from my first two years teaching where I felt as if every decision I made was being criticized. I never felt as though I did anything right. I had a parent call me a child predator which is so far from the truth that it brought me to tears. I entered this profession because I love students. I love their energy and enthusiasm. I usually felt as though I was killing both of these things during my first two years. In the name of learning and discipline I found myself saying crazy, and maybe even ugly, things at times. It was almost like an out-of-body experience. I would look down on myself and think, "I can't believe I just did (or said) that!! I don't really feel that way! Do I?"

I still am not sure where I stand as far as students' learning goes. Sometimes I still may be guilty of caring too much about trying to prepare them for tests and not enough about their actually learning the material. Most days it is easier and less stressful for me to just go with the "test prep" approach. It requires less energy and thinking, and I'm as guilty of not wanting to think as my students on some days. I think I am lucky because I am part of a system that is trying not only to help us prepare students for the standardized tests of the system but also trying to help us learn how to teach students so that they retain information and their learning becomes meaningful. My current administration is helping to keep me from getting too lazy and pushing me to remember what is truly important.

Samantha

Samantha's teaching was featured in Chapter 8, where her teaching assignment of vocational English led her to focus on character development as a prerequisite to readiness for school engagement and academic performance. Here, she is depicted during her first year of full-time teaching at a large suburban school with a dedication to faculty members' intellectual freedom. The school was one of several in the district, and had a reputation for being the least restrictive. The individual schools within the district were granted local control, and so rather than all being subject to a single plantation-style central administration's edicts, each could institute its own culture. The broader district-wide setting, then, allowed her school's administration to operate according to its own priorities and values, an ethos that shaped what was possible for teachers.

In this setting she was able to teach in ways that emerged from her own good judgment, a condition that creates possibilities for eupraxis, or at least as close an approximation thereof as may be available in public school teaching. Although her large suburban school was quite different from the second, and far smaller and more rural, school that Natalie taught in, the two provided similar opportunities for teaching according to professional judgment rather than in response to top-down management's priorities and imperatives.

Samantha's administration's trust in her decision-making allowed her to teach in ways she felt contributed to her students' growth. In contrast with Natalie's first job, where a corporate climate created an accountability mentality that made test scores paramount in the minds of community stakeholders, Samantha's school made teachers accountable to students, based on what they observed and reflected on in their own classrooms, and on their beliefs about what matters in education.

Beliefs about Teaching

Samantha's projected teacher identity was grounded in teachers from her apprenticeship of observation. Her favorite teachers, she said, "were really funny. They were really fair.... You didn't just read something and answer questions. They did a lot of different activities. You never really knew what exactly what we were going to do that day when we went in there." Her experiences teaching in a Montessori school had helped her appreciate the value of children's self-directed learning.

Teachers she found exemplary provided a supportive classroom environment that she hoped to replicate, one that accommodated diverse learners and treated all students fairly. These reflective practitioners were adaptable and resilient when lessons went awry. Samantha admired teachers who promoted exploratory, activity-based, independent, and integrated learning. Positive instruction was useful, active, engaging, performative, open-ended, multimodal, discussion-oriented, integrated, interest-driven, differentiated, and so engrossing that students would not go off task. She aspired to become a reflective practitioner with the willingness to adapt her plans in thoughtful response to the performance of her students.

She disliked teachers who were "very dry, very dull, and if you were struggling you didn't seem to get much sympathy." Such teachers were "very traditional, very, 'Let's do this and answer the questions, and let's do that,'" instead of teaching through "multidisciplinary, hands on sorts of things." During a practicum, she had been horrified by a teacher who was "very sarcastic to her kids." Teachers she hoped not to emulate tested students on verbatim, established knowledge with no interpretive or constructive learning opportunities.

Samantha's wish not to emulate formalist teachers might mean that if she had observed Natalie in her first job, she would not have wanted to emulate her. But Natalie herself was not the problem, as evidenced by her reflection that she felt as though she was having an out-of-body experience teaching in that setting; Natalie would not have wanted to emulate herself either. Teachers are often solely held accountable for their teaching. Yet as the examples throughout this book demonstrate, what teachers do is not necessarily who they are. Blaming teachers for how they teach overlooks too many factors of setting to make for a responsible conclusion. They are always situated within multiple, conflictual contexts that pull them in many directions, often in ways they reject but have little agency to resist, especially at the most vulnerable point of their careers: the beginning. These contexts are not confined to the school itself, but extend into the community and beyond.

Full-Time Job

Samantha took her first job at Danforth High School (DHS). Demographically, Danforth was similar to the school in which she had done her student teaching, reviewed in Chapter 8. It was also demographically similar to the county in which Natalie took her first job. However, Danforth was different from both in the overall ethos of the administration and faculty in terms of how to engage potentially disaffected students with the curriculum. The district's granting of local control to its schools allowed Danforth to create its own culture and values. It faced the same accountability mandates imposed by the state that affected other teachers from her program, but responded to them with greater confidence in its faculty to interpret them and prepare their students for them.

At DHS, the primary structural influence was her instructional team, which shared a common planning period to coordinate cross-disciplinary projects, such as "an autobiography journey through life" for ninth graders. She was not entirely free to teach as she chose, yet felt far more autonomy than she had experienced during student teaching.

When she was interviewed at the beginning of her first year at DHS, Samantha's two most frequent attributions to influences on her instructional thinking were to herself as the originator of ideas and to her students as influences on her thinking. Her colleagues and the English curriculum were next in influence. She made little reference to her teacher education program and her apprenticeship of observation, instead attributing her teaching to factors with presence and immediacy in her environment.

Samantha's teaching addressed a different range of problems than she had faced during student teaching. She mentioned "control" only once, instead referring extensively to planning in the constructivist tradition, suggesting that her focus was more on instruction than on discipline, although socializing students to school and classroom norms was among her concerns. Her instruction in grammar sought to contextualize language use in relation to the students' writing (including writing essays, writing creatively, and writing in a workshop setting) and public speaking. She also hoped to differentiate her instruction so that diverse learners could have equal access to success.

DHS did not include students of great affluence or school affiliation; they were not much different from the students she taught in student teaching where a character curriculum was imposed to civilize their rude behavior. Rather, it had a different ethos, one that enabled Samantha to put a student-centered practice to work. Tracing the source of her enactment of a student-centered pedagogy is difficult if evidence from the research is all we have to go on. She had been exposed to both formalist and constructivist teachers during her apprenticeship of observation. Her teacher education program had emphasized connections and student-centered teaching without providing specific practices to achieve them. Student teaching had suggested the importance of shaping up kids' character through acculturation to behavioral norms. Attributing her gravitation to a student-centered pedagogy at DHS to any single source seems speculative. It's safer to assume that an aggregate for influences helped to make this set of practices appealing to her. She rarely mentioned any influence beyond those at DHS, so if those prior experiences did affect her, they did so subconsciously, an area of mentation impossible to pinpoint with any confidence. I next review what the observation cycles of her first year of Danforth yielded in terms of following her practice of student-centered teaching methods.

Observation cycle #1. During the first observation cycle, Samantha taught a mystery unit in the context of a cross-disciplinary "Me Project" coordinated with teachers from other subject areas. Samantha said, "This is my first real attempt at putting together a unit," an opportunity available through the open-ended expectations for teaching and learning available at Danforth, in contrast to the prepared modules she had taught during student teaching.

Samantha said that her students had "a hard time because they don't have very good reading skills, they don't have very good writing skills, and they really aren't independent enough to really do this." Her struggling students, she believed, lacked "study skills, organizational skills" and the capacity "to be very tolerant of each other and very patient." As had been the case during student teaching, her teaching involved socializing ninth graders to high school behavioral expectations.

She felt that she could help with their socialization toward expected norms by providing them with an engaging curriculum, a view shared by her colleagues and thus engrained in the school's approach. She did have to coordinate her curriculum and instruction with her teaching team for the Me Project, but how she did so was entirely up to her. Her decisions followed from her reflection on her students' needs, a consideration she was entrusted to undertake based on her own judgment that her students needed "to see English and reading and writing as something that's actually fun rather than this, oh, this big chore." To learn about her students' interests, she administered a survey. Students indicated that they liked mysteries and would like to read them, leading Samantha to design a mystery unit around the play *Arsenic and Old Lace*.

Students worked in self-selected peer groups to list characters, clues, the solution to the crime, and a plot outline. The unit included opportunities for writing on personal opinions and evaluations, such as reflections on the craziest and most sane characters in *Arsenic and Old Lace*, and journal writing on how they would create a detective. In addition to these constructivist opportunities, Samantha administered objectivist assessments so that "different kids who test different ways will be able to at least do well on parts of it."

Samantha's instruction drew primarily on school-based influences—particularly herself and her students, but also her colleagues and her principal—for both the socialization of students and integrating the unit with the Me Project. She did not follow her original design strictly. Rather, she reflected on how the instruction was working and made appropriate adjustments.

Observation cycle #2. During the second week of November, Samantha focused on writing and reading poetry. Students began with a journal assignment to write either a poem or a short story, after which students read what they had written. Samantha then led a discussion of Ernest Thayer's poem "Casey at the Bat." She focused first on formal elements such as stanza divisions and rhyme scheme, followed by what she called a "reader's response" session in which students gave personal opinions about the poem. She then shifted to writing the students had done outside class, with students sharing stories in small groups.

On the next day Samantha began with a quiz over "Casey at the Bat" and poetry terms, allowing students to use notes during the quiz. She next randomly assigned students to groups, telling them to act as junior editors for a publishing company who had to pick five from a group of eight untitled poems to recommend to the chief editor (Samantha) for inclusion in a volume of poetry, accompanied by an argument for their selection, which the students worked on for the remainder of the class.

For the most part, she attributed this instructional plan to herself, although the students figured prominently in her thinking. The students, she felt, needed a break from reading the fiction emphasized in the mystery unit, and so she shifted to a requirement from the curriculum to teach poetry terms. Her plans thus were situated within requirements, yet responsive to her students' degrees of engagement and endurance for any one emphasis. She hoped to promote learning and engagement, primarily through constructivist pedagogical tools, aside from the formalist requirement of teaching literary elements. She drew on an assignment modeled by her English Education professors, who had recommended having students classify poems according to themes. Samantha adapted and extended this task to produce the mock editorial panel activity. The school's allowance for reflective practice and attention to students' experiences gave Samantha latitude not evident in many of the cases reviewed in this book. She was given the freedom to consider what her students were ready for, choose poems from outside the official curriculum, and ramp up an idea from campus to produce a more compelling and agentive experience for her students, one that involved their literary discernment in making judgments about what to recommend for the anthology.

Observation cycle #3. In the spring, Samantha introduced a unit on Harper Lee's novel *To Kill a Mockingbird*, a standard in the curriculum that Samantha approached with caution given the racial themes, the Southern context, and the presence in her class of a single African American student who had previously been the target of racially insensitive conduct by a classmate. Samantha hoped to help her students become, as she said, "more tolerant of other people." Toward that end, she assigned them a research project in which they selected and investigated a human rights activist from history. After listing ten vocabulary words from the novel, she addressed unruly behavior and lack of respect in the class, and gave the students the opportunity to vote on whether or not to spend the remainder of class in the school library researching their human rights activists, which they elected to do.

The next day, the class spent twenty minutes on journal entries in response to a prompt based on *To Kill a Mockingbird*: "Tell about a haunted house or an odd person who lived in your neighborhood when you were a kid." After she collected their writing, the students worked in groups to generate rules that discourage offensive behaviors, which they discussed as a class. This inductive approach stood in contrast to the prescriptive character curriculum required during her student teaching. The class then read *To Kill a Mockingbird* aloud for the remainder of the period.

Samantha explained this instruction in relation to a unit on *Romeo and Juliet* they had just completed, one that left students "all tired of it. We'd written journals and taken quizzes and done study questions and drawn character maps." In recognition of their fatigue, she departed from the rest of her instructional team by not concluding *Romeo and Juliet* with a "big bang presentation thing." Rather, she shifted the research requirement to *To Kill a Mockingbird*, a decision suggesting the degree of autonomy she was provided at Danforth. She further had the independence to determine how to explore the novel: "I don't want our discussions and our writing to be so plot-driven. I really am aiming . . . for a much more introspective, thoughtful type of response from them in the writing. . . . The quizzes are basically just to make sure they're reading."

Samantha found that Danforth was "so free and open that I'm sure I could do anything." Her students made decisions as mundane as taking a vote on whether or not to work in the library, and as critical as establishing rules of conduct to guide them in potentially explosive discussions of racial inequality and discrimination. Her planning was flexible, such that she could suspend assessment decisions when the students "take me somewhere that I didn't even know we were going." Samantha's openness to her students allowed their interests, temperaments, levels of endurance, and determination of rules of order to inform her guidance of their learning, within but not restricted to the bounds of the curriculum and her responsibilities to her cross-curricular teaching team. She relied on both informal attention to their engagement and formal tools such as a survey at the beginning of the year, through which her students "told me that they would be interested in finding out about Civil Rights activists who weren't well known," rather than reading again about "Rosa Parks and Martin Luther King and Malcolm X." Their weariness with studying a small set of civil rights icons throughout their education led her to provide latitude in conducting research on a civil rights leader of their choice.

By the end of her first year at DHS, Samantha was arriving at most of her instructional decisions through reflective practice. This setting thus encouraged eupraxia, the "good practice" that is available when teachers have freedom within available structures. Her reflections enabled her to reconsider assignments in light of how her students responded to them. She made some changes, she said, in the hopes that the revisions "will yield better results and thus I think better assessments." These reflections on assignments and their value took place at the daily level and unit level, and in significant ways. "Rather than having a big huge test at the end," she said, she decided to let her students "put together a portfolio of, you know, reflections over what we've talked about and what we've done."

At DHS, Samantha was *expected* to use her good judgment to make instructional decisions based on her own appraisal and her reflective attention to the needs and interests of her students. Although this sort of practice was central to her teacher education program, she rarely mentioned it when explaining her decisions. Possibly that influence was subconscious, yet the research continually prompted her to name influences, and her courses on campus rarely came up when she was asked for attributions to her choices. With fewer extraneous factors influencing her teaching, Samantha found the setting of Danforth to enable her version of eupraxia, one in which she focused on her students as the primary motivation for her decisions about what and how to teach. In so doing, Danforth also enabled Samantha to develop a more coherent conception of teaching English, one more aligned to her ideals than had been available during student teaching, and one far different from Natalie's experiences at O'Connor MS and its highly restrictive corporate assessment regimen.

In order for reflection to serve eupraxis, the school setting needs to provide teachers with the intellectual confidence and latitude to become flexible in relation to how students respond to instruction. This setting involves colleagues, administration, and a community that supports open-ended teaching that follows from teachers' informed judgment of how their classrooms work. At DHS, the administration enabled eupraxis by allowing teachers the authority to interpret the curriculum in light of what they felt were their own strengths and priorities, and the students' needs in relation to it. With voice in the conduct and direction of the class, Samantha's ninth graders were less resistant than were her seniors during student teaching, who were assumed to lack character and were subjected to modules designed to improve it. Her students at

Danforth had a stake in what and how they were learning, opening the possibility for eupraxia to become available to Samantha.

Discussion

This chapter has provided a set of contextual extremes that in turn produced very different kinds of instruction and levels of job satisfaction. Natalie worked in a school system, situated in a large corporate county, that assumed that teachers are not capable of designing their own curricula or assessing students validly, and thus need an external apparatus to ensure instructional quality as measured by an endless series of tests. Economists with an interest in education find such measures to be necessary and appropriate. Koedel (2018), for instance, believes that "as grades inflate, standardized tests keep us grounded," because, he believes, teachers easily cave in when students and parents pressure them to inflate grades and lower expectations. Teachers, in this conception, are not trustworthy observers of their students or assessors of their work, and must be monitored as much as students themselves. Corporate oversight is required, and tests are the measure by which lax teachers are kept disciplined, regardless of what they are testing and what teachers find appropriate.

If Samantha represents thoughtful, student-oriented teachers, then her experience suggests that schools would benefit from greater confidence in teachers' judgment. If Natalie represents the same sort of teacher whose decision-making is highly restricted, then it's understandable why teacher morale is so low when corporate mentalities govern curriculum, instruction, and assessment (MetLife, 2013).

This chapter has focused on how factors beyond schools shape what is possible for teachers, regardless of their beliefs or academic preparation. Rather than positioning schools in opposition to universities, these studies show schools to be functions of their broader settings, and not necessarily in conflict with campus values. Samantha's two teaching settings produced very different forms of instruction, even with respect to the challenge of student socialization, a value of both settings subject to very different approaches to instruction. Danforth was highly aligned with campus values, rendering the two-worlds pitfall moot. But Danforth was situated within a community that allowed its administration to adopt and enforce reflective practice as a primary value. Danforth was viewed as the most progressive of its county's several high schools, suggesting that other school contexts interpreted the district's value on local control to enforce more formalist pedagogies.

For Natalie, the decisions were all centralized and top-down, allowing people far removed from the classroom to dictate the terms of instruction and assessment, people so distant that teachers could not negotiate differences with them, as Natalie could with Leila. Natalie squirmed throughout her experience there and finally bailed out, ultimately landing in a less corporate, less affluent, less complex system where she could teach more through relationships than a curricular system designed to produce a monoculture and uniform student product.

This chapter demonstrates how settings can both shape concept development and produce resistance, if not open defiance, to demands for standardization and homogenization of teaching and student outcomes, measured through reductive bottom-line means. Teachers are often working within and against broad, heavily institutionalized systems that extend well beyond school walls. They include corporate pressures from business interests, politicians, and university economists who believe that test scores tell the only story worth hearing, and who believe that teachers are weak-willed and malleable in the face of resistance to rigor. I assert that teachers like Samantha are not caving in when they change plans. Rather, they are strong and resolute in the quality of their judgment, and when allowed and encouraged to teach in relation to their students and how they interpret what they need socially and academically, are more than capable of making good decisions that allow for greater levels of engagement and success.

That flexibility might lead economists like Koedel (2018) to assume that grade inflation is the only explanation for students doing well, and that this problem must be curbed by more "objective" tests. But failing more students does not indicate good or even "rigorous" teaching, and there's good reason to believe that teaching that results in failure is quite poor, insensitive, and misguided. Good teachers like Samantha and Natalie, when allowed by their circumstances, shift their instruction to engage students and lead to greater success, and thus better grades. The settings of instruction, then, set the stage for how achievement is defined and measured, and how teachers participate in that process. In order for their involvement to matter, they need the sort of respect that Danforth accorded Samantha. Unfortunately, that degree of respect is increasingly eroding as corporate pressures influence the purpose and process of public education.

12

Conclusion

In introducing this volume, I acknowledged that most of the data were collected several years ago. At times, I've wondered how relevant those data might be a few years down the road. Times, after all, do change, and schools along with them. Engelmann (1991) argues that "schools are engaged in what amounts to a continual reform or reorganization for reform" (p. 295), usually, he says, quite poorly. Some changes are initiated and managed from the top of the food chain, such as policy mandates (Bowe, Ball, & Gold, 1992) whose success follows from the quality of the leadership of the school principal (Hall & Hord, 1987). Some involve deliberate efforts by multiple, distributed stakeholders working toward positive, democratic change (Wagner, 1994). Whether they represent "reform" or "deform" is a matter of perspective (Cuban, 2011).

In addition to these systemic changes and many others, some (e.g., Coyle, 2009) argue that kids themselves are different these days, a consequence of the newer forms of socialization that surround them. These mediators include technology, which has altered many school practices (Davies & West, 2014), even as many districts serving less affluent families can't afford to run a full school week or year (Walker, 2019), much less provide cutting-edge technologies for teachers and students. Such schools often lack sufficient bandwidth for connected learning because they must dedicate their capacity to online testing (Johnson, Sieben, & Buxton, 2018), making online affordances more available to some districts than others. The declining financial support for schools (Leachman, Masterson, & Figueroa, 2017), evident in the access-to-digitality-divide, has created many new challenges for teachers, including limited technology hardware and connectivity. Technology itself has not been a panacea, especially when new technological tools are not accompanied by new psychological tools that enable knowledgeable application (Kim, 2012).

The proliferation of testing represents yet another change, along with other shifts subject to neoliberalism's gravity (Kontopodis, 2012). These ideological and economic forces affect teacher educators as well, making them accountable through the performance assessments required of their TCs (Baltodano, 2012). These assessments are, like other "reforms," ideologically undergirded and designed to align instruction with a specific set of values that set a particular pedagogical trajectory, at least until TCs graduate and become subject to other value systems and practices (Smagorinsky, 2018a).

Yet the more things change, the more they stay the same. Note, for instance, the age of many of the citations I used to make points about school change, and how serviceable they remain. Changes on the surface can mask stability in the deeper structures of school life. Campbell and Twenge (2014), for instance, agree with Coyle (2009) that students from each generation are socialized differently by changing environments, yet they find that basic patterns of developmental maturation have remained constant. Although specific conditions and behaviors may change, they fit archetypes and developmental processes that have endured across the span of time.

At the school level, much also remains the same. Schools, like all organizations, might undergo "reform," yet simultaneously are built to sustain their hierarchies (Leavitt, 2003) so that they promote stability and *status quo* positioning. Although contexts have changed, the fact that contexts shape human development, including teachers' lives, has endured. Some of the factors in settings take different forms from decade to decade, yet the historical traditions that shape policies and practices, while evolving, have consistent elements and forms of influence (Applebee, 1974). What seems inescapable is that people are socialized through immersion in settings governed by culture, including its traditions and relationships. Older data thus may have explanatory power over time in spite of broader shifts in society and schools, due to the ways in which the constancy of traditions allows studies of human concept development to have meaning beyond the era of data collection.

When I was doing the analysis of the final studies undertaken for this line of inquiry with Meghan Barnes, reported in Chapters 3 and 4, I asked her if the studies seemed old to her as a millennial who was younger than the teachers in the research. No, she said, not at all; the teachers we analyzed, she said, sounded exactly like the TCs she had taught as a TA that semester. I thus have some confidence that data that tell enduring stories can age quite well, and can be useful for informing considerations of teacher education in subsequent generations of teachers and teacher educators. When the focus is on concept development more than on the latest trends in education, the question of mediation appears to be of lasting relevance, even when the specific mediators change. Educational traditions are more lasting than the specific instantiations that follow from them with each generation, making attention to their mediational roles in concept development relevant over time. I hope that the narratives and analyses I report have more than historical value, and that they resonate with current and future experiences of early career teachers developing conceptions of how to teach English and Language Arts, and perhaps other subjects as well.

Takeaways

In each chapter, I've drawn conclusions about the issues under consideration, and I hope to not belabor those points here. At the same time, a compendium of what I consider to be salient may have value for readers interested in what I think I've learned from studying beginning teachers for a few decades, and what I've learned from aggregating cases that have to this point stood on their own individually. I'll close, then, with what I think is available from this effort to aggregate and synthesize the case studies in a single, integrated volume.

New Realizations

The opportunity to look at a larger set of cases has enabled me to see some things I missed the first time through, either due to my compartmentalized focus on the individual cases analyzed one by one or due to my lack of interpretive knowledge and sophistication at the time of the writing. I had missed, for instance, the central insight of Chapter 5 regarding the possibility that people from outside the dominant culture, often through racialized identities, may decide not to teach because of cultural mismatches that make schools alienating places for them. It was clear to me when I did the original analysis that Penny was out of sorts in an authoritarian school because of her cultural orientation to time. Yet I did not recognize—possibly because the case study analyses were conducted several years apart—that a White classmate from the same university was also misaligned with the school, yet persisted with a teaching career.

No doubt I benefited from my ongoing immersion in cultural psychology (Cole, 1996), critical race theory (Bell, 1995), post- and decolonial theories (Bhambra, 2014), Indigenous epistemologies (Smith, 2005), and other perspectives that help bolster Vygotsky's points about cultural mediation within communities and institutional structures. My continual growth in understanding these perspectives, both through reading and through engaging with data during analytic sessions conducted with my doctoral students, has helped me see what I had originally missed. Only by looking deliberately across the cases did I see more clearly how two TCs from the same program in the same school with similarly frustrating experiences might project themselves into teaching careers quite differently. Their trajectories were, I infer, a function of broad cultural matches and mismatches that extended beyond the contexts that had served as the focus of the initial analyses.

Binaries

Aggregating the cases across this book's contents has confirmed my reservations about working according to binaries such as the two-worlds pitfall or the teacher-centered versus student-centered dichotomy or continuum, depending on how it's invoked. The studies I've compiled here find too many complications and contradictions within both schools and universities for there to be a clean distinction into two discrete worlds or sets of practices, even as they are, broadly speaking, governed by different values.

Similarly, classroom life is too complex to be divided into binaries that position instruction as centered on either the avid, self-motivated student or the oppressive, dominant teacher, or even as hugging the middle of a single pedagogical binary. Teachers are more likely to vacillate among traditions invoked to meet different demands, given that they and their students are situated within broader forces that shape them in manifold ways that defy simple bifurcation into two distinct worlds. Rather, the availability of multiple swirling paradigms surrounding and infusing each suggests that any social world provides contradictory settings whose overlap makes ideologically pure actions virtually impossible to undertake.

These studies also challenge the idea that universities are hothouses of innovation that teachers reject as part of their anti-reform mentality, as argued by Terhart (2013).

Rather, teachers, students, schools, and universities are complex and contradictory, embodying different values in relation to different social mediators. Teacher education is but one of many settings in which people learn to teach. The factors that matter to individual teachers may shift in relation to what is imperative at the moment, which itself may be subject to the vicissitudes of those who surround them and how those in power impose consequences for which traditions they instantiate in their instruction.

The Idealistic Claims of Seamlessness, and Their Seams

Claims to seamless relationships between university programs and school-based mentors and other support systems represent an ideal that cannot be realized in reality. Claiming seamlessness, I would argue, not only masks inevitable fissures in relationships between universities and schools but also shields university faculty from having to address disjunctures when they occur, and obscures contradictions that TCs need to be aware of as they navigate the two environments. It similarly tends to mask internal contradictions within each of the two settings, given that for seamlessness to be available, there cannot be conflicts within either. It's difficult enough to construct and maintain a single seamless social organization, much less mesh two into a unified whole.

Field Experiences and Their Role in Assimilation

Programs with a heavy emphasis on field experiences run the peril of rendering teacher education coursework irrelevant, unless very deliberate opportunities for analysis and reflection are built into the program, and possibly not even then. Extensive field experiences are likely to serve the purpose of assimilation into schools, which have the leverage of offering job security to vulnerable teachers who conform to their ways, a much stronger incentive than is earning good grades in their role as university student seeking to please teacher education faculty. I make this point as being complementary with, rather than in opposition to, my general concerns about the binary of the two-worlds pitfall. It's possible for schools and universities to have different general concerns and respond to different gravitational forces, while also being internally contradictory and sharing traits with one another.

Field-based programs, as I understand the experiences of the participants in the research I report, make schools the primary center of gravity affecting beginning teachers' pedagogical trajectories, and often (if not always) their pedagogical concept development, or at least their teaching practices. As several research participants have shown, how they teach and what they believe can be quite different. But how they teach determines how they will be evaluated in the high-stakes world of job retention, no matter what they are taught in teacher education programs.

Mediated Concept Development, Not Theory versus Practice

Teacher education programs also need to work at the level of the concept, rather than emphasizing primarily either theory or practices detached from principles that enable their adaptation to new situations. As the research reported in this volume suggests, these concepts need to be robust and clear in university programs, rather than fuzzy and nebulous, if they are to work in any practical and reasonably consistent way. Theory and practice need to be integrated so that beginning teachers see how educational theories have clear practical applications, and how teaching practices may, through the abstractable principles from theory, be adopted and modified for a variety of school and classroom settings and circumstances.

My colleagues and I (Smagorinsky et al., 2003) have argued that the problem with teacher education is not too much theory, but too little concept. That claim has held up well in my synthesis of research reported in this volume, although our characterization of concept development as a twisting path in 2003 has shifted away from the idea that a single pathway is there to follow (Smagorinsky, 2013), given the multiple and competing destinations and practices impressed on beginning teachers from different stakeholders. Teachers are often blamed for being contradictory and inconsistent (Ash, Kuhn, & Walpole, 2009). I urge teacher educators instead to consider the likelihood that when people are immersed in contradictory settings, they will find it difficult to act in consistent ways. Their conduct is thus not necessarily a sign of weak intellect or poor judgment. Rather, it is a fairly predictable outcome of meeting a host of imperatives requiring different responses.

For teachers to be consistent, their surroundings need to be consistent. But it matters which sort of surroundings become consistent. Federal programs like No Child Left Behind and Race to the Top, and independently generated programs like the CCSS, have sought to make instructional contexts more similar to one another. Yet many teachers or analysts find these efforts at imposing uniformity to work against the best interests of students and teachers (Baker, Oluwole, & Green, 2013; Sunderman, Tracey, Kim, & Orfield, 2004; Troia & Graham, 2016). Even, however, when programs are designed to produce uniform instruction, other traditions and practices often remain in play (Gilbert, 2014). Finding a clear pathway amid the chaos, including the disorder that follows from standardization, is unlikely for most teachers in most settings.

Socialization via the Apprenticeship of Observation

The apprenticeship of observation should be understood as neither strictly conservative nor fatalistic in the formation of teacher identities and approaches to theory and practice. The case studies reported in this volume show a great variety of classroom experiences of beginning teachers, including those associated with both formalist and progressive traditions, structures, and practices. The teachers in these studies articulated, very consistently, a strong preference for hands-on, activity-based, and meaning-centered instruction in the Deweyan tradition. Their ability to adopt these practices in their own teaching depended on the contexts in which they taught, including the teaching assignments, school and community value systems, MT preferences and dispositions, student characteristics, policy mandates, political and ideological environments, and other factors.

In schools of the present day, there may be a general conservative bias, one currently shaped and reinforced by neoliberal policies (Hill & Kumar, 2009). Although testing mandates have made school more authoritarian in the last two decades, they have been accompanied by the continued development and availability of progressive teaching methods emphasizing inquiry, meaning construction, and activity, widely available online. It's likely, then, that teachers now and in the future will be exposed to a variety of teaching practices over the course of their schooling; and, if they are like the teachers in this study, they will prefer constructive activity to rote learning and will seek to make their classrooms as open-ended and engaging as possible within the confines of authoritarian mandates, perhaps subversively as recommended by Gilbert (2014), perhaps within more generous confines in schools allowing a degree of teacher autonomy.

Teacher Education's Effects on Beginning Teachers' Practice

Teacher education does appear, generally speaking, to affect beginning teachers' practice. Grossman (1990) found that beginning teachers with university training are indeed different from those without. More recently, Teach for America (TFA)—with its minimalist "boot camp" preparation and reliance on intelligence and good intentions—has struggled to produce results or persistence among its recruits, even as it has succeeded in becoming "a well-connected multi-million dollar corporate behemoth with many ties to the same big money groups busily dismantling public education" (Greene, 2016, n. p.; cf. Blanchard, 2013; Cohen, 2013). Evidence from outside TFA's own glossy reports (e.g., TFA Editorial Team, 2018) suggests that having no preparation to teach leaves beginning teachers ill prepared for classrooms (Darling-Hammond, Holtzman, Gatlin, & Heilig, 2005). Teachers who have been through teacher education programs feel better prepared than those who don't (Ingersoll, Merrill, & May, 2014; Johnson, Berg, & Donaldson, 2005; Whitney, Golez, Nagel, & Nieto, 2002), in spite of the long-standing negative portrayal of such programs in the popular press (e.g., Kramer, 1991; Wilson, 2019) and the critical perspectives from within the academy (e.g, Grossman, Hammernessa, & McDonald, 2009; Levine, 2006).

Meanwhile, schools exert powerful, consequential influence on teachers, who must be responsive to the micropolitics of schools for job appointments and retention (Blase & Blase, 2003). This inevitable shift in evaluative weight as beginning teachers go from school to work can complicate the influence of teacher education, no matter how transformative the claims are on behalf of university programs (Darling-Hammond, 2010). These assertions need to be attentive to the tremendous diversity of such programs and their settings. In the United States alone there are roughly 27,000 teacher preparation programs in 2,000 institutions (National Council on Teacher Quality, 2018), each different. This variability has led me to argue against "best practices" in both classrooms (Smagorinsky, 2009) and university teacher education (Smagorinsky, 2018a). I would extend this claim to the idea that there is no such thing as a "model program" in teacher education, as asserted by Davis and Cabello (1989) and others, given that each program is situated differently and is populated by different sorts of people, and thus is not amenable to being taken to scale, replicated, or transferred wholesale to other contexts. Teacher education programs are too unique, and the settings of their implementation too complex and contradictory, to be reproducible in another context.

Parting Thoughts

The revolution in education that so many have predicted has never arrived (Mirel, 2003), and it's worth considering why. I think that Vygotsky's (1987) outline of concept development as a function of cultural mediation helps explain why teacher education is not capable of producing the sorts of changes in schooling that its ideals and rhetoric so hopefully assert is necessary and possible. There is too little agreement on the purpose of society in general, the role of schooling in a democracy, the specific traditions that produce a well-educated person, the structure and practice of teacher education, and much else in order for beginning teachers to proceed on a clear developmental pathway toward enlightened instruction, however defined. I hope that the issues I've raised in this research synthesis help to moderate idealistic claims, and help my fellow teacher educators recognize the limitations of our work, even as we try to do it well. Too much is out of our control for our values to be realized in full in our work with prospective and practicing teachers. And that's only to be expected given the nature of culturally mediated human development in the multiple contexts of learning to teach.

References

Acker, S. (1994). *Gendered education: Sociological reflections on women, teaching, and feminism*. New York, NY: Open University Press.

Addington, A. H. (2001). Talking about literature in university book club and seminar settings. *Research in the Teaching of English, 36*, 212–48.

Alsup, J. (2006). *Teacher identity discourses: Negotiating personal and professional spaces*. Urbana, IL, and New York, NY: National Council of Teachers of English and Routledge.

American Association of University Women. (1995). *The AAUW report: How schools shortchange girls*. New York, NY: Marlowe.

Andrews, P. (2017). Is the "telling case" a methodological myth? *International Journal of Social Research Methodology, 20*(5), 455–67.

Anyon, J. (1980). Social class and the hidden curriculum of work. *Journal of Education, 162*(1), 67–92.

Apple, M. W., & King, N. R. (1977). What do schools teach? *Curriculum Inquiry, 6*, 341–58.

Applebee, A. N. (1974). *Tradition and reform in the teaching of English: A history*. Urbana, IL: National Council of Teachers of English.

Applebee, A. N. (1993). *Literature in the secondary school: Studies of curriculum and instruction in the United States* (NCTE Research Report No. 25). Urbana, IL: National Council of Teachers of English.

Applebee, A. N. (1996). *Curriculum as conversation: Transforming traditions of teaching and learning*. Chicago, IL: University of Chicago Press.

Applebee, A. N. (2013). Common Core State Standards: The promise and the peril in a national palimpsest. *English Journal, 103*(1), 25–33.

Applebee, A. N., & Langer, J. A. (2009). What is happening in the teaching of writing? *English Journal, 98*(5), 18–28.

Appleman, D. (2015). *Critical encounters in secondary English: Teaching literary theory to adolescents,* 3rd ed. New York, NY: Teachers College Press.

Aristotle. (350 BCE). *Nicomachean ethics* (W. D. Ross, Trans.). Retrieved September 17, 2018 from http://constitution.org/ari/ethic_00.htm

Ash, G. E., Kuhn, M. R., & Walpole, S. (2009). Analyzing "inconsistencies" in practice: Teachers' continued use of round robin reading. *Reading & Writing Quarterly, 25*, 87–103.

Atwell, N. (1987). *In the middle: Writing, reading, and learning with adolescents*. Portsmouth, NH: Heinemann.

Au, W., & Ferrare, J. J. (Eds.) (2015). *Mapping corporate education reform: Power and policy networks in the neoliberal state*. New York, NY: Routledge.

Baker, B. D., Oluwole, J. O., & Green, P. C. (2013). The legal consequences of mandating high stakes decisions based on low quality information: Teacher evaluation in the Race-to-the-Top era. *Education Policy Analysis Archives, 21*, 1–67.

Bakhtin, M. M. (1981). *The dialogic imagination: Four essays by M. M. Bakhtin* (M. Holquist, Ed.; C. Emerson & M. Holquist, Trans.). Austin, TX: University of Texas Press.

Bakhtin, M. M. (1986). *Speech genres and other late essays* (C. Emerson & M. Holquist, Eds.; V. W. McGee, Trans.). Austin, TX: University of Texas Press.

Bakhurst, D. (2007). Vygotsky's demons. In H. Daniels, M. Cole, & J. V. Wertsch (Eds.) (2007), *The Cambridge companion to Vygotsky* (pp. 50–76). New York, NY: Cambridge University Press.

Baldassarre, V. A. (1997). *Frameworks to draw upon in designing programmes for beginning teacher in Europe. Comenius project 71599*. Brussels, BE: Association for Teacher Education in Europe.

Ballenger, C. (1999). *Teaching other people's children: Literacy and learning in a bilingual classroom*. New York, NY: Teachers College Press.

Baltodano, M. (2012). Neoliberalism and the demise of public education: The corporatization of schools of education. *International Journal of Qualitative Studies in Education, 25*(4), 487–507.

Barnes, M. E. (2016). Recalculation in teacher preparation: Challenging assumptions through increased community contact. *English Education, 48*(2), 149–76.

Barnes, M. E., & Smagorinsky, P. (2016). What English/Language Arts teacher candidates learn during coursework and practica: A study of three teacher education programs. *Journal of Teacher Education, 67*(4) 338–55.

Barrett, S. E., Abdi, H., Murphy, G. L., & Gallagher, J. M. (1993). Theory-based correlations and their role in children's concepts. *Child Development, 64*, 1595–616.

Bawarshi, A. S., & Reiff, M. J. (2010). *Genre: An introduction to history, theory, research, and pedagogy*. Fort Collins, CO: Parlor Press and the WAC Clearinghouse.

Beach, R. (1993). *A teacher's introduction to reader-response theories*. Urbana, IL: National Council of Teachers of English. Retrieved September 27, 2018 from https://files.eric.ed.gov/fulltext/ED355523.pdf

Belgarde, M. (1992). *The performance and persistence of American Indian undergraduate students at Stanford University*. Unpublished doctoral dissertation, Stanford University.

Bell, D. A. (1995). Who's afraid of critical race theory? *University of Illinois Law Review*, 893–910.

Berchini, C. (2016). Curriculum matters: The Common Core, authors of color, and inclusion for inclusion's sake. *Journal of Adolescent & Adult Literacy, 60*(1), 55–62.

Berchini, C. (2017). Critiquing un/critical pedagogies to move toward a pedagogy of responsibility in teacher education. *Journal of Teacher Education, 68*(5), 463–75.

Berchini, C., & Tanner, S. J. (Eds.) (2019). Working through Whiteness and white supremacy in English Education. Special theme issue of *English Education, 51*(2).

Berkeley, G. (1901). *The works of George Berkeley* (A. C. Fraser, Ed.). Oxford, UK: Clarendon Press. Retrieved September 27, 2018 from https://archive.org/stream/worksofberkeley01berkuoft/worksofberkeley01berkuoft_djvu.txt

Berliner, D. C. (2014). Exogenous variables and value-added assessments: A fatal flaw. *Teachers College Record, 116*(1), 1–31.

Bettelheim, B. (1987). *A good enough parent: A book on child-rearing*. New York, NY: Knopf.

Beyer, L. E. (Ed.) (1996). *Creating democratic classrooms: The struggle to integrate theory and practice*. New York, NY: Teachers College Press.

Bhambra, G. K. (2014). Postcolonial and decolonial dialogues. *Postcolonial Studies, 17*(2), 115–21.

Bickmore, S. T., Smagorinsky, P., & O'Donnell-Allen, C. (2005). Tensions between traditions: The role of contexts in learning to teach. *English Education, 38*, 23–52.

Biddle, B. J., & Berliner, D. C. (2003). *What research says about unequal funding for schools in America*. San Francisco, CA: WestEd. Retrieved April 22, 2015 from http://www.wested.org/online_pubs/pp-03-01.pdf

Blanchard, O. (2013, September 23). I quit Teach for America. *The Atlantic*. Retrieved August 14, 2019 from https://www.theatlantic.com/education/archive/2013/09/i-quit-teach-for-america/279724/

Blase, J., & Blase, J. (2003). *Breaking the silence: Overcoming the problem of principal mistreatment of teachers*. Thousand Oaks, CA: Corwin.

Bleich, D. (1975). *Readings and feelings*. Urbana, IL: National Council of Teachers of English.

Borko, H., & Eisenhart, M. (1992). Learning to teach hard mathematics: Do novice teachers and their instructors give up too easily? *Journal for Research in Mathematics Education, 23*, 194–222.

Bowe, R., Ball, S. J., & Gold, A. (1992). *Reforming education and changing schools: Case studies in policy sociology*. New York, NY: Routledge.

Braaten, M. (2019). Persistence of the two-worlds pitfall: Learning to teach within and across settings. *Science Education, 103*(1), 61–91.

Braddock, R., Lloyd-Jones, R., & Schoer, L. (1963). *Research in written composition*. Champaign, IL: National Council of Teachers of English.

Brizee, A., Tompkins, J. C., Chernouski, L., Boyle, E., & Williams, S. (n. d.). Literary theory and schools of criticism. *Purdue OWL*. Retrieved July 16, 2018 from https://owl.english.purdue.edu/owl/owlprint/722/

Brownell, W. A. (1948). Learning theory and educational practice. *Journal of Educational Research, 41*, 481–97.

Bruner, J. (1987). Prologue to the English edition. In R. Rieber & A. Carton (Eds.), *The collected works of L. S. Vygotsky* (Vol. 1; N. Minick, Trans.; pp. 1–16). New York, NY: Plenum.

Buchmann, M. (1987). Teaching knowledge: The lights that teachers live by. *Oxford Review of Education, 13*(2), 151–64.

Bullough, R., Jr. (1989). *First-year teacher: A case study*. New York, NY: Teachers College Press.

Byrne, E. (1993). *Women in science: The snark syndrome*. New York, NY: Falmer.

Campbell, S. M., & Twenge, J. M. (2014). Is it kids today or just the fact that they're kids? Disentangling generational differences from age differences. In E. Parry (Ed.), *Generational diversity at work: New research perspectives* (pp. 69–80). New York, NY: Routledge.

Carpini, D. D. (2004). "Must be willing to teach composition": The rhetoric and practices of the small college job search. *Composition Studies, 32*(2), 31–52.

Casner-Lotto, J. (2006). *Are they really ready to work? Employers' perspectives on the basic knowledge and applied skills of new entrants to the 21st century U.S. workforce*. The Conference Board, Corporate Voices for Working Families, the Partnership for 21st Century Skills, & the Society for Human Resource Management. Retrieved July 16, 2018 from http://www.p21.org/storage/documents/FINAL_REPORT_PDF09-29-06.pdf

Castles, A., Rastle, K., & Nation, K. (2018). Ending the reading wars: Reading acquisition from novice to expert. *Psychological Science in the Public Interest, 19*, 5–51. doi:10.1177/1529100618772271

Cherian, F. (2007). Learning to teach: Teacher candidates reflect on the relational, conceptual, and contextual influences of responsive mentorship. *Canadian Journal of Education*, *30*(1), 25–46.

Cherif, A. H., Adams, G. E., Movahedzadeh, F., Martyn, M. A., & Dunning, J. (2014). Why do students fail? Faculty's perspective. *Higher Learning Conference Collection of Papers 2014*. July 12, 2018 from https://cop.hlcommission.org/Learning-Environments/cherif.html

Cherng, H.-Y. S., & Helpin, P. F. (2016). The importance of minority teachers: Student perceptions of minority versus White teachers. *Educational Researcher*, *45*(7), 407–20.

Chiu, C. (2016, August 25). A call for deliberate diversification of the teaching force. *Huffington Post*. Retrieved July 10, 2018 from https://www.huffingtonpost.com/teach-plus/a-call-for-deliberate-div_b_11696142.html

Cibulka, J. G. (2009). *Meeting urgent national needs in P-12 education: Improving relevance, evidence, and performance in teacher preparation*. Washington, DC: National Council for Accreditation of Teacher Education.

Coffin, C., Curry, M. J., Goodman, S., Hewings, A., Lillis, T. M., & Swann, J. (2003). *Teaching academic writing: A toolkit for higher education*. New York, NY: Routledge.

Cohen, D. K., & Moffitt, S. L. (2010). *The ordeal of equality: Did federal regulation fix the schools?* Cambridge, MA: Harvard University Press.

Cohen, R. (2013, July 8). Teach for America struggles in Minnesota. *Nonprofit Quarterly*. Retrieved August 14, 2019 from https://nonprofitquarterly.org/teach-for-america-struggles-in-minnesota/

Cole, M. (1996). *Cultural psychology: A once and future discipline*. Cambridge, MA: Harvard University Press.

Coleman, D., & Pimentel, S. (2012). *Revised publishers' criteria for the Common Core State Standards in English Language Arts and literacy, grades K–2*. Common Core State Standards. Retrieved August 18, 2018 from http://www.corestandards.org/assets/Publishers_Criteria_for_K-2.pdf

Collins, B. (2019, April 16). *Wis. teacher on leave in probe of "slave games."* St. Paul, MN: Minnesota Public Radio News. Retrieved May 23, 2019 from https://blogs.mprnews.org/newscut/2019/04/wis-teacher-on-leave-in-probe-of-slave-games/

The Colorado Writing Tutors Conference. (2000). *Theory and practice in the writing center (or theory versus practice?)*. Lakewood, CO: Author. Retrieved August 31, 2018 from http://www.ppcc.cccoes.edu/owl/Call2002.htm

Common Core State Standards. (2018a). *English Language Arts standards: Language—Grade 9–10*. Retrieved August 31, 2018 from http://www.corestandards.org/ELA-Literacy/L/9-10/

Common Core State Standards. (2018b). *English Language Arts standards: Introduction—Key design consideration*. Retrieved August 31, 2018 from http://www.corestandards.org/ELA-Literacy/introduction/key-design-consideration/

Cook, L. S., Smagorinsky, P., Fry, P. G., Konopak, B., & Moore, C. (2002). Problems in developing a constructivist approach to teaching: One teacher's transition from teacher preparation to teaching. *The Elementary School Journal*, *102*, 389–413. Retrieved August 18, 2018 from http://www.petersmagorinsky.net/About/PDF/TESJ/TESJ2002.pdf

Coyl, D. D. (2009). Kids really *are* different these days. *Phi Delta Kappan*, *90*(6), 404–7. https://doi.org/10.1177/003172170909000605

Cozzarelli, C., Wilkinson, A. V., & Tagler, M. J. (2002). Attitudes toward the poor and attributions for poverty. *Journal of Social Issues*, *57*(2), 207–27.

Crane, R. (Ed.) (1952). *Critics and criticism*. Chicago, IL: University of Chicago Press.

Crawford, D. M., Cheadle, J. E., & Whitbeck, L. B. (2010). Tribal vs. public schools: Perceived discrimination and school adjustment among indigenous children from early to mid-adolescence. *Journal of American Indian Education, 49*(1), 86–106.

Crowley, S. (1998). *Composition in the university: Historical and polemical essays*. Pittsburgh, PA: University of Pittsburgh Press.

Cuban, L. (1993). *How teachers taught: Constancy and change in American classrooms 1890–1990*. New York, NY: Teachers College Press.

Cuban, L. (2009). *Hugging the middle: How teachers teach in an era of testing and accountability*. New York, NY: Teachers College Press.

Cuban, L. (2011). *Larry Cuban on school reform and classroom practice: The status quo is always changing*. Retrieved August 15, 2019 from https://larrycuban.wordpress.com/2011/09/09/the-status-quo-is-always-changing/

Cuban, L. (2013). *Inside the black box of classroom practice: Change without reform in American education*. Cambridge, MA: Harvard Education Press.

Cuban, L. (2019, April 26). *Larry Cuban on school reform and classroom practice: Making schools business-like: The longest school reform in U.S. history? (Part 1)*. Boulder, CO: National Education Policy Center. Retrieved May 31, 2019 from https://nepc.colorado.edu/blog/longest-school-reform

Darling-Hammond, L. (2010). Teacher education and the American future. *Journal of Teacher Education, 61*(1–2), 35–47.

Darling-Hammond, L., Holtzman, D. J., Gatlin, S. J., & Heilig, J. V. (2005). Does teacher preparation matter? Evidence about teacher certification, Teach for America, and teacher effectiveness. *Education Policy Analysis Archives, 13*(42). Retrieved August 15, 2019 from http://epaa.asu.edu/epaa/v13n42/

Darling-Hammond, L., Wei, R. C., Andree, A., Richardson, N., & Orphanos, S. (2009). *Professional learning in the learning profession: A status report on teacher development in the United States and abroad*. Palo Alto, CA: National Staff Development Council and The School Redesign Network at Stanford University. Retrieved May 23, 2019 from https://learningforward.org/docs/default-source/pdf/nsdcstudy2009.pdf

Dasgupta, N., & Stout, J. G. (2014). Girls and women in science, technology, engineering, and mathematics: STEMing the tide and broadening participation in STEM careers. *Policy Insights from the Behavioral and Brain Sciences, 1*(1), 21–29.

Davies, R. S., & West, R. E. (2014). Technology integration in schools. In J. M. Spector, M. D. Merrill, J. Elen, & M. J. Bishop (Eds.) *Handbook of research on educational communications and technology* (4th ed., pp. 841–53). New York, NY: Springer.

Davis, N., & Cabello, B. B. (1989). Preparing teachers to work with culturally diverse students: A teacher education model. *Journal of Teacher Education, 40*(5), 9–16.

Dean, D. M. (2000). Muddying boundaries: Mixing genres with five paragraphs. *English Journal, 90*(1), 53–56.

Delpit, L. (1995). *Other people's children: Cultural conflict in the classroom*. New York, NY: The Free Press.

Demko, M. (2010). Teachers become zombies: The ugly side of scripted reading curriculum. *Voices from the Middle, 17*(3), 62–64.

Dewey, J. (1899). *The school and society*. Chicago, IL: University of Chicago Press.

Diamond, J. (1997). *Guns, germs, and steel: The fates of human societies*. New York, NY: W. W. Norton.

Dixon, J. (1975). *Growth through English: Set in the perspective of the seventies*, 3rd ed. Oxford, UK: Oxford University Press.

Dutton, Y. C., & Heath, C. (2010). Cultural evolution: Why are some cultural variants more successful than others? In M. Schaller, A. Norenzayan, S. J. Heine, T. Yamagishi, & T. Kameda (Eds.), *Evolution, culture, and the human mind* (pp. 49–70). New York, NY: Psychology Press.

Ebbinghaus, H. (1885/1913). *Memory: A contribution to experimental psychology* (H. A. Ruger & C. E. Bussenius, Trans.). New York, NY: Teachers College Press.

Edwards, M. (2017, Dec. 12). *"We need more Native teachers": Wyoming DOE hears input on reservation schools*. Retrieved August 24, 2018 from http://www.wyomingpublicm edia.org/post/we-need-more-native-teachers-wyoming-doe-hears-input-reservation-s chools#stream/0

Egalite, A. J., Kisida, B., & Winter, M. A. (2015). Representation in the classroom: The effect of own-race teachers on student achievement. *Economics of Education Review*, *45*, 44–52.

Ehrenhaft, G. (2018). *Barron's writing workbook for the new SAT*, 4th ed. Hauppauge, NY: Barron's Educational Series.

Ellis, V., Edwards, A., & Smagorinsky, P. (Eds.) (2010). *Cultural-historical perspectives on teacher education and development: Learning teaching*. New York, NY: Routledge.

Emig, J. (1971). *The composing processes of twelfth graders* (NCTE research report No. 13). Urbana, IL: National Council of Teachers of English.

Engelmann, S. (1991). Change schools through revolution, not evolution. *Journal of Behavioral Education*, *1*(3), 295–304.

ERIC Clearinghouse on Reading English and Communication. (1995). *From theory to practice: Classroom application of outcome-based education*. ERIC Digest. Bloomington, IN: Author. Retrieved August 18, 2018 from http://www.ed.gov/databases/ERIC_Di gests/ed377512.html

Feiman-Nemser, S., & Buchmann, M. (1985). Pitfalls of experience in teacher preparation. *Teachers College Record*, *87*, 53–65.

Florio-Ruane, S. (2001). *Teacher education and the cultural imagination: Autobiography, conversation, and narrative*. New York, NY: Routledge.

Four Arrows (Ed.). (2006). *Unlearning the language of conquest: Scholars expose anti-Indianism in America*. Austin, TX: University of Texas Press.

Four Arrows. (2013). *Teaching truly: A curriculum to indigenize mainstream education*. New York, NY: Peter Lang.

Freedman, L. (2013, June 28). The developmental disconnect in choosing a major: Why institutions should prohibit choice until second year. *The Mentor: An Academic Advising Journal*. Retrieved September 3, 2018 from https://dus.psu.edu/mentor/201 3/06/disconnect-choosing-major/

Gabel, S. L. (Ed.) (2005). *Disabilities studies in education: Readings in theory and method*. New York, NY: Peter Lang.

Gajdamaschko, N. (1999). Lev Semenovich Vygotsky. In M. A. Runco & S. R. Pritzker (Eds.), *Encyclopedia of creativity*. Vol. 1, Ae-H (pp. 691–98). San Diego, CA: Academic Press.

Gallagher, P. (1996). Making education work. *Elements*, *2*. Retrieved August 18, 2018 from http://www.ul.ie/~childsp/Elements/issue2/gallag.html

García, O., & Wei, L. (2014). *Translanguaging: Language, bilingualism and education*. New York, NY: Palgrave Macmillan.

Gardner, W. L., Gabriel, S., & Lee, A. U. (1999). "I" value freedom but "we" value relationships: Self-construal priming mirrors cultural differences in judgment. *Psychological Science*, *10*, 321–26.

Garn, G., & Brown, C. (2008). Women and the superintendency: Perceptions of gender bias. *Journal of Women in Educational Leadership*, 6(1) 49–71.

Gay, G. (2000). *Culturally, responsive teaching: Theory, research, & practice*. New York, NY: Teachers College Press.

Gibaldi, J. (2003). *MLA handbook for writers of research papers*, 6th ed. New York, NY: Modern Language Association.

Gilbert, C. (2014). A call for subterfuge: Shielding the ELA classroom from the restrictive sway of the Common Core. *English Journal*, 104(2), 27–33.

Gilligan, C. (1982). *In a different voice: Psychological theory and women's development*. Cambridge, MA: Harvard University Press.

Goldberg, A. E. (2006). *Constructions at work: The nature of generalization in language*. New York, NY: Oxford University Press.

Goodlad, J. I. (1984). *A place called school: Prospects for the future*. New York, NY: McGraw-Hill.

Graham, S., & Perin, D. (2007). *Writing next: Effective strategies to improve writing of adolescents in middle and high schools—A report to Carnegie Corporation of New York*. Washington, DC: Alliance for Excellent Education. Retrieved October 21, 2010 from http://www.all4ed.org/files/WritingNext.pdf

Greene, P. (2016, February 17). What went wrong with Teach For America. *The Progressive*. Retrieved August 14, 2019 from https://progressive.org/public-school-shakedown/went-wrong-teach-america/

Grisham, D. L., & Brink, B. (2000). *Model classrooms: A theory to practice link for preservice teacher education*. Vancouver, WA: Southwest Washington Educational Partnership. Retrieved August 18, 2018 from http://www.vancouver.wsu.edu/programs/edu/swep/ModelClassroom.pdf

Gross, S., & Schulten, K. (2014, September 18). "The Giver" and "the dark side of young adult fiction." *New York Times*. Retrieved May 29, 2019 from https://learning.blogs.nytimes.com/2014/09/18/text-to-text-the-giver-and-the-dark-side-of-young-adult-fiction/

Grossman, P. L. (1990). *The making of a teacher: Teacher knowledge and teacher education*. New York, NY: Teachers College Press.

Grossman, P., Hammernessa, K., & McDonald, M. (2009). Redefining teaching, re-imagining teacher education. *Teachers and Teaching: Theory and Practice*, 15(2), 273–89.

Grossman, P. L., Smagorinsky, P., & Valencia, S. (1999). Appropriating tools for teaching English: A theoretical framework for research on learning to teach. *American Journal of Education*, 108(1), 1–29.

Grossman, P. L., & Stodolsky, S. S. (1994). Considerations of content and circumstances of secondary school teaching. In L. Darling-Hammond (Ed.), *Review of Research in Education, Vol. 20* (pp. 179–222). Washington, DC: American Educational Research Association.

Grossman, P. L., & Thompson, C. (2008). Learning from curriculum materials: Scaffolds for new teachers? *Teaching and Teacher Education*, 24(8), 2014–26.

Gutiérrez, K. D. (2008). Developing a sociocritical literacy in the third space. *Reading Research Quarterly*, 43(2), 148–64.

Hall, G. E., & Hord, S. M. (1987). *Change in schools: Facilitating the process*. Albany, NY: State University of New York Press.

Harber, C. (Ed.) (2004). *Schooling as violence: How schools harm pupils and societies*. New York, NY: RoutledgeFalmer.

Harris, Y. R., & Graham, J. A. (2007). *The African American child: Development and challenges*. New York, NY: Springer.

Hemsley-Brown, J., & Sharp, C. (2003) The use of research to improve professional practice: A systematic review of the literature. *Oxford Review of Education*, *29*(4), 449–70. Retrieved September 2, 2018 from http://epubs.surrey.ac.uk/479/1/fulltext.pdf

Herrnstein, R. J., & Murray, C. (1994). *The bell curve: Intelligence and class structure in American life*. New York, NY: Simon and Schuster.

Hickman, M. B., & McIntyre, J. D. (Eds.) (2012). *Rereading the new criticism*. Columbus, OH: The Ohio State University Press.

Hill, D., & Kumar, R. (Eds.) (2009). *Global neoliberalism and education and its consequences*. New York, NY: Routledge.

Hillocks, G. (1986). *Research on written composition: New directions for teaching*. Urbana, IL: National Conference on Research in English and Educational Resources Information Center.

Hillocks, G. (1995). *Teaching writing as reflective practice*. New York, NY: Teachers College Press.

Hillocks, G. (2002). *The testing trap: How state writing assessments control learning*. New York, NY: Teachers College Press.

Hillocks, G., McCabe, B. J., & McCampbell, J. F. (1971). *The dynamics of English instruction, grades 7–12*. New York, NY: Random House. Retrieved August 18, 2018 from http://www.petersmagorinsky.net/Books/Dynamics/Dynamics_home.htm

Holland, D., & Leander, K. (2004). Ethnographic studies of positioning and subjectivity: An introduction. *Ethos*, *32*(2), 127–39.

Hyland, N. E. (2005). Being a good teacher of Black students? White teachers and unintentional racism. *Curriculum Inquiry*, *35*(4), 429–59.

Hymes, D. H. (1974). *Foundations in sociolinguistics: An ethnographic approach*. Philadelphia, PA: University of Pennsylvania Press.

Ingersoll, R., Merrill, L., & May, H. (2014). What are the effects of teacher education preparation on beginning teacher attrition? *Consortium for Policy Research in Education* (Vol. RR-82). Philadelphia, PA: Consortium for Policy Research in Education, University of Pennsylvania.

Jackson, P. W. (1968). *Life in classrooms*. New York, NY: Holt, Rinehart, & Winston.

Jackson, P. W. (1992). *Untaught lessons*. New York, NY: Teachers College Press.

Jacobs, D. T. (1998). *Primal awareness: A true story of survival, transformation and awakening with the Rarámuri Shamans of Mexico*. Rochester, VT: Inner Traditions International.

Jean-Marie, G., & Martinez, A. (2007). Race, gender, & leadership: Perspectives of female secondary leaders. In S. M. Nielsen & M. S. Plakhotnik (Eds.), *Proceedings of the Sixth Annual College of Education Research Conference: Urban and International Education Section* (pp. 43–48). Miami, FL: Florida International University. Retrieved August 18, 2018 from http://coeweb.fiu.edu/research_conference/

Jenson, E. (2008). *Brain-based learning: The new paradigm of teaching*. Thousand Oaks, CA: Sage.

Jilot, J. (2016, November 14). Here's the truth about why there are so few Native American teachers. *Educationpost*. Retrieved July 11, 2018 from http://educationpost.org/heres-the-truth-about-why-there-are-so-few-native-american-teachers/

Johnson, L. L., Sieben, N., & Buxton, D. (2018). Collaborative design as mediated praxis: Professional development for socially just pedagogies. *English Education*, *50*(2), 172–98.

Johnson, S. M., Berg, J. H., & Donaldson, M. L. (2005). *Who stays in teaching and why: A review of the literature on teacher retention.* Cambridge, MA: Project on the Next Generation of Teachers.

Johnson, T. S., Smagorinsky, P., Thompson, L., & Fry, P. G. (2003). Learning to teach the five-paragraph theme. *Research in the Teaching of English, 38,* 136–76.

Kahl, D. H., & Venette, S. (2010). To lecture or let go: A comparative analysis of student speech outlines from teacher-centered and learner-centered classrooms. *Communication Teacher, 24*(3), 178–86.

Kahle, J. B., & Kronebusch, M. (2003). Science teacher education: From a fractured system to a seamless continuum. *Review of Policy Research, 20*(4), 585–602.

Kahn, E. A., Walter, C. C., & Johannessen, L. R. (2009). *Writing about literature, 2nd Edition.* Urbana, IL: National Council of Teachers of English.

Kallos, D. (1999). Recent changes in Swedish teacher education. *TNTEE Publications, 2,* 165–74.

Kaufman, J. E. (2004). Language, inquiry, and the heart of learning: Reflections in an English methods course. *English Education, 36*(3), 174–91.

Kearsley, G. (1994–2001). Explorations in learning & instruction: The theory into practice database. *Jacksonville State University Encyclopedia of Psychology.* Retrieved August 18, 2018 from http://tip.psychology.org/

Kelly, S. (2009). Tracking teachers. In L. J. Saha & A. G. Dworkin (Eds.), *International handbook of research on teachers and teaching* (pp. 451–61). New York, NY: Springer.

Kennedy, M. N. (1998). *Learning to teach writing: Does teacher education make a difference?* New York, NY: Teachers College Press.

Kentli, F. D. (2009). Comparison of hidden curriculum theories. *European Journal of Educational Studies, 1*(2), 83–88.

Kiuhara, S. A., Graham, S., & Hawken, L. S. (2009). Teaching writing to high school students: A national survey. *Journal of Educational Psychology, 101,* 136–60.

Kim, M. S. (2012). Cultural-historical activity theory perspectives on constructing ICT-mediated metaphors of teaching and learning. *European Journal of Teacher Education, 35*(4), 435–48.

Kinloch, V., & Smagorinsky, P. (Eds.) (2014). *Service-learning in literacy education: Possibilities for teaching and learning.* Charlotte, NC: Information Age Publishing.

Kinneavy, J. L. (1971). *A theory of discourse.* Englewood Cliffs, NJ: Prentice-Hall.

Koedel, C. (2018, September 21). *As grades inflate, standardized tests keep us grounded.* Washington, DC: Thomas B. Fordham Institute. Retrieved September 26, 2018 from https://edexcellence.net/articles/as-grades-inflate-standardized-tests-keep-us-grounded

Kontopodis, M. (2012). *Neoliberalism, pedagogy and human development: Exploring time, mediation and collectivity in contemporary schools.* New York, NY: Routledge.

Kramer, R. (1991). *Ed school follies.* New York, NY: Free Press.

Krueger, V. (1989). Reflections: Victoria Krueger. In B. Perrone, H. H. Stockel, & V. Krueger, *Medicine women, curanderas, and women doctors* (pp. 225–29). Norman, OK: University of Oklahoma Press.

Labaree, D. F. (2004). *The trouble with Ed Schools.* New Haven, CT: Yale University Press.

Larsen-Freeman, D. (2000). *Techniques and principles in language teaching.* New York, NY: Oxford University Press.

Laser, M. (2015, October 13). Novelist teaches freshman writing, is shocked by students' inability to construct basic sentences: Have we lost this essential skill and can it be recovered? *The Hechinger Report.* Retrieved September 7, 2018 from https://heching

erreport.org/novelist-teaches-freshman-writing-is-shocked-by-students-inability-to-construct-basic-sentences/

Latour, B., & Woolgar, S. (1979). *Laboratory life: The construction of scientific facts*. Princeton, NJ: Princeton University Press. Retrieved September 28, 2018 from http://home.ku.edu.tr/~mbaker/cshs503/latourlablif.pdf

Lave, J. (1988). *Cognition in practice*. New York, NY: Cambridge University Press.

Leachman, M., Masterson, K., & Figueroa, E. (2017, November 29). *A punishing decade for school funding*. Washington, DC: Center on Budget and Policy Priorities. Retrieved August 12, 2019 from https://www.cbpp.org/research/state-budget-and-tax/a-punishing-decade-for-school-funding

Leavitt, H. J. (2003, March). Why hierarchies thrive. *Harvard Business Review*. Retrieved August 12, 2019 from https://hbr.org/2003/03/why-hierarchies-thrive

Leont'ev, A. N. (1981). *Problems of the development of mind*. Moscow, RU: Progress Publishers.

Levine, A. (2006). *Educating school teachers*. Princeton, NJ: The Education Schools Project. Retrieved May 29, 2019 from https://files.eric.ed.gov/fulltext/ED504144.pdf

Levy, J. (1995, May 22). How to tell the real thing. *Times Higher Education*. Retrieved August 18, 2018 from http://www.timeshighereducation.co.uk/161713.article

Lillge, D. (2019). Uncovering conflict: Why teachers struggle to apply professional development learning about the teaching of writing. *Research in the Teaching of English*, *53*(4), 340–62.

Lipsitz, G. (2006). *The possessive investment in whiteness: How white people profit from identity politics*. Philadelphia, PA: Temple University Press.

Loewen, J. W. (1996). *Lies my teacher told me: Everything your American history textbook got wrong*. New York, NY: Touchstone.

Lortie, D. C. (1975). *Schoolteacher: A sociological study*. Chicago, IL: University of Chicago Press.

Lott, J. G. (1996, March). *High schools are from Mars, colleges from Greece: Why we exist eons apart*. Paper presented at the annual meeting of the Conference on College Composition and Communication, Milwaukee. ED 402 613.

Luria, A. R. (1976). *Cognitive development: Its cultural and social foundations* (M. Lopez-Morillas & L. Solotaroff, Trans.). Cambridge, MA: Harvard University Press.

MacLean, M. S., & Mohr, M. M. (1999). *Teacher-researchers at work*. Berkeley, CA: The National Writing Project.

Madkins, T. C. (2011). The Black teacher shortage: A literature review of historical and contemporary trends. *Journal of Negro Education*, *80*(3), 417–27.

Majors, Y. J. (2015). *Shoptalk: Lessons in teaching from an African American hair salon*. New York, NY: Teachers College Press.

Marshall, J. D., Smagorinsky, P., & Smith, M. W. (1995). *The language of interpretation: Patterns of discourse in discussions of literature*. NCTE Research Report No. 27. Urbana, IL: National Council of Teachers of English.

McCann, T. M. (2014). *Transforming talk into text: Argument writing, inquiry, and discussion, grades 6–12*. New York, NY: Teachers College Press.

McCann, T. M. (2018). How George Hillocks taught us to teach English. *Illinois English Bulletin*, *105*(2), 41–58. Retrieved August 12, 2019 from http://www.petersmagorinsky.net/TEBD/Books/McCann_IEB_18.PDF

McCutcheon, G. (1988). Curriculum and work of teachers. In L. E. Beyer & M. W. Apple (Eds.), *The curriculum: Problems, politics, and possibilities* (pp. 191–203). New York, NY: State University of New York Press.

McKinney, C. (2017). *Language and power in post-colonial schooling: Ideologies in practice*. New York, NY: Routledge.

Meighan, R. (1981). *A sociology of education*. New York, NY: Holt.

MetLife. (2013). *MetLife survey of the American teacher: Challenges for school leadership*. New York, NY: Author. Available at https://www.metlife.com/assets/cao/foundation/MetLife-Teacher-Survey-2012.pdf

Mewborn, D. S., & Tyminski, A. M. (2006). Lortie's apprenticeship of observation revisited. *For the Learning of Mathematics, 26*(3), 30–33.

Milner, R. (2013). *Policy reforms and de-professionalization of teaching*. Boulder, CO: National Education Policy Center. Retrieved August 3, 2018 from https://greatlakescenter.org/docs/Policy_Briefs/Milner_Deprof.pdf

Mirel, J. (2003). Old educational ideas, new American schools: Progressivism and the rhetoric of educational revolution. *Paedagogica Historica: International Journal of the History of Education, 39*(4), 477–97.

Mirel, J., & Goldin, S. (2012, April 17). Alone in the classroom: Why teachers are too isolated. *The Atlantic*. Retrieved May 23, 2019 from https://www.theatlantic.com/national/archive/2012/04/alone-in-the-classroom-why-teachers-are-too-isolated/255976/

Mitchell, J. (1984). Typicality and the case study. In R. Ellen (Ed.), *Ethnographic research: A guide to general conduct* (pp. 237–41). London, UK: Academic Press.

Modica, M. (2015). "My skin color stops me from leading": Tracking, identity, and student dynamics in a racially mixed school. *International Journal of Multicultural Education, 17*(3), 76–90.

Moje, E. B., Luke, A., & Street, B. (2009). Literacy and identity: Examining the metaphors in history and contemporary research. *Reading Research Quarterly, 44*(4), 415–37.

Moll, L. C. (2000). Inspired by Vygotsky: Ethnographic experiments in education. In C. D. Lee & P. Smagorinsky (Eds.), *Vygotskian perspectives on literacy research* (pp. 256–68). New York, NY: Cambridge University Press.

Moore, C. M. (2012). The role of school environment in teacher dissatisfaction among U.S. public school teachers. *SAGE Open*, 1–16. DOI: 10.1177/2158244012438888

Morgan, D. N., & Pytash, K. (2014). Preparing preservice teachers to become teachers of writing: A 20-year review of the research literature. *English Education, 47*, 6–37.

Morgan, H. (2009). What every teacher needs to know to teach Native American students. *Multicultural Education, 16*(4), 10–12. Retrieved July 11, 2018 from https://files.eric.ed.gov/fulltext/EJ858583.pdf

National Center for Educational Statistics. (2017a). *Fast facts: Back to school statistics*. Retrieved July 10, 2018 from https://nces.ed.gov/fastfacts/display.asp?id=372

National Center for Educational Statistics. (2017b). *The condition of education 2017*. Retrieved July 10, 2018 from https://nces.ed.gov/programs/coe/pdf/coe_svc.pdf

National Council for Accreditation of Teacher Education. (2008). *Professional standards for the accreditation of teacher preparation institutions*. Washington, DC: Author. Retrieved April 1, 2016 from http://www.ncate.org/Portals/0/documents/Standards/NCATE%20Standards%202008.pdf

National Council of Teachers of English. (2005). *Position statement on multimodal literacies*. Retrieved August 18, 2018 from http://www.ncte.org/positions/statements/multimodalliteracies

National Council on Teacher Quality. (2018). *2018 teacher prep review*. Washington, DC: Author. Retrieved August 15, 2019 from https://www.nctq.org/dmsView/2018_Teacher_Prep_Review:733174

Newell, G. E., Tallman, M., & Letcher, M. (2009). A longitudinal study of consequential transitions in the teaching of literature. *Research in the Teaching of English, 44*, 89–126.

Newman, D., Griffin, P., & Cole, M. (1989). *The construction zone: Working for cognitive change in school*. New York, NY: Cambridge University Press.

Nieto, S. (2000). *Affirming diversity: The sociopolitical context of multicultural education*. New York, NY: Longman.

Noguchi, R. R. (1991). *Grammar and the teaching of writing: Limits and possibilities*. Urbana, IL: National Council of Teachers of English.

Nunnally, T. E. (1991). Breaking the five paragraph theme barrier. *English Journal, 80*(1), 67–71.

Nystrand, M. (1986). *The structure of written communication: Studies in reciprocity between writers and readers*. Orlando, FL: Academic.

Paris, D., & Alim, H. S. (Eds.) (2017). *Culturally sustaining pedagogies: Teaching and learning for justice in a changing world*. New York, NY: Teachers College Press.

Pasternak, D., Caughlan, S., Hallman, H., Renzi, L., & Rush, L. (2017). *Secondary English teacher education in the United States: A historical and current analysis*. London, UK: Bloomsbury.

Petruzzella, B. A. (1996). Grammar instruction: What teachers say. *English Journal, 85*(7), 68–72.

Phi Delta Kappa. (2016, August). *Critical issues in public education: The 2016 Phi Delta Kappa survey*. Arlington, VA: Author. Retrieved September 3, 2018 from http://pdkpoll2015.pdkintl.org/?utm_source=PDK+International&utm_campaign=001b5b18ef-PDK_PDK_Poll_Results8_30_2016&utm_medium=email&utm_term=0_867590cd6a-001b5b18ef-32572437

Philip, T. M., Souto-Manning, M., Anderson, L., Horn, I., Andrews, D. J. C., Stillman, J., & Varghese, M. (2018). Making justice peripheral by constructing practice as "core": How the increasing prominence of core practices challenges teacher education. *Journal of Teacher Education*. https://doi.org/10.1177/0022487118798324

Phillion, J., & He, M. F. (2009). Using life-based literary narratives in multicultural teacher education. *Multicultural Perspectives, 6*(3), 3–9.

Phillips, D. C. (1995). The good, the bad, and the ugly: The many faces of constructivism. *Educational Researcher, 24*(7), 5–12.

Piaget, J. (1954). *The construction of reality in the child*. New York, NY: Basic Books.

Pianta, R. C., & Hamre, B. K. (2009). Conceptualization, measurement, and improvement of classroom processes: Standardized observation can leverage capacity. *Educational Researcher, 38*, 109–19.

Rabinowitz, P. J. (1987). *Before reading: Narrative conventions and the politics of interpretation*. Ithaca, NY: Cornell University Press.

Rancière, J. (2010). *Dissensus: On politics and aesthetics* (S. Corcoran, Ed. & Trans.). New York, NY: Continuum.

Ransom, J. C. (1941). *The new criticism*. New York, NY: New Directions Publishing.

Ray, B. (2015). *Style: An introduction to history, theory, research, and pedagogy*. Fort Collins, CO: Parlor Press and the WAC Clearinghouse. Retrieved September 3, 2018 from https://wac.colostate.edu/books/referenceguides/style/

Rejan, A. (2017). Reconciling Rosenblatt and the New Critics: The quest for an "experienced understanding" of literature. *English Education, 50*(1), 10–41.

Rheingold, H. L., & Cook, K. V. (1975). The contents of boys' and girls' rooms as an index of parents' behavior. *Child Development, 46*, 459–63.

Richardson, V. (2003). Constructivist pedagogy. *Teachers College Record, 105*(9), 1623–40.

Rita, C., Richey, R. C., Klein, J. D., & Tracey, M. W. (2011). *The instructional design knowledge base: Theory, research, and practice*. New York, NY: Routledge.

Rose, S. K. (1983). Down from the Haymow: One hundred years of sentence-combining. *College English, 45*(5), 483–91.

Rosenblatt, L. (1938). *Literature as exploration*. New York, NY: Appleton-Century.

Sadovnik, A. R., & Semel, S. F. (2010). Education and inequality: Historical and sociological approaches to schooling and social stratification. *Paedagogica Historica, 46*(1–2), 1–13.

Safire, W. (1984). *I stand corrected: More on language*. New York, NY: Times Books.

Sang, G., Valcke, M., van Braak, J., & Tondeur, J. (2010). Student teachers' thinking processes and ICT integration: Predictors of prospective teaching behaviors with educational technology. *Computers & Education, 54*(1), 103–12. doi:10.1016/j.compedu.2009.07.010

Schaller, M., Norenzayan, A., Heine, S. J., Yamagishi, T., & Kameda, T. (Eds.) (2010). *Evolution, culture, and the human mind*. New York, NY: Taylor & Francis.

Schoon, K. J., & Sandoval, P. A. (1997). The seamless field experience model for secondary science teacher preparation. *Journal of Science Teacher Education, 8*, 127–40.

Schuh, K. L. (2004). Learner-centered principles in teacher-centered practices? *Teaching and Teacher Education, 20*(8), 833–46.

Scribner, S. (1997). Mental and manual work: An activity theory orientation. In E. Tobach, R. J. Falmagne, M. B. Parlee, L. M. W. Martin, & A. S. Kapelman (Eds.), *Mind and social practice: Selected writings of Sylvia Scribner* (pp. 364–74). New York, NY: Cambridge University Press.

Shanahan, T. (2013). Letting the text take center stage: How the Common Core State Standards will transform English Language Arts instruction. *American Educator*, Fall, 4–11, 43.

Shaughnessy, M. P. (1977). *Errors and expectations: A guide for the teacher of basic writing*. New York, NY: Oxford University Press.

Slater, G. B. (2015). Education as recovery: Neoliberalism, school reform, and the politics of crisis. *Journal of Educational Policy, 30*(1), 1–20.

Sleeter, C. E. (2001). Preparing teachers for culturally diverse schools: Research and the overwhelming presence of whiteness. *Journal of Teacher Education, 52*, 94–106.

Smagorinsky, P. (1995). The social construction of data: Methodological problems of investigating learning in the zone of proximal development. *Review of Educational Research, 65*, 191–212.

Smagorinsky, P. (1997). Personal growth in social context: A high school senior's search for meaning in and through writing. *Written Communication, 14*, 63–105.

Smagorinsky, P. (1999). Time to teach. *English Education, 32*, 50–73.

Smagorinsky, P. (2001). If meaning is constructed, what is it made from?: Toward a cultural theory of reading. *Review of Educational Research, 71*, 133–69.

Smagorinsky, P. (2002). *Teaching English through principled practice*. Upper Saddle River, NJ: Merrill/Prentice Hall.

Smagorinsky, P. (Ed.) (2006). *Research on composition: Multiple perspectives on two decades of change*. New York, NY: Teachers College Press and the National Conference on Research in Language and Literacy.

Smagorinsky, P. (2008). The method section as conceptual epicenter in constructing social science research reports. *Written Communication, 25*, 389–411.

Smagorinsky, P. (2009). Is it time to abandon the idea of "best practices" in the teaching of English? *English Journal, 98*(6), 15–22.

Smagorinsky, P. (2010). The culture of learning to teach: The self-perpetuating cycle of conservative schooling. *Teacher Education Quarterly, 37*(2), 19–32.

Smagorinsky, P. (2011). *Vygotsky and literacy research: A methodological framework.* Boston, MA: Sense.

Smagorinsky, P. (2013). The development of social and practical concepts in learning to teach: A synthesis and extension of Vygotsky's conception. *Learning, Culture, and Social Interaction, 2*(4), 238–48.

Smagorinsky, P. (2017). Misfits in school literacy: Whom are U. S. schools designed to serve? In D. Appleman & K. Hinchman (Eds.), *Adolescent literacy: A handbook of practice-based research* (pp. 199–214). New York, NY: Guilford.

Smagorinsky, P. (2018a). *Teaching English by design: How to create and carry out instructional units, 2nd Edition.* Portsmouth, NH: Heinemann.

Smagorinsky, P. (2018b). Literacy in teacher education: "It's the context, stupid." *Journal of Literacy Research, 50*(3), 281–303.

Smagorinsky, P., Anglin, J. L., & O'Donnell-Allen, C. (2012). Identity, meaning, and engagement with school: A Native American student's composition of a life map in a senior English class. *Journal of American Indian Education, 51*(1), 22–44.

Smagorinsky, P., & Barnes, M. E. (2014). Revisiting and revising the apprenticeship of observation. *Teacher Education Quarterly, 41*(4), 29–52.

Smagorinsky, P., Boggs, G. L., Jakubiak, C. A., & Wilson, A. A. (2010). The implied character curriculum in vocational and nonvocational English classes: Designing social futures for working class students and their teachers. *Journal of Research in Character Education, 8*(2), 1–23.

Smagorinsky, P., Cook, L. S., Jackson, A. Y., Moore, C., & Fry, P. G. (2004). Tensions in learning to teach: Accommodation and the development of a teaching identity. *Journal of Teacher Education, 55*, 8–24.

Smagorinsky, P., Cook, L. S., & Johnson, T. S. (2003). The twisting path of concept development in learning to teach. *Teachers College Record, 105*, 1399–436.

Smagorinsky, P., & Daigle, E. A. (2012). The role of affect in students' writing for school. In E. L. Grigorenko, E. Mambrino & D. D. Preiss (Eds.), *Writing: A mosaic of new perspectives* (pp. 293–307). New York, NY: Psychology Press.

Smagorinsky, P., Gibson, N., Moore, C., Bickmore, S., & Cook, L. S. (2004). Praxis shock: Making the transition from a student-centered university program to the corporate climate of schools. *English Education, 36*, 214–45.

Smagorinsky, P., Jakubiak, C., & Moore, C. (2008). Student teaching in the contact zone: Learning to teach amid multiple interests in a vocational English class. *Journal of Teacher Education, 59*, 442–54.

Smagorinsky, P., Lakly, A., & Johnson, T. S. (2002). Acquiescence, accommodation, and resistance in learning to teach within a prescribed curriculum. *English Education, 34*, 187–213.

Smagorinsky, P., & O'Donnell-Allen, C. (1998a). The depth and dynamics of context: Tracing the sources and channels of engagement and disengagement in students' response to literature. *Journal of Literacy Research, 30*, 515–59.

Smagorinsky, P., & O'Donnell-Allen, C. (1998b). Reading as mediated and mediating action: Composing meaning for literature through multimedia interpretive texts. *Reading Research Quarterly, 33*, 198–226.

Smagorinsky, P., Rhym, D., & Moore, C. (2013). Competing centers of gravity: A beginning English teacher's socialization process within conflictual settings. *English Education, 45*, 147–83.

Smagorinsky, P., Sanford, A. D., & Konopak. B. (2006). Functional literacy in a constructivist key: A nontraditional student teacher's apprenticeship in a rural elementary school. *Teacher Education Quarterly, 33*(4), 93–110.

Smagorinsky, P., Shelton, S. A., & Moore, C. (2015). The role of reflection in developing eupraxis in learning to teach English. *Pedagogies: An International Journal, 10*(4), 285–308.

Smagorinsky, P., & Taxel, J. (2004). The discourse of character education: Ideology and politics in the proposal and award of federal grants. *Journal of Research in Character Education, 2*(2), 113–40.

Smagorinsky, P., & Taxel, J. (2005). *The discourse of character education: Culture wars in the classroom*. Mahwah, NJ: Erlbaum.

Smagorinsky, P., & Whiting, M. E. (1995). *How English teachers get taught: Methods of teaching the methods class*. Urbana, IL: Conference on English Education and National Council of Teachers of English.

Smagorinsky, P., Wilson, A. A., & Moore, C. (2011). Teaching grammar and writing: A beginning teacher's dilemma. *English Education, 43*, 263–93.

Smagorinsky, P., Wright, L., Augustine, S. M., O'Donnell-Allen, C., & Konopak, B. (2007). Student engagement in the teaching and learning of grammar: A case study of an early-career secondary school English teacher. *Journal of Teacher Education, 58*, 76–90.

Smith, L. T. (2005). Building a research agenda for Indigenous epistemologies and education. *Anthropology and Education Quarterly, 36*(1), 93–95.

Smitherman, G. (2006). *Word from the mother: Language and African Americans*. New York, NY: Routledge.

Smolucha, F. (1992). A reconstruction of Vygotsky's theory of creativity. *Creativity Research Journal, 5*(1), 49–67.

Smylie, M. A. (1994). Redesigning teachers' work: Connections to the classroom. In L. Darling-Hammond (Ed.), *Review of Research in Education, vol. 20* (pp. 129–78). Washington, DC: American Educational Research Association.

St. Pierre, E. A. (2014). A brief and personal history of post qualitative research toward "post inquiry." *Journal of Curriculum Theorizing, 30*(2), 2–19.

Stephens, D., Boldt, G., Clark, C., Gaffney, J., Shelton, J., Story, J., & Weinzierl, J. (1999). Learning (about learning) from four teachers. *Research in the Teaching of English, 34*, 532–65.

Stoeker, R. (1991). Evaluating and rethinking the case study. *The Sociological Review, 39*(1), 88–112.

Stotsky, S. (1999). *Losing our language: How multicultural classroom instruction is undermining our children's ability to read, write, and reason*. New York, NY: Free Press.

Sunderman, G. L., Tracey, C. A., Kim, J., & Orfield, G. (2004). *Listening to teachers: Classroom realities and No Child Left Behind*. Cambridge, MA: The Civil Rights Project at Harvard University.

Taber, K. S. (2011, January 4). Understanding the nature and processes of conceptual change: An essay review. *Education Review, 14*(1). Retrieved May 30, 2019 from http://www.edrev.info/essays/v14n1.pdf

Taylor, C. (1985). *Philosophical papers: Volume 1, Human agency and language*. New York, NY: Cambridge University Press.

teAchnology. (n. d.). *Piaget's theory of constructivism*. Retrieved July 11, 2018 from http://www.teach-nology.com/currenttrends/constructivism/piaget/

Terhart, E. (2013). Teacher resistance against school reform: Reflecting an inconvenient truth. *School Leadership & Management, 33*(5), 486–500.

TFA Editorial Team. (2018). *Our Texas impact*. New York, NY: Author. Retrieved August 15, 2019 from https://www.teachforamerica.org/stories/our-texas-impact

Thomas, P. L. (2014, February 2). *New criticism, close reading, and failing critical literacy again*. Available at http://radicalscholarship.wordpress.com/2014/02/02/new-criticism-close-reading-and-failing-critical-literacy-again/

Tremmel, R. (2001). Seeking a balanced discipline: Writing teacher education in first-year composition and English education. *English Education, 34*, 6–30.

Troia, G. A., & Graham, S. (2016). Common core writing and language standards and aligned state assessments: A national survey of teacher beliefs and attitudes. *Reading and Writing, 29*(9), 1719–1743. https://doi.org/10.1007/s11145-016-9650-z

Tulviste, P. (1991). *The cultural-historical development of verbal thinking*. Commack, NY: Nova Science Publishers.

U.S. Department of Education. (2016). *The state of racial diversity in the educator workforce*. Washington, DC: Author. Retrieved July 10, 2018 from https://www2.ed.gov/rschstat/eval/highered/racial-diversity/state-racial-diversity-workforce.pdf

Valsiner, J. (1998). *The guided mind: A sociogenetic approach to personality*. Cambridge, MA: Harvard University Press.

Vosniadou, S. (Ed.) (2008). *International handbook of research on conceptual change*. New York, NY: Routledge.

Voutira, E. (1996, April). The "It's too theoretical" syndrome. *Refugee Participation Education and Training, 21*, 3–6. Retrieved September 7, 2018 from https://www.researchgate.net/publication/27379261_The_'It's_too_theoretical'_syndrome

Vygotsky, L. S. (1998). Pedology of the adolescent. In *The Collected Works of L. S. Vygotsky, Volume 5, Child Psychology* pp. 3–186 (R. W. Rieber, Ed.; M. J. Hall, Trans.). New York, NY: Plenum.

Vygotsky, L. S. (1987). Thinking and speech. In *The Collected Works of L. S. Vygotsky* (vol. 1, pp. 39–285) (R. Rieber & A. Carton, Eds.; N. Minick, Trans.). New York, NY: Plenum.

Vygotsky, L. S. (1978). *Mind in society: The development of higher psychological processes* (M. Cole, V. John-Steiner, S. Scribner, & E. Souberman, Eds.). Cambridge, MA: Harvard University Press.

Wagner, T. (1994). *How schools change: Lessons from three communities revisited*. Boston, MA: Beacon Press.

Walker, T. (2019, March 29). After moving to a four-day school week, there may be no going back. *neaToday: News and Features from the National Education Association*. Retrieved May 31, 2019 from http://neatoday.org/2019/03/29/4-day-school-week-here-to-stay/

Watson, A. (2018). Navigating "the pit of doom": Affective responses to teaching "grammar." *English in Education, 46*(1), 22–37.

Weaver, C. (1996). *Teaching grammar in context*. Portsmouth, NH: Heinemann.

Weaver, M. (1998). *The feminist bridges project: Bridging feminist theory and practice*. Wooster, OH: The College of Wooster Department of Political Science.

Weber, M. (1930). *The Protestant ethic and the spirit of capitalism*. New York, NY: Scribner.

Wells, A. S., Fox, L., & Cordova-Cobo, D. (2016). How racially diverse schools and classrooms can benefit all students. *The Century Foundation*. Retrieved July 11, 2018 from https://medium.com/the-century-foundation/how-racially-diverse-schools-and-classrooms-can-benefit-all-students-c8d7749f3fcd

Werner, H. (1957). The concept of development from a comparative and organismic point of view. In D. B. Harris (Ed.), *The concept of development* (pp. 125–48). Minneapolis, MN: University of Minnesota Press.

Wertsch, J. V. (1985). *Vygotsky and the social formation of mind.* Cambridge, MA: Harvard University Press.

Wertsch, J. V. (1991). *Voices of the mind: A sociocultural approach to mediated action.* Cambridge, MA: Harvard University Press.

Wertsch, J. V. (1995). E-mail message, XLCHC, January 28.

Wertsch, J. V. (2000). Vygotsky's two minds on the nature of meaning. In C. D. Lee & P. Smagorinsky (Eds.), *Vygotskian perspectives on literacy research: Constructing meaning through collaborative inquiry* (pp. 19–30). New York, NY: Cambridge University Press.

Wesley, K. (2000). The ill effects of the five paragraph theme. *English Journal, 90*(1), 57–60.

Whitney, L., Golez, F., Nagel, G., & Nieto, C. (2002). Listening to voices of practicing teachers to examine the effectiveness of a teacher education program. *Action in Teacher Education, 23*(3), 69–76.

Wideen, M., Mayer-Smith, J., & Moon, B. (1998). A critical analysis of the research on learning to teach: Making the case for an ecological perspective on inquiry. *Review of Educational Research, 68,* 130–78.

Wiley, M. (2000). The popularity of formulaic writing (and why we need to resist). *English Journal, 90*(1), 61–67.

Wilhelm, J., & Smith, M. W. (2017). *Diving deep into nonfiction: Transferable tools for reading any nonfiction text.* Thousand Oaks, CA: Corwin.

Williams, J. M. (1981). The phenomenology of error. *College Composition and Communication, 32*(2), 152–68.

Williams, R. (1977). *Marxism and literature.* New York, NY: Oxford University Press.

Willinsky, J. (1991). *The triumph of literature/The fate of literacy: English in the secondary school curriculum.* New York, NY: Teachers College Press.

Wilson, N. (2019, April 5). What they don't teach you at the University of Washington's Ed School. *Quillette.* Retrieved August 15, 2019 from https://quillette.com/2019/04/05/what-they-dont-teach-you-at-the-university-of-washingtons-ed-school/

Wines, M. (2019, May 30). Deceased G.O.P. strategist's hard drives reveal new details on the census citizenship question. *New York Times.* Retrieved May 31, 2019 from https://www.nytimes.com/2019/05/30/us/census-citizenship-question-hofeller.html?action=click&module=Top%20Stories&pgtype=Homepage

Zeichner, K. M., & Gore, J. M. (1990). Teacher socialization. In W. R. Houston (Ed.), *Handbook of research on teacher education* (pp. 329–48). New York, NY: Macmillan.

Zeichner, K. M., & Tabachnick, B. R. (1981). Are the effects of teacher education "washed out" by school experience? *Journal of Teacher Education, 32*(3), 7–11.

Zepeda, S., & Mayers, R. S. (2006). An analysis of research on block scheduling. *Review of Educational Research, 76*(1), 137–70.

Zuidema, L. A., & Fredricksen, J. E. (2016). Resources preservice teachers use to think about student writing. *Research in the Teaching of English, 51,* 12–36.

Index

accommodation (Piagetian)   63, 64, 84, 85
accommodation (to unwelcome requirements)   125, 127, 136
accountability   9, 46, 89, 147, 154, 203, 204, 206, 208, 209
acculturation/enculturation   xiv, 35, 40, 87, 93, 94, 97, 130, 138, 142, 155, 175, 177, 182, 205, 210
acquiescence   125, 128, 136, 150
affect/emotion   6, 13, 14, 17, 59, 61, 102, 105, 150, 152, 154, 168, 170, 198, 200, 209
Anglo-normativity   95
apprenticeship of observation   16, 25, 35–8, 40, 45–7, 52, 66, 86, 101, 123, 130, 132, 140, 158, 177, 182, 208, 210, 221
appropriation   7, 20, 23, 26
arena   4, 20, 21, 82
assessment   2, 6, 16, 32, 42, 46, 51, 54, 59–62, 66–8, 75, 76, 79, 88, 96, 102, 104, 110, 111, 117, 119–22, 124, 125, 128, 129, 133–5, 137–9, 148, 151, 160, 163, 174, 177, 185, 192, 193, 200, 201, 203, 204, 206, 211, 213, 214, 217
assign and repair teaching   189
assimilation (Piagetian)   63, 64, 84, 85
assimilation (to school norms)   65, 155, 170, 171, 173, 220
Atlas.ti   32
authoritarian instruction   15, 16, 36, 38, 41–3, 45, 46, 55, 63, 83, 86, 90, 101, 110, 112, 114, 118–20, 122, 123, 128, 132, 143, 154, 155, 157–60, 163–5, 167, 170, 171, 181, 182, 185, 202, 219, 222
autonomous text   41
autonomy   146, 193, 210, 212, 222

bathtub   115–17
behavioral expectations   12, 164, 166, 211

best practices   13, 222
binary   2, 23, 41, 51, 55, 59, 80, 102, 103, 106, 154, 155, 159, 181, 195, 196, 199, 200, 219, 220
block schedule   16, 68, 164, 168, 169, 188

case study   ix, 2, 161, 219
Center on English Learning and Achievement (CELA)   viii, ix, x, xiv, 1, 3, 24, 158
character education   ix, 50, 142, 146, 148, 150, 155, 164, 165
Chicago School of literary criticism   103, 104
choice   29, 41, 59, 60, 68, 69, 75, 77, 109, 116, 117, 119, 127, 143, 164, 167–9, 179, 181, 187, 193, 194, 213
closed-ended teaching   140, 162–4
codes of power   74, 76, 153, 178
coding (data)   24, 32, 33, 43, 44, 58, 62, 65, 73, 77, 78, 163, 189, 190
cohort design   ix, xii, xiii, 1, 24, 37–43, 57, 63, 72, 73, 77, 84, 85, 87, 88, 114, 157, 167, 170, 189, 191
Common Core State Curriculum (CCSS)   6, 95, 102, 178, 179, 221
communicative competence   178, 188
competing centers of gravity   11, 24, 111, 156, 157, 169, 170, 220
complex (Vygotskian)   5, 8–10, 63, 84, 99, 119, 129
concept (Vygotskian)   xiii, xv, 1–19, 22–5, 29, 32, 33, 35–7, 39–42, 45, 47, 49–55, 57, 59, 60, 63, 65, 66, 68–71, 74, 75, 77, 81, 82, 85–7, 89, 93–7, 99–107, 110–14, 117, 119–22, 126, 129, 133, 136, 138–42, 145, 146, 148, 151, 152, 154, 155, 157–61, 164, 165, 167, 169–71, 175, 180–2, 187–92, 195–7, 200, 202, 214, 218, 220, 221, 223
concept map activity   24, 26, 27, 55–7, 63, 65, 70, 71, 74, 80, 84, 85, 87, 99, 114

conceptual home base xii, xiv, xv, 42, 77
conceptual tools 23, 112
constructivism 16, 23, 32, 36–8, 40–5, 47, 52, 53, 55–61, 63, 65, 67–9, 74, 75, 79, 81, 83–7, 89, 91, 94, 99–103, 106, 107, 111–15, 117–20, 154, 158, 169, 180, 182, 185, 187, 188, 191, 192, 197, 202, 210–12
contradiction in environments xiii, 4, 17, 18, 45, 46, 49–52, 54, 55, 61–3, 65, 74, 77, 78, 91, 96, 97, 99, 101, 102, 104–6, 110, 111, 113, 115, 120, 140, 152, 171, 178, 219–21, 223
corporate climate 199, 202–4, 206, 208, 213–15, 222
county/district curriculum 54, 108, 121–3, 125–9, 131, 136, 139, 140, 196, 203, 204, 206, 207, 214
course assignments 141, 161
creativity 8, 14, 15, 17, 43, 44, 60, 68, 85, 86, 93, 108, 114, 129, 132, 136–8, 153, 158, 162, 182, 184, 204, 210
cultural heritage instruction 101, 106, 169, 170
cultural-historical theory 1, 2, 4, 14, 17, 80
cultural tools 5, 11, 13, 15, 93
culture xiv, xv, 1, 2, 4–6, 11–15, 17, 19, 20, 22, 23, 35, 37, 40, 42, 45, 49, 50, 59, 61–3, 67–9, 71, 74–7, 79, 80, 83, 86–9, 93–5, 97, 100, 103, 105, 107, 124, 125, 130, 138, 142, 143, 148, 152, 155, 156, 158, 159, 161, 167, 170, 175, 177, 178, 182, 202, 205, 208–10, 214, 218, 219, 223
curricular conversations 100
curriculum guide 108, 125
curriculum materials 31, 108, 110, 154, 168, 180, 196
curriculum sequence 164

deep structure of institutions 62, 67, 79, 89, 95–7, 117, 119, 141, 155
developmentally-appropriate teaching 61, 62, 164
dialogism 2, 75, 163
Disability Studies in Education 62
dispositions 5, 15, 16, 42, 43, 50, 59, 60, 68, 70, 75, 86, 108, 121, 142, 143, 146, 147, 150–2, 158, 160, 164, 165, 171, 182, 186, 193, 194, 201, 221
diversity 53, 58, 61, 62, 66–9, 71, 74, 76, 79–81, 94, 95, 97, 124, 161, 174, 222
doubleness of epistemology 104, 106, 111

engagement/disengagement 2, 5, 11, 17, 33, 50, 54, 60, 61, 64, 76, 103, 105, 111, 132, 141, 142, 146, 147, 151, 154, 163, 168, 174, 181, 183, 185, 195, 196, 200, 204, 208, 212, 213, 215
equilibrium (Piagetian) 63, 84, 85
eupraxis 199, 200, 208, 213

field-based teacher education programs 44, 58, 70, 161, 170, 171, 189, 190, 202, 220
field experiences xiii, 21, 25, 26, 40, 42, 51, 52, 54, 58, 64–6, 73, 111, 115, 116, 154, 157, 170, 220
file cabinets 110, 169, 196, 201
first-order mediational experiences 16
five-paragraph theme 32, 106, 121, 130, 131, 134–40, 154, 173, 176, 177, 189, 190, 192, 196
five-sentence paragraph 132
formalism 36, 43, 46, 54, 67, 75, 79, 82, 83, 103–11, 114, 116, 119, 120, 122, 123, 128–30, 132, 133, 135, 136, 139, 140, 143, 151, 152, 154–60, 168–70, 173–8, 180–2, 184–8, 190–3, 196, 200–2, 206, 209, 210, 212, 214, 221
fuzzy concepts 99, 111, 114, 119, 160, 165, 170, 189, 192, 221

genetic (developmental) method 20
goals 5, 6, 13, 19–24, 29, 30, 37, 62, 75, 77, 79, 106, 115, 126, 128, 129, 142, 179, 180, 202
graphic organizer 169

heterogeneity principle 17
heteroglossia 50
hidden curriculum 62, 79, 141, 142, 155, 159, 165
higher mental functions 14
high-leverage practices 13
high-stakes tests 20, 54, 102, 110, 120, 121, 128, 130, 131, 203, 220

ideals   3, 36, 63, 74, 77, 116, 120, 126, 129, 145, 155, 159, 162, 163, 167, 168, 170, 171, 188, 190, 191, 196, 213, 223
identity   22, 89, 96, 97, 127, 128, 164
Individualized Education Program   144
inquiry   75, 84, 100, 164, 188, 191, 197, 218, 222
intertextuality   2, 163

lamination (metaphor)   69, 96, 97
lasagna gardening (metaphor)   96
literary criticism   6, 43, 64, 70, 100, 103, 122, 171, 173, 174
literary terms   108
local control   208, 209, 214

mandate   16, 32, 54, 110, 120–2, 127, 129, 134, 136, 138–40, 154, 166, 168, 177, 179, 184–6, 190, 193, 203, 206, 207, 209, 217, 221, 222
mediated concept development   2, 220
mediation   1, 2, 4–6, 14, 16, 17, 20, 21, 49, 52, 53, 156, 158, 187, 218, 219, 223
meta-experience   14, 17
mimetic tradition   83, 86, 157
morale   42, 214
motive of the setting   21, 134
multiple worlds pitfall   51, 83, 157

National Council for Accreditation of Teacher Education (NCATE)   40, 50, 161
Native American culture   61, 62, 79–81, 87–9, 94, 95
neoliberalism   16, 46, 199, 217, 221
new criticism   6, 41, 102–5, 110
No Child Left Behind   221

observation cycles   27–9, 31, 163, 164, 168, 190–2, 194, 204, 205, 210–12
open-ended teaching   38, 41, 43, 46, 54, 59, 63, 67, 75, 77, 85, 93, 94, 106, 109, 114, 134, 153, 158, 160, 162, 163, 167, 168, 181, 188, 191–3, 197, 198, 202, 204, 209, 210, 213, 220
orthogenetic principle   10, 11, 52

pacing chart   164, 168, 177, 205
pedagogical tools   3, 19, 22–4, 32, 33, 51, 71, 78, 162, 163, 170, 191, 192, 212

pedagogical traditions   36, 99, 101, 110, 132
phonics instruction   82, 117–19
Piagetian age-based stage theories   2, 55–8, 61–3, 67, 68, 74, 84, 94, 166
policy   2, 50–2, 59, 74, 94, 102, 121, 186, 187, 199, 217, 218, 221
possessive investment in whiteness   80
practical concepts   10, 17, 18
prescribed curriculum   115, 123, 125, 127, 142
program coherence   xii, xiii, xiv, xv, 11, 46, 63, 66, 70, 77, 99, 101, 113, 120, 181
progressivism   viii, xv, 16, 36, 38, 45, 46, 51, 52, 55, 67, 69, 74, 76, 80, 84, 104, 105, 107, 109, 117, 123, 132, 145, 146, 152, 154–60, 164, 165, 167, 170, 171, 178, 181, 187, 190, 195, 214, 221, 222
projected teacher identity   38, 84, 159, 160, 163, 168, 181, 182, 188, 191, 200, 208
prolepsis   5, 6, 20, 21, 35, 45, 141
Protestant work ethic   50, 145, 153, 155, 165
pseudoconcept   5, 8–10, 63, 84, 99, 119, 129
psychological tools   22, 23, 217

Race to the Top   221
reader response instruction   6, 54, 68, 103, 104
Reading Wars   117
reflective practice   44, 73, 185, 212–14
reform   171, 217–19
reproduction of the social division of labor   142, 153
resistance   46, 123, 125, 127–9, 133, 136, 143, 145, 151, 152, 193, 194, 196, 214, 215
risk   21, 40, 75, 159, 160, 178, 183

Sapir-Whorf hypothesis   5
scaffolding   11, 23, 61, 67, 68, 75, 106, 107, 123, 189–91
school curriculum   viii, 6, 16, 24, 29–31, 41, 43, 46, 51, 58–60, 62, 64–9, 74–6, 79, 81, 84, 85, 92–5, 97, 101, 104–6, 108–10, 115, 117–30, 134, 136, 139, 141–8, 150, 152–6, 159, 162, 164–6,

168, 169, 173–7, 179–83, 186–8, 191, 192, 195, 196, 200, 203–7, 209–14
scientific/academic concept   5, 7, 8, 14, 182
seamless transition/relationship   70, 73, 77, 97, 124, 146, 152, 155, 158, 165, 169–71, 190, 202, 220
Second-order mediational experiences   16
sentence combining   183, 185
setting   4, 7, 8, 10, 11, 13–17, 19–24, 28, 29, 31, 33, 36, 44, 46, 52, 58–60, 65, 78–81, 83, 86, 102, 105, 107, 109, 111, 114, 117, 119, 120, 122, 129, 132–4, 136, 138–42, 144, 147, 155, 157, 166, 167, 171, 181, 187, 188, 195–7, 199, 200, 203, 208, 209, 213–15, 218–23
snark syndrome   37
social concept   xv, 6, 11, 15, 112, 140
socialization   13–15, 35, 36, 44, 56, 63, 74, 83, 84, 86, 93, 95, 97, 141, 158, 170, 200, 211, 214, 217, 221
speech genres   2, 50, 62, 79
spontaneous/everyday concept   5, 7, 8, 13, 14, 182
state curriculum   32, 59, 74
state writing assessment   32, 134, 135, 137, 138, 206
status   62, 69, 70, 94, 102, 153, 173, 175, 178, 203
stress   61, 88, 93, 136–9, 208
structural fragmentation   xiii, 39, 40, 42, 73, 100, 132, 181
structuralism   104
student-centered instruction   16, 44, 45, 65, 68, 75, 78, 101–6, 109–11, 120, 123, 126, 127, 129, 132, 139, 140, 143, 145, 146, 154, 157, 158, 160, 163–5, 169, 170, 189–93, 195, 200–4, 206, 210, 219

teacher-centered instruction   41, 42, 101–3, 106, 129, 180, 195, 219
teaching grammar/language   42, 44, 60, 64, 68, 75, 76, 82, 101, 106, 108, 112, 122, 123, 130, 132, 135, 145, 148, 153, 162, 168, 173–7, 179–96, 204, 210
teaching literature   vii, 3, 6, 25, 31, 40, 41, 43, 44, 52, 54, 57, 60, 68, 75, 90, 91, 100–9, 114, 120, 125, 130, 134, 138, 139, 141, 144, 145, 148, 150, 151, 159, 162, 166, 169, 173, 175, 177, 186–8
teaching writing   viii, 3, 25, 30–2, 43, 54, 57, 60, 68, 70, 75, 77, 78, 82, 90, 103, 105–10, 114, 115, 117, 118, 121, 130–41, 144, 154, 158, 161, 162, 173, 174, 176–80, 182, 183, 185, 189, 193–7, 200, 203–7, 210–12, 219
technology/software   5, 26, 40, 50, 54, 58, 61, 67–9, 75, 76, 193, 194, 217
telos   11, 12, 16, 19, 21, 38, 139, 141, 157, 181
tensions   62, 83, 101, 102, 104, 105, 158, 173, 175, 176, 178, 180, 181, 183, 184, 194
theory and practice binary   3, 4, 8, 23, 54, 60, 61, 67–9, 74–6, 84, 86, 124, 162, 170, 183, 185, 220, 221, 163, 167
tightly-held curriculum   125, 129
time, Native American fluid conception of   87–95
tracking   74, 142, 159
"traditional" instruction   41, 44, 46, 59, 60, 81–7, 91, 93, 94, 97, 101–3, 112, 114, 115, 119, 122, 209
translanguaging   178
trial and error teaching   13, 15, 110, 159, 189, 192
two-worlds pitfall   3, 4, 49, 51, 52, 54, 55, 58, 59, 61, 63, 66, 67, 70, 73, 74, 77–9, 83, 88, 94, 99, 101, 102, 105, 110, 117, 132, 155, 157, 159, 160, 166, 174, 175, 180, 185, 195, 199, 214, 219, 220

University of Chicago M.A.T. program   xi, xii, xiii, xiv, 77, 78

vocabulary instruction   85, 132, 151, 154, 188, 189, 204, 212
vocational education   75, 124, 141–6, 148, 152–5, 159, 162, 165, 194, 208

whole language   31, 80, 86, 114, 117–19
worksheets   59, 60, 85, 86, 117, 151, 153, 160, 163, 183, 185, 186, 192, 200–2, 204, 205
writing workshop   31, 60, 77, 205, 206

www.ingramcontent.com/pod-product-compliance
Lightning Source LLC
Chambersburg PA
CBHW050324020526
44117CB00031B/1758